THIRD EDITION

THE EMPOWERED WRITER

An Essential Guide to Writing, Reading, and Research

K.M. Moran
Eric Henderson

OXFORD
UNIVERSITY PRESS

OXFORD
UNIVERSITY PRESS

Oxford University Press is a department of the University of Oxford.
It furthers the University's objective of excellence in research, scholarship,
and education by publishing worldwide. Oxford is a registered trade mark of
Oxford University Press in the UK and in certain other countries.

Published in Canada by
Oxford University Press
8 Sampson Mews, Suite 204,
Don Mills, Ontario M3C 0H5 Canada

www.oupcanada.com

Library and Archives Canada Cataloguing in Publication

Henderson, Eric-, author
The empowered writer : an essential guide to writing, reading & research
/ K.M. Moran, Eric Henderson. — Third edition.

Includes index.
Revision of: Henderson, Eric-. Empowered writer.
ISBN 978-0-19-902361-5 (softcover)

1. English language—Rhetoric. 2. Report writing. 3. Academic writing.
I. Moran, Kathleen M.-, author II. Title.

PE1408.H388 2017   808'.042   C2016-907799-3

Cover image: Henry Georgi/Getty Images

Printed and bound in Canada

3 4 5 — 19 18 17

Brief Contents

Contents

PART ONE Writing and Reading   1

PART TWO   Essays   123

6   The Expository Essay   124

7   Introductions, Thesis Statements, and Conclusions   146

PART FOUR Grammar   305

13 Sentence Essentials   306

APPENDICES

Readings

Sample Professional Essays

Sample Student Essays

From the Publisher

Oxford University Press is pleased to present the third edition of *The Empowered Writer*, a four-in-one text covering rhetoric, research, and grammar with integrated readings. This approach gives students a detailed yet widely applicable and accessible guide for developing skills in writing and research.

Tailored specifically to college and university students in undergraduate composition courses, this text offers an effective method for developing skills in research, writing, and personal and business communication. Key principles are illustrated through sample professional and student essays and reinforced through classroom-tested exercises that encourage students to empower themselves as writers in training, to participate actively in honing their skills, to make informed choices, and to think critically about how and why they write.

This revised edition features new essays on topics relevant to students in Canada, including the experiences of immigrant students, poverty, environmental protection, and the legacy of residential schools. The summary writing chapter (Chapter 5) appears earlier in the book to reflect the order of instruction at the college and university level. New margin notes direct students to related topics in other chapters, and a new appendix provides essay templates for easy reference. The documentation chapter (Chapter 12) includes the latest in APA and MLA documentation styles.

We hope that, as you browse through the pages that follow, you will see why we believe *The Empowered Writer* remains the most exciting and innovative textbook for Canadian students of writing and composition.

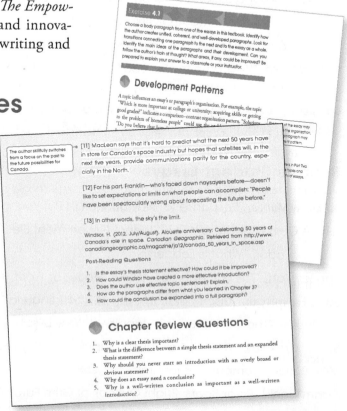

Exceptional Features of *The Empowered Writer*

Abundant exercises. Well over a hundred exercises designed to be completed individually or in groups provide students with ample opportunity to practise and refine their skills. Exercises include

- post-reading questions
- chapter review questions
- documentation exercises
- grammar exercises

High-interest professional essays.
Accessible selections cover topics
of particular interest to students—including experiences
of immigrant students, environmental protection, and the legacy
of residential schools. Marginal
annotations highlight techniques
for students to follow or avoid.

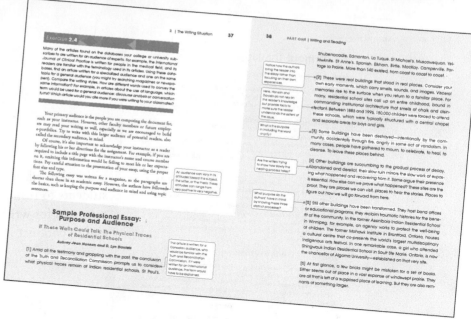

Sample student essays. Numerous examples of student
writing, many of which are new to this edition, illustrate important rhetorical techniques and demonstrate
to students that their best work can stand alongside
the work of professionals.

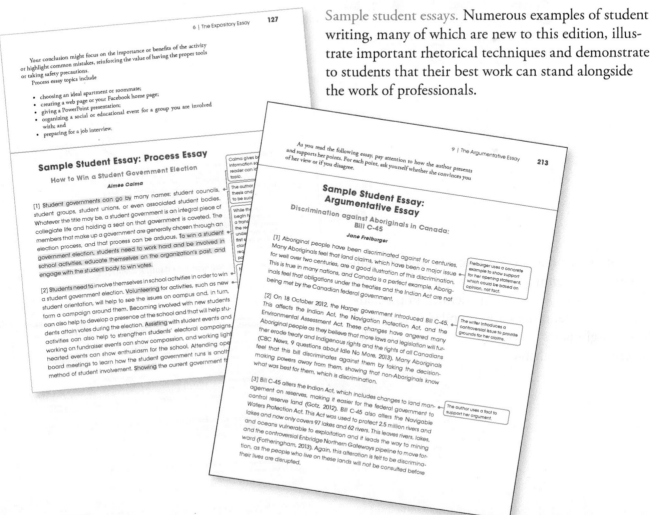

8   PART ONE | Writing and Reading

Critical Thinking

What Is Critical Thinking?

When you think critically, you weigh and evaluate evidence and come to a conclusion. Critical thinking can be defined as "a series of logical mental processes that lead to a conclusion." These processes may include

Critical thinking is a series of logical mental processes that lead to a conclusion.

- analyzing the author's statements;
- comparing these to what you already know or what other authors say;
- evaluating the validity of statements;
- questioning the credibility or the source of information;
- rethinking your position on the topic; and
- synthesizing (putting together) the information with what you already know.

Because critical thinking involves many related activities, such as examining an issue and getting more information from other sources, it can take some time. The best way to succeed is to slow down and to be more careful in your thinking so that you can complete each stage.

*See pages **–** for tips on becoming a careful reader who asks important, relevant questions.*

Many of your assignments will require you to form conclusions about what you have read. You trigger your critical thinking skills whenever you read a work to comment on it, such as during a classroom discussion, or to use it for support in your essay.

Applying Critical Thinking

The highest level of critical thinking involves making the best choice from a range of possibilities. When you read an essay or book or evaluate a real-life situation, you are usually not directly told what to think. A writer or situation might present the evidence and leave you to infer the meaning. When you infer, you arrive at a probable conclusion based on what you read or see. The best inference is the most probable one after all the evidence is weighed.

Exercise 1.3

Consider the following situation:

You invite a new friend for a coffee, but she does not show up. The next day, you meet her unexpectedly and ask her what happened. She pauses for a few seconds and then says matter-of-factly, "I was abducted by aliens, and they just released me."

Critical-thinking focus. The authors encourage students to think critically about their plans and purposes for writing in order to structure their work and to conduct research effectively.

---

3 | Paragraph Essentials   65

If speed limits were abolished on highways, the necessity for law enforcement officers to patrol the highway for speeders would be curtailed. As a result, police chiefs might have more officers to assign to special community projects, such as MADD or drug awareness projects in elementary schools. These officers could spend their time on a variety of social and community projects that would benefit a large number of youths precisely at the time when they need this guidance. In addition, more officers could be allotted to other important areas that are typically understaffed today, such as surveillance and patrol duty to prevent drug smuggling. Surely the presence of police in the community or their dedication to large-scale projects such as drug smuggling would be more beneficial to public safety than having them patrol the highways.

Connecting Paragraphs by Using Transitions

Your reader must be able to follow your thoughts from one paragraph to the next. Most readers expect a new paragraph to introduce a new topic. As the relationship between topics may not always be clear, it is important to use transitions so that the reader can connect the ideas in different paragraphs. A transition can be a word, phrase, or clause. It can occur at the end of a paragraph as a wrap or at the beginning of the next paragraph as part of the topic sentence. Remember that you must conclude each paragraph so that the reader understands that you are finished discussing that particular topic.

A transition connects ideas from one sentence or paragraph to the next.

*See "Transitions between Sentences" on page **.*

When connecting paragraphs, avoid the kinds of transitions used to connect sentences within paragraphs, such as *for example, consequently, moreover*. They are not usually strong enough to connect one paragraph's main idea to the next one.

When making connections between paragraphs, avoid brief one-word transitions. They usually are too weak to link main points, though they can be useful within paragraphs to link subpoints.

The following sentence begins with a dependent clause (underlined) before introducing the paragraph's topic (italicized). The dependent clause acts as a transition, showing that the previous paragraph focused on the fostering of independence through home schooling. The independent clause introduces the new topic.

Chapter 13 focuses on sentence construction.

Although the qualities of independence and self-motivation are important in a home-schooled education, *its flexibility enables the child to learn at his or her own pace, matching progress to the child's natural learning processes.*

Student writer Marissa Miles

This sentence combines an indirect reference to the preceding paragraph with the topic sentence of the current one:

Helpful marginal notes. Writing tips, content summaries, and a running glossary reinforce important ideas. Boldfaced key terms are defined in the margins, and the definitions are compiled in a glossary. New margin notes provide cross-references to related material in other chapters.

Updated and thorough coverage of documentation. The authors outline both APA and MLA documentation styles, making the book a valuable resource for students in a wide variety of disciplines. The instructions have been updated according to the most recent style manuals.

---

of the polar bear population could become extinct by 2050 (WWF, 2012). The way the human race continues to use and abuse the planet, undoubtedly the climate change supporting scientists will be correct about the polar bears' extinction unless immediate and corrective actions are engaged by people united. Can the human race pull it together, or are the polar bears' days truly numbered? Only time will tell.

References

Amstrup, A. C. (1993, April). Human disturbances of denning polar bears in Alaska. *Arctic Institute of North America, 46*(3). 246–250. Retrieved from http://arctic.journalhosting.ucalgary.ca/arctic/index.php/arctic/article/view/1349/1374

Castro de la Guardia, L., Derocher, A. E., Myers, P. G., Terwisscha van Scheltinga, A. D., Lunn, N. J. (2013, September). Future sea ice conditions in Western Hudson Bay and consequences for polar bears in the 21st century. *Global Change Biology, 19*(9), 2675–2687. doi:10.111/gcb.12272

Walsh, J. J., Dieterle, D. A., Chen, F. R., Lenes, J. M., Maslowski, W., Cassano, J. J. . . . Christensen, J. (2011). Trophic cascades and future harmful algal blooms within ice-free Arctic Seas north of Bering Strait: A simulation analysis. *Progress in Oceanography, 91*(3), 312–344.

World Wildlife Fund (2012). *Effects of climate change on polar bears*. Retrieved from http://assets.worldwildlife.org/publications/398/files/original/Effects_of_Climate_Change_on_Polar_Bears_fact_sheet.pdf

World Wildlife Fund. (n.d.). *Marine problems: Pollution*. Retrieved from http://wwf.panda.org/about_our_earth/blue_planet/problems/pollution/

> APA requires that the references begin on a new page at the end of the essay.

 MLA

Like APA, MLA style is parenthetical, meaning that it includes in-text citations. However, the reference list is replaced with a works cited list, and the information is presented differently.

> MLA in-text citations include the author's surname and page or paragraph number(s).

MLA In-Text Citations

MLA in-text citations include the author's surname(s) and page number(s) in parentheses. Separate the items with a single space; do not use a comma unless

---

that it is the most current edition. The examples in this chapter are styled according to the following manuals:

American Psychological Association. (2010). *Publication manual of the American Psychological Association* (6th ed.). Washington, DC: Author.

Modern Language Association of America. (2016). *MLA Handbook* (8th ed.). New York, NY: Author.

The MLA also publishes the *MLA Style Manual and Guide to Scholarly Publishing.*
The following sections provide the basic standards for documenting sources in APA and MLA, with examples to illustrate each format. For more samples and updates, check the associations' respective websites (www.apastyle.org/ and https://style.mla.org/). If you use the websites for help, always double-check the information with at least one other site and take note of when the website was last updated, if possible. If you have run out of resources or simply don't have any more time to spend on finding citation rules, use common sense and adapt the rule closest to your particular case. You can also ask a reference librarian or your instructor for hard-to-find formats.

> APA and MLA are both parenthetical styles, meaning that parentheses are used to enclose brief bibliographical information about the source within the main text.

APA

APA style is parenthetical—whenever you directly quote or paraphrase an author in your essay or use an author's idea, you include a citation in parentheses in the sentence. You also provide a more complete description of all the sources in a reference list, which appears on the final page(s) of your essay.

APA In-Text Citations

Generally, APA in-text citations include the author's surname, the work's year of publication, and (for direct quotations or paraphrases) the relevant page number at the end of the sentence. Separate the items with commas and use the abbreviation *p.* or *pp.* for *page* or *pages* (do not italicize the abbreviations). In most cases, the end punctuation comes after the closing parentheses.

> APA in-text citations include the author's surname, year of publication, and page number(s).

(Ashton, 2008, p. 12).

If the sentence gives the author's name (i.e., uses a signal phrase) and does not include a direct quotation, do not repeat the name in the parenthetical citation. Include the publication year and page number(s) immediately after the author's name.

 Sandy Crashley's essay "The Cost of Buying Happiness: Why Less is More" (see Chapter 11, pp. 254–7) uses the APA format.

Ashton (2008, p. 12) found that . . .

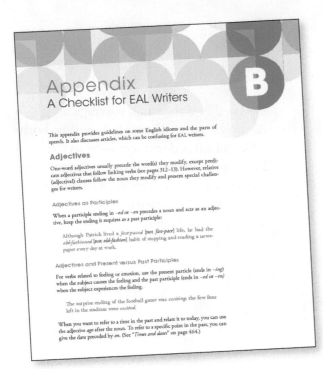

Checklist for EAL writers. Students of English as an additional language will benefit from this appendix, which clarifies common idiomatic words and phrases and matters of usage that native English speakers often take for granted.

Essay templates. Templates for expository and argumentative essays appear in Chapter 7 and 9 and again in Appendix E for quick and easy reference.

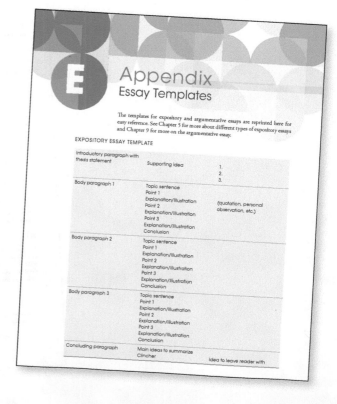

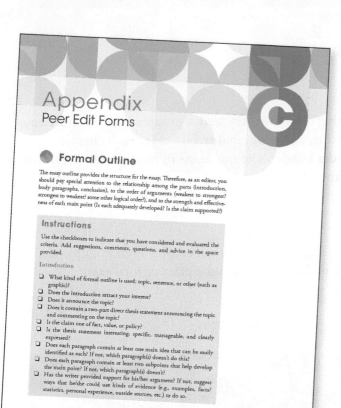

Peer editing forms. These forms help students to evaluate the work of their classmates.

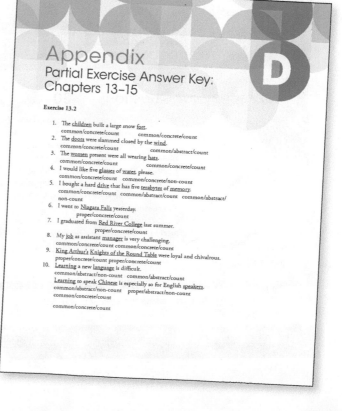

Partial answer key. Answers to most of the grammar exercises allow students to check their progress. Unanswered exercises can be assigned as graded coursework.

Online Resources

For Instructors

- An instructor's manual features learning objectives, key terms, group work and take-home assignments, in-class writing assignments, and additional resources for each chapter.
- A comprehensive test generator provides hundreds of questions in multiple-choice, fill-in-the-blank, short-answer, and essay formats.

For Students

- A student study guide includes self-grading practice quizzes, consisting of multiple-choice and short-answer questions; a practice mid-term exam; and a practice final exam.

www.oupcanada.com/Empowered3e

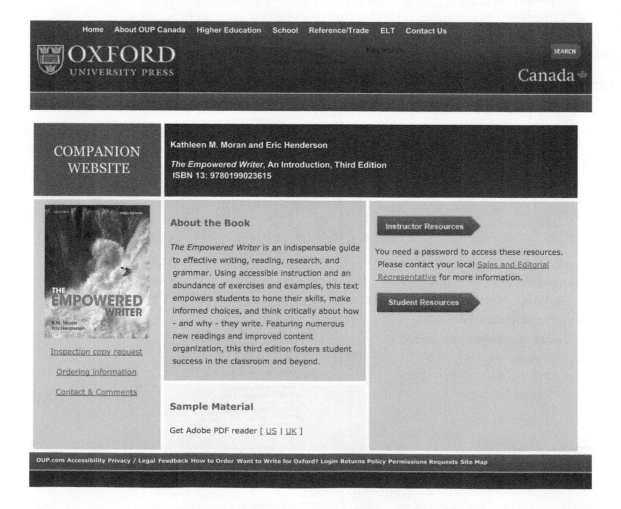

Preface

Many books help students learn how to write at the college or university level. The third edition of *The Empowered Writer* differs by addressing the same material in a more academic manner. For example, the student samples are genuine, coming from students who have taken courses with us or our colleagues. The professional essays—which have doubled in number in this edition—also follow the rules set out in this text. While a few samples use a journalistic style, students are rarely asked to analyze an essay that does not follow the stylistic rules they have been learning.

Because critical thinking is an essential skill for any successful writer at this level, the term is introduced and explained in detail from the outset and its application is stressed throughout the book. Students are also introduced to the differences between expository writing and argumentative writing; clear examples, often with annotations, are provided so that the students can see the differences. In addition, an extensive section about research and how to properly integrate and present sources in an essay outlines the most current practices used in APA and MLA documentation.

Writers at this level are typically required to use a more elaborate writing style than they are accustomed to. Unfortunately, many students think that this style requires using more words rather than choosing the most accurate words or phrases. The later chapters help students build on grammar rules they already know, allowing their grammatical structures to reflect a higher level of writing. A section on style helps students learn to write clearly and concisely, developing a valuable skill for the workplace.

We have included a chapter to deal exclusively with summary writing, both as a stand-alone task and as a means to incorporate research material in an essay. Again, the student summaries that we have included were written by former students. Several of these summaries relate to the full-length essays found in *The Empowered Writer*, which means that students can try their hand at summary writing and compare their work with what others have produced.

Finally, the book includes chapter objectives, extensive exercises, and chapter review questions. We also include post-reading questions at the end of most sample essays, designed to help students connect content with technique. By involving the student and encouraging the completion of these exercises, we hope that students will consider writing a satisfying task.

Acknowledgements

I would like to thank all my students who have helped make this book possible. You have made this journey so much fun!

K.M. Moran
October 2016

The authors and publisher would like to acknowledge the following reviewers, along with those who wish to remain anonymous; your thoughtful comments and suggestions have helped to shape *The Empowered Writer*:

Veronica Abbass, Seneca College
Trevor Arkell, Humber College
Emily Ballantyne, Dalhousie University
Jennifer Chambers, Sheridan College
Marie-Josée Chapleau, College of the North Atlantic
Paula Crooks, Conestoga College
Mark Feltham, Fanshawe College
Lynn Gresham, Conestoga College
Tom Gwin, Red Deer College
Gaye Hickman-Barr, Kwantlen Polytechnic University
Chandra Hodgson, Humber College
Amanda Johnstone, Conestoga College

Viktoria Jovanovic-Krstic, University of Toronto and Humber College
Navneet Kumar, Medicine Hat College
Annette Lapointe, Grande Prairie Regional College
Louise Lloyd, Conestoga College
Roneen Marcoux, University of the Fraser Valley
Lindsey McRae-Graine, Humber College
Wendy Morgan, Fleming College
Julie Morris, Sheridan College
Graham Pearce, College of New Caledonia
Carolyn Speakman, Lethbridge College
Fred Wood, Fleming College

PART ONE
Writing and Reading

1

Basic Skills Development

In this chapter, you will learn

- the roles of writing, thinking, and reading in creating and understanding texts;

- reading strategies and their processes;

- the value of critical thinking; and

- methods for reading unfamiliar words and improving your vocabulary.

The writing process involves more than just writing words. This chapter will explain the importance of writing, thinking, and reading. You will explore the importance of critical thinking in reading and writing. You will also examine how to infer word meaning and expand your vocabulary.

An Integrated Approach

Writing is hard work, but there are practical strategies that make the experience more rewarding. The writing skills you develop now will serve you well in the future because good writing involves organizing your thoughts logically, choosing your words carefully, and creating documents that make sense to your readers.

 Chapter 2 discusses writing for the workplace.

> Good writing involves organizing your thoughts logically, choosing your words carefully, and crafting documents that make sense to your readers.

Writing and Thinking

Writing is inseparable from thinking. Like many writers, when you have an idea, you may discuss it with friends, create a mind map, or draw pictures and label them. By doing these activities, you translate concepts into words that make sense to you. Once you have written the words, you have to ask yourself whether they reflect exactly what you meant to say. Words are more concrete than ideas, but getting words onto the page is simply one important step in the process.

Exercise 1.1 asks you to write about something you enjoy. Writing about a familiar topic is often easier than writing about an unfamiliar one. This book will help you go from this exercise to writing research papers and will show you how the process is similar for all types of writing.

Exercise **1.1**

Write about a skill or hobby that you enjoy—do not stop to edit yourself. When you've finished, answer the following questions in one or two paragraphs:

1. What is your goal in pursuing this skill or hobby? Has the goal ever changed?
2. How would you attain your goal? What other approaches could you take?
3. Which do you enjoy more: working toward a goal or achieving it? Why?

Writing and Reading

Reading and the writing process are closely connected. When we read, we interpret the writer's thoughts according to what we already know (see Figure 1.1). This includes our knowledge of words, our understanding of the world, and our emotions. Reading expands our knowledge. By studying the works of other writers, we improve our own writing. Therefore, good readers are often good writers.

A good reader not only reads the words but also examines the text's ideas and how they are presented. Read this paragraph and then consider the following questions:

Music was far more creative in the 1980s than it is today. The punk and prog rock movements had expanded into new wave, which mixed influences of both genres. Sounds and instruments were driven by evolving technology. Musicians experimented with sounds more than at any other time, and music videos brought a whole new element to music. Fans could not only hear the music, but they could also see the musicians. These stars became trendsetters, the likes of which have not been seen since. Pop music of the 1980s was, of course, the usual drivel that has been produced by every generation and is analogous to today's cult of rap and hip-hop, which all sounds unimpressively alike.

1. Why did the writer use specific words? What words would be more or less objective?
2. What did the writer mention that you already knew? What didn't you already know about the subject?
3. Did the writer state anything that you disagree with? If so, why do you disagree?
4. Are the writer's statements logical?

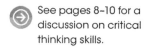 See pages 8–10 for a discussion on critical thinking skills.

By examining writing in this way, you are beginning to develop critical reading and thinking skills.

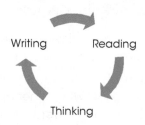

Writing   Reading

Thinking

FIGURE 1.1	The critical writing cycle

You should be able to identify the main ideas in a piece of writing, especially if you are summarizing it. Try to identify the writer's purpose in writing, the intended audience, the writer's style, or specific strategies used to communicate meaning or tone. By analyzing any of these elements, you can enlarge your own understanding and appreciation of the writing process and thereby become a more effective writer.

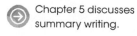 Chapter 5 discusses summary writing.

You should also note when the author is being subjective rather than objective. Authors often include their opinions, such as in the first sentence in the paragraph about 1980s music. There is no factual basis for the statement; it is simply based on how the author feels. To be objective, the author would need to include facts, such as sales numbers, to prove a point. Make sure you include facts, statistics, or secondary sources to back up your opinion so that your writing is not completely subjective.

 # Reading Strategies

When we read, we examine words and continually interpret their associations, which combine to create an overall meaning. Many of us also respond best to the text when it evokes memories, emotions, or even desires. When we have such responses, we become active readers.

Consider the following text, which begins an article about procrastination.

> You know the people who walk confidently into an algebra test without trying to burn last-minute formulas into their brains? They may seem like homework cyborgs, but they're real, and you can become one of them—once you learn to keep procrastination under control.
>
> The first step: Understanding that procrastination isn't caused by laziness! Most of us put things off to avoid negative emotions—from awkwardness to boredom to anxiety. But the truth is, you'll save yourself tons of stress if you outsmart those sneaky feelings that get in your way—and it's easier than you think.
>
> Kaminski, M. (2015, October). Why can't I stop procrastinating?
> *Choices, 31*(2), 14–15. Retrieved from http://ra.ocls.ca/ra/login
> .aspx?inst=conestoga&url=http://search.ebscohost.com.eztest.ocls.ca/login
> .aspx?direct=true&db=a9h&AN=109479211&site=eds-live&scope=site

What do you think "homework cyborgs" and "burn last-minute formulas into their brains" mean? You probably don't think that people literally burn things into their brains, but you understood what Kaminski meant because you thought critically about the wording. You analyzed it for meaning as you read and made personal connections. For example, we all know students who "pull all-nighters" because they did not start studying for an exam early enough and students who seem to do nothing but study. Even though Kaminski makes general statements about procrastination, you were probably able to identify with the statements you read.

If you continued to read the article, you could make certain **inferences** and conclusions based on the writer's statements and the way they were presented. For example, Kaminski discusses the typical types of procrastinators. She doesn't specifically state what type of procrastinator you may be (if you are one), but you could make that inference. As you read on, you could test her

Inference is a conclusion we make based on the evidence presented; the corresponding verb is *infer*.

logic and consistency and compare it to your own experience by asking questions such as

1. Are the claims logical? Does the writer support them with proof? Does the writer link ideas in an understandable way?
2. Are they valid considering what you know about the subject?
3. Are they truthful?
4. Is the information reliable?
5. Does the author provide enough proof in step 1 for you to agree with the beginning of the piece?

Chapter 7 explores kinds of claims and evidence; Chapter 8 examines claims and logical arguments.

Reading at the college and university level means reading–thinking–writing, where you

1. focus on understanding;
2. use critical thinking to test the validity of the statements; and
3. analyze and evaluate the work, considering the methods and strategies that the writer uses to make it effective (or not).

Selective reading is a reading strategy with a goal, such as scanning for main points or reading for details.

Scanning is a reading strategy in which you look for key words or sections of a text.

Focused reading is a close and detailed (i.e., word-by-word) reading of a specific, relevant passage.

When you ask these kinds of questions, you respond critically to a work by considering the validity and logic of the claims and deciding if the evidence supports the author's arguments.

As you write assignments, you often complete the cycle of reading–thinking–writing: you read a text; you think about it critically; and you write about those thoughts, making them clear and concrete. You can then restart the cycle by rereading the piece, rethinking it, and perhaps further clarifying your thoughts by writing about them again. Responding to essays and thinking about the writers' conscious choices will lead you to reflect on your own writing processes and help you make sound and conscious choices.

College and university courses require different types of reading. For instance, sociology involves seeking particular patterns of information; mathematics and chemistry may have to be read very carefully; but familiar economic theory may be reviewed briefly. There are different types of **selective reading**, such as scanning and focused reading, in which you look for specific information.

Scanning is reading with a purpose. When you scan, you read for the main points or to identify another specific feature. To scan effectively, you often need to know where to look. If you want to know the subject of a reading, you might scan the introduction or look at the first sentence of each paragraph (this is often a topic sentence that tells you what the paragraph is about). You could also scan the table of contents or reference list for key words.

Focused reading concentrates on smaller blocks of text. Sentences are read carefully for detail and sometimes for tone or style. Focused reading is specialized reading—you become a specialist (historian, literary critic, sociologist, mathematician) in your reading of the text.

Scanning and focused reading are often combined. For example, following these stages will help you conduct thorough research:

1. Begin by scanning catalogue entries, journal indexes, book contents pages and indexes, reference books, and other types of sources in order to find materials to support your essay topic.

2. Once you have located most of your sources, scan them to determine which are the most valuable for your purpose so that you can focus on the most useful.
3. Scan individual articles, books, and websites to identify the main ideas.
4. Focus to understand the main ideas and to see how they fit with your **thesis statement** or with the ideas of other writers.

Scanning and focused reading are deliberate reading strategies. You should ask yourself specific questions as you read to get as much from the text as possible. Table 1.1 outlines some basic tactics for scanning and focused reading.

The **thesis statement** is the main point of, or what you are trying to prove in, your essay.

 Chapter 10 explores various research strategies.

 See pages 6–7 for guidelines and strategies for selective reading.

TABLE 1.1 Basic Strategies for Scanning and Focused Reading

Scanning	Focused Reading
Know your purpose for reading and what you are looking for.	Identify important or relevant passages.
Know where to look.	Break down the passage to find complex material—for example, separate main points from subpoints and claims from supporting details and examples.
Skip much of the text, isolating only the most relevant areas.	Read the passage first for comprehension; then apply active reading skills.
Quickly scan (skim) the text.	Read the text slowly.
Take notes and cross-reference.	Summarize, paraphrase, and directly quote.

Exercise 1.2

An index is an alphabetical listing of content and is found at or near the end of a book. Scan the index of one of your textbooks, looking for a term in a topic that interests you (for example, *sexuality* or *deviance* in a sociology text or *depression* or *motivation* in a psychology text). Scan the entries under this topic and then scan the relevant pages to find the term's definition. (Introductory textbooks are probably your best choice because they often include definitions of both general and specialized terms.)

Critical Thinking

What Is Critical Thinking?

Critical thinking is a series of logical mental processes that lead to a conclusion.

When you think critically, you weigh and evaluate evidence and come to a conclusion. **Critical thinking** can be defined as "a series of logical mental processes that lead to a conclusion." These processes may include

- analyzing the author's statements;
- comparing these to what you already know or what other authors say;
- evaluating the validity of statements;
- questioning the credibility or the source of information;
- rethinking your position on the topic; and
- synthesizing (putting together) the information with what you already know.

Because critical thinking involves many related activities, such as examining an issue and getting more information from other sources, it can take some time. The best way to succeed is to slow down and to be more careful in your thinking so that you can complete each stage.

 See pages 13–16 for tips on becoming a careful reader who asks important, relevant questions.

Many of your assignments will require you to form conclusions about what you have read. You trigger your critical thinking skills whenever you read a work to comment on it, such as during a classroom discussion, or to use it for support in your essay.

Applying Critical Thinking

The highest level of critical thinking involves making the best choice from a range of possibilities. When you read an essay or book or evaluate a real-life situation, you are usually not directly told what to think. A writer or situation might present the evidence and leave you to infer the meaning. When you infer, you arrive at a probable conclusion based on what you read or see. The best inference is the most probable one after all the evidence is weighed.

Exercise **1.3**

Consider the following situation:

> You invite a new friend for a coffee, but she does not show up. The next day, you meet her unexpectedly and ask her what happened. She pauses for a few seconds and then says matter-of-factly, "I was abducted by aliens, and they just released me."

What can you infer from her statement? Is there more than one possibility? Which is the most likely? What could you say or do to ensure that your conclusion is the most probable one? Use the following headings to complete your answer.

Possible inferences

Probable inferences

How to ensure that your inference is correct

As a critical thinker, you question assumptions, including your own; test the evidence; and accept or reject the conclusions after careful analysis. When questions arise, the critical thinker seeks answers within the text but may also consider relevant personal experience or outside sources. For example, in the situation described in Exercise 1.3, you might ask the woman's friends about her belief in aliens or about her sense of humour.

In analyzing an argument as a critical thinker, you should carefully evaluate all the writer's claims and look for failures in logic or misuse of emotion. You should also think about points that the writer doesn't raise. Is he or she avoiding certain issues? Fact-based writing can produce contradictory findings. For example, two researchers investigating the connection between television viewing and violence may arrive at very different yet credible conclusions. What can account for the conflicting results? Answering this question also involves critical thinking.

Reading and Critical Thinking

When a writer makes a claim that experts have debated for years—for example, that cats are smarter than dogs—readers often question it. Making the best inference requires weighing several factors:

- *Writer's credibility*: Is the writer considered an expert? What is the nature of his or her expertise? Could he or she have a bias, such as hating dogs?
- *Nature of the thesis or main points*: Specific points are stronger and often easier to prove than general ones. Since there are many different dog breeds, it would be difficult to generalize about the intelligence of all dogs.
- *Basis of the statement*: A claim may depend on an underlying assumption, such as a particular definition. There are various ways to define and measure intelligence. Those who think a dog is more intelligent

 Chapters 2 and 6 examine thesis statements.

may point to trainability as the intelligence factor, while cat fanciers may point to adaptability or independence. Another thing to determine is whether fact has been separated from fiction.

- *Method*: How does the writer attempt to prove his or her point? Does he or she use fact or opinion?

- *Support*: A credible writer provides evidence. You must evaluate the nature of this material and the way the writer uses it. What kind of evidence does the writer use? Does he or she rely too much on one kind of evidence or one source? How many sources are used? Are they current (recent studies may be more credible than older ones)? Does the writer ignore some sources (e.g., those that find dogs more intelligent than cats)?

- *Conclusion*: While analysis and questioning are important when you read the work, you will be synthesizing information in order to say something definitive about it and/or about the writer. Your goal is to determine whether the weight of evidence supports the writer's claim. You might consider how weaker points affect the validity of the findings. Are there any gaps or inconsistencies in the chain of reasoning? Is the writer's conclusion logically supported?

Exercise **1.4**

We use critical thinking and inferences in our everyday lives. For each of the following scenarios, choose the best inference from the list and justify your choice.

1. You arrive at your 8:30 class, having missed yesterday's, and are surprised to see an empty classroom. None of your classmates is waiting in the hall, and there is no sign stating that the instructor is ill.

    Inferences:

    a. You have mistaken either the time or the room.

    b. The instructor cancelled class yesterday.

    c. The instructor is ill, but no one put up a notice.

    d. No inference is possible. (What further information is needed?)

2. Matt invites Dee to a movie. Shrugging, Dee agrees. When Matt suggests a romantic comedy, Dee says she isn't in the mood. He suggests an action flick; Dee replies, "You know I don't like them." Finally, he suggests a drama starring her favourite actor, but Dee says she didn't really enjoy her last film.

    Inferences:

    a. Matt is pressuring Dee too much.

    b. Dee is finding it hard to decide on a movie.

c. Dee really doesn't want to go to a movie tonight.

d. No inference is possible. (What further information is needed?)

3. It is Todd's roommate's turn to cook dinner. When Todd gets home, his roommate is glued to the TV and the kitchen looks untouched. "Wow! Something smells great," enthuses Todd.

Inferences:

a. Todd has a poor sense of smell.

b. Todd is sarcastically voicing his displeasure.

c. Todd is trying to give his roommate a hint that he should start dinner.

d. No inference is possible. (What further information is needed?)

4. Brad is helping Kodi train for the 600-metre race by recording his time after every complete circuit of the track. Kodi does the first circuit in 60 seconds and the second in 65.

Inferences:

a. He will probably do the third circuit in about 55 seconds.

b. He will probably do the third circuit in about 65 seconds.

c. He will probably do the third circuit in about 70 seconds.

d. No inference is possible. (What further information is needed?)

Exercise 1.5

In the following blog post, Lawrence Cunningham uses critical thinking to analyze the book publishing industry and its future given the increased use of digital reading devices. Read the essay and answer the post-reading questions, using your critical thinking skills and ability to make logical inferences.

Where Are the Books?

[1] Books have lined the shelves of the offices of all my colleagues at every school where I have worked. In my early days of teaching, or when spending a term as a visitor, I'd wander into a learned neighbor's office to get acquainted. The titles and content of those books announced a person's intellectual background and interests. They were instantly and extensively a topic of earnest discussion. If my interlocutor should be interrupted by a call or an assistant popping in, I'd amuse myself by grazing over the titles, scanning the shelves that added up

(continued)

to an inventory of knowledge. On their shelves and mine, students attending office hours would likewise find easy icebreakers.

[2] When visiting the homes of friends, especially new friends but longer-term friends as well, it has always interested me to see what books are stacked on their shelves, in the living room, the study, along hallways. At parties, these books have been great conversation starters, fountains of discourse and debate. You could even pick them up and hand them over, citing the passage on a given page where you recalled a point being made particularly well.

[3] My wife and I, when house hunting the last time around, inspected two dozen apartments before falling in love with the homey charm of the one where we live now. As an anonymous broker showed us through the absent homeowners' place, we'd scan the stacks of books that gave a sense of the people who lived there—lovers of art history, a denizen of Wall Street, devotees of history, biography, the Civil War. Stephanie and I would joke, when viewing that rare apartment empty of books, that the absence of books was an absence of warmth and that we would not trust the people who lived there. "Where are the books?" we'd ask in bewilderment as we rode down the elevator, never to return.

[4] Today, with reading so often done and "books" acquired digitally, stored in pixels on hand-held devices, we see fewer new titles gracing the offices of colleagues and teachers, the homes of friends. No longer on display, they can no longer be conversation pieces. The average age of books on shelves is rising steadily and even these [are] becoming anachronistic. Shelves are given over to decoration, clocks, cups, bells, photographs. My wife and I wonder, "What will our kids think, 10 or 20 years from now, when they see an apartment without a single book in it?" Maybe nothing. We would be horrified.

[5] But exactly what the future holds is uncertain. One of my recent books, *The Essays of Warren Buffett*, is selling briskly in both print and digital, though with vastly more sales in print than digital, yet it costs $35 in print and half that in digital. Time will tell.

Cunningham, L. (2013, March 26). Where are the books? *Concurring opinions.* Retrieved from http://concurringopinions.com/archives/ 2013/03/where-are-the-books.html

1. Why do you think Cunningham feels it is important to have icebreakers, such as book titles, when meeting new colleagues?
2. What does the word *interlocutor* mean? Why do you think Cunningham uses this rather than a similar word?
3. What does the author's opinion of books and the vocabulary he uses tell you about his perception of his audience?
4. Arrange the following items from most to least important: Cunningham's credibility, the credibility of the blog that published the post, Cunningham's support for his claim, and your own or your friends' experiences with books. Give reasons to support your answer.
5. Cunningham states that he would not trust people who did not have books in their houses. Do you feel the same way? How does his opinion affect your view of him and how you feel about the blog post?

Responding Critically and Analytically through Questions

You will examine different elements of a text at various stages in your reading. This section discusses the activities involved in pre-reading, first reading, and second reading.

Pre-Reading

Pre-reading can give you valuable information to help plan your reading; that is, it can give you an agenda. When you select a source, ask yourself, "How much and what parts of it are useful to me?" Some sources could provide you with methods and points of view for analyzing data. Information about the writer could alert you to his or her qualifications, the intended readership, and any biases he or she might have. A science or social science article may contain an abstract, a concise summary that precedes the article and overviews the writer's hypothesis, method, and results. Reading abstracts can help you find the articles that are most relevant to your own reading or research interests.

Ask yourself the following questions when working at the pre-reading level.

 Chapter 9 discusses how to write abstracts.

- *What is the title of the work?* Non-fiction work (a book, journal article, or report) needs to tell the reader what the work is about. The title can convey information about content, organization, and tone. It may also indicate whether the author plans to tell you about the topic or argue some aspects of it. Of course, you should not decide whether a source will be useful to your research solely by its title, but it is often a good starting point. For example, what assumptions can you make about works with the following titles?

By reading each word of a work's title carefully, you can often determine whether it will be useful to your research.

Perry-Globa, P., Weeks, P., Zelinski, V., Yoshida, D., & Colver, J. (2007). *Perspectives on Globalization.* Toronto, ON: Oxford University Press.

Clarkson, S., & Wood, S. (2010). *A Perilous Imbalance: The Globalization of Canadian Law and Governance.* Vancouver, BC: University of British Columbia Press.

Both titles contain words that inform their readers whether the author discusses or argues a topic. The title of the first book suggests that readers will look at different viewpoints about globalization, such as how it affects individuals. The second indicates that the book looks at globalization from a distinctly Canadian perspective, with a focus on law.

- *How long is the text?* Few people begin reading without leafing through the pages to find the ending; this impulse reveals how much reading time is required. You should make sure you have time to complete your first reading in one sitting to get a sense of the whole. With a longer essay or a book, you can do this with individual sections or chapters.
- *Who is the author?* Do you know anything about him or her? Is he or she featured in your textbooks? Is this a person your instructor has mentioned?
- *What are his or her profession and nationality?* Are any other important or defining characteristics given, such as experience in the field?
- *Does he or she belong to or have affiliations with a specific organization, group, or community?* For example, is this person employed by the Government of Canada? Is he or she part of a cultural group being written about or studied?
- *Does he or she seem to be an expert in the field?* What shows you this? Is he or she affiliated with an academic institution or organization? Are the author's other works listed?
- *Why was the work written?* Was it written to convince readers of a particular opinion or point of view? If so, how would this affect the way you use it?
- *Is the work divided into parts?* Are there headings and subheadings throughout? Do they tell you about content or organization? Extra spacing between paragraphs could also indicate divisions. In a book, look for chapter titles and subheadings within individual chapters.
- *When was the work written?* An essay might include the publication date in a footnote at the bottom of the first page or at the end. In a book, the publication date usually appears on the copyright page (at the front of the book). A recent date does not necessarily make the work recent; for example, the book may be a reprint of a much earlier edition. On the

other hand, if the book has been revised since it was first published, changes or updates may make it especially useful. Essays that appear in an edited collection were probably first published earlier than the collection itself (though essays are sometimes commissioned for a volume and would then bear the same date).

- *To whom is the work addressed?* Who was it written for? If an essay, what publication does it appear in, and what does this information tell you? The publication could be a refereed scholarly journal, one in which the articles have been evaluated by knowledgeable peers. Such articles are usually reliable sources if you are writing a research essay.

- *If a book, who is the publisher?* Is it an academic or a university press? Again, if you are writing a research essay, a scholarly publication might be a more reliable source than a book aimed at a wide, non-specialized audience.

- *What is the level of language used?* If the language seems difficult or specialized, you may have to do a little background reading or exploratory research. At the very least, you will need to read carefully, defining words by their contexts wherever possible and making sure that you have your dictionary handy.

 See pages 21–22 for coverage of word meanings.

- *Is there an abstract that summarizes the entire essay?* Usually, an abstract precedes an essay. In a book, the preface, introduction, or foreword might give you a summary. The editor of an essay collection often summarizes the essays in an introduction or a foreword.

Exercise **1.6**

Many of your textbooks include references to journal articles, books, and other media. These may be found in the notes, bibliography, or suggestions for further reading (perhaps at the end of each chapter). Choose two journal or book titles from a textbook in your favourite subject, analyze them word by word, and describe what you think each is about.

First Reading

It's a good idea to read the essay or chapter once for content and general impressions. As you read, underline or highlight passages that interest you. You may also write comments, thoughts, associations, criticisms, questions, or additions in the margin.

 Research note-taking will be covered in more depth in Chapter 10.

When reading, remember to ask questions that will help you read critically. It is important to think consciously about the issues in the list provided here. As you become more familiar with reading and critical thinking, these questions will become second nature and you will find that you answer them without even thinking about them.

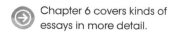

Tone is the writer's attitude (e.g., subjective, objective, formal, or informal) to the subject matter.

Jargon is language that is specific to a field or a group.

Chapter 6 covers kinds of essays in more detail.

- *What are your impressions of the first few paragraphs?* Did they draw you into the work?
- *Is there a distinct introductory section?* What does it tell you about the topic being discussed?
- *What is the tone?* Tone is the writer's attitude to the subject matter—for example, subjective, objective, formal, or informal.
- *What kinds of words are used?* Is the vocabulary level simple, sophisticated, general, specific, or specialized?
- *Is jargon used?* Jargon consists of words and expressions used in a particular discipline or among members of a group. This vocabulary may not be understood by people outside the group. Jargon sometimes becomes part of everyday speech, such as ASAP (from the military) and STAT (from the medical community).
- *What kind of essay is it?* Is it persuasive, expository, personal, narrative, descriptive, or a combination of different kinds?
- *What is the essay/chapter about?* Do you know anything about the subject? Do you know of (or have you read) other works on the subject?
- *Can you identify the thesis?* Do you agree or disagree with it?
- *Can you identify the main points?* For example, are they in paragraph topic sentences?
- *Do the points seem well supported?* Is there always enough detail provided?
- *What kinds of sources does the writer use?* Does he or she use footnotes, endnotes, or parenthetical references?
- *Is the text easy to follow?* Are the points clearly expressed or is the meaning sometimes ambiguous? Note the problematic areas. Are these passages unclear because they contain unfamiliar words? Can you determine word meanings from the context or should you use a dictionary?
- *Does the author always seem confident and certain about what he or she is saying?* Does he or she ever express reservations or doubt? Does he or she appear to contradict himself or herself?
- *Does he or she seem to change his or her position at any point?* Does he or she explain the change or support it with evidence?
- *Does the work shift its focus?* If so, is there an apparent reason for it?
- *Does the work seem to build?* Does it get stronger or weaker? Where?
- *Is there a distinct concluding section?* Is it satisfying? Does it address the questions raised in the introduction?

Exercise **1.7**

Using the same material from Exercise 1.6, choose five of the questions on page 16 and further analyze the book or journal. Write a short description (no more than one or two sentences) for each question and, if relevant, provide examples. Would either title be appropriate for use in an essay? Why or why not?

The following is a typical first reading of an essay. The reader's responses are provided in the marginal annotations.

Sample Professional Essay: First Reading

Bear Cub: Rogue Wildlife Is Par for the Course on Canada's Northernmost Green

Eva Holland

[1] It was morning by the time a golfer discovered the carcass. Massive and partially devoured, the moose lay dead on the fairway. The night before, the ungulate had wandered out of the shelter of the trees lining the green, and a grizzly bear had taken it down right there on the mani-cured grass. Not much can shut down the Dawson City Golf Course during its short summer season, which starts as soon as the ice breaks up and the ferry can go back on the water. But in 2013, a bear-versus-moose death match did just that. Management closed the course for 36 hours while conservation officers disposed of the carcass and set traps in case the grizzly returned to claim his leftovers.

[2] Located at 64 degrees north, just half a day's drive south of the Arctic Circle, the course is the most northerly natural green in Canada. Here's how you find it: First, follow dusty, tourist-heavy Front Street until it dead-ends at the Yukon River, which is so silt-choked it looks like choc-olate milk. Nudge your pickup onto the open-deck ferry and feel the vessel shudder as it fights the current to cross. Next, wind up a hill out of the valley on a narrow paved highway that'll take you to Alaska if you keep going. Instead, turn left, following the blue signs marked with a stick-figure golfer in mid-swing. Dodge the six-inch-deep ruts that mar the dried-mud-and-gravel surface. Engage your four-wheel drive, if you've got it. The chewed-up road climbs along a cliff edge before it

Notice the use of the author's language. She uses the word par—*a golf term—to entice golfers to read this article.*

The author uses a synonym so that her writing does not become repetitive. She assumes that, even if readers do not know the word, they will be able to understand it based on the previous sentence.

The author places her thesis in the middle of the paragraph. What is her purpose in doing so?

The author uses directions much like residents of rural Canada do. What effect does this have on the readers?

slopes down into dense boreal forest. Suddenly, the tall, spindly spruce trees part, and fairways appear on the left and right like an oasis.

> Why is the fact that this is a boreal forest important?

> Why does the author compare a golf course in northern Canada to a desert oasis?

[3] Early last June, a rust-riddled Ford F-250, its bed loaded with grey-brown silty dirt, sat parked at the edge of the green at Hole 3. Under a high early-summer sun that wouldn't set until nearly midnight, a man with a shovel walked from the green to the truck and back again, scooping earth from the pile and scattering it across the half-grown grass.

> The author uses many words that create a visual image for the readers, making it much easier to identify with what she is describing.

[4] Aside from encounters with rogue wildlife—a moose that likes to stomp holes in the eighth green; a black bear that spent the summer of 2014 outside the crew's quarters—maintaining the greens is the toughest part of running the course, which is used mainly by locals. Yukon winters mean temperatures below –40 degrees for days at a time, and each spring thaw reveals dead brown patches.

> Here the author is supporting her thesis, which is about the challenges of maintaining a golf course that is so far north.

[5] Matt Smith, slight and dark-haired with a deep tan, is the superintendent of grounds; sanding the greens gives his newly seeded grass a fighting chance. Down south, at a big corporate golf course, he'd have spreaders and sanders—machines to help with the job. But here, he does it by hand, spreading the loose soil, raking it smooth, then flattening it with a drum roller. Smith gathers the soil himself from a spot on the side of the road just down the hill, loading it into a Bobcat and carrying it back to the truck. "Ideally, I'd be using a coarse sand," he says. But he'd have to truck it in from Whitehorse, a six-hour drive away. "You've gotta work with what you got, right?"

> Again, the author is supporting her thesis.

[6] To keep the course running, Smith has to make sure that an array of aging machines remains functional. The facilities run on solar power—with a diesel generator as backup—and fresh water is trucked in. (He pumps the non-potable water for the sprinkler system from the marsh below the eighth and ninth holes; last summer, when a valve for the main suction line fell off into the muck, Smith spent three hours swamp-diving to retrieve it.) He's used to having a gun on hand: there's a 12-gauge for shotgun starts or in case of a bear or moose emergency.

> Why does the author make a distinction between fresh water and non-potable water? What is non-potable water?

> Why does the author include this fact?

[7] Smith's main concern, though, isn't facing down megafauna. The real mischiefmakers are the ravens, who swoop down and snatch balls as helpless golfers look on. (Rule number 10 on the scorecard reads,

"No penalty if you lose a ball to ravens.") On that June morning, Smith finishes raking, slams the truck's tailgate shut, and throws his rake and shovel on the ever-shrinking pile of dirt in the bed. Then he slides into the driver's seat and rumbles on through the rough.

> The author ends her piece by re-emphasizing how much work is involved in keeping the course open.

—Holland, E. (2016, February). The bear cub: Rogue wildlife is par for the course on Canada's northernmost green. *The Walrus*. Retrieved from http://thewalrus.ca/bear-club. Reprinted with permission from Eva Holland.

Exercise **1.8**

Choose one of the articles that you used in Exercises 1.6 and 1.7. Using the strategies discussed in the section on first reading, read through the article and make annotations based on the most relevant items in the bulleted list. Examine the points you have noted and identify the strongest ones by asking these questions: Are there particular arguments or statements that you feel are stronger than others? Are there any sections that you feel weaken the essay? Are there any words you do not understand based on the context? If so, do you need to look them up in a dictionary?

Second Reading

In your second reading of a work, you apply critical and analytical skills. To develop such skills, ask yourself these questions as you read:

 Chapters 4 and 5 discuss specific writing strategies, such as anecdote and narration.

- *Is the introduction effective?* What makes it effective or ineffective?
- *What specific strategies does the writer use to draw you into the work?* For example, does he or she use questions, quotation, anecdote, narration, description, or analogy?
- *Is the author's purpose in writing clear from the start?* Why is she writing this and for whom?
- *Who is the intended audience?* Is the choice of words always appropriate for this audience?
- *Why does the writer use the tone that he or she does?* Is she targeting a specific audience, such as golfers looking for a unique course, or is she writing for people who design golf courses?
- *Does the author try to persuade you to change your mind about something?* Or does the author intend to explain or explore something, describe something, or tell a story?

- *Is the main point of the work announced in the introduction?* What is the thesis statement? Can you put it in your own words?
- *How are the points backed up?* What kinds of evidence are used? Does the writer use examples, illustrations, facts, statistics, authorities, personal experiences, or analogies?
- *How does the writer organize the work?* Is one method used more than any other—for example, compare/contrast, definition, cause and effect, narration, description, or division?
- *Does the author appear reliable and fair?* Is she using judgmental language?
- *How are the main points arranged?* Is the strongest point placed near the beginning, middle, or end? Is the most effective order of points used?
- *Does the work depend more on logic or on emotion?* Do you relate to the images she creates with words, or do the facts give you more information?
- *Does the writer appeal to a set of values or standards?* Does she imply that the wildlife is in danger or that golfers have rights over nature?
- *Are there any lapses in logic?* Does the writer assume that you understand her ideas when, in fact, you need more information?
- *If the points are not always clear, why not?* Is there specialized language, insufficient background, poorly constructed paragraphs, faulty or ineffective writing style, or inconsistencies or contradictions in the argument?
- *Is the conclusion effective?* What makes it effective or ineffective? Does it accurately wrap up the essay or does it leave you feeling that something is missing?

It is very important to remember that critical thinking is more than just reacting to the text and either agreeing or disagreeing with the author. When you think critically, you delve deeper into the topic and examine your feelings, impressions, and values. Critical thinking can make you uncomfortable, as you may be asked to examine yourself or your views in a new way.

One easy method to examine how you think is to note your reaction to your friends' social media posts. If a friend posted the latest study about the links between autism and vaccines, would you repost the article? Doing so is fine on social media, but at college or university, you need to look at such texts closely. You could turn to the media or to your school's databases to see what is being said about this latest study. However, you must remember that there may be a bias in the writing you examine. Thinking critically means you are always looking for any prejudice.

As stated earlier, articles in peer-reviewed journals are often the best source of information because they are supported by research and examined by other experts in the field. Scientific studies are often based on previous research, so the findings are likely similar. By reading the results of studies on a possible vaccine–autism connection, you can begin to form your own opinion about your friend's post. You can also see how misinformation can be distributed by people who react to postings emotionally rather than rationally, and you can identify language that is used to create an emotional response.

We can think critically about anything. What is your initial reaction to the statement "Everyone hates Nickelback, but everyone loves Neil Young." Do you agree or disagree? A critical thinker or reader does not just accept the statement. For example, how can it be true that everyone hates Nickelback when the group has reached international audiences and has sold millions of albums? Neil Young is in his seventies, so how relevant is he to your generation? Anyone who thinks critically will examine the statement for overgeneralization: Does "everyone" really love or hate certain musicians? He or she will also do some research to find out why this statement was made and may question whom the speaker or author consulted to generate this kind of statement. Did he or she just speak to friends who shared the same musical tastes? Did he or she speak to random people? How was the sample taken? By examining the words of others carefully and looking at overgeneralizations, assumptions, and broad statements, we become critical thinkers who are not easily swayed by these types of statements.

 # Word Meanings

The texts you read in college or university may be more challenging than what you are used to. A reliable, current dictionary—whether in print or online—is part of the key to understanding these books and articles. That said, looking up every word you don't understand would require too much time. If you interrupt your reading too often, you may lose your train of thought and miss important points. When reading, you must know the exact meanings of some important words but only approximate meanings for many others.

> Avoid online dictionaries that are not affiliated with a reputable publisher; the sources are often not cited and the definitions may not be accurate.

Use a dictionary only to confirm a guess or when you have no idea what a word means; otherwise, try to determine meanings through context clues (the surrounding words) or similarities with words you already know. The meanings of important nouns, verbs, adjectives, and adverbs are often revealed through context. If an author thinks the typical reader won't know a certain word, he or she may define it, use a **synonym**, or rephrase it to make the meaning clearer. The author may also let the surrounding words clarify the meaning and **connotation** of the unfamiliar word.

> A **synonym** is a word that means the same thing as, and can therefore replace, another word.
>
> **Connotation** means the feeling or an idea that the word creates.

Let's look at a few examples. Specialized words, such as words borrowed from another language or culture, are defined for general audiences:

The *waribashi* (disposable wooden chopsticks) are provided for free at many Japanese restaurants.

Particularly important concepts may be given an expanded definition:

The theory of culture shock—the cycle of liking, disliking, and then accepting the new culture one is in—is widely accepted among linguists and social researchers.

Even in highly specialized writing, the author may define terms the reader might not know:

Even though the Danish government eliminated thimerosal (the preservative that anti-vaccination people believe causes autism) from its vaccines in 1992, rates of autism have continued to increase.

Thompson, C. (2009). "The anti-vaccination movement: Just the latest battle in the Science Wars." *This*. Retrieved from https://this.org/2009/10/28/science-irrationality/

Rather than being stated directly in a clause or phrase, a definition can be implied in the preceding sentence:

Ruttenbur and the soldier have a joint house and property in the game, even though the soldier is married in real life. Such in-game polygamy is common.

Thompson, C. (2012, September 12). "Game theories." *The Walrus*. Retrieved from http://thewalrus.ca/game-theories/

When a writer doesn't define a word, you may be able to infer its meaning by looking at the words around it and at the idea he or she is trying to express. In the following example, the statement after the semicolon helps to reveal the meaning of *mediated*:

Results from the emotions questionnaire indicated that the personality changes were mediated by the emotions experienced while reading; a person's emotional state is known to influence his or her scores on personality tests.

Oatley, K. (2008, June 25). "The science of fiction." *New Scientist*. Retrieved from https://www.newscientist.com/article/mg19826621-700-the-science-of-fiction/

In the next example, the author's use of *either . . . or* shows the contrast between two words. Since you probably know that *virtuous* means "morally good," you can infer that *insidious* must mean something bad ("deceptive" or "treacherous"):

We are blinded by cuteness, and the very traits that make a character either virtuous or insidious are lost on us.

Poplak, R. (2005, May 1). "Fear and loathing in Toontown." *This Magazine*.

What follows a word may suggest its meaning, not by defining or rephrasing but by expanding or illustrating through examples:

> He has a lot of chutzpah—his exaggerated swagger, his condescending tone, and his overinflated ego all point to this.

Exercise **1.9**

Using context clues, your knowledge of similar words, or a suitable dictionary, write a one-sentence definition for each italicized word in these two passages. If you determine the meaning through context or other clues, look up the word in a dictionary and compare your definition with the "official" one.

1. In *virtual* spaces, questions of moral behavior seem to have been passed over entirely, perhaps because, until recently, few games have been specifically designed to allow people to virtually participate in morally *reprehensible* behavior. The record-breaking sales of the Grand Theft Auto series guarantee that this will soon change. Such a huge market for the game has shown that there is a collective desire to *immerse* oneself in virtual *misbehavior*.

   Tuplin, A. (2008, October 11). "Virtual morality." *Adbusters*. Retrieved from
   http://www.adbusters.org/article/virtual-morality/

2. Sadly, *segregationist rhetoric* has consistently *hijacked* the debate over black-focused schools, overshadowing what's really at stake. *Proponents* of the concept say it bears no resemblance to segregation, and that they can't afford to worry about the political *optics* when they have the chance to do something—anything—to address the crisis in black education in not only Toronto but the country as a whole.

   Wallace, A. (2009, July 8). The case for all-black schools.
   This Magazine. Retrieved from https://this.org/2009/07/08/
   case-for-afrocentric-black-schools/

Reading carefully to determine both the immediate context and the main idea of the sentence or passage can help you determine a word's meaning. If you are still in doubt, look up the word. By examining a word's **denotations** (dictionary definitions) and at least one of its connotations, you are well on the way to making it part of your writing vocabulary.

> **Denotation** is the literal meaning of a word.

Improving Vocabulary

Broadening your vocabulary is very important. Each profession has its own specialized vocabulary that you will learn as you progress to your final certification.

Your instructor may explain these new words, or they may be defined in the glossary of a textbook.

Another way to improve your vocabulary is to read. The more you read, the more you discover new vocabulary. Some magazines, such as *Reader's Digest*, include vocabulary-building exercises, and you can find games like these, along with word search puzzles, crossword puzzles, Scrabble, and Boggle, online. You can also look in a thesaurus to discover synonyms for words you already know. Then you can try out the new word when writing an essay. Just make sure the meaning is appropriate by checking it in a dictionary.

Once you have learned new words, it is important to use them so that they become part of your vocabulary. You can maintain a word journal, but it is important to add to it and review it regularly. Select new vocabulary that you can work into conversations. Your friends may ask you to explain the meaning; by doing this, you help them increase their knowledge as well. You can also learn from others in the same way. The important thing is to become comfortable with new words. Practise using them as often as possible so that they become part of your everyday vocabulary.

Jonathon Gatehouse includes many inferences in his essay on Olympic athletes. He expects you to be able to link his ideas to the thesis without him explaining how they relate. While reading, try to identify the main points that appear to be inferences and decide whether they are clear or if direct statements would be better. Also note any words that are unfamiliar to you.

Sample Professional Essay: Inferences and Vocabulary

Almost Famous Canadian Olympians

Jonathon Gatehouse

Anonymity is the rule, not the exception, on the world's biggest sporting stage

> In informal writing such as this essay, sentence fragments and comma splices can often be found. If you are not familiar with these, Chapter 14 discusses them in detail.

> The author is giving concrete examples to illustrate his thesis.

[1] Don't get her wrong, representing Canada at the Beijing Olympics was one of the great experiences of Sultana Frizell's life. Marching in the Opening Ceremonies, wearing the red maple leaf and, when it came time to chuck her four kilograms of steel, the unimaginable thrill of standing on the field at the Bird's Nest stadium in front of 91,000 people. But the truth was that few were there to watch her, or the other women's hammer throwers. The cheering and the attention was reserved for the men's 400-metre heats taking place on the track at the same time. Back home, her event wasn't being carried on TV; it was relegated instead to live streaming on the CBC website. Her parents

couldn't even watch. Their house in the countryside near Perth, Ontario, only has dial-up.

[2] And Frizell—who shattered her own Canadian record and entered the world's top 10 with a toss of 75.04 metres earlier this season—knows that it won't really be any different this time around in London. "When it comes to the Olympics, hammer throwing is definitely the smelly kid on the playground," the 28-year-old says with a laugh. The Games motto—*citius, altius, fortius*, translates to "faster, higher, stronger." There's nothing in there about "equal."

> The author expects you to infer the thesis, which is that certain sports will not be noticed at the Olympics.

[3] Anonymity is the rule, not the exception, on the world's biggest sporting stage. There will be 10,500 athletes representing 205 nations competing at the 2012 Summer Games, and the vast majority of them are destined to return home just as overlooked as when they arrived. With 302 medal events in 26 different sports spread out over 17 days, there is simply too much for the average fan to follow. And for every star like Usain Bolt, who became an instant global icon by streaking to victory in the men's 100-metre sprint in Beijing, there are hundreds of Olympians who would be overjoyed just to be recognized by anyone other than their friends and family.

> The topic sentence clearly supports the thesis.

[4] Vancouver's Inaki Gomez started out as a swimmer, specializing in the 200-metre butterfly, before a car accident early in his teens left him with a damaged disc in his neck and changed his athletic path. Unable to train in the pool, he switched his focus to the track and discovered a talent and passion for race walking. He was the provincial boys champion his last two years of high school. During his time at the University of British Columbia, he placed fifth at the World University Games and was named the school's outstanding male athlete. He is ranked number one in Canada over the 20-kilometre distance, and is aiming to place among the top 15 in the world in London. And in a sport where one foot has to be on the ground at all times, his average pace-per-kilometre is just a tick over four minutes—something few runners can sustain. But all that doesn't buy you much respect. He sees the people gaping as he powers past them on the sea wall in Stanley Park, and hears their sniggering, and sometimes even the taunts and insults. It's part of being a race walker—at least in North America—and you simply have to learn

> The author gives another example of an overlooked sport in Canada.

to let it roll off your back. "Anything that anybody would say about our sport we've heard at one point or another," says the 24-year-old. "You become thick-skinned about it."

Like all good writers, the author acknowledges differences.

[5] There are a few places where the sport is truly cherished. Earlier this spring, Gomez competed at the International Association of Athletics Federations (IAAF) World Cup in Saransk, Russia, a place he refers to as the "Mecca of race walking." The national training centre since Soviet days, and the capital of the Republic of Mordovia, the city is a little off the beaten track—the few images linked to Google maps include a picture of goats standing at the feet of a statue of Lenin—but the locals know their stuff. Gomez was impressed to see banners depicting the sport's greats hanging from the lampposts, and awed by the tens of thousands who lined the streets to watch the race. Their support helped inspire him to a fourteenth-place finish in the strongest field he has yet encountered in his young career.

[6] Gomez expects the atmosphere in London to be similar—the race walking course runs along the mall in front of Buckingham Palace and it is one of the Games' few unticketed events, open to anyone who cares to come and watch. But he's also realistic about how much attention his own efforts are likely to garner back in Canada. For most fans, race walking is a peripheral sport at best. It would probably take an Olympic medal to even start changing that, but for now Gomez is content with the knowledge that fellow Olympians understand he is every bit as much an athlete as they are. "They know the level of intensity and effort that we put into it," he says.

The author helps explain why the athletes continue to train despite the lack of recognition.

[7] The enormous scope of the Summer Games—which boasts 11 more sports and almost four times as many athletes as the Winter quadrennial—guarantees not every event will find a place in the sun. But in recent years, the International Olympic Committee has moved to limit the size of the competition, and winnow away some of the less popular pursuits. When BMX bike racing became an official medal event in 2008, it was at the expense of the 1000-metre track cycling time trial. Golf and rugby sevens will join the Olympics at Rio 2016, taking the spots of baseball and softball, which were turfed for failing to attract enough nations (and TV viewers), despite their popularity in the Americas and

parts of Asia. The churn has been fairly constant over the years. All told, more than 50 sports have now come and gone since the first modern Games in 1896. Rope climbing was a medal event on five different occasions. There was once an Olympic swimming obstacle race where competitors had to clamber over rowboats, and a contest to see who could glide the furthest after diving into the pool. The 1900 Paris Games had a live pigeon-shooting contest—Léon de Lunden of Belgium won gold with 21 confirmed kills. And for three Olympics starting with Los Angeles in 1984, solo synchronized swimming was a sport. Tastes change.

[8] But the temptation to judge sports on the basis of how many spectators or how much media attention they attract does disservice to the athletes. There are no easy paths to the Olympics.

> In an academic essay, paragraphs must be longer than two sentences.

[9] Cory Niefer began shooting competitively 24 years ago, when he was a pre-teen army cadet in Yorkton, Saskatchewan. The Canadian air rifle champion for more than a decade, he missed out on a 2008 Olympic berth by a couple of millimetres, placing second at the 2007 Pan Am Games. Sticking with his dream meant enduring another four years of travel and penury, but the 36-year-old will finally be there in London, competing in two disciplines, standing and prone. In preparation, he's taken a year away from his work as a sports psychologist in Saskatoon (the federal government provided him with four months' worth of funding) and thrown himself into training. An average day now begins with an hour of stretching and visualization, followed by two range sessions totalling five hours, and then a couple of more hours in the gym working on his cardio, core strength, and flexibility. "As shooters, we have to do our physical training outside of our technical training," he says.

[10] Hitting a 1-centimetre-wide bullseye from 10 metres away is no simple matter—just the beating of your heart is enough to throw off your aim. A perfect shot demands that you are both perfectly still and entirely relaxed at the moment you squeeze the trigger. Niefer likens it to holding an incredibly difficult yoga pose. "Most sports are all about movement; ours is about non-movement," he explains. "You can't use your nervous energy or adrenalin." The opening round is more of a marathon, with competitors given an hour and 45 minutes to fire 60 shots. And then when the medals are on the line, it becomes a sprint, 10 shots with no

more than 75 seconds between them. "There's a huge mental component," says Niefer. "And that's where my talent really lies."

[11] Donna Vakalis of Toronto will also have to contend with those challenges on the range, but in her case they will come toward the end of a five-event day. The 32-year-old architect is one of two Canadian women competing in the modern pentathlon, which combines fencing, a 200-metre swim race, a round of show jumping on an unfamiliar horse, and a 3-kilometre run interspaced with stops to shoot at targets with a pistol. "It's probably the Games' most exciting and eccentric event," she says. Introduced by the founder of the modern Olympics, Pierre de Coubertin, in 1912, it is meant to replicate the experiences of a nineteenth-century soldier carrying a message across enemy lines.

> The author discusses further ways sports are not recognized. How does this situation compare to that in other countries?

[12] Vakalis knows that few Canadians share her enthusiasm for the sport. And the indifference even extends to the federal government and the groups that help Olympians—she receives a total of $6,000 a year in funding from her province and federation and pays for the rest of her training and travel on her credit cards. Attempts to convince her bank to extend her a line a credit have been met with incredulity. And her sponsors are a couple of friends who allow her to live in their home rent-free, and the Toronto company that gives her boxes of power bars. "If you have any riches, you part with them to become a pentathlete," she says. But the scant prospects of fame, fortune, or even recognition haven't diminished her satisfaction and excitement over having made it to London. "The reward is the competition itself, and the training," says Vakalis, who started the pentathlon in her teens, long before the women's event became part of the Olympics in 2000. "I'm doing it for me."

[13] Sultana Frizell has a similar explanation for why she continues to sweat and strain in pursuit of excellence, but surely little glory. The hammer throw is the only track and field event that's excluded from the IAAF's "Diamond League," a globe-circling series of stadium competitions featuring large cash prizes. The rationale is that heavy metal balls tear up the infield too badly, and pose a potential threat to other competitors and officials. Instead, there's the "IAAF Hammer Throw Challenge," nine events in far-flung places like Korea and Senegal, where the winner takes home US$2,000, the silver medallist $1,500, and the

third-place finisher $1,000. They're fun, but hardly big time. "For the one in Eugene, Oregon, we had about 100 people watching, which was great," says Frizell. "And in the Czech Republic there was a crowd of about 50."

[14] No wonder then that her all-time favourite competition isn't the challenge circuit or even the Olympics, but a festival in Fränkisch-Crumbach, a German town of 3,000 about an hour outside of Frankfurt, that's held each June. The locals set up the throwing cages on a field behind the grocery store and turn out en masse to cheer. There's a beer garden and sausage vendors. "By the end of the competition there are 1,000 drunk-ass Germans who are just so excited you are there," enthuses Frizell. "It's amazing." (Do a little digging on YouTube and you will find a video of the 6-foot, 220-pound former figure skater performing a cartwheel at the medal ceremony to show her appreciation.)

[15] She's looking forward to once again hitting the centre stage in London and competing in front of 80,000 people in the main stadium. And if few people are actually paying attention when her big moment comes, it doesn't really matter. This time her mother will be on hand to watch, just in case there's no TV coverage, or Internet problems back home. And her friends on the field will be cheering. "We know we're not the premier event," she says. "So we try to motivate ourselves. We get excited for each other." After all, even without the hype, it's still the Olympics. ●

> The author ends with the inference that, despite the lack of recognition, the athletes still have attained the dream of competing in the Olympics.

—Gatehouse, J. (2012, July 12). Almost famous Canadian Olympians: Anonymity is the rule, not the exception, on the world's biggest sporting stage. *Maclean's*. Retrieved from http://www.macleans.ca/society/almost-famous. Originally published by Maclean's magazine on July 10, 2012. Used with permission of Rogers Media Inc. All rights reserved.

Post-Reading Questions

1. Look at the title, the author, and the name of the publication. Was the title an accurate indicator of what was in the article? What main ideas did you think the author would address? Did he address them?
2. Reread the article carefully, underlining words or phrases you do not clearly understand. Can you infer the meaning from the context? Check your inferences against the dictionary definition. Read through all the definitions to ensure your knowledge is correct.
3. Go through the questions on pages 19–20. After reading the article a second time, what differences did you note between readings?

4. The author begins and ends by discussing Sultana Frizell. Do you think this was an effective way to end the essay? Why or why not?
5. What vocabulary did you learn in this article that you could include in your own speaking and writing?

 # Chapter Review Questions

1. How does essay writing as discussed in this chapter differ from what you have learned previously?
2. How does improving your reading skills affect your essay writing?
3. What role does critical thinking play in essay writing? In reading?
4. What are the different types of reading strategies you may use at college or university? What are the strengths of each?
5. What are some effective ways to build your vocabulary? What others were not mentioned in this chapter?

2

The Writing Situation

In this chapter, you will learn

- the importance of purpose in the writing process;
- the importance of audience in the writing process;
- the stages of essay writing; and
- the steps involved in writing a critical response to an essay.

To write a strong essay that has the reader in mind, you must have a clear understanding of why and to whom you are writing. This chapter will help you assess your purpose and audience by showing you the factors to consider before you begin writing. You will also learn the important steps good writers use when drafting an essay for college or university and how to write a critical response to an essay.

Writing Purpose

Purpose is your reason for writing, as well as how you approach the task.

Before you begin writing, you need to think about your purpose. Deciding purpose could address either broad or specific concerns and involve any number of the following questions. If you are uncertain about your writing purpose, try to clarify it by asking your instructor or by using techniques such as pre-writing.

- Will you be choosing your own topic or were you given one? If the latter, will you have to narrow the topic?
- What kind of writing will you be doing? What form will it take (response, essay, research proposal, lab report)?
- What main activities—informing, explaining, arguing, narrating, describing, summarizing—are involved?
- Does the assignment stress learning something new or does it ask you to apply concepts and practices already taught?
- What specific skills will you need to demonstrate? How important is each to the overall assignment? For example, will you have to define, summarize, synthesize, analyze, compare and contrast, or classify? If the assignment includes a specifically worded question or statement, pay particular attention to verbs such as *evaluate, assess, summarize, explore, explain, argue for or against, discuss, or describe*. Each term indicates a different purpose for the assignment.
- Will you be using your own ideas? Will you be basing them on memory, observation, opinions, readings, or class or group discussions?
- What is your interest in the topic? How can you discover your interest level and develop it further, if necessary?
- What level of knowledge and specialization does the assignment require?
- Will the assignment test new approaches to an old problem (inventiveness, imagination, creativity)?
- Should your language be formal, like that of most academic disciplines? Will some informality, such as the use of contractions and informal wording, be acceptable?
- Will you be using other people's ideas? Will you get them from books and articles or other sources (e.g., interviews or surveys)?
- How much and what kind of preparatory reading do you expect to do?
- Will you be submitting work in progress, such as pre-writing assignments, a self-survey, a proposal, an outline, a plan, or a rough draft?
- Is there a specified word or page length? Will marks be deducted if you write outside this range?
- How much time have you been given for the assignment? An in-class exam would require a different assessment of purpose than that of an essay assigned weeks in advance.

Thinking about these questions is a good way to understand an assignment's requirements. You can, for example, do a self-survey such as the one in Table 2.1. The information in the table is valuable for any writer, as it helps keep him or her on track.

TABLE 2.1 Self-Survey Table

Question	Response	Where To Begin/What Needs To Be Done
Choice of topic?	Was given category (technology); need to narrow topic.	I'm interested in Smartphone apps, but I need to make the topic more specific; brainstorming works best for me.
Kind of writing?	Formal research essay.	I've done some online research in one of my courses but nothing on this scale before.
Main activities?	Mainly informing and explaining, but I'll be summarizing the results of studies and relating statistics.	I need to reread the sections in the text on exposition and summarizing.
Specific skills?	Many skills are relevant: analyzing, synthesizing, and summarizing; evaluating will be important because there are a lot of strong opinions about MMPORGs; I'll likely start by defining MMPORGs and divide RPGs into different categories.	We're just starting to cover research, so obviously I need to become familiar with research methods and what's involved in synthesizing information from diverse sources.
Interest and knowledge?	My interest and knowledge levels are high, but I'm not very familiar with the academic studies done on apps.	It might be hard to be objective all the time since I think that apps are misunderstood by adults and educators due to recent studies; I need to be careful and not let opinion or bias creep in.
Language?	Formal language, which means no contractions; I need to know if I can use developer slang.	I'm not always sure what is formal versus informal usage; I'll seek clarification from the instructor or the text.
Sources?	Three secondary sources are required; need to think about CARS (credibility, accuracy, reasonableness, and support); need to use APA citation style.	I'm not sure how many studies have been done on the topic; because the topic is current, I likely won't be using many books, but I may have to use some online sources, especially publisher's web pages; I'll need to check if these are considered reliable sources.

(continued)

TABLE 2.1 (Continued)

Question	Response	Where To Begin/What Needs To Be Done
Preparatory reading?	Not really, other than maybe some background on apps.	Look for apps history, books/websites on apps; talk to friends who develop apps?
Work in progress?	1) proposal; 2) outline; 3) first draft; 4) final draft; note dates for peer editing in the syllabus.	I know that I will be asked to submit an informal proposal, explaining my interest and knowledge about the topic; by this point, I hope to have narrowed my topic.
Length requirements?	About 1,500 words.	Can I go over without penalty? How strict is the word count? Right now, it looks hard to do in 1,500 words, which is why I need to work on narrowing the topic right away.
Time requirements?	We have four weeks before the final version is due, with due dates for the stages of the project.	I need to draw up a schedule to visit the library and begin preliminary research; I think I'll need to spend a lot of time on my outline since I find it easier to write a rough draft with a solid outline to work from.

Exercise 2.1

Using Table 2.1 as a guide, create a self-survey for a current or recent writing assignment. Identify the questions relevant to the task, write your responses, and briefly state what you know and/or what you need to find out to satisfy the writing purpose.

A Is for Audience

Audience refers to your intended readers and their expectations.

Almost everything is written for an **audience**—readers with common interests, attitudes, reading habits, and expectations. For example, a children's book will look and read much differently than a text for one of your courses. Each is designed for the people using it. Student writers must also "design" each essay for a particular audience or reader. This type of writing is different from writing in a journal or writing for yourself, where you are probably the only audience.

Reader-Based Writing

Reader-based writing focuses on the reader, not on the writer. It is geared toward the audience the essay was designed for. To write this way, you need to consider who your audience is and where its interests and values lie.

If your instructor allows you to use informal wording, you can address the audience directly by using the pronoun *you*. You may also be able to discuss events by using *I*. Here are two examples of informal prose:

- Did you enjoy studying Shakespeare in high school?
- When I chose a roommate, I was looking for someone who was fun. I should have looked for someone who could pay the rent.

However, in formal prose, these pronouns are usually replaced with *one* or nouns such as *reader*. The reader is rarely addressed directly. The following statements are formal:

 Chapter 16 elaborates on the distinction between formal and informal prose.

- All students are required to complete at least one art credit in order to graduate.
- When examining the requirements, one should pay close attention to what needs to be done first.

Exercise **2.2**

Choose one of the sample essays in this book and determine whether the writing is formal or informal. Are there places where the writer has changed from one type to the other? How does the style of writing affect the way you feel about the piece? Write a paragraph analyzing the essay. Focus on whether the style increases the writer's credibility, as discussed in Chapter 1, page 9. You may also want to use some of the questions about first and second readings, on pages 16 and 19–20.

Reader-based writing must be error-free and have a clear meaning. Ideas need to be expressed directly and concisely. Your work should have no obvious lapses in logic, nor should you assume a reader knows something just because you know it. You may have to define certain terms or clarify specific points. It is best to assume that the reader knows a little less about the subject than you do.

 Chapter 16 discusses the clear expression of ideas.

Readers should not have to fill in gaps. Take this sentence:

Of all the bills-of-lading submitted, only 20 per cent had errors.

The writer should have helped a general reader by giving additional information, such as what a "bill-of-lading" is and what the errors were.

Exercise **2.3**

Rewrite the following sentences, adding detail for the audience wherever necessary.

1. Of the 1,500 students enrolled, only 750 actually completed the ECE course.
2. In order to improve the world economy, many governments are introducing stimulus packages.
3. More than 75 per cent of PET bottles are being thrown into landfill sites.
4. Some people compare Canada's GST to Britain's VAT.
5. LTE networks have become a selling feature for Canada's wireless providers.

Audience Factors

Consider the following basics about an audience when you prepare to write:

- *knowledge*: background, expertise, or familiarity with the topic
- *interest level*: extent of interest or potential interest
- *orientation*: the attitudes and emotional or ethical positions that define a typical reader

By thinking about these factors, you stand a better chance of reaching your audience. Suppose you want to explain a particular skill that you are an authority in. You must first consider how much your readers know about it. You would not write for readers who know as much as you do, unless you want to alert them to a special area they might not know about. For example, you might write an essay about surviving in the extreme cold for either a general audience of winter sports enthusiasts or the more specific audience of out-of-bounds skiers.

It is important to note that meeting audience expectations does not necessarily mean telling its members what they want to "hear" but doing everything you can to make it more likely that they will hear and understand you. For example, if you don't meet their expectations of using familiar terms or explaining unfamiliar ones, they may not pay attention to your points. Writing *to* your audience is more effective than writing *for* your audience.

Exercise **2.4**

Many of the articles found on the databases your college or university subscribes to are written for an audience of experts. For example, the *International Journal of Clinical Practice* is written for people in the medical field, and its readers are familiar with the terminology used in its articles. Using these databases, find an article written for a specialized audience and one on the same topic for a general audience (you might try searching magazines or newspapers). Compare the writing styles. How are different words used to convey the same information? For example, in articles about the use of language, which term would be used for a general audience: *discourse analysis* or *conversation turns*? Which article would you cite more if you were writing to your classmates?

Your primary audience is the people you are composing the document for, such as your instructor. However, other faculty members or future employers may read your writing as well, especially as we are encouraged to build e-portfolios. Try to write with this larger audience of potential readers, also called the secondary audience, in mind.

Of course, it's also important to acknowledge your instructor as a reader by following his or her directions for the assignment. For example, if you are required to include a title page with the instructor's name and course number on it, omitting this information would be failing to meet his or her expectations. Pay careful attention to the presentation of your essay, using the proper font size and type.

The following essay was written for a magazine, so the paragraphs are shorter than those in an academic essay. However, the authors have followed the basics, such as keeping the purpose and audience in mind and using topic sentences.

> An audience can vary in its attitudes toward the subject, the writer, or the thesis; these attitudes can range from very positive to very negative.

Sample Professional Essay: Purpose and Audience

If These Walls Could Talk: The Physical Traces of Residential Schools

Aubrey Jean Hanson and D. Lyn Daniels

[1] Amid all the testimony and grappling with the past, the conclusion of the Truth and Reconciliation Commission prompts us to consider what physical traces remain of Indian residential schools. St Paul's.

> This article is written for a Canadian audience, who would be familiar with the Truth and Reconciliation Commission. If it were written for an international audience, the term would have to be explained.

Shubenacadie. Edmonton. La Tuque. St Michael's. Muscowequan. Yellowknife. St Anne's. Spanish. Elkhorn. Birtle. MacKay. Camperville. Portage la Prairie. More than 140 existed, from coast to coast to coast.

Notice how the authors bring the reader into the essay rather than focusing on their own experiences.

[2] These were real buildings that stood in real places. Consider your own early moments, which carry smells, sounds, and images. Visceral memories rise to the surface when you return to a familiar place. For many, residential school sites call up an entire childhood, bound in commanding institutional architecture that smells of chalk and disinfectant. Between 1883 and 1996, 150,000 children were forced to attend these schools, which were typically structured with a central chapel and separate areas for boys and girls.

Here, Hanson and Daniels do not rely on the reader's knowledge but provide facts to make sure the reader understands the extent of the issue.

[3] Some buildings have been destroyed—intentionally by the community, accidentally through fire, angrily in some act of vandalism. In many cases, people have gathered to mourn, to celebrate, to heal, to cleanse. To leave these places behind.

What is the purpose in including the word angrily?

[4] Other buildings are succumbing to the gradual process of decay. Abandoned and derelict, their slow ruin mirrors the slow work of exposing what happened and recovering from it. Some argue their presence is essential. How else can we prove what happened? These sites are the proof. They are places we can visit, places to hear the stories. Places to figure out how we will go forward from here.

Are the writers trying to show the slow pace of the healing process?

[5] Still other buildings have been transformed. They host band offices or educational programs; they reclaim traumatic histories for the benefit of the community. In the former Assiniboia Indian Residential School in Winnipeg, for example, an agency works to protect the well-being of children. The former Mohawk Institute in Brantford, Ontario, houses a cultural centre that co-presents the world's largest multidisciplinary Indigenous arts festival. In one remarkable case, a girl who attended Shingwauk Indian Residential School in Sault Ste Marie, Ontario, is now the chancellor of Algoma University—established on that very site.

What purpose do the authors have in mind by showing these three distinct processes?

[6] At first glance, a few bricks might be mistaken for a set of books. Either seems out of place in a vast expanse of windswept prairie. They are all that is left of a supposed place of learning. But they are also remnants of something larger.

[7] A loop of rope hangs from a tree in Alert Bay, British Columbia. It's part of an old swing, worn down by the weight of children moving back and forth, enjoying a little escape. But it is also an unexplained, ominous evocation of death—of young students in care, of adults who could no longer carry the darkness, of their children who were forced to shoulder the burden of pain, shame, and isolation.

> Notice that Hanson and Daniels use an ominous tone here. What were your first thoughts when you read "a loop of rope hangs from a tree"? Does it bring to mind images of the American South during the civil rights movement? Why do they use this image?

[8] A window frames a cloudy sky. The view is punctured by ragged glass, damage caused by a bullet or rock or some other projectile. A former student and a late-night drive-by. An afternoon stunt by some passing teenagers. Vandalism that's not senseless, but rather a symbolic ejection of anger that broods like an unwelcome stranger.

[9] A crooked shed stands against the sky in Birtle, Manitoba, warped by wind and age. The reclaimed earth is suffused with a sense of abandonment, but children once worked these fields. Atop twisted planks, the shed's roof seems insupportable, poised for an imminent collapse. But collapse is also a kind of release—tension escaping a rotten structure.

[10] Handprints and a small footprint appear on the back door of Muscowequan Indian Residential School in Lestock, Saskatchewan. Someone actively refused to be passively marked by this place. It's an act that speaks to the strength and resilience of those who continue onward even as these buildings deteriorate.

> The writers use words such as *strength* and *resilience* to draw the audience in so that readers can understand how Indigenous people feel about residential schools.

[11] There is something reassuring about these crumbling, disintegrating sites. Time passes. Things change. Can the paternalism that built these buildings also wear away and make room for new beginnings? There's a dilemma, of course. If the memories of what happened wither away, maybe it will mean things have gotten better. Or it will mean that people have forgotten, and that they are capable of making the same mistakes again. Forgetting helps some people heal. Remembering helps others learn.

[12] Challenges remain for First Nations, Métis, and Inuit children. Failure rates, dropout rates, and suicide rates all are too high. This is the legacy of Indian residential schools: these buildings still loom in many communities. Twenty-first-century classrooms need to foster—not

> Hanson and Daniels discuss subjects that the audience has knowledge of. They are asking you, the reader, to understand that the rates are higher than in the rest of Canada.

assault—Indigenous communities, individuals, cultures, languages, and knowledge.

[13] All Canadians need to look for what cannot be seen in these pictures alone. People's lives were touched, scorched by these places. Tuberculosis killed too many children. Others were punished with electric shocks, or strapped in public with their pants down. In 1937, four young boys froze to death trying to run away from the Lejac Residential School. There are many stories like theirs, and these images remind us that we need to hear them.

> Whom are the authors addressing? How do you feel as a reader?

[14] Civilization. Assimilation. Integration. Reconciliation. Evolving rhetoric. Aggression. Violence. Racism. Legislation. Repression. Omission. Oppression. Colonialism. Cultural genocide. What terms are you comfortable using?

> Why do the writers ask you, the reader, this question? What is their purpose?

[15] Education can give us hope, and we are hopeful educators. Hopeful for today's and tomorrow's First Nations, Métis, and Inuit students. Hopeful that all children will learn about Indigenous histories and perspectives, because testimony is more than an individual responsibility. It is a collective one. Hopeful that all Canadians—young and old, Aboriginal and non-Aboriginal, in school and out—will acknowledge the physical remains of residential schools as powerful sites of memory and remembering, and will work to build something better.

> The authors do not use complete sentences here. Is it effective? Why or why not?

> The authors walk us through the negative aspects of the residential schools; however, what is their current purpose?

Hanson, A. J., & Daniels, D. L. (2015, September). If these walls could talk: The physical traces of residential schools. *The Walrus*. Retrieved from http://thewalrus.ca/if-these-walls-could-talk. Reprinted with permission from Aubrey Jean Hanson and D. Lyn Daniels.

Post-Reading Questions

1. What is the authors' purpose? Does it change in the article?
2. How would the writers have changed the essay if it was for a specialized audience?
3. How do Hanson and Daniels view the audience? Do they believe you would view the topic positively, neutrally, or negatively?
4. Do the authors explain points well enough? Could any explanations be improved?
5. How would the inclusion of cited research have affected the impact of this article?

Writing for the Workplace

As in your school writing, your workplace writing has a specific audience with particular expectations. For example, people are often overwhelmed by the number of messages they receive at work each day. They need to be able to scan a message to determine its importance. Therefore, your writing should be clear and concise. By meeting this expectation, your audience works more efficiently and is more likely to understand and respond to your message.

Depending on your job and the field you work in, you may be asked to write for a variety of situations. You may have to write blog posts, tweets, emails, or reports. While these types of writing seem very different from essays, some of the same basic principles apply. Critical thinking skills are extremely valuable here, as you have to decide on the purpose, the audience, the tone, and the content.

The purpose of your message will dictate whether you want to use an informative or persuasive approach. If you are informing employees of a straightforward policy change, such as switching from cheques to direct deposit, the informative approach works best. However, if you are changing the start times of shifts, you may have to use the persuasive approach, as many people might be upset about this matter.

Always consider your primary and secondary audiences when composing a message. Many business messages are read by people who are not necessarily the intended audience. For example, you may send your manager an email requesting that desks be rearranged to facilitate greater communication and collaboration between employees. He or she may forward the email to his or her manager, which means you now have a secondary audience. The message may also go to your colleagues, another secondary audience. You need to be aware of all potential audiences when you write your message.

A further consideration is whether the message is going to people in your department or to a more general audience. This understanding will help determine what vocabulary to use. If you work in the sales department and are discussing "early adopters" with other salespeople, you do not need to define this jargon; however, if you are writing to people who do not know the term, you will have to explain that it refers to customers who are quick to buy new products. It is important to tailor your message to your audience: if your readers already know words that you define, they will become bored; if you do not define words that are new to them, they will become overwhelmed. Either way, they will stop reading, and no message is effective if no one reads it.

Tone is important when you compose a document. You want to avoid being overbearing or condescending when writing your message. Think of how you would react if you were given your own message. Always be polite. Never compose a message in anger; if you feel you must reply to a message that upset you, make sure that you have calmed down before responding.

See pages 50–51 for instructions on creating an outline.

When composing business documents, remember that organization is a key factor, just as when you are writing an essay. Take time to create an outline, even if it is rough. Ensure all the points you want to make are covered, as this will help you avoid having to resend messages. It is especially easy to ignore this step with emails. Sending several messages about the same topic wastes everyone's time and signals that you are not an efficient worker or communicator, which can be harmful on the job. No one wants to promote someone who does not communicate well.

Exercise **2.5**

1. What are three characteristics about writing for the workplace?
2. What are the dangers of not understanding your audience?
3. What is the difference between a primary and a secondary audience?
4. If a message is not clear and concise, what problems can occur?
5. What attitudes will the audience expect you to have? What ones might disturb or offend your readers, making them less likely to accept your points?

 # Stages in Essay Writing

Body paragraphs are the middle paragraphs of an essay that help prove the thesis by presenting facts, arguments, or other support.

An essay consists of an introduction containing a thesis statement, **body paragraphs** with clear topic sentences and examples, and a conclusion that restates the thesis. As the writer, you have to choose what information to include and decide how to best organize your thoughts so that your readers clearly understand your ideas. To accomplish these goals, you generally complete five stages:

- **pre-writing (inventing)**: finding a topic and developing a thesis statement
- **researching**: finding background information and supporting evidence (could involve intensive library resources or simply consist of examining your knowledge about a topic)
- **organizing**: determining the order of points; outlining
- **composing (first draft)**: putting your ideas in paragraph form
- **revising (final draft)**: revising and editing to achieve the finished version

Although various factors could affect how much time you spend on each stage, you should always plan for enough revision time to ensure that your writing is grammatical, mechanically correct, and clear.

Pre-Writing

Pre-writing strategies should clarify your thoughts about a subject and enable you to generate useful ideas, some of which you will use in your essay and others you will discard. Pre-writing often brings you to the point where you can write a tentative thesis statement and, in many cases, determine your main points.

If your instructor hasn't given you a topic, the pre-writing stage begins with finding one. First, though, it is important to recognize the difference between a subject and a topic. A **subject** is a broad category that contains many potential topics. Modern technology, climate change, and energy sources are subjects. A subject could be more specific than these examples: the Internet, changing weather patterns, and alternative energy sources could also be considered subjects. A **topic** differs from a subject in being narrower, or more focused. Similarly, a **thesis statement** is even more focused because it makes a specific comment about the topic or tells the reader how you will approach it. Figure 2.1 visualizes this relationship and Table 2.2 offers examples of each category.

> Pre-writing helps you clarify your thoughts about a subject, enables you to generate useful ideas, helps you create your thesis, and may determine your main points.

A **subject** is a broad category that contains several possible topics. A **topic** is narrower, or more focused, than a subject. A **thesis statement** is even more focused because it makes a specific comment on the topic or tells the reader how you will approach it.

 Chapter 6 explores thesis statements in more detail.

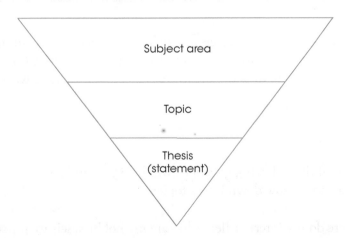

Subject area

Topic

Thesis (statement)

FIGURE 2.1	**Subjects versus topics**
	Sample source

TABLE 2.2 Subject, Topic, and Thesis

Subject	Topic	Thesis
Music	Pop music	Pop music reflects the tastes of generations.
Censorship	Censorship in the twentieth century	How censorship in the twentieth century has shaped literary tastes.
The Internet	Information available on the Internet	How the Internet has shaped people's understanding of the world around them.

Exercise 2.6

Decide whether each item in the following list is a subject, topic, or thesis.

1. Corporations are only contributing money to colleges and universities so that they can influence students and curriculum.
2. Students should use public transportation.
3. Home economics, shop, and business studies help high school students become well rounded.
4. Parents encourage violence in sports.
5. Greed is responsible for the global economic difficulties.
6. Jazz is one of America's greatest musical genres.
7. Students in other countries are models for activism.
8. Religious freedom is a human right.
9. Pets should be used for therapy.
10. Studying foreign languages is unnecessary today.

> All pre-writing strategies could be considered meeting places between you and your topic. Because they are designed to "free up" your thoughts and feelings, don't hesitate to experiment with variants on these methods.

Several pre-writing strategies will help you develop your topic, including questioning, brainstorming, freewriting, and clustering (or mapping). You may find that one of these techniques or a combination works best for you.

Questioning

Asking yourself the following questions will help you find a subject, which you can then start to narrow down into a topic:

- Where do my interests lie? What are my hobbies, leisure pursuits, reading interests, extracurricular activities?
- What would I like to learn more about? A familiar topic isn't always a good choice because you might assume that you don't need to do any research. Thinking this way may prevent you from fully exploring the topic.
- Are sufficient sources available? Consider not only research sources but also questionnaires, interviews, experts, statistics, etc.
- What topic might other people like to learn about? What topic could benefit society or a specific group (for example, students at my college or university)?
- Can I think of a new angle on an old topic? A neglected area can be a new opportunity for exploration. For example, many Canadians feel that their country is safer than the United States because of the lack of guns. But who has guns in Canada? Should we really feel safe?

Once you have determined a subject, you can learn more about it by asking the traditional journalistic questions (Who? What? When? Where? Why? and How?). Let's say your subject is "roommates." Your questions might look like this:

- Who are the best (or worst) roommates?
- What are the qualities of an ideal roommate?
- When is the best time to start looking for a roommate?
- Where can you find a roommate?
- Why are roommates necessary (or unnecessary)?
- How do you get along with a roommate?

Questioning is often a good strategy for an expository (or explanatory) essay in the sciences and social sciences. In these disciplines, your thesis can be framed as a specific question or series of questions that you try to answer.

> **Questioning** is a pre-writing strategy that frames a possible thesis as a specific question or series of questions that the writer will try to answer.

Brainstorming

Brainstorming is a tried-and-true method for exploring a subject. In this approach, you write words, phrases, or sentences that you associate with a subject and can look for ways to connect or categorize some of the items. You can often combine brainstorming with other pre-writing methods. For example, if you began by asking the journalistic questions about the subject "roommates," you could brainstorm answers to "What are the qualities of an ideal roommate?" You could continue to use these two methods by asking why the most important qualities on the brainstorming list contribute to a perfect roommate. Although brainstorming can produce a list that looks something like an outline, the object is to come up with as many points as possible and to link them in some way. You don't need logical connections at this point.

Brainstorming can be helpful for all kinds of essays. It can be done alone or in groups, which makes it particularly useful in collaborative projects, where all participants can give input.

> **Brainstorming** is writing words, phrases, or sentences that you associate with a subject.

Freewriting

In **freewriting**, you write without stopping for a span of time, usually 5 to 10 minutes. You can freewrite without a subject or topic in mind and see where your thoughts lead you or you can begin with a specific idea. You might stray and start writing about something else, which is fine. Don't censor or edit yourself or concern yourself with spelling or grammar. There is often no need for any punctuation or capital letters. The most important principle is that you keep writing without lifting your pencil or pen from the page or fingers from the keyboard. Focus on flow and process. If you get stuck, write anything, such

> **Freewriting** means writing without stopping. It is important to let your ideas flow without editing or censoring them.

as "I can't think of anything to say" or "What's the point of this?" until another idea or association comes to you.

If you enjoy freewriting and find it beneficial, you can follow it with a looping exercise. In **looping**, you underline potentially useful words, phrases, or sentences; choose the best one; and use it as the beginning point for another round of freewriting. You can also summarize the most useful phrases into a sentence and use it as your starting point.

Although freewriting is a popular pre-writing strategy, you can use it at any point in the writing process because it has several functions:

- It can free you from writer's block. A typical problem in beginning to write is feeling that you have nothing to say.
- It enables you to express undiscovered feelings and associations; in other words, it gives you access to thoughts or feelings you might not have known about. This feature makes freewriting helpful for personal essays.
- When used with looping, it can help you narrow down a topic and, sometimes, come up with a thesis and main points.

In the following freewriting and looping sample, the writer discovers a potential thesis for an essay. In this case, writing for five minutes yielded an interesting topic that was complete enough to serve as a thesis statement (shown by double underlining):

> Bureaucracy can be very disturbing you can get parking tickets even when there is no parking left and you are forced to park by the yellow line and you think you'll be gone early enough in the morning where was the bureaucracy when you needed them to make the decision in the first place and it can also lead to you having to take english 100 over again because you didn't get the B- required for the elementary post-degree program even though you feel your writing should be at least a high B or A average and the teacher says just be more clear and some comma errors and gives you a mediocre mark who's to say that the best teachers are the ones who get the A average because I think the best teachers are the ones who know what it's like to struggle because they have learned hard work and they have also learned patience these two things are the most important things being a teacher or they are up there anyway.
>
> —Y.M.

Choosing to freewrite on "bureaucracy," Y.M. began with a complaint about parking, which triggered a complaint concerning his mark in a previous English course. He continued to follow this train of thought as he complained about how the teacher had marked his writing. This led him to consider the qualities of a good teacher; he discovered that being a good teacher has nothing to do with marking or education but with the idea of having to struggle and overcome obstacles. Y.M. could test this claim by finding evidence to support it.

Clustering

Clustering, or **mapping**, is a technique that represents ideas graphically. Unlike questioning, brainstorming, and freewriting, clustering is spatial and enables you to visualize the interrelations among your thoughts. On a blank piece of paper, you circle your topic and then think of related words or phrases, which you record and circle, connecting each with the word or phrase that gave rise to it.

Figure 2.2 is the result of a group clustering exercise that began with the subject "vitamins" and produced the thesis statement, "Due to media hype and the promise of good health, more people than ever are taking vitamins before they really know the risks involved." The statement needs further work, but it is a solid start. The dotted lines in the figure represent other possible connections, which you can often find in this method.

The pre-writing strategy of **clustering (or mapping)** involves circling words and phrases and connecting them to other words. Doing so allows you to visualize the relationship among thoughts.

FIGURE 2.2   Clustering diagram about "vitamins"

Clustering allows you to form distinct groups of related words and phrases, which can help you develop your main points and provide a structure for your essay. It is often useful for starting an argumentative essay, which relies heavily on logical connections.

After your pre-writing stage, you will have enough ideas and have made enough connections to have your topic. You may also be ready to express your thesis.

Thesis Statement

As we've previously discussed, a thesis statement expresses the main point of your essay or what you will be attempting to prove. This statement has two parts: the topic and the comment. In the thesis, "Life in residence at the University of the South Pole helps prepare one for life after university," "Life . . . South Pole" is the topic and "helps . . . university" is the comment. The comment tells the reader how you will be addressing the topic, or what your focus will be.

Not every topic can be turned into an effective thesis statement. If your topic is too broad, it will be difficult to plan or write more than a general overview because there is so much you could say. If your topic is too specific, you could be limited by its scope, and you may have problems researching if there is limited material available.

Exercise **2.7**

The following topics are arranged from broadest to narrowest. Indicate the ones that could be turned into an effective thesis.

1. Species extinction
   Threatened species in Canada
   Threatened species in Canada's Arctic
   Threatened polar bear habitats in Canada's Arctic
   Threatened polar bears living near Coats Island in Hudson Bay
2. Smartphones
   Use
   Apps
   Popularity of gaming apps
   The need for friends to complete quests on gaming apps
3. Nutrition
   Dieting
   Fad diets
   The Atkins diet
   Loss of muscle mass while on the Atkins diet

Research

Research is indispensable to college- and university-level reading, thinking, and writing. To begin researching, you must have a topic for your essay. You might still be working on your thesis, but it should be clear to you by the time you finish this step.

If your essay is research-oriented, you will do most of your research in a library or another place where you have access to written and electronic material. However, not all evidence comes from outside sources. Personal interviews and personal observations may also be allowed, and you can do these anywhere. Research may also involve determining what you already know about a topic and considering how you will use this knowledge in your essay.

> Research can come from personal interviews or published sources, such as newspapers or journals.

Once you have done some research, you can often explain or analyze a topic. If you want to write about how immigration affects Canada, you could look at newspaper and magazine articles, read studies about the immigration experience, and interview immigrants. With this material, you could examine the issue from different perspectives. By knowing your topic and your audience, you can fill in necessary knowledge gaps without overwhelming the audience with irrelevant information that they probably already know.

 Chapters 10 and 11 discuss the research process.

Organization

Organization is mainly about the **outline**, an integral part of writing successful essays. Even seasoned writers use an outline before beginning a new piece of work. An outline gives you a specific plan that can save you time and prevent you from getting off-track as you draft your essay. You do not always need to follow your outline completely, and it may change over time, but it is extremely important that you do not skip this step if you want to write a well-organized, articulate paper.

> An **outline** is a representation of your points and supporting material. Creating an outline is a crucial stage in essay writing, enabling you to see the arrangement of your ideas before you begin a draft.

Two kinds of outlines are the scratch and the formal. A scratch (or sketch) outline represents only your main points, usually indicated just by a word or phrase. It provides a rough guideline and gives you flexibility in developing your points. It may be adequate for a short essay and equally helpful for an in-class essay, when there is little time for a formal outline. The formal outline includes main points and subpoints, revealing more of your essay's structure. In a formal outline, you can see at a glance how the parts interrelate—which is especially useful if the essay is long or complex, such as a comparison and contrast or research essay. A formal outline is a good choice if you lack confidence in your organizational skills because it can remind you of your original plan.

> An outline written before or during the first draft should be considered an organizational aid that can be altered or adapted as your thinking changes or as you come across new evidence.

 Chapter 12 provides an example of an outline.

Exercise 2.8

Look at the outline for "The Cost of Buying Happiness" on pages 244–5 and then read the essay. Do the paragraphs follow the outline? How do you think the outline helped the writer?

Organizing an Outline

Chapters 9 and 12 provide detailed discussions of outlines for particular types of essays.

An outline is a vertical pattern of ideas and supporting information. Your main points are the headings; under each, you list ideas connecting to them—related, less important points, expansions of the main point, examples, evidence—which are subheadings.

Although the outline typically proceeds from general (main) points to specific subpoints, the ordering principle of emphasis is also involved. The order of points helps determine how much emphasis each receives. For example, the last point made in an argument is usually the most emphatic. You can order the points in the body of your essay according to a logical method, such as the strength of the argument presented in each (this is particularly important in an argumentative essay). There are several ways to order your points logically:

- *Climax order*: Begin with your weakest, or least important point, and proceed to the strongest, most important.
- *Inverted climax (dramatic) order*: Begin with your strongest point and end with your weakest.
- *Mixed order*: Begin with a moderately strong point and follow with the weakest argument before concluding with the strongest.

The number of main points and the strength of the opposing argument are factors that can help you determine which method is best for your topic.

Creating an Outline

Here are some general guidelines for making an outline:

1. Decide on your topic and the main point you want to make about it; you can use brainstorming, question–answer, clustering, or freewriting to develop ideas.
2. Divide the outline into introduction, paragraphs for development, and conclusion.
3. Plan for a minimum of five paragraphs total unless told otherwise or your essay is very short.

4. Ensure that you have one main idea per paragraph.
5. Ensure that the main points are ordered logically and effectively.
6. Divide your main ideas (points) into subpoints (at least two per paragraph) that develop the main idea.
7. Represent the relationship between main ideas and their points of development (or subpoints) graphically by indenting subpoints or, more formally, alternating letters and numbers to show the level of development (e.g., I, A, 1, a).

 Chapter 5 discusses outlining further and provides a template that can help you get started.

Composing: First Draft

Getting words on paper in sentence and paragraph form is the most challenging stage for most writers. The traditional first draft is based on the outline.

When you begin your first draft, don't worry if your introductory paragraph is incomplete. You can just write your thesis statement and begin the first paragraph. Start with your topic sentence and then create sentences for your subpoints. Include the support (such as examples, anecdotes, or statistics) for each subpoint and craft a concluding sentence. Repeat this process for each body paragraph. Once you have completed them all, try to draft a concluding paragraph. This conclusion can be a summary of everything that you have said in the body of the essay. Finally, you can turn to writing the introduction.

Remember that these paragraphs are just a rough draft. Sentences can be added or deleted once the draft is complete or even as you continue writing. You may find that the organization of your outline is not the most logical. What you thought worked best in the first paragraph may not fit there after all. You may discover that a point is not relevant to your topic. Feel free to move ideas around, eliminate them, and/or replace them. As mentioned in the previous section, your outline does not have to dictate exactly how you will write your paper. When you begin to write, your ideas may branch beyond what you originally considered. This does not mean the outline is useless; it helps you develop your ideas in a more mature fashion.

In the first draft, your focus should be on putting your ideas in sentence and paragraph form.

Composing on the Computer

You can create your outline and write your first draft on paper or on computer. Both systems have advantages. Drafting on paper, even if only an outline, provides more room to add notes. Some people write a draft on paper so that they can draw circles and lines between similar ideas. Others feel that seeing an idea on paper increases their creativity, as the blank page becomes a challenge to fill.

Drafting on a computer can save time, as you can add or revise ideas quickly. You can use different colours and fonts to identify new thoughts or ideas that you want to add to the document. You can also cut whole sections and place them elsewhere to create a better sense of coherence in your paper.

However, there are challenges to keep in mind: computers crash, files get lost, and printers run out of ink.

Keeping Copies

When you are writing your document, it is important to keep copies of previous drafts.

Whether you work on paper or on computer, it is important to keep copies of your previous drafts. For computer writing, save a clean copy on your hard drive, not the desktop, at various stages and label it clearly so you can find it if you need it later. For example, you should save a clean copy of your outline. You could use the course number, the document type, and the year for your label, as in *ENG101_HydeOutline1_2017*. Create a system that works best for you.

Many students work from their outline file, adding details and creating a draft of their essay. To do this with your writing, copy your outline into a new file, save it, and work from this version so that you retain a clean outline. Following our example, the new file could be called *ENG101_HydeDraft1_2017*.

After finishing this first draft, you can repeat the process so you have a new document (e.g., *ENG101_HydeDraft2_2017*) to work from as you revise. By creating new files as you progress, you can revert to the older file and start again on a fresh copy if you decide you don't like the changes you made or you find that you cut information you didn't want to delete.

Alternatively, most word-processing programs have track changes and comment functions you can use to make side notes or write reminders to yourself. These are especially useful in the editing stages. For example, you can add a comment in the margin, such as "Find a better quote." One thing to keep in mind is that these comments and changes don't always transfer to the subsequent documents when you are saving new drafts.

Make sure that you regularly save your work to your hard drive. A good rule is to save a document every 15–20 minutes. Save it to another source as well, such as a USB key, so that you have a backup if your computer crashes. Most colleges and universities give students access to the school network, so you can save documents there. (Make sure you know exactly where to save your document; saving it to the computer's desktop is generally not a safe location. Get help from the computing staff if you're unsure.) A final alternative is to pay a company to store your data for you in a cloud. Many reputable firms can be found on the Internet. Ask your librarians or IT department staff for suggestions.

Revising: Final Draft

The final draft probably is the most undervalued stage of the writing process. Many students think that the final draft is the place to apply a few necessary touch-ups. They may assume they were supposed to "get it right the first time." However, professional writers almost never do, so why should this be expected of student writers?

Remember that the first and even the second draft are usually rough attempts to put your thinking into words. To change the rough into final requires a new focus: the written document. When you revise, you want to build on its strengths and repair any weaknesses. This process could involve any or all of the following:

- **F**ine-tuning
- **O**verviewing purpose and audience
- **C**larifying meaning
- **U**nderscoring ideas
- **S**olidifying structure

The acronym FOCUS can help you recall the parts of the revision process. There is no correct order, except that fine-tuning should always be the final stage (it appears first to make the acronym).

Overviewing Purpose and Audience

The first task in revising is to determine whether the essay fulfills its purpose and speaks to your intended audience. This step seldom results in major changes, but you may decide you need to adjust your introduction or modify the body of the essay. For example, you might find that a relatively unimportant point in your outline turned out to be very important in your draft and thus need to rewrite a part of the introduction to be consistent with this new emphasis. On the other hand, you might find that you have overdeveloped a point that is only slightly related to your thesis and decide to delete part of the relevant body paragraph. You might also find that some of your words were too informal for your audience and need to be replaced.

Clarifying Meaning

Try reading complicated or unclear parts of the essay aloud. Will your audience understand your meaning? These unclear passages should receive your close attention. Wherever a sentence seems awkward or too long, consider rephrasing it for directness and clarity.

It is hard to be objective when you look back at what you have written, particularly if you have just written it. Leaving time between completing the first draft and revising will help you see your essay more objectively. Having someone else read your paper can give you valuable input, especially if he or she can point to unclear passages. Seeing where other people have difficulty will highlight these places for close attention. The problem may be as simple as a word that is out of place or that means something different from what you thought. Such seemingly small errors can obscure the meaning of an entire sentence and affect the impact of a paragraph. Work on these unclear or awkward passages.

> Usually, the first and even the second draft are essentially rough efforts to put your thinking into words.

> Getting someone else to read your paper can give you valuable input, especially if he or she can point to unclear passages. Seeing the places where other people have difficulty will highlight them for close attention.

Underscoring Ideas

Your body paragraphs should reinforce your thesis and support your points. Reviewing this part of the essay might mean going back to your notes, outline, or early drafts to see if you can further support any undeveloped ideas. You might decide to include an example or analogy to make an abstract or a general point more concrete and understandable. Don't settle for "almost"; ask if all your points are as strong as they could be.

If you get stuck developing an idea at this stage, try a brief pre-writing session. Remember that you can use pre-writing strategies at any point in the process; their main purpose is to generate ideas.

Solidifying Structure

To improve your structure, return to your outline. Do you see any weaknesses in the outline that you didn't notice before? Does your essay's structure reflect your original plans? Can you make it more logical or effective? If the essay's structure seems strong, look at each paragraph as a mini-essay with a topic sentence, a well-developed main idea, and a concluding thought. Not all paragraphs need to be constructed this way, but all do need to follow a logical sequence. Is each paragraph unified, coherent, and adequately developed? Are paragraphs roughly the same length or are some too short or long?

When you revise, you want to make your essay stronger, clearer, and more readable. When a writer makes a change to a draft, it is often because he or she discovered a better way to express an idea. After all, you know much more about your topic now than you did at any other stage.

Fine-Tuning

Working on the final draft could involve some large-scale adjustments and will almost certainly involve some small-scale ones. In the fine-tuning stage, you shift focus to individual sentences and words. Make sure each sentence is grammatical, your expression is clear and concise, and you have used appropriate transitions between sentences. You can also refine your style by checking for sentence variation. Can you combine short, simple sentences into longer, more complex ones or can you use different sentence types to make your points more interesting?

Finally, print out your final paper and read it carefully. Look for typos, spelling, grammar, and punctuation mistakes, faulty sentence structure, and **mechanics** errors. You often see errors on paper that you miss on the computer screen.

The final draft usually focuses on five main stages: **f**ine-tuning, **o**verviewing purpose and audience, **c**larifying meaning, **u**nderscoring ideas, and **s**olidifying structure (FOCUS).

 Chapter 17 explains efficient writing and editing strategies, as well as proofreading guidelines.

Applied to formatting, **mechanics** includes margin size, spacing between sentences, font size and type, and page numbers; applied to writing, it includes abbreviations, capital letters, hyphenation, and numbers.

The Critical Response

An in-class or out-of-class **critical response** assignment may require you to analyze an essay you have never seen before. To do so, you need to exercise your active reading skills, beginning with content comprehension. Your response should demonstrate effective critical thinking and your ability to analyze such elements as the writer's purpose, audience, and strategies. Depending on the nature of the assignment, you may be able to use your own perspective on and/or experience about an issue. You may be asked to focus mainly on the essay itself or on the author references.

A critical response can be considered argumentative: a strong response will convince readers that your thesis is valid and well supported. Although a critical response often clarifies your thoughts or reveals your feelings about an issue, you should not force your opinions on the text. The main function of a critical response is to engage with the text and, through this engagement, to share your views with others.

Below are some of the objectives and conventions of response writing. Remember to pay careful attention to the guidelines you're given, as they can vary greatly from instructor to instructor and from assignment to assignment.

- Your first sentences could include an overview or generalization about the text or the central issue(s) it raises.
- If your reader is unfamiliar with the text, briefly summarize its main ideas (or its plot, if the text is a literary work or a movie).
- Include a thesis statement that briefly indicates your approach to the essay, topic, or issue.
- Don't forget that you are primarily reacting to a text; it should remain front and centre in your analysis. If you use personal experience or observation, it should help support a point but never replace analysis.
- You don't need to research the topic, unless your instructor requires it.
- The length of a critical response can vary considerably, from a couple of well-developed paragraphs to 500 words or more, depending on the nature of the assignment and length of the work you are analyzing.
- You may be required to respond to more than just the text, for example, to another student's response as well. In that case, you will need to filter your perspective through that of another reader, considering both the validity of his or her views and your agreement or disagreement. Sometimes, your instructor will help get you started by posing specific questions.
- In addition to analyzing what is in the essay, you can consider what is not there. What has the writer left unsaid?

The main function of a **critical response** is to engage with a text and, through this engagement, to share your views with others.

 Summarizing skills are an important asset when writing a critical response. Chapter 9 examines how to summarize others' work.

Chapter 1 provides a more complete list of questions applicable to a wide range of readings.

The following questions are often relevant to a critical response.

- Does the author appear reasonable? Does he or she use reason effectively, establishing a chain of logic throughout? Are there failures in logic?
- Does the author succeed in making the issue relevant to the reader? Does he or she appeal to the reader's concerns and values? How does he or she do (or not do) this?
- Is the tone inviting, openly challenging, or neutral?
- Is the order of points appropriate? Are all points well supported?
- What, specifically, would strengthen the writer's argument?
- Does the essay appear free of bias? Is the voice as objective as possible given the argumentative stance? If the author openly declares an opinion, is it a good strategy?
- Does the author acknowledge the other side? How does he or she respond to the opposing viewpoint (e.g., fairly, effectively)?
- Does the author make emotional appeals? Are any extreme or manipulative?

To provide an example of a critical response, we have included Cathy Gulli's essay about putting young offenders in solitary confinement, followed by a student's reaction. After reading the latter, discuss with a classmate whether it satisfies the requirements of a critical response. Then, write a 350–500 word response to Gulli's essay.

Remember that the original essay may be more informal than your critical response to it. For example, the writer may not have cited sources or may have used slang or colloquial language. Check with your instructor before using an informal style.

Sample Professional Essay: Critical Response

Why Do We Still Put Young People in Solitary Confinement?

Cathy Gulli

Gulli adds this explanation to clarify the meaning for her audience.

[1] As the provincial advocate for children and youth in Ontario, part of Irwin Elman's job is to watch out for young people detained in a youth justice facility, which is essentially a jail for anyone aged 12 to 17 who is serving time, or awaiting trial or sentencing. There are 20 across the province, and they all operate under the same legislation and the

Ministry of Children and Youth Services. At any point during their stay in custody, young people have the legal right to call the provincial advocate. Elman has fielded many complaints, but even he is alarmed by the serious violations exposed in a landmark report compiled by his office and released this week on the use of solitary confinement.

> Here she states her focus for the essay.

[2] "It's a Matter of Time: Systematic Review of Secure Isolation in Ontario Youth Justice Facilities" reveals a startling portrait of injustices and indignities occurring within some of the very institutions intended to uphold the rule of law and respect for human rights. Among the most egregious offences that have happened since 2009, the earliest year studied: young people have been confined for days or weeks longer than is prescribed by provincial law or supported by international research; the use of isolation has increased among the youngest, most vulnerable, subset of detainees, those aged 12–15; youth have endured "dehumanizing conditions" inside the cells such as extreme temperature fluctuations and waiting hours for staff to dispose of their bodily waste; they have been denied their legal rights to access a lawyer or the provincial advocate—and have been taunted as "sissies" by staff for such requests.

> Based on the preceding words, what does the word *egregious* mean? Why did Gulli use this word rather than a better-known one?

> Notice that the author uses a word that many understand to show how the youth are viewed by those in authority. How does this choice affect you, as the reader?

[3] Solitary confinement is a lawful practice in Canada, albeit an increasingly controversial one. It is supposed to be used as a last resort to manage behaviour, especially physical aggression; once a threat has ended, youth must be released. In Ontario specifically, the Child and Family Services Act states that individuals under 16 cannot be confined for more than 8 hours in one day or 24 hours in a week; those older than 16 cannot be held for more than 72 hours unless approved by a provincial director. And yet, the report shows that, in 633 cases, young people were held in isolation for more than 24 hours. Three-quarters were confined for between 1 and 3 days; one-quarter was held for 3 to 17 days. (There was a decrease in the use of solitary confinement across all facilities from 1,021 in 2009 to 701 in 2014; that may reflect the fact that fewer youth have been placed in custody.)

> Gulli uses facts to support her point so that you, as the reader, know she is voicing facts, not just an opinion.

[4] Elman realizes staff in a crisis situation only have a few tools and strategies to use, including isolation, but he is convinced that prolonged isolation is never warranted. "If your hope is to help young people turn

their lives around, on what planet does anybody think that putting them in a room with very little in it for days in a row is going to help?" he says. "It makes no sense."

> Note that, in a formal essay, you need to provide a concluding sentence. Do not end with a quotation.

[5] In compiling the report, the advocate's office obtained data from the Ministry of Children and Youth Services and interviewed young people at all 20 justice facilities. (The information pertains to April 2009 to March 2010, and the calendar years of 2013 and 2014.) Many of the youth described "inhumane" conditions. Some said they weren't able to shower, or that the water temperature fluctuated between extreme hot and cold. Some were not given blankets at night; any bedding was taken away during the day. They felt degraded when receiving food through a slot in the cell door. Books were prohibited. Eighty youth were denied a Bible or prayer mat. One told the advocate that solitary confinement turns youth "into crazy, mad, angry people." Another described hearing "kids go crazy—yelling, punching walls until their knuckles bleed cause they can't take it anymore."

> Gulli has a specific opinion about this treatment. Can you think of a counter argument? Critical thinking involves looking at both sides.

[6] These revelations are especially distressing given the arguments against solitary confinement by experts in human rights, child welfare, medicine, and neuroscience. The United Nations says solitary confinement, which it defines as isolation for more than 22 hours, should be "absolutely prohibited" in youth under 18, and individuals who are mentally ill. "Prison psychoses" syndrome is now established by researchers as a consequence of solitary confinement, and can cause problems including "perceptual distortions, paranoia . . . and self-harm."

[7] In its journal last year, the Canadian Medical Association argued that "other options" should be explored for handling young inmates, citing the potential "long-term or permanent" health effects, including altered brain activity, "depression, phobias and personality changes, which may affect the offender's ability to successfully reintegrate into society upon release."

> The author cites a well-known source to support her argument regarding solitary confinement.

[8] To Dr Jean Clinton, a professor and youth psychiatrist at McMaster University who has consulted on child welfare, "solitary confinement is a guaranteed exacerbation of trouble." Many young people in custody have endured childhood maltreatment; they may be developmentally

> Again, she cites a doctor associated with a well-known Canadian university. Is the intended audience Canadians only? Why or why not?

delayed, or have a mental illness or learning disability; many have experienced racism or multi-generational trauma as descendants of residential school survivors (black and Aboriginal youth are overrepresented); some have fetal alcohol spectrum disorder, or suffer from an addiction. At the same time, the brains of adolescents are not fully formed, says Clinton, so "leaving them inside a cell with nothing in it but their anger and repeating thoughts" sets them up for more problems.

[9] Youth have a "biological drive for sensation-seeking," she says, and interacting with others helps to form the neural pathways that create identity. Without positive stimulation and relationships, their brain development is stunted. Gratefully, the opposite is also true, says Clinton: "Neuroplasticity means that this is an amazing opportunity for change and growth."

[10] That is the view of Stephen de Groot, a former professor of social work at the University of Manitoba, who has developed a "relationship- and strengths-based approach" for facilities. The goal is to teach young people how to "emotionally and socially self-regulate" partly by staff modelling that behaviour. That can occur in ways as simple as eating lunch together, and as significant as having youth set personal goals to achieve. "Just by changing the focus [of their time in custody]," he says, "we see differences in kids' behaviours."

[11] But change doesn't come easily. Since 2010, de Groot has worked with both the Ministry of Children and Youth Services and many of the justice facilities cited in the advocate's report to implement his relational approach, "but there's a lot of resistance to it." That's because staff often feel their control is being taken away; some say their safety is at risk—perhaps justifiably so: they do not wear protective gear or possess weapons; their "de-escalation" tools come down to communication, restraints, isolation, and physical strength. "We do have staff who are injured," says Diane Irwin, executive director at St Lawrence Youth Association (SLYA), a justice facility outside of Kingston, Ontario, "sometimes severely."

> Is this a fair representation of the opposite side of the argument? Is the author biased? Why do you feel this way?

[12] At SLYA it has taken two years and "many long, long sessions" with de Groot for the entire staff to "buy in," says Irwin. Today, she says they have seen success, with youth more comfortable in custody, and staff

saying their job is easier; there have only been two youth grievances, and no one has quit. Solitary confinement is still used, but that happens less often and for less time; that decision is now made by a team, including a supervisor. "My biggest point to our staff is if our ultimate goal is to help youth be productive citizens and not reoffend, you want them to pay attention to your teachings. And they're not going to if they don't respect you and if you don't have a relationship with them."

> Gulli places the negative before the positive here. Does that affect how readers will feel about how different facilities operate?

[13] The recent changes at SLYA speak to the variability between how facilities operate. The advocate's report showed that, while serious problems with the use of solitary confinement have occurred at some justice facilities, others have rarely held young people in isolation. That reveals "a lack of safeguards that would ensure a child within one facility would be cared for in the same ways as a child in another," says Kim Snow, a professor and child welfare researcher at Ryerson University who analyzed the report's data. There also appear to be no indicators to suggest that young people who are more prone to aggression are relegated to certain facilities. That alone is evidence that alternatives to solitary confinement exist.

> The author creates doubt in the reader's mind and then uses the word *vague* to describe the ministry's response. How does the word choice affect readers' view of the ministry?

[14] For its part, the ministry has appointed an expert panel to review its residential services, which includes justice facilities; the findings will be reported by the end of the year. It remains to be seen whether the advocate's recommendations, including a ban on the use of solitary confinement for more than 24 hours, are adopted. In response to several specific questions from *Maclean's*, the ministry replied vaguely that it "will review [the] thoughtful and important recommendations." In the meantime, Elman says the stunning misuse of solitary confinement is akin to sentencing a young person twice: "When you put them in an institution and control every moment of every day, they're punished," he says. "You don't need to make it any worse."

—Gulli, C. (2015, August). Why do we still put young people in solitary confinement? *Maclean's*. Retrieved from http://www.macleans.ca/news/canada/why-do-we-still-put-young-people-in-solitary-confinement. Originally published by Maclean's magazine on Aug. 31, 2015. Used with permission of Rogers Media Inc. All rights reserved.

Post-Reading Questions

1. Has Gulli clearly supported her argument? Give examples of passages that support your answer.

2. Besides using argument, what other organizational patterns are in this essay?
3. What type of audience is Gulli writing for?
4. What was the writer's purpose for writing this piece? Did she achieve it?
5. How could Gulli be more objective in this piece? Choose at least two of her points and reword them to show less bias.

Sample Student Essay: Critical Response

Response to "Why Do We Still Put Young People in Solitary Confinement?"

Julianny Vahlis

[1] Solitary confinement is inhumane for young people in Canada while in Venezuela people are being killed by young people. This is a topic that needs to be treated wisely. It is a fact that taking basic rights from young people is inhumane, but the law should not take it easier on them either. Elman states that, if your hope is to help young people turn their lives around, on what planet does anybody think that putting them in a room with very little in it for days in a row is going to help? I do not know if solitary confinement is going to help, but those youth need some kind of disciplinary action. There should be consequences for their actions. There should be a way to help these people, but also a way to protect the people that work around them. "We do have staff who are injured," says Diane Irwin, executive director of one of the facilities outside Kingston, Ontario.

> Note that Vahlis looks at both sides of the argument.

> Here she uses both the argument quoted in the original article and her own views based on her personal experience and beliefs.

[2] In my country, the law protects children and teenagers, so what happens when youth make minor offences in Venezuela? Nothing happens because, according to the law there, children and youth should not go to prison and if they do go, it is for a short period of time. I would not like Canada to become a country where young offenders are protected but citizens who might never commit a crime are not.

> Again, she draws from personal experience. How could she have made her argument stronger?

[3] In the article, Dr Jean Clinton states that solitary confinement is a guarantee of trouble. In my personal experience, not giving them any kind of disciplinary action guarantees a bigger offence after coming out of prison. In my experience, this becomes a never-ending cycle

> What solution do you think Vahlis would suggest?

because the law feels sorry for the minor, the minor does not change, and the cycle continues. The problem needs a solution. When I was in my country, I was robbed by a 13-year-old. This caused me feelings of sadness, disappointment, and anger. It is not that I wanted human rights taken from him, but I wanted some kind of justice or solution.

[4] I believe that it is good to apply relationship-based methods for improving behaviour, as Professor Stephen de Groot is doing in Ontario; however, responsibilities should also be given to these youth to show them the cost of their actions. I do not want to be hard with what I say. I just want to point out a reality that Canada might face if youth do not face consequences for their actions.

> Vahlis obviously feels very strongly about this topic. Do you agree or disagree with her final statement? Why?

Post-Reading Questions

1. Has Vahlis written a good response? Give specific examples to support your thoughts.
2. What specific points has she chosen to address from the original essay?
3. What, if any, important points should she have included? What, if any, should she have excluded?
4. How has the perspective of the original article influenced Vahlis's response?
5. Are there any areas in this critical response essay that are unclear or did Vahlis judge her audience appropriately? Give examples to support your answer.

 # Chapter Review Questions

1. Why is it important to understand your audience?
2. What is the difference between reader-based and writer-based prose?
3. Why is it important to have a clear purpose in mind when writing?
4. What is the difference between a topic and a thesis?
5. What are the different ways you can begin writing your essay? Which one is most effective for you?
6. What are the five stages in essay writing? Why is each important?
7. What is a critical response assignment?
8. What acronym can you use when revising your final draft? What is each step?
9. How can revising your draft improve your essay?

3

Paragraph Essentials

In this chapter, you will learn

- how to construct an effective paragraph;
- why it is important to write coherently;
- what techniques improve paragraphs; and
- how effective paragraph structure reflects effective essay structure.

Like an essay, a paragraph must have a beginning, middle, and end. If any element is missing, such as the topic sentence, the paragraph could lack unity and coherence and you could lose the reader's attention. In addition, paragraphs must be connected to each other to help the reader follow the essay's points. This chapter will help you create unified and coherent paragraphs so that your essay keeps the reader's interest.

Introducing the Paragraph

Like an essay, a paragraph must be organized to serve specific functions:

- to introduce an important point
- to develop that point
- to convey both the important point and its development clearly to the reader

A paragraph and an essay both have a beginning, middle, and end. The beginning announces what is to follow, usually in the topic sentence of the paragraph or the thesis statement of the essay. Without a clear topic sentence, the points will lack force and the paragraph will not be cohesive. The middle of the paragraph develops the main point, and the ending provides a satisfying conclusion. The final sentence may act as a summary of the paragraph's main idea, much like the conclusion of an essay.

You may have been taught to end a paragraph by leading into the next one. Doing so can be very difficult, and it can become tedious for the reader if you end each paragraph this way. Instead, try to focus on wrapping up the topic in your paragraph effectively before introducing the next topic. Above all, do not try to end a paragraph with a sentence that both concludes your main idea and introduces the next one, as it will likely confuse a reader.

Topic Sentence

The topic sentence, usually the first sentence in a paragraph, introduces the paragraph's main idea.

 See Chapter 6 for an expository essay template and Chapter 7 for an expository writing template.

The **topic sentence** introduces the main idea in the paragraph. Therefore, it is usually the most general sentence; the other sentences in the paragraph illustrate or expand on the main idea in some way. The topic sentence is usually the first sentence in the paragraph for the same reason that the thesis statement usually appears in the introduction (first paragraph) of the essay: it provides a logical starting point and makes the paragraph easy to follow.

Paragraph Wrap as Conclusion

A **wrap** is the last sentence of a paragraph that sums up the main point and recalls the topic sentence.

Using a paragraph **wrap** is a satisfying way to conclude a paragraph as it reminds the reader what the paragraph was about. It is especially effective in a longer paragraph where the reader might lose track of the main idea. However, the wrap doesn't just repeat the topic sentence; it reinforces its importance by using different words.

In the following paragraph, student writer Jordan Van Horne successfully wraps the main idea, which is introduced in the first (topic) sentence:

If speed limits were abolished on highways, the necessity for law enforcement officers to patrol the highway for speeders would be curtailed. As a result, police chiefs might have more officers to assign to special community projects, such as MADD or drug awareness projects in elementary schools. These officers could spend their time on a variety of social and community projects that would benefit a large number of youths precisely at the time when they need this guidance. In addition, more officers could be allotted to other important areas that are typically understaffed today, such as surveillance and patrol duty to prevent drug smuggling. Surely the presence of police in the community or their dedication to large-scale projects such as drug smuggling would be more beneficial to public safety than having them patrol the highways.

Connecting Paragraphs by Using Transitions

Your reader must be able to follow your thoughts from one paragraph to the next. Most readers expect a new paragraph to introduce a new topic. As the relationship between topics may not always be clear, it is important to use **transitions** so that the reader can connect the ideas in different paragraphs. A transition can be a word, phrase, or clause. It can occur at the end of a paragraph as a wrap or at the beginning of the next paragraph as part of the topic sentence. Remember that you must conclude each paragraph so that the reader understands that you are finished discussing that particular topic.

A **transition** connects ideas from one sentence or paragraph to the next.

 See "Transitions between Sentences" on page 69.

> When making connections between paragraphs, avoid brief one-word transitions. They usually are too weak to link main points, though they can be useful within paragraphs to link subpoints.

When connecting paragraphs, avoid the kinds of transitions used to connect sentences within paragraphs, such as *for example, consequently, moreover*. They are not usually strong enough to connect one paragraph's main idea to the next one.

The following sentence begins with a dependent clause (underlined) before introducing the paragraph's topic (italicized). The dependent clause acts as a transition, showing that the previous paragraph focused on the fostering of independence through home schooling. The independent clause introduces the new topic.

 Chapter 13 focuses on sentence construction.

> <u>Although the qualities of independence and self-motivation are important in a home-schooled education,</u> *its flexibility enables the child to learn at his or her own pace, matching progress to the child's natural learning processes.*
>
> Student writer Marissa Miles

This sentence combines an indirect reference to the preceding paragraph with the topic sentence of the current one:

Chapter 4 discusses the various ways to develop a main point in a paragraph or throughout an essay.

Another crucial function of genetic engineering is its application to the pharmaceutical industry.

Student writer Neil Weatherall

Exercise **3.1**

In each set of sentences, choose which one makes the best topic sentence.

1. Topic: The 100-mile diet
   a. In small communities, stores often use local products to produce their own wares.
   b. Eating locally is one way to sustain the local economy and farming community.
   c. For example, on Vancouver Island, most grocery stores sell dairy products from Island Farms and other regional dairies.

2. Topic: Smartphones
   a. Recent studies have found that the brain cannot handle all the multi-tasking we try to do.
   b. We interrupt our meals, leave conversations, and forget to concentrate on our driving in order to answer our smartphones.
   c. Smartphones dominate the lives of many people in society today.

3. Topic: Physical education classes
   a. Physical education classes teach skills and knowledge not usually stressed in other classes.
   b. Skills like physical coordination and teamwork are developed in PE classes.
   c. PE classes allow more opportunities for social interaction, which is an essential skill in building future relationships and careers.

Paragraph Unity

A **unified paragraph** focuses on one central idea that is announced in the topic sentence and that all sentences relate to.

Each paragraph should focus on one central idea announced in the topic sentence. It is usually best to place your topic sentence at the beginning because it anchors the thought in the paragraph. In a **unified paragraph**, all sentences relate to the main idea being presented.

Although the principle of one idea per paragraph is logical, it may sometimes be difficult to tell where one idea ends and the next one begins. This is especially true in a rough draft, where you are trying to get your ideas down and may not always pay attention to paragraph structure. Therefore, an important question to ask when revising is whether each paragraph contains one main idea.

During revising, you may see that one paragraph is much longer than the others. In such cases, you can determine a logical place to divide the paragraph into two shorter ones. Consider combining very short paragraphs, as they may seem underdeveloped. Be sure to use logical transitions between connecting sentences.

> Although there is no perfect paragraph length, some instructors give students an ideal range—such as between four and seven sentences—to ensure that each paragraph is sufficiently developed but is not complicated or hard to read.

Exercise **3.2**

In each of the following paragraphs, one sentence is off-topic, affecting the paragraph's unity. Identify this sentence and explain why it doesn't belong.

1. The requirement to display the new driver sign on your vehicle is a reasonable one. It allows other drivers to recognize that the driver may be inexperienced. These drivers may drive more cautiously around the novice driver. It also alerts law enforcement officials to the fact that the driver is learning how to cope in traffic. However, officers have been known to pull over a new driver even if they have no legitimate reason to do so. Since alcohol consumption is often high in teenagers, the sign in the rear window enables police to monitor for drunk driving more effectively. The requirement is therefore beneficial for both other drivers and the police.

2. The ability to concentrate during classes can easily be affected by a student's lack of activity. Most students find it difficult to sit around for six hours each day with only a lunch break, during which they might also do nothing but sit and eat. Exercise gives students relief from simply passively taking in information hour after hour. It especially helps children with high energy levels who find it hard to sit still. In addition, exercise is a solution to the ever-growing problem of obesity. By breaking up the day with at least one compulsory period of activity, students will be able to retain more information and perform better academically.

Paragraph Coherence

It is often easy to identify a paragraph that contains off-topic ideas, but identifying a paragraph that lacks **coherence** may be more difficult. The word *cohere* means "stick together." A coherent paragraph is easy to follow because the writer has used strategies to connect one sentence to the next.

> A **coherent** paragraph is easy to follow because its sentences are connected to each other.

Here is the opening of an essay about the need for a nutritious diet. Although the ideas are quite simple, the paragraph is difficult to follow. Try to determine why this is the case.

Most children throughout Canada depend on their parents to provide them with the proper nutrients each day. There are many contributing factors that make this ideal unachievable, and this lack can cause children to cultivate a serious disease known as obesity.

Now consider a rewritten version of this paragraph. Why is it easier to follow?

Most Canadian children depend on their parents for adequate daily nutrition. However, many factors can prevent them from achieving their nutritional ideal, which may result in obesity, a serious medical disorder.

Part of the problem in the original paragraph lies in the word choice: *cultivate* and *disease* are not the best words in this context. The careful use of repetition and transitions in the second example helps the words and ideas stick together. The writer replaced *this ideal* with *their nutritional ideal*, linking *ideal* back to *nutrition* in the first sentence. Adding the transition *however* and replacing *and* with *which* clarifies the relationship between ideas.

In another example, student writer Walter Jordan evokes the new awareness shown by a friend after his grandfather's death. Coherence is achieved largely through the use of repetition, rhythm, and parallel structures, all of which are discussed in the following sections.

On previous trips, we had noticed the smell of nature when we woke and filled our lungs with fresh air, but this time he noticed the smell of the water and of the rain-sprinkled flowers. We had often looked at the stars on a clear night, but this time he spoke of the deep darkness of the sky; we had always seen the ground we stepped on, but this time he saw the footsteps left behind us.

> Understanding the meaning of words is important for both reading and writing. Not understanding a word when you are reading can affect your understanding of the essay. Not understanding the meaning of a word when writing can affect your reader's understanding of your essay.

 Chapter 1 discusses strategies for learning word meanings.

Word Choice

Usually, more than one word can convey your intended meaning. Considering what word to use may be a question of choosing the best one for the given context. However, whenever you use a word that is not part of your everyday vocabulary, you should confirm its meaning by looking it up in a dictionary. Exchanging your writing with someone else will also help you perfect your word choice. Pay attention to any passages that strike him or her as unclear.

Logical Sentence Order

Your writing is closely connected to your thinking—you need to make your thought process clear to your reader. You can achieve this objective by ensuring that the sentences in your paragraphs follow a logical order. If your ideas do not connect, the paragraph will be incoherent. Any gaps in a paragraph need to be filled in, perhaps by inserting a sentence.

Repetition and Synonyms

Repeating key words or phrases in a paragraph can reinforce your main idea and help your reader understand it. Think of alternative words and expressions, such as synonyms. Use a thesaurus, but check a synonym's dictionary definition to ensure that the word is appropriate and matches your intended meaning. Experienced writers consider the rhythm of the sentence, often placing the repeated or key words at strategic points in the paragraph.

Remember that selective repetition is not the same as being repetitious, which can occur when you needlessly repeat a word or an idea.

Parallel Structures

Experienced writers also use parallel, or balanced, structures to achieve coherence. Charles Dickens often employed this strategy: "It was the best of times; it was the worst of times" (*A Tale of Two Cities*). Parallel sentences can also repeat structures to make the ideas clearer, such as "In order to remain healthy while in school, students should eat well, exercise regularly, and sleep enough."

 Chapter 15 provides more information about parallelism.

Transitions between Sentences

Transitional words and phrases guide the reader from one sentence to the next, signalling the exact relationship between them. Although adding the right transitional words will give the paragraph coherence, failing to use a transition to connect two ideas can make following the paragraph's development difficult. Do not begin a sentence with the FANBOYS: *for, and, nor, but, or, yet*, and *so*. They should be used only to connect two main ideas within a sentence. Some of the most useful transitions are listed in Table 3.1.

TABLE 3.1 Transitions

 Chapter 14 discusses transitional words and phrases further.

Purpose	Examples
Limit	*admittedly, although, it is true that, naturally, of course, though*
Show cause and effect	*accordingly, as a result, because, consequently, for this reason, if, otherwise, since, so, then, therefore, thus*
Illustrate	*after all, even, for example, for instance, indeed, in fact, in other words, of course, specifically, such as*
Emphasize	*above all, assuredly, certainly, especially, indeed, in effect, in fact, particularly, that is, then, undoubtedly*

(continued)

Show sequence or addition	*after, again, also, and, as well, and then, besides, eventually, finally, first . . . second . . . third, furthermore, in addition, likewise, next, moreover, or, similarly, too, while*
Contrast or qualify	*after all, although, but, by contrast, conversely, despite, even so, however, in spite of, instead, nevertheless, nonetheless, on the contrary, on the one hand . . . on the other hand, otherwise, rather (than), regardless, still, though, whereas, while, yet*
Summarize or conclude	*finally, in conclusion, in effect, in short, in sum (summary), so, subsequently, that is, therefore, thus, to summarize*

Unfortunately, transitional words and phrases can be overused. Too many can clutter the paragraph and the essay. Wordy transitions such as *in spite of the fact that*, *due to the fact that*, *first and foremost*, *finally*, *in conclusion*, and *in the final analysis* also produce clutter and should be avoided.

A transitional word or phrase can only assist the reader to move from one idea to the next; it is not a substitute for a link in the writer's thought process. You must write with the reader in mind and leave no holes in thought. Your reader must be able to follow your logic every step of the way. In the following passage, the writer has left something out, and no transitional word alone can bridge the gap:

Society relies on an unbiased newscast in order to gain a true perspective on current events. Front-line employees are entering the TV news field underage and under-educated, thus often producing ill-informed reporting.

The writer quickly moves from a generalization about the need for "unbiased" reporting to an example of one of the causes of "ill-informed reporting" without connecting the two ideas. He or she could have stated that today's newscasts are sometimes biased or ill-informed and proceed to give examples of or solutions to this problem.

Society relies on an unbiased newscast in order to gain a true perspective on current events. However, newscasts today are sometimes biased or ill-informed. This may be because front-line employees are entering the TV news field underage and under-educated, thus often producing poor reporting.

A unified and coherent paragraph, then, refers to one central idea and contains sentences that connect logically to each other. Figure 3.1 illustrates these qualities—the sentences are represented by arrows and are numbered (e.g., S1 means sentence 1).

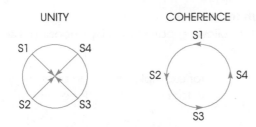

FIGURE 3.1	Unity and coherence

Exercise **3.3**

Find the gap in the following passage and provide a logical link to make it coherent.

> The surprise attack on Pearl Harbor forced the United States to be more aggressive in world politics. This interventionist policy has recently evolved into a series of pre-emptive strikes on those perceived as a threat to US security.

Exercise **3.4**

Coherence through sentence order

All but one of the following sentences are from Jim Kjelgaard's *Kalak of the Ice* (1949). Put them in the most logical order to form a coherent paragraph and discard the irrelevant one. Supply any necessary links between one sentence and the next. Be prepared to justify the order you used.

> and looked with bright eyes at the water below.
> From the height at which he had flown, a floating chip of ice had looked like a dead fish. But now he could afford to miss no opportunity to get food.
> Suddenly the gull planed down toward the open water.
> The gull squawked querulously, crossed the lead, and reversed his direction.
> Then, within inches of the surface, he flapped upward again.
> A lone white gull hovered over the open lead,
> Not often was the gull guilty of such error.
> His last meal, a few shrimp, had been eaten twenty hours ago.
> Desperate hunger prodded the bird.
> He banked, and flew slowly up the lead with bent head.

(continued)

Coherence through transitions

Fill in the blanks in the following paragraph by choosing the appropriate transition from this list:

moreover	for example	unfortunately
but	in fact	for example
above all		

Note: One transition has been given to you, and one should not be used in the paragraph.

> Massive energy consumption is having a negative impact on the planet. ___, in the summer of 2006, western Europe experienced some of the hottest weather on record. Moreover, this temperature increase is not an isolated occurrence. ___, almost every credible scientist today believes that the earth is experiencing climate change due to the emissions of greenhouse gases from cars and coal-burning power plants. Ninety per cent of the energy used in the US comes from fossil fuels: oil, coal, and natural gas, ___ problems arise from other sources, too. ___, nuclear power plants leave radioactive by-products, making storage difficult. ___, dams are not much better as nearby populations must be relocated, and the surrounding habitat is destroyed.

Exercise 3.5

The following paragraph features repetition (in *italics*) and transitions (in **boldface**) to make the writing coherent.

> **In contrast to** allopathy, in Traditional Chinese Medicine (TCM) organs are viewed as "networks"—**that is**, functional physiological and psychological domains—**rather than** discrete anatomical structures. All *our* organs are related; **in fact**, *our* body, [*our*] behavior, and the environment we are in are also interconnected. **In other words**, TCM focuses more on the *context* where the disease exists than on the disease itself. Such emphasis on *context* implies that the way[s] people get sick and can be treated are highly personalized.
>
> People with different *symptoms* may have the same underlying problem, requiring similar treatments; yet people with the same *symptom* may need completely different remedies. While we are equally

endowed with our basic parts, our lungs, heart, kidneys, liver, and so on, our way of coordinating these parts is individualized. **For example**, if arthritis is due to an invasion of "heat" (inflammation), it is different from the same condition with a different cause—**for example**, "cold" (reduced circulation) or "dampness" (accumulation of fluids). **In the first case**, practitioners would administer cooling herbs; **in the others**, warming or diuretic herbs would be used.

Student writer Grace Chau

1. Identify the topic sentence, the repetitive devices, and transitions in this paragraph. Do you think that the writer made a good choice in numbering the points? Why or why not?

Critics of the World Trade Organization (WTO) argue that its approach to globalization causes more harm than good because it undermines democracy. The WTO is undemocratic in several respects. First, ambassadors from member nations are appointed, not elected. Second, the coalition known as the "Quad," comprised of the European Union, the United States, Japan, and Canada, holds almost all the real power. In theory, at least, such decisions as new membership, rule changes, and rule interpretations of WTO rules should be voted for with a three-quarters majority. In practice, however, the Quad determines the WTO agenda. Third, WTO trade talks are held in secret to avoid public criticism and scrutiny. Furthermore, an organization that is not elected controls trade so effectively that it possesses the power to supersede the power of elected communities, states, and even nations on any issue, however ambiguous, related to trade.

Student writer Tao Eastham

2. Identify the topic sentence, the repetitive devices, and transitions in this paragraph, which is an introduction to a book chapter. Based on the text, what topic do you think will be developed in the next paragraph? Give evidence to support your answer.

The news media's power to trivialize anything that comes to their attention is almost magical. News service advertisements talk about providing a "window on the world" or a report on "history in the making." But the nightly television newscast and the daily newspaper fall far short of these ideals. Instead, we get a fast-paced smorgasbord of unconnected and disembodied news stories where meaning

· *(continued)*

and context are lost in the rapid-fire delivery of colourful prose and dramatic pictures. As a result, much of what passes for news is instead isolated, unconnected, and almost meaningless bits of information—in effect, the news is trivialized. This trivialization operates at both the structural level of news gathering and dissemination, and at the level of individual news stories. We have termed this style "the trivialization effect."

Adapted from Rutland, R. A. (1973). *The newsmongers: Journalism in the life of a nation: 1690–1972.* New York, NY: Dial Press.

The essay "Everything You Need to Know about Impostor Syndrome" was written for a general audience; its purpose is to show the readers that feeling like an impostor is common but can be avoided. When reading the piece, consider whether the author meets the criteria for good paragraphs. Are the points linked logically? How successfully does the language help you better understand the article?

Sample Professional Essay: Good Paragraphs

Everything You Need To Know about Impostor Syndrome

Sydney Loney

> The author introduces the topic with a real-life example that many people can understand or sympathize with, creating interest.

[1] Tara Sutton is an award-winning war correspondent and documentary filmmaker from Toronto. She has a master's degree in journalism from New York's Columbia University, and she was the first foreign reporter to enter Fallujah, Iraq, after the siege in 2004 to document human rights abuses during the Iraq War. She's also given talks all over the world. But, sometimes, Sutton feels like a fraud.

> Loney uses headings to notify the reader what is coming. This technique is often used in longer essays and reports so that readers can identify sections of interest quickly.

[2] "When I was in Iraq, I was the only video journalist and I was freelancing," says Sutton. "Everybody else had security experts and crews and flak jackets, and I didn't have any of that stuff. I'd lie there at night thinking, 'You're so useless. You don't know what you're doing. Why are you even here?' I always felt so inferior, like I wasn't as qualified as everyone else."

WHAT IS IT?

[3] Though impostor phenomenon, or impostor syndrome, as it's commonly called, was first identified in 1978 to describe high-achieving people who dismiss, minimize, or ignore evidence of their abilities, Sutton only recognized the symptoms in herself after reading an article about it in *The New York Times*. Since then, high-profile people—from Mike Myers (who famously said, "I still expect that the no-talent police will come and arrest me") to Facebook COO Sheryl Sandberg—have publicly admitted that they had a problem.

> In this paragraph, the author gives a brief history of the syndrome.

[4] In an article published in the *International Journal of Behavioral Science*, research estimates that 70 percent of us will, at least once in our lives, fear being exposed as frauds, no matter how successful we are. "People who feel like impostors have a hard time internalizing and owning their accomplishments and, instead, ascribe them to things like luck, timing, connections or computer error," says Valerie Young, the author of *The Secret Thoughts of Successful Women: Why Capable People Suffer From the Impostor Syndrome and How to Thrive in Spite of It.*

> The writer introduces statistics about the syndrome and includes quotes from an expert, balancing the anecdotal examples from the previous paragraphs.

[5] These feelings are especially common for students and people in creative fields such as writing, acting, and music. "You're judged subjectively and are perceived as being only as good as your last book, film, show or assignment," says Young. "You have to continually prove yourself in ways you wouldn't if you were in an accounting department or in customer service." That self-doubt is also more common among women, minorities, and people who grew up poor or working class. "Whenever you're in a group for whom there are stereotypes about competence, you're more susceptible," says Young.

> With this paragraph, the author moves from a general discussion of impostor syndrome to the specific types of people who are more likely to experience it.

> In an academic essay, do not end a paragraph with a quotation.

HOW TO MAKE IMPOSTOR SYNDROME WORK FOR YOU

[6] Alicia Liu first blogged about her brush with impostor syndrome in 2013, and she has revisited the topic several times since. The Canadian computer programmer, who now lives in San Francisco, wrote about how feeling like a fake made her reluctant to speak up for fear of sounding stupid. "The stakes were even higher because I was the only female engineer on nearly every team I've been on, so I felt I was

> Loney gives another real-life scenario, which reinforces the description of impostor syndrome in a way that people can identify with.

representing my gender," she wrote. "I quietly avoided doing things I didn't think I'd be good at, even though the only way to get better is to do them." That's one of the problems with impostor syndrome—it can hold you back from learning. It may even make you overprepare, which "leads to unnecessary work and potential burnout," says Liu.

[7] But Pamela Catapia, a registered clinical counsellor in Vancouver, says there can be benefits to feeling this way. "If you have impostor syndrome, you're likely a caring, conscientious, talented person who has both the desire and the capacity to improve the world," she says. She points to her clients as evidence; many of them tell her they feel like impostors, but, for the most part, they're actually extremely competent with unrecognized or underutilized leadership skills.

> Here, the author offers a counterargument to her article by mentioning the benefits of impostor syndrome.

[8] While Catapia admits that impostor syndrome can lead to procras-tination, self-sabotage, anxiety and overwork, she says it is possible to make those feelings work for you. The secret is to recognize the good and the bad of impostor syndrome—and hang on to the good. "If over-preparing for things is working, keep that strategy. But if you're feeling burned out and exhausted, dial it down," she says. Young agrees. "I don't like to hear people say 'stop being a perfectionist,' because that's not helpful. You do things because you're getting something out of it. So I ask people, 'What's the good part about being a perfectionist that you want to keep?' If you care deeply about the quality of your work—not everyone does—keep that part, but let go of any shame you might feel over minor and very human imperfections."

> The author uses a transition to indicate a continuation of the discussion.

[9] Sutton credits impostor syndrome with helping her become a better journalist, though she didn't realize it at the time. "The benefit of feeling that way is that I asked so many questions. I had no assumptions that I knew what was going on," she says. "It also led me to do a lot more listening than talking."

[10] There are still days when Sutton's self-doubt resurfaces, especially when it comes to public speaking. "Whenever I start to write a speech, I feel like I don't have anything to say. Now I know it's just a feeling, but in the beginning, I believed it was true."

MAKE PEACE WITH YOUR INNER CRITIC

[11] Though impostor syndrome can push us to achieve, it can also do more harm than good, leading to anxiety, procrastination and burnout. Here's what to do if the negatives start to outweigh the positives.

> The writer recalls the previous discussion before continuing with advice for handling impostor syndrome.

1. KNOW THAT YOU'RE NORMAL

[12] We often assume that struggling with confidence in a new situation is proof that we're impostors, says self-help speaker and author Valerie Young. But those feelings are normal. "Of course you're going to feel off base at first," she says. "If you're starting a new job, instead of thinking, 'I don't belong here,' try, 'This is going to be hard for a while. This is new for me, and mastering or taking on new things is hard.'" She adds that, unless you're a narcissist, you should have feelings of self-doubt every now and then. "If it's your first time doing something, you haven't had time to develop the confidence that comes from prior experience."

> By separating the main points of advice with numbered headings, Loney draws attention to them and makes it easier for readers to retain the information.

> Notice that Loney repeats the credentials of the people quoted, reinforcing their position.

2. PUT IT IN CONTEXT

[13] Consider why feelings of inadequacy are there in the first place, says computer programmer Alicia Liu. "It's not merely a personal issue—though impostor syndrome is too often framed as purely personal. For me, it also reflected the discrimination and stereotyping in the tech industry and wider culture." Your own experience may be rooted in childhood or exacerbated by dismissive coworkers or cultural stereotypes. "You need to sort through your beliefs about yourself and your talents and to examine which belong to you and which came from others," says clinical counsellor Pamela Catapia. "Think about the beliefs that protect, guide and encourage you to grow versus the ones that shame and control you and keep you stuck." When you acknowledge how other people's attitudes might be holding you back, it's easier to feel worthy and confident.

3. CHANGE YOUR MIND

[14] "If you want to stop feeling like an impostor, you have to stop thinking like one," says Young. "This means reframing the way you think about competence, failure and fear. If you get an assignment that feels beyond you, instead of thinking, 'I have no idea what I'm doing,' the

reframe is, 'Wow! I'm really going to learn a lot,'" she says. And remember, your body doesn't know the difference between fear and excitement—sweaty palms and a dry throat come from both. "As you're walking to the podium or going to meet with your boss, just keep thinking, 'I'm excited.' The best part is that, over time, you will be."

> The article ends on a positive note, which reiterates the point that impostor syndrome can be overcome.

Loney, S. (November 2016). Everything you need to know about impostor syndrome. *Canadian Living.* Retrieved from http://www.canadianliving.com/life-and-relationships/money-and-career/article/everything-you-need-to-know-about-impostor-syndrome. Reprinted with permission from Sydney Loney.

Post-Reading Questions

1. How does Loney maintain paragraph unity throughout this essay?
2. Does the writer use paragraph wraps successfully? Give some examples to support your answer.
3. Does the author maintain coherence throughout the essay? What method does she use to ensure her writing is understandable?
4. What types of transitions does the author use?
5. Does Loney conclude her essay effectively? Give reasons to support your answer.

 # Chapter Review Questions

1. Why is it important to create a coherent paragraph?
2. What are some advantages in using transitions when writing paragraphs?
3. How are topic sentences and paragraph wraps different?
4. Why is paragraph unity important?
5. What are some types of transitions that you can use in your writing? How do they differ from each other? How can they help you express your thoughts differently? Create some sentences and try switching transitions.

4

Paragraph and Essay Development

In this chapter, you will learn

- how to identify organizational methods for writing paragraphs and essays;

- how to develop your essay through substantial paragraphs; and

- how to combine organizational methods within an essay.

To write an interesting, informative essay, you must consider many factors, such as audience and formality. You also need to decide how to make it logical and easy to follow. For example, you could use one main pattern for your essay but different patterns for paragraphs. This chapter will introduce you to various organizational writing patterns and help you determine how to organize your essay and its paragraphs into a unified, coherent, and well-developed whole.

Developing Your Essay

As discussed in Chapter 3, an effective paragraph is unified, coherent, and well developed. A unified paragraph focuses on one topic. A coherent paragraph makes sense and provides logical connections so the reader can follow the writer's train of thought. A well-developed paragraph contains supporting information that is organized in a consistent pattern and thoroughly expands a point. The same applies to an essay as a whole: an essay focuses on one topic, with each body paragraph explaining a particular part.

> A unified paragraph or essay focuses on one topic. A coherent paragraph or essay makes sense and provides logical connections so the reader can follow the writer's train of thought. A well-developed paragraph or essay contains supporting information organized in a consistent pattern.

The following paragraph from a student essay about safe injection sites clearly illustrates these concepts. The author connects drug use and disease, showing unity. Repeated words, such as *problem*, and synonyms, such as *situation*, provide coherence. Finally, the paragraph is well developed, as it illustrates the drug problem in Victoria before discussing the solution, which is the essay's main focus.

> Victoria is an urban centre with a heroin and drug-related disease problem. This situation is easy to see when one is walking through the downtown core. The problem may not be as severe as Vancouver's, but it is necessary to take proactive actions to prevent the spread of AIDS and hepatitis. Having been involved with The Youth Empowerment Society downtown and working with street youth in Victoria, I see the need for such a program in Victoria; the personal health of users, old and young, is at stake.
>
> Student writer Kerry Hinds

A writer often chooses one main method of development for the essay but uses other methods in supporting paragraphs. For example, he or she may set out to examine a cause–effect relationship but use different methods from paragraph to paragraph to introduce, clarify, illustrate, or expand the main points.

> The **development pattern** determines how an essay or a paragraph will be organized.

Choosing the appropriate **development pattern** is one of the keys to writing a complete and interesting essay. The pattern you choose for your body paragraphs and the essay overall depends on such factors as the kind of essay, its primary organizational method, your purpose in writing, your topic, your audience, and your main points and their order (e.g., climax, reverse climax). If you are writing a persuasive essay for an audience who may not agree with your point of view, you could use your less controversial arguments in your first body paragraph and move to the more controversial ones. You could also begin by defining an issue and explaining its importance or relevance before continuing with your argument or explanation. The development patterns discussed in the next sections can be used for both body paragraphs and essays.

Exercise **4.1**

Choose a body paragraph from one of the essays in this textbook. Identify how the author creates unified, coherent, and well-developed paragraphs. Look for transitions connecting one paragraph to the next and to the essay as a whole. Identify the main ideas of the paragraphs and their development. Can you follow the author's train of thought? What areas, if any, could be improved? Be prepared to explain your answer to a classmate or your instructor.

Development Patterns

A topic influences an essay's or paragraph's organization. For example, the topic "Which is more important at college or university: acquiring skills or getting good grades?" indicates a comparison–contrast organization pattern. "Solutions to the problem of homeless people" could use the problem–solution pattern. "Do you believe that homeless people are a problem?" places the problem of homelessness as much more important than the solutions.

> The topic of the essay may determine the organization, but each paragraph may use a different pattern.

One way to generate patterns of development is to ask the questions in Table 4.1. Each question leads to a particular method for developing an essay or paragraph. If, for example, your topic is "fast food," you could use any of these methods to develop it.

> The chapters in Part Two discuss the types and components of essays.

TABLE 4.1 Questions and Methods of Development

Question	Method of Development
What is it?	Definition
When did it occur?	Chronology (time)
What does it look like?	Description
How can it be told?	Narration
How do you do it? or How does it work?	Process ("how to")
Why should/does it affect me?	Personal
What kinds/categories are there?	Classification/division
What causes/accounts for it? What is the result/effect?	Cause–effect
What is the answer?	Question–answer
How can it be shown?	Example/illustration

(Continued)

TABLE 4.1 (Continued)

Question	Method of Development
How can it be (re)solved?	Problem-solution
What are the advantages/ disadvantages?	Cost-benefit
How is it like something else?	Analogy
How is it like and/or unlike something else?	Comparison and contrast

Definition: What Is It?

Defining a topic tells your reader what you will be discussing in your essay, helps you understand the topic better, and helps you organize your main points.

Defining a topic not only tells the reader what you will be talking about but also helps you understand your topic better and organize your main points. Does *fast food* mean a Big Mac or microwave meals? Both could be considered fast food but are not the same. In the following example, the writer concisely defines *cloud computing* and uses the division pattern to expand the definition.

> Cloud computing is a technology that allows users to access information and documents without being tied to one computer or network. These clouds also allow users to share documents, and anyone can make changes as the need arises. Networks established within companies require users to log in to the company network where data is stored in order to access documents. Storage is often limited on these networks, and documents are difficult to update by many different users. Cloud computing, on the other hand, means that people can access many different networks and systems, and users can share documents with others easily. Multiple people can access shared documents and make simultaneous changes. Also, storage space can be increased, for a fee, as the user's needs increase. No longer is a person tied to one computer or network.

 See Chapter 6 for a description and sample of a definition essay.

Chronology: When Did It Occur?

Chronology means tracing a topic's development over time.

A **chronological** pattern traces the topic's development over time. When did fast food first appear? When did it truly begin to affect people's lives? Tracing the evolution of fast food in the last 15 years might provide the audience with an appreciation of how the industry has changed. Applying this method of development could also involve a cause–effect or problem–solution approach.

Student writer Courtenay O'Brien uses chronology to develop her paragraph on the Olympics:

The earth shook as father and son wrestled high above the clouds; Kronos, the dreaded father who ate his children, battled his powerful son to rule the Earth. However, Zeus, whom the Fates had protected as a child from Kronos's mighty jaws, triumphed once again, becoming, in the words of Homer, "father of gods and men"; his children would honour his victory as a celebration known as Olympia. From 776 BCE the Olympic Games occurred every four years to celebrate Zeus's success. By 260 CE the Games' importance had deteriorated so much that they were held only occasionally, until the Roman Emperor Theodosius outlawed them completely in 394 CE. The Olympic Games were founded on a profound religious significance, specific ideals about athletes, and strict rules that enabled the Games' long existence and prohibited the inclusion of women. As Olympia changed, the founding principles that had originally made Olympia so significant were disregarded, eventually leading to the end of the ancient Games.

Description: What Does It Look Like?

Description can be used at any point to add concrete, physical detail, but it should play a limited role. You could use a spatial pattern by describing a fast-food burger from the top bun through its condiments and the meat to the lower bun. Description can also create a visual image (such as some of those noted below), an auditory reference (such as the sound of a robin's song), or even a memory of a smell (such as the scent of roses). It is important to be as concrete as possible so that the reader clearly understands what you mean. Instead of using the sentence "It was a dark and stormy night," make the reader "live" the experience: "The thunder was so loud that the windows rattled, and the rain fell so violently that it bounced off the pavement." This type of wording leads to less audience misunderstanding.

Description adds concrete, physical detail to an essay.

This paragraph describes Fallingwater, a house designed by Frank Lloyd Wright.

When Wright came to the site he appreciated the powerful sound of the falls, the vitality of the young forest, the dramatic rock ledges and boulders; these were elements to be interwoven with the serenely soaring spaces of his structure. But Wright's insight penetrated more deeply. He understood that people were creatures of nature, hence an architecture which conformed to nature would conform to what was basic in people. For example, although all of Fallingwater is opened by broad bands of windows, people inside are sheltered as in a deep cave, secure in the sense of hill behind them. Their attention is directed toward the outside by low ceilings; no lordly hall sets the tone but, instead, the luminous textures of the woodland, rhythmically enframed.

The materials of the structure blend with the colorings of rocks and trees, while occasional accents are provided by bright furnishings, like wildflowers or birds outside. The paths within the house, stairs and passages, meander without formality or urgency, and the house hardly has a main entrance; there are many ways in and out. Sociability and privacy are both available, as are the comforts of home and the adventures of the seasons. So people are cosseted into relaxing, into exploring the enjoyment of a life refreshed in nature. Visitors, too, in due measure experience Wright's architecture as an expansion of living.

> Hoffman presents a visual image so that readers can imagine the building, even if they have never seen it.

Hoffman, D. (1993). *Frank Lloyd Wright's Fallingwater: The house and its history* (2nd rev. ed.). Mineola, NY: Dover.

Narration: How Can It Be Told?

> **Narration** (the telling of a story) can be an effective way to introduce or reinforce your topic.

A story can lend drama to an argument or illustrate a point. **Narrating** an incident, or even including some dialogue, can be an effective way to introduce or reinforce your topic. Narration is used in personal essays but can also be used in other types, as in the following sample about the legendary origins of coffee. Because description and narration are generally considered informal, ask your instructor before using them extensively in a formal essay.

Legend has it that one day, Kaldi, an Ethiopian goat-herder, noticed his goats were so frisky when they returned from grazing that they "danced." Curious about the source of their excitement, Kaldi followed them the next day and observed the animals eating the berries of a nearby tree. Kaldi grabbed some berries himself and soon experienced a slow tingle that spread throughout his body. According to the legend, Kaldi was soon "dancing" alongside his goats.

Pendergrast, M. (1999). *Uncommon grounds: The history of coffee and how it transformed our world.* New York, NY: Basic Books.

Process: How Does It Work?

> Relating a **process** focuses on the steps in a sequence.

Although a process-analysis essay is usually a fact-based paper that relates the chronological, step-by-step stages of a **process**, this method of development can also be used in an argumentative essay—for example, if you wanted to convince a reader that one game system is easier to operate than another. This method can be applied to less technical subjects, such as "How to Impress Your Boss or Professor in 10 Easy Steps." Remember that relating a process focuses on the steps in a sequence. Returning to our fast-food topic, you could describe the regimented process of burger production from the time a customer places an order to the time he or she receives the food.

 See Chapter 6 for a description and sample of a process essay.

Here is an excerpt from a process-analysis essay:

The traditional method of painting icons is a long process, requiring a skilled, experienced painter. The artist takes a wooden panel, one with the least amount of resin, knots, and risk of splitting, and covers it with cheesecloth. A gesso is then made from rabbit-skin glue and calcium carbonate (chalk). It is applied to the panel 7 to 10 times and then polished by hand until it is mirror-like. The original is traced to perfection and then transferred onto the gessoed surface. After this, gold leaf is laid on everywhere it is required (backgrounds and halos, for example). Egg tempera paint is freshly made from powdered pigment and egg yolk and is applied from the darkest dark to the lightest light with an egg-white glaze spread on between each coat.

Student writer Magda Smith

Personal: Why Should It Affect Me?/How Does It Affect Me?

A **personal essay** focuses on an aspect of the writer's life or a significant experience. In a successful personal paragraph or essay, the writer is able to make his or her experience seem relevant to the reader. However, don't use this method extensively in a formal essay.

> A **personal essay** focuses on an aspect of the writer's life or a relevant experience.

To present your personal experience with fast-food restaurants, you might consider your childhood visits to them, when the busy, exciting atmosphere was more important to you than the food. Student writer Brian Gregg begins his expository essay on college binge drinking with a recent personal experience; such an approach would be particularly appropriate if his audience were mostly college or university students.

Exam time is approaching at my college, and stress levels are at an annual high. For this reason, when Friday night arrives, I know I will be drinking—and I definitely will not be alone. Last weekend, my friends and I went to a typical residence party. If I can remember correctly, there were about 15 people noisily crowded into a room the size of a large closet, and many more were herded in the hallways. According to a study in the *American Journal of Public Health*, today's North American college students have the highest binge drinking rate of any group, even when compared to their peers who do not go to school; furthermore, alcohol is associated with many social problems on college campuses and is the most widespread and preventable health issue for the more than six million students in America (Wechsler et al., 1995, p. 921).

Classification/Division: What Kinds Are There?

In **classification** or **division**, you begin with many items—for example, commonly known members of the animal kingdom—which you organize into more manageable groups: mammals, birds, fish, reptiles, and amphibians. Each category could in turn be organized into still smaller units. For mammals, these groups could be rodents, primates, and carnivores. Fast-food burgers can easily be classified into hamburgers, chicken burgers, fish burgers, or veggie burgers. Another example is film categories (G, PG, 14A, 18A, and R); the differences could be analyzed by applying the same criteria to each category.

In division, you are more concerned with the whole than with the individual parts. You break a subject into parts in order to better understand or explain the whole (the subject). For example, to illustrate how essay structure works, you can divide it into introduction, body paragraphs, and conclusion. The paragraph on cloud computing (see p. 82) uses division to explain the difference between types of data saving.

Cause–Effect: What Is the Cause? What Is the Result?

You can use the **cause–effect** method to organize an entire essay or to analyze a main point in one or more paragraphs. When you use causes, you consider the reasons for an occurrence. A cause–effect essay or paragraph might focus on one effect, which would be accounted for by one or more causes. On the other hand, it could focus on one cause and consider one or more effects. Since fast food has often been blamed for obesity, you could look at studies that link obesity (effect) to unhealthy diets (cause). Cause–effect studies are particularly common in the sciences.

The **antecedent–consequent** organizational method uses time–order relationships in a similar way. (Think of "before and after" photographs.) The following excerpt discusses one cause for stress in first-year students.

> A major cause of stress in first-year students is the need to establish a new social base. Students not only find themselves among strangers, but also often have to rely on these strangers for moral support. Consequently, friendships tend to be forged rapidly but superficially. When students inevitably find themselves dealing with mid-terms, assignments, and an increasingly heavy course load, they need close friends and family for support but are forced to turn to these new acquaintances instead. Intense friendships may be formed during such

times, but often the stress is insurmountable, leading students to give up and head home.

Student writer Alexis Parker

Question–Answer: What Is the Answer?

The **question–answer** method is effective when you ask a question in the topic sentence and answer it in the paragraph. Questions such as Who? What? When? Where? Why? and How? can be applied to any topic. Posing a relevant question engages the audience because it invites an answer. Student writer Robert Tyre begins his essay by asking two questions, suggesting that the piece will focus on these related areas of foreign policy:

> In the post–Cold War era, do military solutions still have a place or is diplomacy able to solve all our foreign policy questions? Does the United Nations still have a useful purpose or will military coalitions like NATO usurp its role entirely? With increasing world tensions and the current American-led wars in Iraq and Afghanistan, many people around the world are asking these questions.

The **question–answer** method involves posing questions and explaining their answers. Questions such as Who? What? When? Where? Why? and How? can be applied to almost any topic.

Example/Illustration: How Can It Be Shown?

Using concrete **examples** is a way of supporting a point and clarifying an abstract idea. Examples can often be combined with other methods, such as cause–effect, cost–benefit, or comparison and contrast (see pp. 86–90). If you were using the cause–effect method to develop the point that fast food saves valuable time (an effect), you might talk about the convenience of drive-throughs at fast-food restaurants. Examples are very important in most writing, whether they are brief expansions of a point or more fully developed explanations.

Using concrete **examples** is one of the best ways to support a point and clarify an abstract idea.

Brief expansion:

Graffiti art can be seen as a political message on a sidewalk, a limerick on a bathroom wall, a doodle on a desktop, or even a digital image on the Internet.

Fully developed explanation:

In 2012, Lance Armstrong, winner of seven consecutive Tour de France titles, admitted to taking performance-enhancing drugs. Armstrong admitted to using erythropoietin (EPO) and testosterone, as well as a technique known as blood doping. Many people find it hard to believe that he managed to evade detection during the many years he raced.

Problem–Solution: How Can It Be (Re)Solved?

The **problem–solution** method of development could focus on a problem, a solution to a problem, or both a problem and solution. A problem with fast food is its nutritional value; proposing ways to make it healthier combines this development pattern with example/illustration. Studies focusing on problem–solution and cost–benefit are particularly common in the social sciences.

In the following essay conclusion, the author restates his thesis that Confederation was not so much a consequence of various causes but the best solution to unanticipated problems.

> Politicians were not entertaining the idea of uniting the British North American colonies until numerous problems arose. Political alliances, foreign raids, railway expansion, industrial booms, and the termination of long-standing agreements would have been significant events on their own, but their convergence before 1867 helped push Canada towards Confederation. The most logical solution to these problems was union. Macdonald, Brown, and other nineteenth-century politicians did not strategically plan Confederation, but rather Confederation offered itself as a solution to the problems imposed on them.
>
> Student writer Chris Hoffart

Cost–Benefit: What Are the Advantages and Disadvantages?

Analyzing something often involves weighing its advantages and disadvantages. Cost–benefit analysis can be applied to almost any topic, as few things in life come without costs or negative consequences. You could apply this method to fast food by focusing on the individual, community, or perhaps even global costs or benefits. The organizational pattern used for a cost–benefit essay depends on whether the essay is expository or argumentative. In an expository essay, the analysis involves the objective weighing of pros and cons. However, if you are arguing that the benefits are more important than the costs, you might consider the costs first and the benefits second, leaving the strongest argument for last. If you took the opposing position, you might begin with benefits, as student writer Jutta Kolhi does in her argumentative essay on genetically modified organisms (GMOs).

> Some scientists believe that releasing GMOs into the environment could reduce pesticide use since crops could be genetically modified to produce a toxin against the pests. Unfortunately, such a toxin could

have adverse effects on other organisms, such as the pollinator species of the plant. Some believe that genetic engineering could reduce
hunger in Third-World countries by allowing more food production.
However, after growing genetically modified crops, the farmer would
be unable to sow the seeds to grow more crops because GMOs seeds are
sterile, forcing the farmer to buy new seeds every year—an unrealistic
expense. Furthermore, introducing GMOs in Third-World countries
would be risky as most countries have limited resources and few safety
measures in place for controlling GMOs.

Analogy: How Is It Like Something Else?

An **analogy** is a comparison between two objects that share a characteristic.
The analogy helps the reader understand the original object. For example, you
could compare fast food to the fast pace of modern society. The following excerpt uses the analogy of a desert to stress the importance of water management
in North America.

> An **analogy** is a comparison that helps the reader to better understand the original object.

> Imagine a hot, torturously dry desert. Throughout this arid wasteland,
> no life exists—not a tree, shrub, or animal alive. Though to many
> residents of Europe and North America this scenario may seem highly
> abstract and incomprehensible, it is the reality faced by many equator-
> ial nations, such as China, Africa, Saudi Arabia, and parts of India.
> Residents of these nations have developed a keen understanding of the
> importance of water, and how best to manage it to enable a basic level
> of existence. However, residents of nations more endowed with water,
> such as Canada, seem largely indifferent to such a reality.
>
> Student writer François Beaudet

Comparison and Contrast: How Is It Like and/or Unlike Something Else?

Comparison and contrast is a method of systematically drawing similarities
and differences between two things. When you compare and contrast, you find
logical bases of comparison and then analyze their similarities and differences.
In arguing that one fast-food restaurant is better than another, you could compare prices, food quality, cleanliness, and staff friendliness. Student writer Bree
Stutt contrasts two different environmental philosophies by defining each:

> **Compare and contrast** involves finding logical bases of comparison and then analyzing their similarities and differences.

> Conservation is a "shallow ecology" approach to viewing the environ-
> ment and the role of humans within it. Conceived by Norwegian phi-
> losopher and linguist Arne Naess in the early 1970s, "shallow ecology"

 See Chapter 6 for a description and sample of a comparison and contrast essay.

begins with "an assumption, often unexamined, that human beings are [the] central species in the Earth's ecosystem, and that other beings, as parts of systems, are of less importance or value." Preservation, on the other hand, is based on Arne Naess's "deep ecology" movement, which places humans within ecosystems and holds that humans are different from, but not more valuable than, other species.

Exercise 4.2

Let's say you are writing an essay about rap music. Your topic sentence depends on the development method you choose. Here are some examples:

- *Definition*: Rap music is defined by some as being no more than talking over someone else's music.
- *Definition and division*: Rap is a unique form of music that is built around heavy bass beats mixed with sharp, quick lyrics. There is a whole spectrum of rap music, ranging from slow ballads to fast-paced songs.
- *Chronology*: The style of rap music has evolved considerably since it first gained popularity with North American youth in the early 1990s.
- *Description or narration*: The lights were dim, and the crowd, writhing to the rhythm of the bass, was pressing forward to the stage.
- *Process*: To create rap music you need a DJ to provide the beats by mixing records and an MC who takes the beats and contributes the vocals.
- *Personal*: When I first heard rap music, I found the lyrics offensive and sexist.
- *Classification*: There are many different forms of rap, including hip hop, hard core, and R&B.
- *Cause–effect*: By using slang, rap music expands people's vocabulary.
- *Cause–effect*: Living in the ghetto, surrounded by "booty" and the "brothers," can sometimes cause young men to chant words to a particular rhythm that has no melody.
- *Cause–effect*: Rap music has been used as a vehicle for an oppressed minority to get its voice heard.
- *Question–answer*: How does rap music manage to offend a broad demographic group while maintaining a strong fan base?
- *Problem–solution*: It may seem somewhat ironic, but many of the problems addressed in rap lyrics could be solved through this very same medium.
- *Cost–benefit*: Though rap may lead young people to openly and healthily question authority, it can lead some adolescents to commit acts of violence against society.
- *Analogy*: Rap can be compared to the insistent and repetitive chants of an evangelist preacher.

- *Comparison and contrast*: Rap and hip-hop music of the late 1980s and early 1990s, with their offensive lyrics and radical counter-cultural appeal, can be compared to the rock-and-roll revolution of the late 1960s and early 1970s.

With these examples in mind, write at least three different topic sentences for each item in the following list. Use a different organizational method for each sentence.

alternative schooling	exercise	same-sex marriages
animal rights	gas prices	sports violence
climate change	Internet piracy	stress
eating disorders	organ transplants	
email	privacy	
evolution	public speaking	

As you read the following essay, look for the different organizational methods that the authors use to develop the piece. Do they rely on one more than on the others? Pay attention to how the authors link ideas both within and between paragraphs.

Sample Professional Essay: Paragraph Development

Picture This: A Photovoice Study of International Students' Food Experience in Canada

Stephanie Amos and Daphne Lordly

INTRODUCTION

[1] International student enrolment in Canadian universities is increasing (1). As international students acculturate or assimilate to the host country, they may experience culture shock, a disoriented state as a result of moving from a familiar culture to an unfamiliar one (2). Acculturation can be influenced by the time frame of the student's sojourn, the cultural attitudes of both the student and the host country, and the degree of cultural dissimilarities between the student's home country and the host country (2, 3). Stress related to culture shock is most prominent during the initial stage of acculturation (2, 4), and may lead to

> The authors define the term *culture shock* so that the readers understand it.

a preoccupation with food (5). Limited access to authentic traditional foods contributes to the stress, and grieving for home can occur (6, 7).

[2] Other authors have reported that changes in students' environments are related to increased unhealthy behaviours, including a decrease in overall diet quality (7–10). Brown et al. (11) found that international students' food had significant meaning in terms of memories of their home country, different tastes in the host country, maintenance of physical health, and eating with others. Little research exists to show how international students are affected by their transition from high school to university or by their sojourn in a new country, or how those factors influence adjustment to food and dietary patterns in the host country. Understanding international students' food experiences can increase knowledge and influence practice decisions that could enhance and improve student experiences.

> By using words such as *acculturation*, *assimilation*, and *sojourn*, are the authors writing to a general or specific audience? If the reader does not know these terms, how might his or her understanding be affected?

PURPOSE

[3] International students' Canadian food experiences were explored through the use of Photovoice, a participatory action, qualitative research method rooted in photo elicitation and ethnography (12).

METHODS

Participants

> In most studies published in academic journals, background about the study is essential so that it can be replicated. Readers also learn more about who participated and why.

[4] The researcher invited the participation of a convenience sample of 15 undergraduate (n=10) and graduate (n=5) international students attending a 13-week university nutrition bridging program at Mount Saint Vincent University. All program attendees agreed to participate. Informed consent was reviewed orally during class time, and participants subsequently signed consent forms. Six participants were Chinese and nine were Saudi Arabian. The study included 13 women and 2 men. Participants' ages ranged from 25 to 30. The Mount Saint Vincent University Research Ethics Board approved the study.

DATA COLLECTION

[5] Data was gathered from three sources: focus group discussion, photographs, and memos. The researcher scheduled three focus groups.

All participants attended two sessions, each approximately 90 minutes long; a third session was cancelled because of attendance issues. All sessions were audiotaped and transcribed using InqScribe 2.2 (Inquirium, LLC, Chicago, IL, 2012).

[6] **The first focus group:** During the first focus group, the researcher facilitated participant introductions and described Photovoice and photo-taking procedures. To create a context for photo taking and inspire critical reflection and discussion, the researcher posed the following major question: What is your food experience like in Canada? She also asked four secondary questions:

> Amos and Lordly rely heavily on description so that readers can clearly understand what was done.

- What meaning does food hold for you?
- What barriers and facilitators to food preparation do you encounter?
- What types of changes have been made to your diet?
- How are you adjusting to Canadian food culture?

[7] Participants adopted and reframed the secondary questions as objectives that guided their photography.

[8] **Photography:** The study included the use of Photovoice, a methodology that allows individuals to identify, reflect upon, and enhance realities within their community (12). The theoretical underpinnings of the method are critical consciousness and feminist theory (12). Participants photograph scenes, people, or objects related to the topic of interest and then discuss the photos with other participants and the researcher in a group setting. The strength of the method is that it empowers marginalized groups to record visually and discuss social concerns that are then brought forward to policymakers (13). The method is well suited to the exploration of health- and food-related concerns as participants see them, because it provides a lens for viewing participants' perspectives and daily lives (4, 14, 15).

[9] Using personal digital or cellphone cameras, participants photographed what they perceived demonstrated their food experience in Canada. Each participant took approximately 5 pictures over 14 days.

From the photographs, each participant chose two photos that best represented her or his food experiences. One participant included a photo brought from home. Participants wrote a descriptive caption for all their pictures, using their own words to describe the relevance of the photograph. The photos and captions were emailed to the researcher before the second focus group.

[10] **The second focus group:** During this session, a PowerPoint presentation displayed participant photos. To begin group discussion of each photograph, every participant read his or her descriptive caption. The researcher asked the group to study each photo objectively by asking, "What is in this picture?" The question "How does this relate to your food experience in Canada?" enabled participants to make connections between aspects of their own subjective understanding.

[11] **Memos:** The researcher provided sticky notes during both focus groups so that participants could record their feelings and responses to the photograph discussions. These memos provided a discreet way to communicate for participants who may have been hesitant to voice their thoughts.

DATA ANALYSIS

[12] Analysis mirrored Wang's participatory method approach to represent participants' food-related experiences creatively (13). Three elements constructed the participatory approach to analysis: selection, contextualization, and coding (16). First, participants took photographs or provided existing photographs, and chose which photos to use in a discussion of their food experiences. Participants then defined the significance of the photograph. Last, participants focused on theme development through discussion. The principal researcher further developed themes through the analysis of memos and the discussion transcription, using an open coding strategy (17). Themes were verified by a second reader and electronically member checked by participants. Data trustworthiness was maintained, following established conventions (18).

RESULTS AND DISCUSSION

[13] Seven key themes, discussed below, emerged from the data: the paradox of Canadian convenience, the equation of traditional foods

Studies in journals are written with the results at the end. This is climactic, in that readers have to wait until the end of the article to find out what was discovered.

with health, traditional food quality and accessibility, support networks, food consumption for comfort, ethnic restaurants, and exploration of non-traditional foods. Maintenance of cultural identity with traditional foods surfaced as an overarching theme.

The Paradox of Canadian Convenience

[14] Participant discussion focused on the prevalence and availability of Canadian convenience foods and negative experiences associated with an increased intake of these foods. The convenience of food was praised, but not the associated perceived negative health effects. Canadian convenience meant an increased intake of fat and sugar and consumption of larger portion sizes in comparison with their home eating practices; these resulted from higher consumption of snacks, fast food, and beverages. Many experienced weight gain or a fear of weight gain associated with an increased consumption of convenience foods. Figure 4.1 captures the perceived proliferation of high-sugar foods in Canadian diets.

> Here the authors use division to emphasize the differences that international students perceive.

[15] Other researchers have reported increased consumption of convenience foods and energy-dense foods among international students (2, 7–11). Moreover, displacement of healthy foods with similar unhealthy foods of the same food group has been noted (19).

FIGURE 4.1 A student's photo representation of and comment on the high sugar content in Canadian foods

Equation of Traditional Foods with Health

[16] All international students felt their home country food was healthier than Canadian food. Individual ingredients in traditional dishes were valued for their health benefits. Participants believed cooking for themselves

"The sugar level of the drinks and jams is higher than my usual intake in my country. In addition, I noticed that lots of juice[s] are not made [with] real fruit, [and] are not healthy enough. Even in jams, the producer[s] often add sugar in their products."

was the best method to ensure that what they ate was healthy. These beliefs created a strong desire to consume traditional foods or organic foods that were perceived as healthy. Some students felt the negative physical health effects of eating Canadian foods. Describing the physical toll on her body, one student commented: "My digestion is not as good as in my country. Yeah, I also find in my stomach, when I . . ., it's changed to when I speak to some people, like the smell in my mouth is not good."

> Amos and Lordly include narration from the study subjects to support the findings.

[17] The study findings are similar to those from previous studies, which suggest international students continue to consume traditional items because of negative perceptions of the new culture's food (20–22).

Traditional Food Quality and Accessibility

[18] Students found access to traditional foods; however, the quality and taste were poorer than similar products in the home country. Chinese students had better access to traditional foods than did Saudi Arabian students. Similarly, Brown (8) and Brown et al. (11) found that international students felt traditional food in the home country tasted better than traditional food prepared in the host country—and the more dissimilar the culture was, the greater the adverse reaction to the new culture's ethnic food availability and quality.

Support Networks

> To begin this section, the authors use a strong topic sentence that many readers can identify with, no matter what culture they are from.

[19] Food played not only a physical role, but a social one. Food preparation, cooking, and eating with other students provided a human connection for students living away from their families. One participant stated: "I usually cook dishes at home with my friends because it is difficult for me to accept all kinds of native food. I prefer to make dishes in the way of my own country's."

[20] Figure 4.2 is a snapshot representation of one participant's family life in her home country, where meeting over a big dinner was common practice; she missed this. Coming together was important, especially to celebrate special events. Acquiring Canadian contacts for traditional ingredients or foods did help participants find an acceptable Canadian

version of a familiar food. Participants also noted the importance of support networks for cultural acceptance between Canadians and themselves. Mealtimes, including the preparation and consumption of food, encouraged cultural acceptance among various cultures.

[21] Counihan and Van Esterik (23) describe food as a medium for cultural companionship that encourages friendship. Previous research also shows the relational value of cooking together, which includes valuing cultural diversity and provides a safe environment in which to communicate with people whose cultures differ in ways other than language and traditions (4, 24, 25).

FIGURE 4.2 A student's photo representation of and comment on family mealtimes in her home country

"Usually more about family, I think. Usually it's more family. So here we just eat for [the sake of] eat[ing]."

Food Consumption for Comfort

[22] Participants found consumption of traditional dishes a source of comfort (26). International students are transported to a safe place within the new culture by preparing and eating traditional dishes. Consumption of traditional food acts as a cushion against the loss of familiarity they experience (11). As a result, international students would often prepare traditional meals for school lunches (Figure 4.3). Brown (8) found that cooking home country food alleviated international students' stress and loneliness. Conversely, consumption of traditional dishes could also increase homesickness (11). In previous studies, international students' avoidance of traditional food and consumption of more host country foods helped minimize homesickness brought on by the nostalgia of eating traditional foods (8, 11). The research suggests international students may have conflicted emotions about consuming traditional foods.

FIGURE 4.3 A student's photo representation of and comment on the importance of food preparation

"I don't like cheese or salad, so I can't have satisf[ying] foods in university. Therefore, I will cook by myself if I have time, and I will bring them to university and reheat them by microwave."

The writers use an example here to explain briefly the problems international students have with ethnic food. However, unless the readers have experienced these ethnic foods, they will be unsure of the point. Greater detail is needed for a more general audience.

Ethnic Restaurants

[23] Participants became very animated when discussing eating out. It was a form of social activity and fulfilled the need to consume traditional cuisine. However, many participants were disappointed by the inauthenticity of the ethnic foods. They were also frustrated by the lack of acknowledgement of religious restrictions around requests for food without pork or alcohol.

[24] Evidence exists of inauthenticity in Canadian ethnic restaurants, as entrepreneurs struggle to meet the needs of two markets: Western and traditional (25). Many entrepreneurs of non-Western ethnicity provide foods to meet Western consumers' needs (22). A dish may have an ethnically appropriate name; however, authentic ingredients are not used or substitutions (to appeal to Western tastes) are made, which result in taste differences (26).

Exploration of Non-Traditional Foods

[25] Canadian culture provides international students with an opportunity to explore foods not readily available in their home country. Participants commented on the vast array and availability of products in Canada, including cheeses, milk, yogurt, and eggs. One said, "We do not have the variety of cheese as much as in Canada." Another commented, "Egg and milk—the material here is really good." A third stated, "Canada has a variety of ingredients, as well, for example, different kinds of cheese sold in everyday supermarket[s]."

[26] Chinese participants accessed Canadian organic food frequently and praised the greater availability of these products in Canada.

International students explored food through the creation of "fusion" dishes, using popular ingredients found in Canadian grocery stores in traditional dishes. The exploration and use of Canadian foods indicate international students' ability to move from their home culture preferences. Jamal (20) attributed students' exploration of mainstream food as a source of adventure and independence from parental control. While international students appreciated traditional foods, they were curious about new tastes.

Cultural Identity and Food

[27] The high frequency of traditional foods in the participants' photographs and comparison between Canadian and traditional foods throughout discussion indicated international students had a strong connection to traditional foods and that their cultural identity was connected to these foods. In fact, an overarching theme throughout the data was the association of participants' cultural identity with food (7).

[28] Garza-Guerrero (7) states that culture shock induces a yearning for familiar objects such as food, and explains why international students establish identity through familiar foods as they acculturate. In an effort to maintain their cultural identity, international students use food as a medium to ease insecurities, socialize with others from their home country, and adapt to the expectations of the host culture (7). Typically, participants were proud of their traditional food in comparison with the host country's food. Bochner (2) affirms that this behaviour is a means to fight cultural insecurities in the host country. The reinforcement of acculturation and identity through food is highly dependent on the opportunities to source, cook, eat, and share food with other international students.

> By including previous research done by others, the authors add to their credibility and show that they know a great deal about the issue.

Study Limitations

[29] Chinese and Saudi Arabian students were represented in the study. The inclusion of students from additional cultures would enrich the data. Language emerged as a barrier. In response, the lead researcher paid special attention to explaining study objectives clearly and confirming

> In a well-written essay or article, the authors need to acknowledge the study's limitations or even the opposing view in order to prove their credibility. If authors ignore these, readers may question how well the authors know the subject.

participant understanding throughout the research process. Academic demands influenced study participation; the final focus group session was therefore cancelled. The intent of the third focus group was to review the results with participants to ensure their food experiences were adequately represented and to serve as a platform to discuss how Canadian universities could better meet international students' food-related needs. While member checking, or participant validation, was accomplished electronically through email, the advocacy interest and contribution from participants was minimal (18).

[30] Finally, the findings represent the experiences of international students at one university. Readers in similar settings may or may not find the results applicable to their own situations (18).

RELEVANCE TO PRACTICE

In this closing paragraph, Amos and Lordly provide an answer to the perceived problem. Note that, in academic essays, writers need to end with a conclusion that does not include new ideas.

[31] International students experience several food-related challenges as they transition to their Canadian studies and life. The study findings suggest current resources could enhance international students' experience. For example, university food integration programs featured as a component of an international student university orientation could introduce students to ethnic restaurants, describe features of Canadian cuisine, and explain how to access traditional ingredients. Such programs would celebrate the ethnic diversity of the international student body and reinforce students' personal identity as they acculturate. Nutrition professionals could explore an expanded role for the university cafeteria in providing suitable culturally authentic food choices. The large numbers of international students attending Canadian universities, as well as the importance they place on maintaining a cultural identity through food, indicate the need for increased attention by residence food committees, university international offices, and the international students' academic disciplines in prioritizing these students' food experiences.

References

1.   Siddiq F, Holterman B, Nethercote W, Sinclair A, White A; Dalhousie University School of Public Administration. *The economic impact of international*

students enrolled in Nova Scotia universities: An expenditure analysis. Halifax, NS: Minister's Post-secondary Education Research Advisory Panel, Department of Education; 2009. Report No. 1.

2. Bochner S. Sojourners. In: David SL, Berry JW, eds. *The Cambridge handbook of acculturation psychology*. 1st ed. Cambridge, UK: Cambridge University Press; 2006. p. 181–91.

3. Berry JW. Acculturation: Living successfully in two cultures. *Int J Intercult Relations*. 2005;29:697–712.

4. Brown L, Holloway I. The initial stage of the international sojourn: Excitement or culture shock. *Br J Guidance Couns*. 2008;36:33–49.

5. Okorocha E. The international student experience. *J Grad Educ*. 1996;2:80–4.

6. Hall J. Food and dietary requirements for international students. *J Int Educ*. 1995;6:53–60.

7. Garza-Guerrero. Culture shock: Its mourning and the vicissitudes of the identity. *J Am Psychoanal Assoc*. 1974;22:408–9.

8. Brown L. The role of food in the adjustment journey of international students. In: Lindgreen A, Hingley MK, eds. *The new cultures of food: Marketing opportunities from ethnic, religious, and cultural diversity*. London, UK: Gower; 2009. p. 37–53.

9. Furukawa T. Cultural distance and its relationship to psychological adjustment of international exchange students. *Psychiatry Clin Neurosci*. 1997;51:87–91.

10. Wengreen H, Moncur C. Change in diet, physical activity, and body weight among young-adults during the transition from high school to college. *Nutr J*. 2009;32(8):1–7.

11. Brown L, Edwards J, Hartwell H. A taste of the unfamiliar. Understanding the meanings attached to food by international postgraduate students in England. *Appetite*. 2010;54:202–7.

12. Wang C, Burris MA. Photovoice: Concept, methodology, and use for participatory needs assessment. *Health Educ Behav*. 1997;24:369–87.

13. Wang C, Redwood-Jones YA. Photovoice ethics: Perspectives from Flint Photovoice. *Health Educ Behav*. 2001;21:560–72.

14. Martin N, Garcia AC, Leipert B. Photovoice and its potential use in nutrition and dietetic research. *Can J Diet Pract Res*. 2010;71:93–7.

15. Thomas HC, Irwin JD. Using Photovoice with at-risk youth in a community-based cooking program. *Can J Diet Pract Res*. 2013;74:14–20.

16. Wang CC, Yi WK, Tao ZW, Carovano K. Photovoice as a participatory health promotion strategy. *Health Promot Int*. 1998;13:75–86.

17. Polit D, Beck CT. Enhancing quality and integrity in qualitative research. In: *Nursing research: generating and assessing evidence for nursing practice*. Lippincott, Williams and Williams; 1998. p. 539.

18. Guba EG, Lincoln YS. *Fourth generation evaluation*. London, UK: Sage; 1989.

19. Perez-Cueto F, Verbeke W, Lachat C, Remaut-De Winter AM. Changes in dietary habits following temporal migration. The case of international students in Belgium. *Appetite*. 2009;52:83–8.
20. Jamal A. Food consumption among ethnic minorities: The case of British-Pakistanis in Bradford. *Br Food J*. 1998;100:221–7.
21. MacDonald JT, Kennedy S. Is migration to Canada associated with unhealthy weight gain? Overweight and obesity among Canada's immigrants. *Soc Sci Med*. 2005;61:2469–81.
22. Cranfield J. The changing landscape of the Canadian food market: Ethnicity and the market for ethnic food. *Can J Agric Econ*. 2012;61:1–13.
23. Counihan C, Van Esterik P. *Food and culture*. New York: Rutledge; 1997.
24. Smart PLJ, Huang C, Pang CL, Kuah KE, Smart A. Negotiating Chinese immigrant food culture in a global setting. *Int Inst Asian Stud Online Newslett*. 1999;19.
25. Kim YY. *Becoming intercultural: An integrative theory of communication and cross-cultural adaptation*. Thousand Oaks, CA: Sage; 2001.
26. Finkelstein J. Rich food: McDonald's and modern life. In: Smart B, ed. *Resisting McDonaldization*. London, UK: Sage; 1999.

Amos, S., and Lordly, D. (2014). Picture this: A photovoice study of international students' food experience in Canada. *Canadian Journal of Dietetic Practice and Research, 75*(2), 59–63.

Post-Reading Questions

1. Explain how the authors maintain paragraph unity.
2. How do Amos and Lordly develop the paragraphs in this essay? Give examples of the methods they use.
3. Why do the authors use headings? Do these replace transitions or add to them?
4. In the introduction, the authors explain culture shock. Is this explanation needed? Why or why not?

 # Chapter Review Questions

1. What are some of the characteristics of effective paragraphs?
2. Why is supporting information important in paragraphs?
3. What are the different types of organizational or development methods used for both paragraphs and essays?

4. Explain when it is appropriate to use each organizational method for developing paragraphs.
5. Why is it important to use concrete wording when describing something?
6. When is using narration acceptable in a formal essay?
7. What is the difference between an essay that discusses causes and one that discusses effects?
8. How are comparison essays and contrast essays different?
9. Why are examples important in writing?
10. Can more than one development pattern be used in an essay? Why or why not?

5

Summarizing Other Writers' Work

In this chapter, you will learn

- how to write a summary;

- how a summary, paraphrase, abstract, and annotated bibliography differ;

- how to paraphrase; and

- how to create an abstract and an annotated bibliography.

Students are often asked to summarize another author's work. Such material can then be integrated into their essays, which can add variety and credibility to their writing. This chapter will help you learn how to write effective summaries and paraphrases. In addition, you will learn how to use and write abstracts and annotated bibliographies.

What Is a Summary?

A **summary** is a short overview or outline of a longer piece of writing. You can write a summary of a sentence, paragraph, or entire essay or report. The summary accurately reflects the original, includes its main idea(s), does not add anything that isn't in the original, and is in your own words.

A **summary** is a shorter rephrasing of an original work.

You may have experience summarizing your thesis and main points in your writing. In the student essay "What Is Leadership?"—reprinted in Chapter 6—the author summarizes his definition of leadership in the concluding paragraph. (The paragraph is broken into separate sentences here.)

Leadership is the coordination of people, resources, and tasks towards the completion of a goal.

> The author restates his definition using different words than earlier in the essay.

Leadership can be demonstrated in many situations, from a doctor trying to save a life in the ER to a university teacher to a military commander.

> The author gives relevant examples from the essay to illustrate his thesis.

Although leadership is often provided by qualified, educated persons, it may sometimes arise from unlikely sources.

> The author reinforces yet another aspect of his thesis, again using different words.

Regardless, leadership is a skill that can be developed through experience and education.

> After an appropriate transition, the author concludes by restating his belief.

When you write an essay, you might also include a summary of another writer's work to

> Although you may have summarized your thesis and main points in your own essays, an important writing skill is knowing how to summarize the ideas of other writers.

- use a source's main idea(s) as background information;
- set up a point of your own (e.g., show how it is similar to or different from the other writer's position); and
- explain the other writer's position as it relates to your thesis.

Summary writing skills are used in essays and stand-alone exercises. For example, your instructor may ask you to summarize an essay or a passage from a textbook to ensure you understand the writer's ideas. (This type of exercise can also help you develop your reading and writing skills.) You may also be asked to complete various summaries and construct an annotated bibliography when writing a research paper. A well-written essay often includes paragraph summaries rather than direct quotations. All these activities have one thing in common: you are presenting someone else's ideas. Therefore, you must clearly understand the material you summarize and carefully represent the original work.

 Chapter 11 discusses summarizing secondary sources.

How to Write a Summary

Summaries may seem intimidating if you haven't written one before. However, the book reports you wrote when you were younger are very similar to a summary. The main difference is that you do not analyze what you have read and thus do not recommend anything in a summary.

Along with the qualities listed on page 105, a well-written summary

- retains the meaning of the original piece;
- includes the subpoints (if it is a longer summary);
- omits examples and illustrations, unless they are very important;
- uses the same order as the original;
- keeps the original's relative importance of ideas; and
- uses concise wording.

Follow these steps when writing a summary of any length:

1. Read the entire work to learn its purpose, thesis statement, intended audience, purpose, etc. Pay attention to the title, as it often signals the content of the piece. Headings also indicate main points.
2. Reread the piece, noting its major points. Write them in your own words to create a summary.
3. Reread the article and your summary to make sure you have stated the points as the original author intended.
4. Make sure you have used your own words. Create your own sentence structures and use synonyms. Using the other author's structure and language is considered plagiarism.
5. Edit and proofread your summary before you submit it.

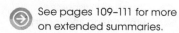 Chapter 11 discusses plagiarism.

Summary Length

As mentioned earlier, a summary is shorter than the original work. The length can range from one sentence to several paragraphs or even pages, depending on how you use the summary. If you are writing a short summary, make sure you capture only the most important points. For example, you may want to summarize an entire paragraph in one sentence because it includes irrelevant material that could distort your purpose and distract your reader. At other times, your instructor (or your manager) might ask you to write an extended summary of an entire report or lengthy essay and share it with others. This chapter includes summaries of various lengths, accompanied by related exercises.

> Summary length is dictated by the intended use. A summary can be as brief as a sentence or two or can be a longer extended summary.

See pages 109–111 for more on extended summaries.

Summarizing Your Sources

Because you are summarizing another writer's work, you must always credit your source. During the research stage, summarize all the main sources you plan to use and carefully record significant direct quotations. This practice can save you from having to find the sources again when you begin writing.

Summarizing a book, article, or Internet source highlights the main points, enabling you to demonstrate your understanding of the source and its applicability to your thesis statement. Summarizing a source's content also avoids too much direct quotation.

Summaries and Argument

If the purpose of your essay is to persuade the reader rather than present facts, you may need to distinguish between fact and opinion. Read the following opening to a professional essay.

> In the course of two years' research for a book on how we think about pain, I've spoken to neurologists, doctors, artists, therapists of every stripe, as well as psychologists—the front-line workers. And frankly, I preferred the people selling healing magnets to most of the psychologists. They were bad communicators. They couldn't make eye contact. They seemed more interested in certain folds in the brain than in helping human beings cope with pain.
>
> Jackson, M. (1999, August 16). "Every breath you take: A former hospital pain specialist puts his faith in the powers of meditation." *Maclean's.*

If you did not acknowledge the writer's words as opinion, you would seriously misrepresent them. Here is an example of a distorted summary:

> Psychologists generally communicate badly and are shifty-eyed.

However, you could correctly acknowledge the author's argument this way:

> Marni Jackson preferred "the people selling healing magnets" to the majority of psychologists she spoke to.

Using Signal Phrases

A **signal phrase** clearly attributes a statement to one or more people. Choose a signal verb that reveals whether the writer is explaining or arguing—verbs such

 Chapter 8 discusses the difference between fact and opinion.

A **signal phrase** indicates that what follows is taken from another source. When you summarize, be especially careful to be specific but not detailed and to use your words but the writer's ideas. Do not be too general or vague or distort the writer's meaning in any way.

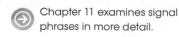

Chapter 11 examines signal phrases in more detail.

as *prefer, believe, claimed,* and *argued* all suggest opinion, whereas *says, states, described,* and *found* do not.

Using appropriate verbs or phrases such as *according to* shows the writer's attitude toward the subject. But do not characterize his or her stance as negative or assume that the writer has a bias. A summary should represent, not judge. The writer may be opinionated; when representing those views, you should not express your own.

Sample Sentence Summaries

The following summaries show how to condense a paragraph into a sentence or two. This type of summary is useful when you want to include key ideas in your essay but do not want to quote extensively. Bear in mind that your instructor may require more detail.

Sample 1:

Helen Thompson was one of the first women to obtain a PhD from the University of Chicago. Her thesis, *The Mental Traits of Sex* (1903), illustrates the main arguments in the similarities tradition. These include the importance of overlap between genders, the requirement of highest methodological standards to demonstrate difference, the search for social explanations of difference, and the demonstration of the specificity of difference.

> Kimball, M. M. (1994). The worlds we live in: Gender similarities and differences. *Canadian Psychology/Psychologie canadienne, 35*(4), 388–404.

Summary:

Helen Thompson's 1903 thesis, *The Mental Traits of Sex*, shows the importance of scientific and social study of the similarities and differences between men and women.

> The summary begins by noting the author, the date of publication, and the title to show where the information came from.

> The summary points out the two types of studies that the author used to make her conclusions.

> Notice how the author of the summary uses different words and a different sentence structure to state the main points.

Sample 2:

It is time for some perspective. With the growing urgency of climate change, we cannot have it both ways. We cannot shout from the rooftops about the dangers of global warming and then turn around and shout even louder about the "dangers" of windmills. Climate change is one of the greatest challenges humanity will face this century. It cannot be solved through good intentions. It will take a radical change in the way we produce and consume energy—another industrial revolution, this time for clean energy, conservation, and efficiency.

> Suzuki, D. (2005). The beauty of wind farms. *New Scientist, 186*(2495), 20.

Summary:
In order to fight global warming, people have to choose to become actively involved and not complain about the necessary changes.

Exercise 5.1

Using the criteria discussed in this section, analyze the following sample from Kimball's essay and the summary. Then, write a summary that meets these criteria.

Sample:

Throughout the history of feminism, from Wollstonecraft to the present, two views of gender differences have been advocated (Cott, 1986). In one, similarities between the sexes have been emphasized, whereas in the other, women's special characteristics that differ from men's have been emphasized.

Summary:

The history of feminism, from Wollstonecraft to the present, shows two different views of gender differences (Cott, 1986). Similarities between the sexes are highlighted in one, but women's special characteristics have been spotlighted in the other.

Exercise 5.2

Choose a paragraph from one of the readings in this textbook and summarize it in one or two sentences.

The Extended Summary

An extended summary includes the elements discussed so far, but it is longer than a few sentences. Although it is mostly in your own words, you may use some from the original (no more than you strictly have to). You must place quotation marks around any phrases—more than three consecutive words—that you cite directly.

Extended summaries are approximately 10–30 per cent of the length of the original. However, if the work you are summarizing requires more expertise

> An extended summary applies the rules for summarizing to an entire work or a main part of it. Although it is too long to use in an essay, this type of summary shows your ability to identify key ideas and put them in your own words. You must also decide whether to include all the main ideas or only the most important ones.

than your audience has, you may need to write more or add a few transitions to make the summary easy to follow. Add no more than necessary for clarity.

How to Write an Extended Summary

You can write an extended summary using these seven steps. (You will recognize some of the instructions from the steps to writing any summary.)

1. Read the work to learn its purpose, thesis statement, intended audience, purpose, etc. Take note of the author, his or her professional credentials, and any other sources used, which can help you determine the elements of the piece.
2. Reread the article, noting its major points, the most important subpoints, and/or key examples. From these points, write an outline using your own words.
3. Read the article and your outline to make sure you have not missed any of the main points.
4. Following your outline closely, write a summary that includes the thesis statement and all the main points (if you're summarizing the entire piece). If you are writing a summary of a specific length and have room for more than the main points, pick the most important subpoints or idea developments to reach the required length.
5. Check your wording against the original. Have you unconsciously used any of the original writer's wording? Have you accurately reworded the points? Have you put quotation marks around phrases and sentences taken directly from the original?
6. Create the title for your extended summary (if required). Include the title of the document you are summarizing, as well as the original author's name. The preferred method is Summary of ["Title of Essay,"] by [Name of Author]. After giving these elements in the title, you may not need to mention them again.
7. Edit and proofread your summary.

> Ensure that your summary is in your own words and that you have put quotation marks around words and phrases taken directly from the source.

It is best to leave time between each step. Sit down and do step 1 all at once. Minimize distractions, as you want to make sure you understand the writer's meaning. Take a break—a few hours or, if you have enough time, even a day—before beginning the next step. But if the work is short and you feel you can concentrate well, you can move on to step 2 immediately.

An extended summary should contain the work's thesis statement and the main ideas. The thesis statement should appear in the introduction of the original, and the main ideas are often the topic sentences of major paragraphs. The topic sentence might not be the first sentence—indeed, some paragraphs might not even have one. Furthermore, not every paragraph will contain a main idea;

the number of paragraphs in the original might not match the number of points in your outline.

Extended Summary Samples

Let's look at samples of extended summaries. The first is preceded by the original essay and the summary's outline.

Sample Professional Essay: Extended Summary

The $15 Minimum Wage Movement Rises Up

Janet Nicol

[1] The fight for a $15-an-hour minimum wage in British Columbia is a fight for women's rights, according to organizers of the campaign. Women make up the majority of those who perform low-wage work across Canada.

[2] "These are not young people living in their parents' basements," Irene Lanzinger, president of the BC Federation of Labour, said about minimum-wage earners. "These are parents, single mothers and new Canadians."

[3] Women make up 63 per cent of workers on minimum wage in British Columbia. Last year, the federation launched its Fight for $15 campaign in partnership with local family-advocacy and anti-poverty groups. The coalition has held rallies and other events to raise public support for the cause. Campaign leaders met with the province's Liberal Premier Christy Clark and Minister of Labour Shirley Bond.

[4] In September, minimum-wage earners in British Columbia received an increase of 20 cents, and now earn $10.45 an hour. British Columbia has the second-lowest minimum wage in Canada after New Brunswick, yet the province has the highest cost of living. Lanzinger said she is "at a loss to explain" the government's unwillingness to make a significant change. "The government wasn't feeling the public pressure," she said. "We were astounded at the small amount."

[5] During the recent holiday season, campaign coordinator Denise Moffatt dressed as the Christmas Grinch on downtown Vancouver streets to draw attention to what she says is the province's stingy stance. Coalition members also handed out lumps of coal to shoppers, letting them know workers were being "scrooged" on the minimum-wage issue by government.

[6] "The increase would make a huge impact on women," Lanzinger predicts, "and would represent a positive economic impact because the wages would go back into the economy. In the past 15 years, BC has been among the worst provinces for child poverty. Poverty has a long-term cost on our education, health care and the criminal justice system."

[7] "Young workers have always been engaged in this issue," Lanzinger added. "They approached our executive to suggest the campaign, which lines up with other fights across Canada and American cities. We thought, if that's what it takes to lift people out of poverty, we'll do it."

[8] The Alberta government is committed to a $15-an-hour minimum wage, to be phased in over three years. According to Statistics Canada, more than 820,000 Canadians work at or below the minimum wage. This represents 5.8 per cent of all workers. Newfoundland and Labrador has the highest proportion of employees working at minimum wage (9.3 per cent), while Alberta had the lowest proportion (1.3 per cent). US cities including Seattle, San Francisco, and New York City have passed laws with timelines for designated employers to implement a $15-per-hour minimum wage.

[9] Contrary to claims by the business lobby, consumers would not end up paying much more if wages go up, Lanzinger believes, because costs are spread over many customers. "Wouldn't consumers want to know the workers serving them are making a decent wage? I have yet to encounter a good argument against this campaign."

[10] British Columbia also should develop a poverty-reduction plan, Lanzinger adds. "Raising the minimum wage is part of the solution. We also need to raise welfare rates and have a social housing plan."

[11] The high cost of child care is another barrier for single mothers entering the workforce. Even at $15 an hour, many workers will continue to struggle to make ends meet, Lanzinger admits, which is why the federation envisions the next step as a "living wage" campaign. "That's way down the road though," she said. "Right now the government has to deal with poverty."

Nicol, J. (2016, Winter). The $15 minimum wage movement rises up. *Herizons*, 6–7.

When you decide on the main points to summarize, paraphrase them as you construct an outline. Remember that the final summarized version must be in your own words and that direct quotes must be placed in quotation marks.

Outline:

[1] Women in British Columbia are fighting for their rights by asking for a $15 minimum wage.
[2] Women make up more than half of the minimum-wage workers in British Columbia.
[3] Only New Brunswick has a lower minimum wage, yet British Columbia is the most expensive place to live in Canada.
[4] Irene Lanzinger, the president of the BC Federation of Labour, believes that a higher minimum wage would improve the province's economy because higher minimum wages mean more money in the economy.
[5] Lanzinger believes that a higher wage would mean less poverty and fewer costs to society.
[6] The campaign for higher wages for women has joined with other young workers who are affected by minimum-wage jobs in order to help eliminate poverty.
[7] Statistics Canada shows that just under a million workers receive minimum wage or less.
[8] Costs for goods and services would not rise very much if minimum wage were $15, as the increased costs would be absorbed by many customers.
[9] Lanzinger also believes that the BC government should reduce poverty with a many-pronged approach, which includes higher minimum wage.
[10] In the future, child care costs should also be investigated, but poverty is the immediate issue.

Nicol's article features many illustrations, such as the passage that discusses minimum wage in other provinces, and discusses cities that have passed legislation to improve pay. Much of the information is used to support the writer's thesis and does not need to be included in the summary. Because some passages simply elaborate on the main points, the summary avoids repetition by not including them:

Summary of "The $15 Minimum Wage Movement Rises Up," by Janet Nicol

Women in British Columbia are campaigning to increase minimum wage to $15 an hour, which they believe is part of the rights women should expect. In British Columbia, women make up more than half of the minimum wage workers, and only New Brunswick pays less for minimum wage, yet British Columbia is the most expensive place to live in Canada. This means that many people live in poverty. The president of the BC Federation of Labour, Irene Lanzinger, believes that a higher minimum wage would be very beneficial to the province's economy, as more money would be in circulation. She also feels that more money would reduce poverty and would improve other social problems. In order to help promote the increase in minimum wage, the campaign joined with other workers who are also affected by this issue. These two groups represent some of the Canadians who work for minimum wage or less. These Canadians make up just less than 6 per cent of workers. While some argue that the costs for goods and services will increase due to a higher minimum wage, Lanzinger disagrees as the increased costs would be absorbed by many customers. In the future, Lazinger would like to see a many-pronged approach taken to reducing poverty in British Columbia, including examining costs for caring for children, but she believes that the government currently needs to focus on the poor.

Our next sample summarizes an essay from Chapter 12 (see pp. 278–81).

Summary of "Polar Bears: Bright Outlook or Grim Future," by Adam Cook

In this essay, the author looks at the future of polar bears, which, while not endangered, are threatened by human activity. Humans have hunted these animals for a variety of reasons and this activity is causing many problems, such as decreased habitat and fewer cubs being born. Hunting has also reduced the food sources that these bears rely on. Air and water pollution has also contributed to the declining numbers of polar bears. Not only does the pollution kill various marine wildlife, but it also results in polar bears not being able to obtain enough food because their food sources are dying. Finally, climate change has a direct impact on the polar bears, as they need ice to hunt and build up their store of fat and nutrients. However, the ice is not lasting as long as the bears need it to. For females, this ice is extremely important, for without food caught while on the ice, their cubs will not survive. Without changes to human behaviour, the polar bears will die out.

 ## Other Ways to Summarize

You can also present another writer's ideas with a paraphrase, abstract, or annotated biography. While some of these terms may overlap with each other or with *summary*, you must be able to recognize the differences so that you can provide your instructor with what he or she wants.

Paraphrase

A **paraphrase** is usually about the same length as the original work. You normally paraphrase an important part of a text, perhaps a whole paragraph or occasionally more. A strict paraphrase is entirely in your own words. Because a paraphrase includes everything of substance from the source, it is unlike a summary, whose main purpose is to condense the original while keeping its basic meaning.

The following example illustrates the differences between summarizing and paraphrasing. The original paragraph is from student writer Barclay Katt's "Tail of Opposites" (see Chapter 6, pp. 134–5).

> Most people have been struck, at one time or another, by the way pet owners come to resemble their pets. It is strange why this is so, and never the other way around—that pets come to look more like their owners. For some reason, the face of the cat or dog is more transferable to the human face than the human face is to that of the dog or cat. Here, it must be admitted that the dog owner is at an advantage. As there are far more breeds of dogs than of cats, the observer cannot help but be impressed by the infinite variety of possible faces of dog owners—from pushed-in pug to the full-blown majesty of Irish wolfhound.

Summary:
Many have noticed that people who own pets often look like their animals, but this comparison is found more often with dog owners than cat owners (Katt, 2017, pp. 134–5).

A **paraphrase** restates the source's meaning using only your own words. Paraphrase when you want to cite a small amount of material that is directly relevant to your point. Include the entire original thought but rephrase it.

A summary is shorter than the original, but a paraphrase is approximately the same length.

 See Chapter 11 for more on paraphrasing, using direct quotations, and citing.

Paraphrase:
It has often been observed that those who own pets look like their animals. However, pets seldom resemble the people who own them. Perhaps this is because people see animals in human faces, but not humans in animal faces. People who own dogs are compared most often to their pets because there are more kinds of dogs than cats. Therefore, people can see many types of breeds in human faces, such as a pug or an Irish wolfhound (Katt, 2017, pp. 134–5).

Exercise **5.3**

Paraphrase the paragraph you summarized in Exercise 5.2.

Abstract

An **abstract** is an overview of your purpose, methods, and results. It can include key phrases or even whole sentences from the full work. Not all the material needs to be reworded.

Articles in peer-reviewed journals have been evaluated by experts before publication.

An **abstract** is an overview of your purpose, methods, and results. Write it after you have finished your essay or, at least, after you have formed your conclusions. However, an abstract appears before the beginning of the essay; it is placed after the title and author notation and before the introduction, enabling readers to decide whether they wish to read the whole piece.

Abstract length varies: an essay abstract is generally 75–100 words; an abstract for a scientific paper is at least twice as long; and some are even longer. A writer will often incorporate key phrases or even complete sentences from the full work into the abstract.

You will often find abstracts at the beginning of papers in peer-reviewed journals and can search for them in the databases at your school library. Reading abstracts can help you determine whether an article will be useful for your essay. However, do not use the abstracts alone; scan the whole article to ensure that it relates to your topic.

Exercise **5.4**

1. Using your school's databases, find articles with abstracts. Choose two articles that you find easy to understand by scanning the contents.
2. Read the abstract for one article and then read the complete work.
3. Read the second article without looking at the abstract first.
4. Compare your understanding of the two articles. Was it easier to understand the first or second article?
5. Write a one-paragraph abstract for the second article and then compare it to the actual one. How do they differ?

Annotated Bibliography

An **annotated bibliography** is an expanded bibliography that often accompanies a large research project, such as a book, dissertation, or other major study. It can take the form of a critical survey, demonstrating the variety of approaches that other writers or researchers have taken to the subject. While an abstract concisely summarizes your own work for potential readers, an annotated bibliography concisely summarizes similar works in the field of study—they tell readers where the writer's particular piece of the puzzle fits into the whole.

Because an annotated bibliography may contain hundreds of entries, each one must be brief. Generally, the entry is a concise presentation of content, focusing on the thesis statement and major points and findings. If the entry refers to a book-length study, the main points may take the form of major section or chapter headings. Sometimes, an annotated bibliography appraises each work's usefulness or contribution to the field.

The following is a sample annotated bibliography entry of Sandy Crashley's "The Cost of Buying Happiness: Why Less Is More," in Chapter 11 (see pp. 254–8).

> The author discusses the minimalist movement and the tiny house movement in relation to how society views success. She examines both movements, and then discusses the characteristics of each. Crashley cites studies that show the effects of a consumer-oriented society. Information from a variety of sources is effectively integrated into the paper to support the author's points. She uses logically ordered subtopics to present a successful overview of the benefits to individuals when they eliminate needless possessions. [78 words]

An **annotated bibliography** summarizes similar works in a field of study. It includes a concise version of the content, focusing on the thesis statement and major points or findings, and can also include an appraisal of the study's usefulness.

Exercise **5.5**

Create an annotated bibliography using the articles from Exercise 5.4.

Summarizing at the Workplace

Preparing a summary is not only a classroom activity. While at work, you may be asked to summarize information for colleagues or your manager. You may be asked to attend a seminar or conference and report on what you learned. You obviously will not give people a very detailed account of the event or give your opinion about how valuable it was. Instead, you will need to apply the same rules you learned here and relate the important information.

Exercise 5.6

Read the following memo and write a summary to present to your instructor. Try to keep the summary length to 10 per cent of the original.

MEMO
TO: Juan Alexandros, District Supervisor
FROM: Gail Fromme, Human Resources Manager
DATE: 12 November 2016
SUBJECT: CHANGES TO WORKPLACE ASSESSMENTS

As of 1 January, we will be implementing a new system to evaluate the managers in each district. This new evaluation includes the latest in psychological testing, which we feel will better predict who will succeed as a manager and whom we need to eliminate.

I will be sending out the new forms within the next few days, once our legal team has vetted them. Please do not share these forms with the staff, as district supervisors will be the only ones using them.

The company would like you to inform the managers that changes will be made to the yearly evaluations. Please notify them that the new evaluations will

1. Include feedback from the staff they manage
2. Include a minimum of 15 hours on-site supervision by the district supervisor
3. Require a self-evaluation, which will be compared to the staff feedback
4. Include a visit to the head office to meet with an evaluation team

Once you receive the new evaluation package, which will include all the necessary new forms and detailed instructions, please read everything carefully. Any questions you have will be answered at the training session we will be having in mid-December. In the meantime, feel free to call me at ext. 267 between 8:30 and 4:00, Monday to Thursday.

The following article contains summarized information. While reading, note whether the author uses adequate transitions between ideas and between what is summarized and what is new material. Also, think about how she summarizes other works to add credibility to her ideas.

Sample Professional Essay: Summarizing

Almost a Million Canadian Kids in Poverty Is an Acute Emergency

Elizabeth Lee Ford-Jones

[1] Hundreds of thousands of Canadian children are growing up without enough.

> The author's thesis or main idea is set out immediately in her title.

[2] UNICEF's most recent report on child well-being in rich countries ranked Canada 17 out of 29 countries assessed, scoring 27th in child obesity, 22nd in infant mortality and 21st in child poverty rates. Sadly, this isn't news. The House of Commons resolved to eradicate child poverty in 1989, but in late 2013, Statistics Canada reported that 967,000 children in this country still lived in low-income homes.

> Note that the writer summarizes what she believes is the most important point of her article. Many writers summarize others' works with a purpose in mind so that they can relate it to their thesis.

[3] These numbers don't simply represent difficult childhoods; they mark a huge group of Canadians who are growing up without the supportive environments they need to develop into healthy adults. They will carry the stress of early adversity throughout their lives.

> As this is an article and not solely a summary, the author includes her opinion.

[4] In 2009, my colleagues and I began a new elective in social pediatrics based out of the Hospital for Sick Children so that medical students could see first-hand the social realities of impoverished Canadian children. The students visit the homes of poor families, sometimes with social workers and infant nurse specialists, and witness the unsettling ways that social environments impact the health of patients.

[5] The stories they report back from the field are deeply troubling, particularly for a country as wealthy as Canada. The students see the impact of neighbourhoods that lack positive activities for children, food

> The author fails to use a parallel structure in this sentence. She uses *lack* to describe the need for "positive activities" but doesn't revise the sentence before discussing the other negative aspects. Therefore, it seems that the children lack food insecurity and long parental work hours. She should state, "lack of positive activities for children and that experience food insecurity, long parental work hours at low-wage jobs that are combined with long public transit times, and the near impossibility . . ."

insecurity, long parental work hours at low-wage jobs combined with long public transit times, and the near impossibility of accessing services such as eye examination, expensive corrective lenses, and dental work for their kids. The students see what parenting low on hope looks like.

[6] In one case, McGill University medical student Maya Harel-Sterling visited an inner-city Canadian mother of 18 years of age who had given birth to a frail baby girl in her bathroom after keeping her pregnancy a secret. In her reflection published by *Paediatrics and Child Health*, "How Did You Sleep Last Night? Have You Eaten Today?" she describes the crowded apartment with four other residents and no room for the baby to crawl or play. The mother sleeps on the floor.

[7] In another household, an elderly grandmother cares for the children while their mother works evenings as a cleaner and their dad drives a pizza delivery truck. The kids spend much of the time with the television on—not a jot of stimulation there.

[8] Mounting evidence in the field of social epidemiology shows that poverty limits the futures of children, especially babies, who lack living environments with family support and opportunities to learn and be active, mentally and physically. We won't resolve this problem without providing access to jobs that pay a living wage and appropriate community supports for every Canadian.

[9] In the April 2014 issue of the *Journal of the American Medical Association*, Neal Halfon, a child health researcher at the University of California, wrote that child poverty levels are persistently high. He wrote that these trends were not due to temporary ups and downs in business but to major shifts in the structure of the economy, which he calls "structural deficits."

[10] The results, including a lack of adequately paying jobs and proper training for skilled work, leave low-income families ill-prepared to give their children the strong start they need for healthy development. This is a problem in both the United States and Canada. Low-income children, especially minorities and Aboriginal people, are growing up with an increased risk of preventable diseases—diseases both medical and mental health related that arise as a result of their early living conditions and will affect us all.

The writer uses the informal *kids* in her title but the more formal *children* throughout the article. When writing for academic purposes, use formal wording.

In this paragraph, the author summarizes the work of Neal Halfon. In an academic essay, you would need to provide information such as the publication date and page numbers.

This is an example of using the original author's words in a summary. There are times that words are used in a certain way, such as for emphasis. You need to retain the original in such cases and place it in quotation marks.

Even in a non-academic essay, a writer needs to start with a topic sentence so that the readers know what the paragraph will be about.

[11] We can address this triad of problems: unacceptable levels of stress ("toxic stress"), which affect cortisol production and set a path of learning and disease problems; lack of access to comprehensive health services; and fundamental disadvantage, including poverty. There are pilot programs in place, but services must be broader and readily available.

[12] Where do we start? What was once considered "a long emergency"—with outcomes manifesting some years later in the life trajectory as ill-health and lack of contribution to society—ought now to be recognized as an acute emergency. Societal structures must change so that the lottery win of life doesn't fall to only a small percentage of families.

> The author begins her final paragraph with a question that is linked to her thesis. She then uses the rest of the paragraph to answer her question and to restate her view that the number of Canadian children living in poverty is an acute emergency.

Lee Ford-Jones, E. (2014, September 8). Almost a million Canadians in poverty is an acute emergency. *The Toronto Star*. Retrieved from http://www.thestar.com/opinion/commentary/2014/09/08/almost_a_million_canadian_kids_in_poverty_is_an_acute_emergency.html

Post-Reading Questions

1. Was it easy to understand when the author switched between new ideas and the summary of others?
2. How did the summarized parts of this article add to your understanding of the author's argument?
3. Do you think the author gave enough information from the UNICEF report? Why or why not?
4. Is the author's point of view clear? How do you think she feels about poverty in Canada? Use examples from the article to support your idea.
5. Why do you think the author chose to write an article like this rather than a typical summary as outlined in this chapter?

Chapter Review Questions

1. What are the key characteristics of a summary?
2. What steps can you follow in writing an extended summary?
3. What is the difference between summarizing and paraphrasing?
4. What is an abstract?
5. What is an annotated bibliography and when is it used?

PART TWO

Essays

6

The Expository Essay

In this chapter, you will learn

- how expository and argumentative essays differ;

- how to organize expository essays; and

- how to write an effective in-class essay.

Essays come in various types, each one with a specific purpose. You need to recognize the differences so that you understand what kind of essay you are asked to write. This chapter introduces you to useful terms and guidelines for answering an essay prompt and helps you understand how to approach a topic for all essay-writing situations.

Expository versus Argumentative Essays

As explained in Chapter 2, there are many reasons for writing an essay. But any essay is either exposition or argument, and these purposes influence how it will be organized. **Exposition** explains or informs; **argument** persuades your audience to change its mind or see your point of view.

Many of the same skills and strategies apply to both kinds of essays. Both can use facts and reliable sources to support main points. Critical thinking is essential for success in either form. Furthermore, your voice should remain objective and your language neutral. For the differences between the types, see Table 6.1.

Exposition is informing, explaining, describing, or defining a topic for the audience. **Argument** is persuading your audience to change its mind or to see your point of view.

 # Types of Essays

Pay attention to the prompts included in an essay assignment. If you are asked to explain the difference between college and high school, you will write an expository essay that compares or contrasts points. If, however, you are asked

TABLE **6.1** Expository versus Argumentative Writing

Expository Writing	Argumentative Writing
Use a fact-based thesis (see page 170).	Use a value- or policy-based thesis (see pages 170–1).
Begin with an open mind and see where your exploration takes you.	Begin by considering your view on an issue and how you can support it.
In your body paragraphs, look at the available evidence and rely on critical thinking for your conclusion.	In your body paragraphs, draw the reader's attention to supporting evidence but do not ignore or distort contradictory evidence.
Research is usually an integral part of expository writing.	Research is not always necessary in argumentative writing, although you may use it to strengthen your argument. By using information from an expert in the field, you add validity to and provide support for your point of view.
If you are writing about a controversial topic, do not take sides, though you may explain both positions by using objective language.	Try to win your argument fairly, by using logic and making use of emotion only where appropriate.

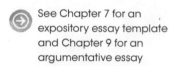
See Chapter 7 for an expository essay template and Chapter 9 for an argumentative essay template.

to explain whether a business diploma is more valuable than a journalism diploma, you will use argument and draw a conclusion based on what you have written. Again, you can use a comparison–contrast structure, but you want readers to understand the validity of your conclusion with argument: you want them to accept your points. Understanding the prompt given or the nature of the assignment is crucial for your success.

Here are examples of each type.

Sample topic for an expository essay:
Explain how inflation influences consumer prices.

The word *explain* is in the prompt, so you will need to inform and explain.

Sample topic for an expository essay that might use some argument:
What can consumers do to combat the effects of inflation?

How might argument be involved? What assumption are you making about the topic that the reader would be expected to agree with?

Sample topic for an argumentative essay:
What must nations do to prevent hyperinflation?

Verbs like *must* and *should* usually signal an argumentative thesis.

How to Write Various Expository Essays

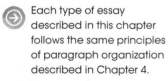
Each type of essay described in this chapter follows the same principles of paragraph organization described in Chapter 4.

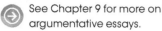
See Chapter 9 for more on argumentative essays.

The remainder of this chapter focuses on the following types of expository essays: process, definition, comparison and contrast, and in-class (or examination). Each discussion includes a sample essay.

The Process Essay

The introduction for a process essay is brief and direct. It may provide background information or include preparation instructions, such as listing equipment needed for the activity. It must include a clear thesis statement.

Arrange each stage in chronological order and discuss each step in detail—don't consider step 2 until you have covered step 1. You may also include what not to do in a process. For short processes, put more than one point in a paragraph. For example, if you are describing how to select a computer, you can include researching online and asking opinions in one paragraph.

Your conclusion might focus on the importance or benefits of the activity or highlight common mistakes, reinforcing the value of having the proper tools or taking safety precautions.

Process essay topics include

- choosing an ideal apartment or roommate;
- creating a web page or your Facebook home page;
- giving a PowerPoint presentation;
- organizing a social or educational event for a group you are involved with; and
- preparing for a job interview.

Sample Student Essay: Process Essay

How to Win a Student Government Election

Aimee Calma

[1] Student governments can go by many names: student councils, student groups, student unions, or even associated student bodies. Whatever the title may be, a student government is an integral piece of collegiate life and holding a seat on that government is coveted. The members that make up a government are generally chosen through an election process, and that process can be arduous. To win a student government election, students need to work hard and be involved in school activities, educate themselves on the organization's past, and engage with the student body to win votes.

[2] Students need to involve themselves in school activities in order to win a student government election. Volunteering for activities, such as new student orientation, will help to see the issues on campus and, in turn, form a campaign around them. Becoming involved with new students can also help to develop a presence at the school and that will help students attain votes during the election. Assisting with student events and activities can also help to strengthen students' electoral campaigns, working on fundraiser events can show compassion, and working light-hearted events can show enthusiasm for the school. Attending open board meetings to learn how the student government runs is another method of student involvement. Showing the current government their

> Calma gives background information so that the reader can identify with her topic.

> The author ends with her thesis and the steps required to be successful.

> While the writer does not begin her paragraph with a transition such as "first," the reader can easily understand that this is the first step because of the clarity of the thesis and steps required in the opening paragraph.

> Note that Calma uses parallel structure to begin each action the reader should follow in order to complete the process successfully. Parallelism is discussed in Chapter 11.

> Again, note the parallelism used.

> Parallelism is used for the next step as well.

willingness and eagerness can help students to be elected because those board members will have a vote in who is to be elected for the next term. Becoming involved in many facets of the school by volunteering for new student events, showing passion and school spirit by helping to raise funds and attend fun events, and appearing at board meetings are key steps to winning a student government election.

In concluding the first paragraph, the author reminds the reader of the crucial steps involved for the first part of the process.

[3] In order to win a seat on the council, students will need to know all they can about the council's history. Learning about past activities, such as referendums and their outcomes, will help to form a campaign and to learn the feelings of the student body. This may be done by reading through older issues of the student newspaper or going through the public minutes of the board meetings to pinpoint key issues to campaign on. Finding out about past accomplishments the student government has achieved will help to strengthen students' campaigns by proving the worth of that government to the student body with measurable proof. By expanding on those accomplishments with future plans of their own, students can figuratively fit into the minds of the student body and ascertain votes. Participating in current campaigns that the government might be running, like whether or not to include a bus pass in student fees, will help to understand the function of the government and how it interacts with the students. Forming a campaign strategy around those interactions can help students to be elected. By learning about the government through its history, building a campaign platform around the government's accomplishments, and participating in current government initiatives, students will have a strong platform and an excellent chance of being elected to government.

The writer gives concrete examples to help the reader fully understand the step she has given for the process.

[4] Engaging with the students is vital to winning a government election. It is a lot easier now in schools to understand the wants of the student body because students use social media platforms in the form of public groups and community pages to voice their concerns about the school. Utilizing these websites to connect with the students and hear their complaints and ideas is essential to gaining the student's trust and votes. The student paper can also be an asset for this purpose; reading the editorial section can illuminate key issues that students feel strongly about, and in turn what campaigning students should focus their election platform on. Understanding the government's code of ethics and

Calma repeatedly states the process's purpose. Repetition can be as effective as using obvious transitions, as discussed in Chapter 3.

its policies is also very important in connecting with the student body when campaigning. By understanding the role of the government and its limitations, campaigning students can base their platform around the council's parameters. Making hollow promises in order to win votes is immoral and, although it might win someone an election, those promises are quickly broken and will raise the ire of the student body. It is always best to campaign truthfully and gain legitimate votes from students who will be proud to have voted for an honest student council member. Visibility during the election is the most important aspect of engaging with students during an election. Creating unique and interesting posters will help to keep campaigning students fresh and foremost in the minds of the voting student body. Using all possible venues to publish those posters can also win students the election; posting them on social media sites, putting flyers in common areas of the school, and handing them out to other students personally will make an excellent and lasting impression. Those impressions will then carry over and help to win the election when it comes time to vote. Engaging with students through the utilization of social media to hear students' thoughts and worries, understanding the government's policies to make attainable and honest promises, and creating memorable posters that are distributed many ways will certainly help to win a student council election.

[5] Getting involved with all aspects of campus by volunteering for events, assisting in fundraising ventures and participating in fun happenings, and attending board meetings will all help to understand the wants and needs of the school, and that understanding may be used to create a successful campaign platform. Learning about the student government's past voting outcomes, learning its accomplishments, and participating in its current initiatives will help to strengthen a platform. Engaging with the student body by hearing its ideas and complaints, understanding the limits of the government and making honest commitments within a platform, and campaigning with thoughtful and interesting posters will keep campaigning students prominently in mind when it comes time to vote for government members. Although bringing all of these pieces together will give students the best chance of winning a seat on their student government, nothing can be guaranteed and they may not win. Elections of any kind are only predictable up to a point and then trust must be placed in the actions and intentions of

> Note that the writer includes what not to do and the reasons for avoiding it.

> While the paragraph wrap is long, it is an effective review of the content.

> The first part of the concluding paragraph effectively summarizes what was stated in the process essay. The author also includes a note of caution but continues with the positive outcome of following her process.

the candidate. If students have a passion for their school and a strong enough desire to participate in their student government, they stand a great chance of accomplishing their goals and winning the election.

Post-Reading Questions

1. By looking at the essay's title, what did you expect to learn from the author?
2. Were your expectations met? Give evidence to support your answer.
3. How could Calma have organized this essay differently?
4. Does the author use any words that are unfamiliar to you? Did you need to look them up in a dictionary? If not, why?
5. Did the author include any new ideas in the concluding paragraph? If so, what are they?

The Definition Essay

A definition answers the question, "What is it?" A definition essay helps the reader clearly grasp a concept and elaborates on a subject, using a variety of organizational methods, such as comparison and contrast.

When writing this type of essay, provide an accurate definition of your topic, as definitions sometimes change. If you fail to give the correct definition, you fail to prove your credibility, which affects the reader's reaction to your essay. For example, if you discuss privacy, you need to be clear that social media and electronic communication have changed the term's meaning.

Some possible topics for definition essays include

- censorship
- consumerism
- freedom
- human rights
- justice

Sample Student Essay: Definition Essay

What Is Leadership?

Andrew Fodor

[1] An unconscious car accident victim enters the emergency room of a local hospital. Nurses, technicians, doctors, and other health-care providers swarm around the patient and begin administering tests and

procedures. The attending physician stands back to assess, monitor, and give orders to the emergency team. The life of the patient depends on the leadership skills of the attending physician.

[2] Leadership is a skill that actively encourages, directs, coordinates, and guides one or more individuals towards the completion of a goal. Leadership is a valuable attribute in nearly all areas of society, such as the military, government, business, education, and families. Although a power structure is often developed to identify or assign an individual, groups of individuals, or organizations to a leadership role, this is not a prerequisite of leadership. For example, the child of a mother undergoing chemotherapy may provide hope, encouragement, and inspiration to his or her family.

[3] A classic example of leadership is a project manager (PM). He or she has a responsibility to complete a project on time, within budget, and to the requirements of the client, usually a third party or company department. The PM must provide direction (a project plan) for the team; delegate responsibility to team members (subprojects); monitor team progress; communicate between management, the project team, and the client; and manage a number of other tasks (for example, team morale).

[4] There are numerous ways to improve an individual's leadership skills; these can often be accomplished by education (such as workshops) and on-the-job experience.

> As mentioned earlier, an academic essay should not include one-sentence paragraphs. The author does not have to follow the rules so closely because his essay is not academic.

[5] Leadership is the coordination of people, resources, and tasks towards the completion of a goal. Leadership can be demonstrated in many situations, from a doctor trying to save a life in the ER to a university teacher to a military commander. Although leadership is often provided by qualified, educated persons, it may sometimes arise from unlikely sources. Regardless, leadership is a skill that can be developed through experience and education.

Post-Reading Questions

1. What concrete words does Fodor use to help the reader understand his concept of leadership?

2. Do you agree with all the examples given? Which, if any, detract from the author's argument?
3. How does the writer establish his credibility?
4. What type of audience is Fodor writing for? Give evidence to support your answer.
5. Explain why this work is a good example of a definition essay.

The Comparison and Contrast Essay

Comparison and contrast can be used as the primary organizational method in either an argumentative or an expository essay. This approach can be more challenging than others, so consider using the four-step approach:

1. Make sure you can actually compare topics. It is not possible, for example, to compare the American health-care system to the Canadian educational system.
2. Make sure the topic is manageable. Comparing high school in two provinces is manageable, but comparing Canada to the United States is not.
3. Carefully choose at least three areas of comparison for your main points. Make sure each is logical and manageable.
4. Carefully organize the essay. You can choose between the block and the point-by-point methods.

Point-by-Point Method

The point-by-point method applies one point of comparison to each subject for each paragraph. In the following outline, the numbers represent your points of comparison and "A" and "B" the items you are comparing:

1. Point of comparison
   A: Subject of comparison
   B: Subject of comparison
2. Point of comparison
   A: Subject of comparison
   B: Subject of comparison
3. Point of comparison
   A: Subject of comparison
   B: Subject of comparison

Block Method

In the block method, consider all the points that relate to your first subject (your first block of material). Then consider all the points that apply to the second subject (your second block). Place the points in the same order. Here is an example:

A: Subject of comparison
   1.   Point of comparison
   2.   Point of comparison
   3.   Point of comparison

B: Subject of comparison
   1.   Point of comparison
   2.   Point of comparison
   3.   Point of comparison

Let's apply the two methods to the instruction "Compare and contrast the benefits of cycling to the benefits of walking."

Point-by-Point Method

1. Transportation
   A: Cycling
   B: Walking
2. Exercise
   A: Cycling
   B: Walking
3. Health
   A: Cycling
   B: Walking
4. Cost
   A: Cycling
   B: Walking

Block Method

A: Cycling
   1.   Transportation
   2.   Exercise
   3.   Health
   4.   Cost

B: Walking
   1.   Transportation
   2.   Exercise
   3.   Health
   4.   Cost

Sample Student Essay: Comparison and Contrast Essay

Tail of Opposites: Meow, Meow, or Woof, Woof?

Barclay Katt

[1] For most people, it is an easy choice. In fact, it is not really a "choice" at all: it is simply the way it is. There are "cat people" and "dog people" in the world, and neither group speaks the language of the other. They are as separate as curds and whey, and when a cat person meets a dog person on neutral turf, the result is a war of words in which the fur is sure to fly. It seems that each group disdains the other; in many other ways, each doggedly or cattily proclaims its separate identity.

[2] Just by walking into a house, you can tell whether the owner is a feline fancier or a canine connoisseur. (The fact that you have made it to the front door tells you something; have you ever heard of a watchcat?) The cat owner will show you to the elegant living room. Elegant? Cat owners possess the most costly furniture, but it is invariably armoured by ugly plastic coverings with, perhaps, a swath of towels wrapped around sofa ends. The dog owner will conduct you swiftly to the humble kitchen table. En route, you will notice the unmistakable "odeur du chien." But in the kitchen, cooking odours will mingle with those of dog, disguising the latter, though not erasing them completely.

[3] Talk to these two different groups of people, and you will again notice a difference. It is not that cat people are snobbish or that they believe themselves superior; the tilt of their noses has nothing to do with it. But there is one thing that they will expect of you: unremitting absorption in the object of their affection—Kitty. You had better be prepared to spend much of your time gazing in adoration at the magnificent specimen. You must also suffer the fastidious attentions of the cat, if it deigns to give them—even if the tribute takes the form of the kneading of its knife-like claws on your thigh.

[4] It is not that dog people are crude or that they have no concern for social graces. But there is one thing that they will expect of you: conviviality, even to the point of garrulousness. Be careful not to turn away from your host too often (resist the temptation to find out where

that annoying series of yips is coming from). Dog owners are famous back-slappers, jabbers, and unapologetic probers of your person. But they will never ask you to share the virtues of their pet and will suddenly lose their warmth if you show too much interest. They are possessive of the bond and discourage interlopers.

[5] Most people have been struck, at one time or another, by the way pet owners come to resemble their pets. It is strange why this is so, and never the other way around—that pets come to look more like their owners. For some reason, the face of the cat or dog is more transferable to the human face than the human face is to that of the dog or cat. Here, it must be admitted that the dog owner is at an advantage. As there are far more breeds of dogs than of cats, the observer cannot help but be impressed by the infinite variety of possible faces of dog owners—from pushed-in pug to the full-blown majesty of Irish wolfhound.

[6] Perhaps it is due to these differences that dog owners and cat owners do not seem able to abide one another; they just never can see eye to eye on anything—or whisker to whisker, for that matter—especially where it concerns the superiority of their own pet. Certainly, the day that cat people and dog people do agree on something will be the day that world peace is finally possible.

Post-Reading Questions

1. Identify the thesis statement in this essay.
2. Identify the method used for comparing and the basis for comparison.
3. As a member of the intended audience, are you persuaded by this point of view? Give reasons to support your answer.
4. Identify any unfamiliar vocabulary and add those words to your vocabulary journal (discussed in Chapter 1). Could different words have been used as effectively?
5. Would another organizational pattern be as effective as the one Katt uses? If so, which one?

The In-Class (or Examination) Essay

You will probably have to do in-class writing while in college or university. This type of essay requires you to demonstrate your knowledge of a subject and your writing skills, as well as your ability to think, read, and write under pressure.

Chapter 1 discusses critical thinking.

You may be able to use a text, notes, or a dictionary; it may just be you, a pen, and some paper.

An in-class, or examination, essay usually tests recall. It also assesses other important qualities, such as organization, time management, critical thinking, and adaptability.

> In-class writing tests your recall, organization, time management, and adaptability skills.

Recall

> It is important to prepare for in-class writing with realistic expectations: the goal is to distinguish essential information from the rest and enable you to focus on what you need to know. Write it, say it, imagine it, experience it, picture it, draw it, test it, repeat it, and understand it.

For an in-class essay, you need to know the terminology of your subject and remember information from lectures, textbooks, and discussions. You also need to know the basics of essay format and structure. If you are asked to write a summary of a text, you will need to know how to summarize; if you are asked to write a critical response to an essay, you will need to know how to analyze and think critically.

An in-class essay tests the application of facts more often than it does the simple recall of basic details. In psychology, you may need to know about B.F. Skinner and his theories of behaviourism, but showing that you understand their implications and impact on the discipline may be more important than describing how he actually performed his tests.

Organization and Time Management

Before you begin to write, spend a few minutes planning how you will answer the questions and how much time you will spend on each one. Stick to your plan: if you find yourself taking too much time on a question, jot one or two points in the margin to follow up on if you have time and move on to the next question.

Read the instructions carefully before beginning. Read every word and underline key words or phrases to reinforce their importance and to keep them in mind as you write (see the next section). Remember that writing skills are connected to reading and thinking skills. If you misread the question or the prompts, you lose credibility because you have not followed directions. This is especially important when the question makes a distinction of some kind: "Answer *three* of the following five questions"; "Respond to *either* question 1 *or* question 2." Pay attention to the verb used to introduce or frame the question—*discuss*, *compare and contrast*, and *explain* give three different instructions.

> When writing an essay, pay close attention to the verb that introduces the question. Words such as *discuss, compare and contrast,* and *explain* provide different instructions.

Finally, plan for at least five minutes per question to review your answers after you've finished writing. Use this time to ensure that you haven't left anything out and that the reader will be able to follow your ideas. Final checks, careful proofreading, and additions such as transitions are important. Instructors prefer to read a thoughtfully revised and carefully proofed essay, even if it has some deletions or some arrows, than one that looks tidy but is unclear in places.

Critical Thinking and Adaptability

To answer the questions properly, distinguish what needs to be addressed and focus on strong, well-chosen points and supporting details. A common weakness of in-class essays is the tendency to generalize or to be too broad; limiting the topic and finding a distinct area to make your own will result in a more manageable essay. Ask yourself the following questions to refine a topic:

- What do you personally know about the topic?
- Have you or anyone you know had experience with it?
- How can you explain the topic using your own knowledge or skills?

Finding where you are knowledgeable is the key to narrowing the topic and to using your strengths.

All essays benefits from examples and illustrations by giving you solid support for your points. Examples and illustrations will also turn the general and abstract into the concrete and specific. Details are essential. Consider using a pre-writing technique, such as questioning or brainstorming, to generate detail.

> Examples and illustrations turn the general and abstract into the concrete and specific.

 Chapter 2 discusses pre-writing.

Student Lindsay Strummer had 90 minutes to write the following essay, which was enough time for her to develop an approach to the topic, thesis statement, and outline. You may not be given this much time to write an in-class essay; as a result, you might not be able to develop each point as thoroughly as she has done.

Sample Student Essay: In-Class Essay

QUESTION

Piracy has been a part of society for centuries. It has been vilified by lawmakers for as long as it has existed, but it has also been romanticized in literature and in the movies. Pirates have adapted to the changes around them in order to profit from others. They are no longer just "sailing the seven seas" but exist even in cyberspace. Explain what Internet piracy is and describe its ramifications to society in general.

ANSWER

[1] The Internet has changed the way people function in daily life. Almost everything can be done online. Shopping, banking, and communicating with others are all tasks that required people to leave their homes, for the most part, up until the mid-1990s. Now, these tasks can be done with a computer and an Internet connection. While this is convenient, and arguably, an advancement, unfortunately, this ease of access has also created a new form of pirate in society: the Internet pirate. Unlike the pirates of old, these people profit from someone else's loss without having to leave the comfort of their home, and, for many, the most concerning part about Internet piracy is that virtually anyone can become a "pirate." This form of piracy is just as detrimental to society as traditional forms still practised.

[2] The most talked about form of Internet piracy involves the theft of music. Until 2011, the music industry was losing money. That did change in 2012, but the profits are not as large as many people seem to think. Making music costs a lot of money. First, there is the musician's share of the profit that must be paid, often in the form of royalties. The cost of the recording sessions must be included in the balance books, as must all the salaries for the people working in the industry. The cost of a CD or music download help cover those costs. However, Internet pirates bypass this by downloading music illegally. Many programs exist that are free and allow music lovers to access digital music without having to pay for their pleasure. While some of these programs or downloads may contain viruses, this does not stop people from accessing them. These pirates often view these activities as victimless crimes; that is not true. Each illegal download costs artists revenue and causes music companies to lose money. Without the money earned from the music being produced, the music industry faces collapse. The more money lost, the less large companies are willing to take risks with unknown artists, as their music is not guaranteed to sell. Therefore, society risks missing out on the newest musician who could become the next superstar.

[3] Software piracy grows every year and is of concern to companies that copyright their material. There are many different ways to access pirated software online. Some websites may offer illegal copies of popular software at discounted rates. Keys are provided, which the pirates

have created. Sometimes these keys work and sometimes they don't. If one buys a key that doesn't work, it is almost impossible to get the money back. In the long run, pirated software obtained this way can wind up costing as much as the legal versions. Another way that one can obtain software is from peer-sharing groups. These people do not see themselves as pirates; however, what they are doing amounts to piracy, as they are stealing the profits from the companies that spend money on research and development.

[4] Another form of piracy that exists on the Internet is that of identity theft. Many people shop and bank online, and while most of the information exchanged is well protected, there are still pirates who hire computer hackers to break through the code that protects an individual's identity. Once one's identity has been discovered, the pirates can then use this information to amass wealth at the expense of the unsuspecting victim. For example, a credit card number can be stolen by a pirate and then used to purchase goods, such as designer clothing, for resale. Unless one checks bank or credit card statements carefully, this piracy can go undetected for months. This is not a victimless crime, as many people wind up paying for this in terms of higher interest rates and service fees. This identity theft can also involve more than just credit cards. Pirates can learn addresses, phone numbers, driver's licence numbers, social insurance numbers, and so much more. Once one's identity is compromised in this way, it becomes very difficult to participate in everyday activities until the information is replaced. This type of piracy costs money for both the victim and society, as wages must be paid to those replacing the identification. Once again, society is being made to pay so that a few may profit without ever having to leave home.

[5] Piracy has been a problem plaguing society for centuries and the newest form, Internet piracy, is just as much of an issue as were the pirates on the high seas. Unfortunately though, today's pirates cannot be seen easily, as they often work from the comfort of their homes and steal from unsuspecting victims. These victims can be large corporations, such as those producing music and software, or they can be individual musicians and unsuspecting home computer users. One of the problems is that anyone can become a pirate by simply

downloading music illegally. Internet piracy costs everyone money and must be stopped.

Student writer Lindsay Strummer

Post-Reading Questions

1. How does Strummer limit the topic? Does she have an area of expertise or specialization that allows her to adapt the topic and capitalize on her knowledge? Give evidence to support your answer.
2. Identify the thesis statement and the main points (the latter take the form of topic sentences for the body paragraphs). Why does the author use this particular order of points?
3. Some of the writer's statements could be challenged. Within the limits of an in-class essay, has the writer adequately supported her points? How has she done so? Has she failed anywhere?
4. Has Strummer directly addressed the question? Suggest other ways that a student writer could respond to it.

Exercise **6.1**

Identify which type of expository essay best fits each of the following topics:

- respective audiences for online games (such as *The Sims* or *World of Warcraft*)
- how tablet computers are changing the way we live
- living in residence versus living in an apartment
- the importance of networking when job hunting
- the value of post-secondary education
- the importance of owning pets.

The following expository essay uses a number of organizing processes, such as definition and description. Notice that the author uses clear examples to explain her points. She includes very clear descriptions so that the readers can visualize what is being discussed, which improves their understanding. Remember that essays, whether expository or argument, can use a variety of organizational patterns and can even have different organizing patterns in individual paragraphs.

Sample Professional Essay: Expository Essay

Help Protect Our Bogs: Why It's Important to Save Our Wetlands

Bev Yaworski

[1] Bogs are one of the five main types of wetlands, which also include marshes, fens, swamps, and shallow water wetlands. You might wonder what makes bogs so important. Besides providing a habitat for rare plants, birds, and mammals, these threatened wetlands have a profound effect on our health by improving air quality.

> Yaworski constructs a clear thesis that supports her title and immediately explains the importance of bogs.

WHAT ARE BOGS?

[2] A bog is a wetland with little water movement and is characterized by acidic, peaty soils (partly decayed organic material). The soils are spongy and poorly drained with acidic water quality and low amounts of nutrients and oxygen, thereby creating materials such as sphagnum mosses and peat.

> The author provides a definition early so that readers understand exactly what she is discussing in the essay.

[3] As wetlands, bogs are saturated with water long enough to promote wetland or aquatic processes as indicated by poorly drained soils, vegetation that thrives in wet conditions, and biological activity adapted to a wet environment. They may feature flora such as blueberries, orchids, and carnivorous plants. Labrador tea, cranberry, and bog laurel may also be evident.

Types of Bogs

[4] Common types of bogs are domed/raised bogs (such as Burns Bog in British Columbia), basin bogs, flat bogs, and shore bogs (such as Pacific Rim National Park). They may be classified according to the type of vegetation present—namely treed, shrubby, or open bogs containing mainly sphagnum moss and minimal plants.

> In an academic essay, each main section must have at least two subsections.

WHY ARE BOGS IMPORTANT?

[5] Bog preservation might not seem like the most urgent environmental concern. But these wetlands are worth protection for reasons that may surprise you.

> Here, she begins to expand on her thesis now that her readers fully understand what bogs are in their many different forms.

Ecological Diversity

[6] "Wetlands such as bogs are some of the most ecologically diverse ecosystems on earth and provide habitat to thousands of wildlife species," says Jasmine Leduc, communications officer, National Capital Commission, which administers Ontario's Mer Bleue Bog. "Bogs provide important habitat for plants, fish, and wildlife, as well as biological productivity and diversity. Close to one-quarter of the worlds' existing wetlands lie within Canada. More than 14 per cent of Canada's surface area is covered by wetlands."

> The author brings in an expert to support her own point of view. This gives the author more credibility for her argument.

Climate Control

[7] Like other wetlands, bogs store and recharge groundwater while accumulating nutrients such as nitrogen, phosphorus, carbon, and sulphur—and may help in regulating climate change. They also contribute toward erosion protection. Bogs are highly valued for their aesthetic and passive recreation opportunities, including bird watching, nature studies, photography, and hiking.

Medicinal Plant Life

[8] Bog plant life has historical connections in providing ingredients for healing treatments. For example, Labrador tea is taken for chest conditions and other medical ailments. (Note, however, that this traditional remedy can be toxic when used in large amounts.) Cranberries—commonly grown in bog environments—are often used in herbal products.

BOGS ACROSS CANADA

> Yaworski discusses some bogs that exist in Canada, thus supporting what she stated earlier about the importance of bogs.

[9] With more wetlands than any other country, Canada is home to a wide variety of bogs.

Mer Bleue Bog (Ontario)

[10] Near Ottawa, Mer Bleue Bog is a 3,500 hectare conservation area and an example of a northern ecosystem, justifying its designation as a Wetland of International Importance under the United Nations Ramsar Convention—an international treaty for wetland

conservation. It is one of the most analyzed bogs on the planet and hosts a research facility measuring carbon dioxide and methane. Approximately 50 per cent of Mer Bleue is a raised boreal peat dome, or sphagnum bog, a system typically occurring in the boreal forests of northern Canada.

[11] It is home to a variety of plants; some are rare, and almost all exhibit unusual characteristics enabling them to survive under challenging conditions. These include the sundew, pitcher plant, bog rosemary, rare orchids, and cotton grass, as well as low heath shrubs. Also present are black spruce and tamarack trees. Mer Bleue provides habitat for significant and rare fauna, including the Fletcher's dragonfly, an insect observed in only a handful of sites worldwide.

Burns Bog (British Columbia)

[12] Located south of Vancouver, Burns Bog, at 3,000 hectares, is the largest raised peat bog on the west coast of North America. It is an estuarine raised peat bog (estuarine because it is at the mouth of the Fraser River).

[13] Raised peat bogs are normally not found this far south. They are mostly found in places such as Ireland, Finland, and Russia. Burns Bog produces moisture-laden breezes that help keep the temperature down in the Metro Vancouver area. Bogs such as Burns Bog store 10 times more carbon than rainforests. Valuable habitat is present for wildlife such as deer, southern red-backed voles, barn owls, and greater sandhill cranes. Burns Bog is also an important stopover for more than 400 migratory bird species.

Kejimkujik National Park (Nova Scotia)

[14] The National Historic Site of Canada is located on the Atlantic coast of Nova Scotia. Along with old-growth forests, this special park features seaside bogs containing large rocks left over from the last ice age. Sphagnum moss rules its vegetation. Slow-growing trees may also be present, but few animals or birds tolerate its windy conditions. Unique plants grow here, including pitcher plants and horned bladderwort—vegetation that trap and consume insects.

THREATS TO BOGS

In a formal academic essay, you need a concluding sentence to end a paragraph.

[15] "Originally, Burns Bog was under attack by drainage for farmland," says Eliza Olson, president, Burns Bog Conservation Society. "This is typical worldwide. Next, industry has become a problem. This is because so little was/is known about the importance of peat bogs worldwide. They have been viewed as wastelands or Mother Nature's cemetery. The biggest challenge is lack of awareness of how important peat bogs are."

[16] "While there are significant efforts underway to halt the loss of wetlands, conditions such as climate change, population growth, and land use changes continue to take their toll," reports Pamela Zevit, program coordinator, South Coast Conservation Program.

[17] "Influencing human nature toward a sustainable future where the value of wetlands is fully recognized and protected remains a great challenge," Zevit adds. "Even though we may understand that conserving our natural capital and the goods and services it provides is essential to life, doing so remains, for the most part, a societal choice. We have the ability and we know it can work, so let's choose wisely."

PROTECTING BOGS

[18] Education, raising awareness, fundraising, volunteering, advocacy—these are all ways to get involved in protecting bog wetlands.

Get Educated

[19] Burns Bog Conservation Society presents regular public education sessions and school field trips. Fundraisers such as Job for the Bog—highlighting International Bog Day—and golf tournaments are held to support educational, environmental programs.

The author does not use a formal concluding paragraph for this essay. However, she does end with thought-provoking ideas about how to help preserve bogs and how to enjoy them.

[20] Mer Bleue Bog also offers many opportunities to learn more about its unique aspects year-round on its 20 kilometres of trails—whether it's hiking, birding, or snowshoeing.

Yaworski, B. (2015, October 1). Help protect our bogs: Why it's important to save our wetlands. *Alive*. Retrieved from http://www.alive.com/lifestyle/help-protect-our-bogs. Excerpted from alive magazine, #396, October 2015. Published by Alive Publishing Group. Reproduced by arrangement with the Publisher. All rights reserved.

Post-Reading Questions

1. Who do you think the audience is for this essay? Justify your answer with relevant quotations from the article.
2. Do the author's methods for developing paragraphs work for this essay? If so, why? If not, how would you have organized the ideas?
3. The author uses specialized language in this piece. What is her purpose in doing so?
4. Most essays do not include headings. Why do you think the author uses them?
5. Does this short essay have enough detail? What would you add to make it more complete?

 # Chapter Review Questions

1. What is the difference between an expository and an argumentative essay?
2. What is the purpose of writing an argumentative essay?
3. What are the benefits of including research in an expository essay?
4. What are some important factors to remember when writing an in-class essay?
5. When you are refining a topic, what are some important factors to consider?

7

Introductions, Thesis Statements, and Conclusions

In this chapter, you will learn

- the structure of an expository essay;

- ways to introduce an essay;

- the importance of creating an effective thesis statement; and

- methods for writing a conclusion.

By this point, you have probably noticed that the requirements for essays at the college and university level are more advanced than those at the high school level. In this chapter, you will examine how to draw your audience into your essay effectively and to keep them engaged through to your conclusion.

The Expository Essay Template

As noted in Chapter 2, it is important to use an outline when drafting an essay because it will help you stay on track and ensure that your essay remains unified, coherent, and well developed. A template (such as the one in Table 7.1) will also help you organize your thoughts into paragraphs. Templates can be expanded or contracted as necessary: if you need more than three body paragraphs, just add to the template. Similarly, not all paragraphs require three

 See also the argumentative essay template in Chapter 9.

TABLE 7.1 Expository Essay Template

Introductory paragraph with thesis statement	Supporting idea	1. 2. 3.
Body paragraph 1	Topic sentence Point 1 Explanation/Illustration Point 2 Explanation/Illustration Point 3 Explanation/Illustration Conclusion	(quotation, personal observation, etc.)
Body paragraph 2	Topic sentence Point 1 Explanation/Illustration Point 2 Explanation/Illustration Point 3 Explanation/Illustration Conclusion	
Body paragraph 3	Topic sentence Point 1 Explanation/Illustration Point 2 Explanation/Illustration Point 3 Explanation/Illustration Conclusion	
Concluding paragraph	Main ideas to summarize Clincher	Idea to leave reader with

points about your topic sentence. Some may need only two, while others may require more. Some points may also need further explanation or illustration.

Table 7.2 provides part of a template for an essay on eating disorders. The first body paragraph, which has more than three points, uses definition to give the reader the necessary background to understand the rest of the essay. The next body paragraph could use chronology to establish an increase in eating disorders over a certain period. The final paragraph may use a cause–effect pattern. Remember that you don't need to use full sentences or have fully developed ideas at this stage. Ideas introduced here can also be modified or moved later. At this point, the main purpose is to write your ideas down and organize them.

TABLE 7.2 Expository Essay Template: Eating Disorders

Introductory paragraph with thesis statement	Eating disorders are a problem for society.	
	Supporting idea	1. explanation of different types 2. why they are on the rise, or at least seem to be 3. medical and psychological impact
Paragraph 1	Topic sentence	When people think of eating disorders, they often think of teenage girls or runway models who starve themselves, but that is only one of the many disorders.
	Subpoint 1	Anorexia nervosa—most known
	Illustration	Find medical definition from journals and explain whom it affects and side effects
	Subpoint 2	Bulimia (binge and purge)
	Illustration	Find medical definition from journals and explain whom it affects and side effects
	Subpoint 3	Compulsive overeating
	Illustration	Find medical definition from journals and explain whom it affects and side effects
	Subpoint 4	Selective eating
	Illustration	Find medical definition from journals and explain whom it affects and side effects
	Conclusion	Many different types of eating disorders, but they all have the same outcome.

Exercise **7.1**

Create a template for each of the following essay topics.

1. The causes of tuition increases.
2. How to alleviate stress during the first year of college or university.
3. How millennials are different from boomers.
4. The advantages of having a diploma or a degree.
5. How the rise of social media has led to increased written communication.

 # The Essay's Introduction

Our template shows that an expository essay starts with an **introduction**. In fact, even if this term is not used, almost everything you read begins with a preview of what follows. The introduction presents the work's main idea (thesis) and often the organizational pattern—whether it is a book, article in a scholarly journal, class essay, sales proposal, or résumé. Your introductions will have one or more paragraphs that fulfill specific functions and should be unified, coherent, and well developed.

    The introduction is one of the most important parts of your essay. Take the time to write one that will draw the reader into your essay, provide necessary information, and satisfy your audience's expectations.

An **introduction** is the opening of a document that presents the main idea (the thesis statement) and the main organizational pattern.

Functions of the Introduction: Reader's Interest

The introduction should create reader interest. Although most of your essay's main points, subpoints, and supporting details will be placed in the body paragraphs, an ineffective introduction can indicate that the rest of the essay is the same. Reader interest can be created through three different organizational patterns.

Reader interest is very important. You need to catch and maintain the reader's attention and interest. Reader interest is especially important when writing for an instructor. If your essay is entertaining and thought-provoking, your mark will probably be higher than if it is mundane.

Logical Introduction

With the **logical approach**, you use the first part of the introduction to build your emphasis. Begin with the general and proceed to the specific, which is your thesis statement and is usually the introduction's last sentence. A logical opening helps you establish the topic's relevance and shows where it fits with your points as they progressively become more specific. Figure 7.1 illustrates this method.

The **logical approach** moves from a broad to a narrow focus.

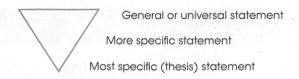

General or universal statement

More specific statement

Most specific (thesis) statement

FIGURE 7.1	Structure of paragraph introduction

In the following introduction, the writer begins with a general claim and gradually brings the subject—Laos's dependence on hydroelectric power—into focus. This development is important for general readers who may not know much about Laos and the topic. Pay close attention to how the writer also creates reader interest.

> The paragraph begins with a general statement before making specific connections between rivers and their uses by civilizations.

> Stock focuses on a specific country and discusses how Laos has used its rivers in the past.

> The author further narrows the topic by mentioning a specific river system and stressing its importance to Laos.

> In the thesis statement, the writer announces the essay's main point, the most specific sentence.

Rivers have always been a central part of civilization. From the banks of the Tigris and Euphrates was born the idea of civilization, and almost all subsequent peoples have relied on rivers for trade, transportation, irrigation, fishing, and drinking water. The Lao of Southeast Asia are one such people, living for thousands of years in villages by the many rivers of that country. They have depended on their waterways for clean drinking water, irrigation for their crops, and fishing. The heart of the Lao river system lies in the Mekong River, the longest river in Southeast Asia. Laos is a landlocked country and is therefore doubly reliant on its rivers as a source of trade. Impoverished by war and political turmoil, Laos has turned to its rivers to provide a new, modern resource: electricity.

Student writer Ian Stock

Another kind of logical approach begins by mentioning something familiar to the reader and proceeds to the unfamiliar. The following opening illustrates this approach:

While the intelligence quotient (IQ) has long been a useful tool to determine one's intelligence, a development in the study of human intellectual experience has expanded to include one's emotional state. It is called emotional intelligence, or EQ.

Student writer Chin-Ju Chiang

> In the **dramatic approach**, the essay's opening is meant to catch the reader's attention in an interesting or thought-provoking way. An **anecdote** is an incident or event that is used because it is interesting or striking.

Dramatic Introduction

The **dramatic approach** can be used in various ways. You can begin with an interesting quotation (but citing from a dictionary is not a good example of this method), a thought-provoking question, a personal experience, an illuminating statistic, a description of a scene, or a brief narrative such as an anecdote.

Unlike the logical approach, you begin with something specific. The idea is to surprise or intrigue your reader gently, not to shock or startle. The dramatic approach is used more often in argument, but it can be used in an expository essay as well, as this example illustrates. In the excerpt, the student writer creates a scenario that enables the reader to experience an unfamiliar martial art as she did.

Imagine a circle of adults and children dressed in white pants with different-coloured cords around their waists. Everybody is clapping and singing in an unfamiliar language—entranced by what is unfolding within the circle. Musicians are playing drums, tambourines, and an instrument that looks like a stringed bow with a gourd attached. There is an inescapable feeling of communal energy within the circle. Uncontrollable curiosity lures the unknowing spectator; peering into the circle exposes two people engaged in an intense physical dialogue. Kicks and movements are exchanged with precision and fluidity, which create a dance-like choreography. What is being witnessed is called a *roda* (pronounced ho-da, it means "circle" in Portuguese). A person's first encounter with this intriguing display of physicality and grace is an experience not easily forgotten. I did not forget my first *roda*, and, consequently, I later began training in this Brazilian form of martial arts—*capoeira* (pronounced cap-where-a).

Student writer Kerry Hinds

> The writer evokes a scene in order to interest the reader, using both descriptive detail and narration (telling a story).

> Putting the reader in the place of the unknowing spectator, Hinds continues to evoke the scene, arousing the reader's curiosity and suspense.

> The writer concisely defines *capoeira* in her thesis statement. Note that her use of personal experience is a strategy designed to create reader interest. Her essay will probably make minimal or no use of personal experience but will explain significant aspects of this martial art.

Exercise 7.2

Rewrite the paragraph on *capoeira* using the logical approach. (You might have to do some research on the topic.)

Mixed Approach

You can also use a mixed approach to attract interest:

- *Dramatic–logical*: You could begin with a question and then use the logical approach to develop the rest of the paragraph.

- *Logical–dramatic*: You could use a "reversal" strategy, beginning with a general statement before dramatically turning the tables and arguing the opposite. Student writer Grace Beal employs this strategy in her essay on the use of fur in today's society.

> The writer makes a general statement.

> Using the logical method, Beal adds detail, becoming more specific.

> The author reiterates her main point before contrasting the caveman's needs with those of society today.

> In her thesis statement, the writer forcefully announces her argumentative claim: killing animals for their fur is now wrong.

Since the beginning of time, people have depended on fur. Cavemen wore animal skins as clothing; furthermore, after killing an animal, such as a buffalo, the flesh would be eaten and the bones would be used in tool-making. They used as much of the animal as possible due to their spiritual beliefs and because, with few other resources, it made sense to waste as little as possible. Wearing fur in that age was a necessity: it was warm, practical, and readily available. Today, it is a far different story. Fur is part of the upscale fashion industry, but killing wild animals for their skin extends beyond fur fanciers; it is a luxury product for many different consumers today, such as car owners with leather upholstery. There are more than 40 different animal species that are killed for their skin, and not a single one needs to be.

Some academic articles do not use any of these introduction types. Instead, they may begin with a direct and concise statement of the problem or purpose and may even include the study's findings. This is often the case with scientific articles designed for those with specialized knowledge of the subject.

Whatever approach you use should be relevant to your topic, purpose, and audience. For example, if you were arguing in favour of euthanasia or another issue with a built-in emotional aspect and knew your audience opposed it, a strong, emotional opening could alienate readers.

Other Functions

The introduction serves three other important functions:

- *Announces your topic and the main points*: The thesis statement gives the main points of the essay and must have two parts: the topic and a comment on it (see pp. 154–5).
- *Introduces the writer*: The introduction is the writer's first chance to establish credibility, presenting himself or herself as being knowledgeable about the topic as well as being reliable and trustworthy. You show your credibility by writing well and by appearing rational, fair, and in control.
- *Indicates how the writer plans to develop the main points*: Organizational patterns, as mentioned throughout this book, include description, narration, definition, chronology, compare and contrast, and cause–effect.

 Chapter 4 discusses paragraph development; Chapter 6 discusses essay development.

Features of the Introduction

The Opening Sentence

In the logical approach, the introduction usually builds to the thesis. Like this statement, the opening sentence needs to be written carefully. An ineffective opening may be too general or abrupt, obvious, overstated (making a false universal claim), or irrelevant, as shown in these examples.

Too general:
In the twentieth century, many historic events have occurred around the globe, especially in Europe, Asia, and America.

Why is this too broad? Does the phrase beginning with *especially* help to make it more specific? How can the statement be made more effective?

Too abrupt:
Changes need to be made to Manitoba's driving laws to address driving while using illegal drugs.

Why is this statement too abrupt? Would it be less so if it were placed somewhere else in the introduction?

Obvious:
As the population continues to rise around the world, the need for transportation will also increase.

What makes this statement too obvious? What changes would make it more appropriate as an opening?

Overstated:
Everyone these days has used a computer at one time or another.

Many people in the world, even in Canada, have not used a computer. There are few situations satisfied by the "everyone" claim. How can the statement be improved?

> Be wary of making "everyone" claims unless your statement truly applies to everyone.

Irrelevant:
Few people know that sea otters can live to the age of 15 years.

This opening could be effective if the statement fell into the "believe it or not" category, but it doesn't. How would you rewrite it?

If you start your essay in any of these ways, the reader may be much more critical of your work than if you open with an effective sentence. An ineffective opening is like receiving a weak handshake when first meeting someone.

> If you have problems writing an introduction, consider writing the rest of the essay first.

Writing an introduction requires time and patience. Don't be discouraged if, after having produced an outline, you cannot quickly write a strong introduction. You might want to return to the introduction after you've written the rest of the essay. In fact, some instructors believe that the introduction should be written last.

Exercise 7.3

In groups, consider the following opening statements and discuss what makes them ineffective. How would you revise them to make them more effective and interesting?

1. Franz Anton Mesmer discovered hypnosis in the 1770s.
2. Although email is a modern communications miracle, it is also the biggest nuisance ever invented.
3. It is said that ignorance is bliss.
4. I guess we would all like to look like a Kardashian if we could.
5. There are many issues surrounding end-of-life treatment of terminally ill individuals.
6. Leprosy is, without doubt, the most brutal disease known to humanity.
7. Why not buy the best-made sports car the world has to offer?
8. The movement of people away from the Catholic Church is mostly due to its teachings on such issues as abortion, women's equality, and homosexuality.
9. Sports are something we all watch.
10. In all American literature, no character ever gave more thought to moral decisions than Huckleberry Finn does.
11. Most people in our society dream of growing up, marrying, and getting a good job so they can start a family.
12. Desperate times call for desperate measures.
13. The importance of education has been reiterated many times.
14. Who was Roger Bannister?
15. Fighting is a part of hockey—no ifs, ands, or buts.

The Thesis Statement: Simple versus Expanded

> A **simple thesis statement** announces the topic and makes a comment on it.

> Chapter 8 discusses thesis statements based on facts, claims, and values.

We mentioned earlier in this chapter that a thesis statement reveals the essay's topic and makes a comment on it. A **simple thesis statement** has these two necessary parts and nothing more. Here is an example:

Life in residence at the University of the South Pole helps prepare one for life after university.

An **expanded thesis statement** gives more detail, usually by including the essay's main points. It answers questions such as "How?" or "Why?" to account for or justify the main idea. This example addresses the question, "How does life in residence prepare one for life after university?"

Life in residence at the University of the South Pole helps prepare one for life after university by making a student independent, by reinforcing basic life skills, and by teaching one how to get along with penguins.

Here's an example of a topic, followed by a simple thesis statement and an expanded one that answers the question "Why?"

Topic:
School uniforms

Simple thesis statement:
Making school uniforms mandatory has many advantages for students.

Expanded thesis statement:
Making school uniforms mandatory has many advantages for students, as they eliminate distractions, encourage a focus on academics, and reduce competition based on appearances.

A simple thesis statement may be sufficient for a short essay, such as one of fewer than 500 words. It can be used in an expository essay in which you attempt to answer a question or solve a problem. In an argumentative essay, an expanded thesis that announces all your points in the introduction will be a forceful start. Check with your instructor for specific guidelines about simple versus expanded thesis statements.

Effective Thesis Statements
An effective thesis statement should be interesting, specific, and manageable.

- *Interesting*: The thesis attracts the reader to the topic and the essay.
- *Specific*: The thesis isn't so general, broad, or obvious that it lacks relevance; it informs the reader about what will follow.
- *Manageable*: The thesis sounds as if it can be reasonably explored in the space of the essay; the writer will successfully carry out what the thesis promises.

A thesis statement may be ineffective because it doesn't meet this criteria or because it has other problems. An unclear thesis statement may confuse rather than inform. For example, the following thesis statement doesn't clearly express the main points of the essay. The writer needs to be more detailed and precise.

> Pets are important in that they can unify and heal and are an inevitable part of human nature.

Do we know what the writer means? As an expanded thesis statement, it is inadequate because it will likely baffle readers, not inform them. This revised thesis is more effective:

> Pets are important in bringing people together, helping them recover from an illness or depression, and enabling them to express important human values, such as love.

> An effective thesis statement begins with the writer's clear thoughts, which produce clear expression. When you use an expanded thesis statement, you must express your main points in parallel structure; otherwise, it could be hard to follow (see Chapter 15, page 393).

A thesis statement may be unclear because it seems to focus on more than one topic. When you revise your essay, your thesis needs to reflect the essay's main point accurately. In this example, we don't know whether the essay is about excessive dieting or body image:

> Many youth are obsessed by dieting today due to the prominence our society places on body image.

To revise this thesis successfully, the writer needs to narrow the topic to one specific area, such as unhealthy diets and the problems they create, the effects of body image on youths, or the relationship between body image and dieting. The last topic would likely involve extensive research and might not be manageable within a medium-length essay.

Avoid a stiff, self-conscious thesis statement that refers directly to you or the essay's purpose. Consider these examples.

Ineffective:
I/This essay will examine the phenomenon of online gambling and argue in favour of strict government regulation of this growing industry.

Revised:
Online gambling is of increasing concern to governments and should be subject to strict regulations.

Your thesis may change as you write your outline or draft and uncover areas about your topic you weren't aware of before.

Exercise **7.4**

1. Using the three criteria for effective thesis statements, evaluate the effectiveness of the following statements for an essay on aliens.

   a. It is probable that aliens exist somewhere in outer space.

   b. It is clear that aliens have infiltrated the highest levels of the Canadian government.

   c. Everyone is curious about the possible existence of aliens.

2. Which of these simple thesis statements is best for an essay on how computers influence people? Rate each according to whether it is interesting, specific, and manageable. Be prepared to explain your decisions.

   a. The computer is one of the most entertaining pastimes we have.

   b. Violence found in computer games is affecting children by increasing the number of shootings in schools.

   c. The computer has helped change the way we live compared to the way our grandparents lived 50 years ago.

   d. Computers take away our free time by creating a dependency that is very hard to escape from once we are hooked.

   e. TV.is losing its influence thanks to the increasing popularity of computers.

   f. A computer is a great babysitter for pre-school-age children.

3. Write an effective thesis statement on the topic of the computer's influence, using any pre-writing technique you feel comfortable with and making sure that you follow the three requirements of a good thesis statement.

4. Identify the following thesis statements by type and make the simple ones expanded.

   a. Regular, moderate doses of stress not only are inevitable in today's world but also can be good for you.

   b. As consumers, we must keep ourselves informed about the activities of the industries we support.

   c. Although poor waste management has already had a significant impact on the planet, future damage can be minimized through recycling, waste reduction programs, and public education.

   d. Education is viewed as a benefit to individuals, but too much education can have negative results.

   e. Many people misunderstand the meaning of success.

A Thesis Statement Checklist

Use the following checklist when writing thesis statements.

1. Have you written a complete thesis statement, not just a topic?
2. Does it have two parts? (simple thesis statement)
3. Have you included your main points in the order they will appear in your essay? (expanded thesis statement)
4. Is there enough detail for the reader to understand your main points (i.e., is the statement clearly phrased and not confusing)?
5. Is it clear what one topic the thesis will focus on (i.e., the statement is not vague and doesn't straddle multiple topics)?
6. Is it worded objectively and not self-consciously (i.e., by mentioning the writer or the essay itself)?
7. Have you arranged your main points in a parallel structure?

Exercise 7.5

In groups, choose a topic from the list and use a pre-writing technique to formulate a simple thesis statement with the three criteria discussed in this chapter.

aliens	nature
backpacking	pets
clothes	Quebec
energy	relationships
Facebook	science
ghosts	taboos
humour	(the) unconscious
indie rock	virtual reality
justice	waste
karma	xenophobia
laughter	youth
malls	Zen Buddhism

Exchange your statement with another group's and evaluate it according to the three criteria. Give one mark for each; half marks are allowed. When all the groups have completed the evaluation process, discuss the ratings and the reasons behind them. Revise your thesis statement according to the feedback your group receives.

Use another pre-writing technique to come up with three main points and reword the simple thesis statement so that it is an expanded one. Exchange the statements again and evaluate them based on points 4–6 in the checklist above. Again, discuss the ratings with the other groups.

Introduction Length

In general, an introduction should be no more than about 15 per cent of the essay's length, but you should check with your instructor for specific guidelines. The length will also depend on whether you decide to include the main points of your essay (expanded thesis) or background information.

Although the introduction should never overbalance the rest of the essay, there is no reason not to include your main points and express them fully if the introduction calls for doing so (see p. 155).

Exercise **7.6**

Evaluate the following introductory paragraphs according to the criteria discussed in the previous pages. Does each function as an effective introduction? Specifically consider the following:

- Which method(s)—logical, dramatic, mixed—did the writer use to create reader interest?
- Is the opening effective? What makes it effective or ineffective?
- Identify the thesis statement. Is it interesting, specific, and manageable? Simple or expanded?
- Has the writer established credibility?
- Is the essay's main organizational pattern apparent?
- Does the paragraph length seem appropriate?

 See Chapter 4 for a review of essay organizational patterns.

1. Clothing has always reflected the times, and a prime example is the bathing suit. From their most cumbersome and unattractive beginnings to the array of styles we see today, bathing suits have always reflected the lives of the women who wore them and the society in which they lived. In the last hundred years, roles of the sexes, improvements in women's rights, changes in the economy, and perceptions of body image have all played a part in bathing suit design. (Student writer Stephanie Keenlyside)

2. What is it about the Italian Mafia that fascinates millions of people? Could part of the answer lie in Hollywood's depiction of a 5' 9", 275-pound Italian named Bruno Francessi who drives a black Cadillac, wears $3,000 silk suits, and claims to have "two" families; or is it the way the media creates celebrity status for Mafiosi people and events? The media and film industry portray a mobster's lucrative lifestyle as the result of thoughtless killings, a regimen of violence and corruption. But to fully understand the mob lifestyle, one must understand how mobsters operate—not what they appear to be on the surface, but the structure, conduct, and economic realities that created their power and enable them to maintain it. As someone who lived close to this power, I know that behind the media perception lies a fundamental belief in and adherence to a system. (Student writer Dino Pascoli)

(continued)

3. The sport of bodybuilding has evolved considerably through the ages. Starting with muscle man competitions, it has now turned into what some would call a "freak show." Bodybuilding is a sport that requires its athletes to display their best aesthetically pleasing physiques on stage; they are judged according to specific criteria. Many factors leading up to the judging itself contribute to the outcome of the competition; for example, nutrition from whole foods and supplements and low body fat percentage from proper diet and cardiovascular training all contribute to the success of the competitors. Steroids, too, are a major factor in professional events like the International Federation of Bodybuilders (IFBB) competitions, where athletes are not tested for drug use. Anabolic steroid abuse plays a large role in bodybuilding, often resulting in adverse health effects. (Student writer Mike Allison)

4. Two 20-year-old Vancouver men were street racing three years ago when one of the cars, a Camaro, struck and killed Irene Thorpe as she crossed the street. The car was going so fast that Thorpe was thrown 30 metres into the air. Both men were convicted of criminal negligence causing death. They were given a two-year conditional sentence to be served at home, put on probation for three years, and had their drivers' licences revoked for five years. Like most street-racing tragedies, this one was preventable. Though the street-racing phenomenon has been around for decades, it is growing exponentially. Recent movies have glorified this activity, enticing young, inexperienced drivers. The increase in street racing has led to an increase in the injuries to racers, spectators, and innocent bystanders. In addition, racing often results in property damage and is associated with assault, weapons offences, and drug and alcohol abuse. To help combat this growing problem, anti-racing legislation needs to be introduced and strictly enforced. Furthermore, an education program needs to be implemented and legal racing venues created. (Student writer Maureen Brown)

5. Why does my cell phone not work? Why do I get radiation poisoning when I travel by plane? Why is the light switch not working? These are the kinds of questions we ask ourselves when solar flares are striking the earth. Solar flares originate from the sun. Every 11 years, the sun switches its magnetic poles, causing the magnetic fields to twist and turn in the atmosphere above sunspots, which are eruptions on the sun's surface. The magnetic field seems to snap like a rubber band stretched too tightly. When one of these fields breaks, it can create energy equal to a billion megatons of TNT exploding. The magnetic fields seem to flip and reconnect after they break. Solar flares occasionally head towards the earth, and even though we are 1.5 million kilometres from the sun, these flares can reach us in fewer than two days. While the earth is experiencing a solar flare, multiple problems can occur—from malfunctions of orbiting objects to disruption in power systems and radio signals. While the flares can produce these problems, they can also create the most beautiful and unusual auroras seen around the world. (Student writer Nicholas Fodor)

Exercise **7.7**

Evaluate the following introduction based on whether the opening is successful, the writer creates interest and appears credible, and the thesis statement is effective. Rewrite the paragraph, correcting any weaknesses you find. You can add your own material or ideas, but try not to increase the length (approximately 130 words).

> Something drastic needs to be done about obesity among teenagers today! Over the last decade, there has been a disturbing trend toward teenage obesity. Teenagers today would rather lodge themselves in front of the TV or play video games for hours on end than get some form of physical exercise. This problem becomes pronounced in high school because physical education is not compulsory in most schools. However, PE classes have a lot to offer. Participation can reduce the risk of heart failure, improve overall fitness, promote good health habits, improve self-discipline and skill development, boost self-confidence, increase academic performance, and enhance communication and cooperative skills. Obesity is an alarming trend among high school students today and should be a concern to both students and their parents.

The Essay's Conclusion

Functions of the Conclusion

The **conclusion** is the final paragraph of an essay. It recalls both the thesis statement and the discussion in the body paragraphs. Put another way, it asks the reader to reconsider the thesis statement based on the evidence from the main points. Unlike an introduction, it often works from the specific to the general (see Figure 7.2). An effective conclusion often includes a clincher statement—an idea to remain with the reader.

> The **conclusion** is the final paragraph of the essay that sums up what was said in the body paragraphs.

    Your conclusion shouldn't surprise the reader, as your points have been thoroughly discussed in the essay. It should be predictable because you have prepared the reader for it, but it should not be a boring restatement of the thesis. This type of conclusion leaves the reader unsatisfied and wondering if you didn't leave enough time to complete the essay properly, got tired of the subject matter, or couldn't be bothered to write an interesting ending.

Introduction

Conclusion

| FIGURE 7.2 | Introduction–conclusion inverted pyramid |

Spend as much time on your conclusion as you do the other parts of the essay so that you give your reader a good impression of your writing. After all, the feelings of your audience are the most important factor in writing for academic and workplace purposes.

Two Kinds of Conclusion

The introduction and conclusion are not identical bookends with the body paragraphs in between. The conclusion can emphasize the importance of the thesis in two ways:

> A **circular conclusion** reminds the reader of the thesis. A **spiral conclusion** restates the thesis and leads the reader beyond it.

- A **circular conclusion** restates the thesis with different words that stress its importance, perhaps suggesting an action if you are arguing for a practical change. It reminds the reader of the thesis and "closes the circle" by bringing him or her back to the starting point. This type of conclusion must show how the thesis statement has been proven, not simply repeat it.
- A **spiral conclusion** suggests a specific way that the thesis could be applied, asks further questions, or proposes other ways of looking at the problem; it refers to the thesis but also leads suggestively beyond it. It might point to results of the thesis or suggest follow-up research.

A conclusion can sometimes include personal reflection, such as considering the way your thesis has affected you or people you know. This kind of conclusion, however, is more acceptable in personal and some argumentative essays than in expository ones. If you have not used personal experience in the essay, do not use it in the conclusion.

Specific things to avoid in the conclusion are

- restating the thesis statement word for word;
- mentioning a new point (the conclusion rewords the thesis and the main points of the essay in an interesting way but does not introduce something new);

- giving an example or illustration to support your thesis (examples belong in your body paragraphs); and
- writing a conclusion that is much longer than your introduction (exceptions are essays that include a lengthy "Discussion" section).

Read your introduction and then your conclusion to check that it is complete and relates to your introduction in a satisfactory way.

Exercise **7.8**

Consider these sets of paragraphs, which form the introduction and the conclusion for three essays. Is it clear from the introduction what the writer will be discussing? What kind of introduction does the writer use? Is it clear from the conclusion what the writer discussed? What kind of conclusion is each writer using?

Write a brief analysis of how the two parts simultaneously intersect and operate independently. Consider strengths and possible weaknesses. Remember that the paragraphs should not only function as effective specialized paragraphs but also display unity, coherence, and development.

1. An expository essay
Topic: A racial incident in Canada's past
Introduction:

One of Canada's most important features, which figures prominently in its self-presentation to the world, is as a peaceful nation that respects the individual and celebrates multiculturalism. The country is known for its cultural and ethnic diversity. Often, however, Canadians idealize their image and push inequality out of their presentation of their country. However, if we look carefully at the history of Canada, there have been many occasions when the clean image of national tolerance has been seriously undermined, such as in the *Komagata Maru* incident in Vancouver in 1914.

Conclusion:

Although much has changed for the better since the beginning of the twentieth century and Canada is justifiably proud of its diversity today, people sometimes ignore past incidents of racial discrimination. Since the *Komagata Maru* incident is not well known, it is important that people hear about it so they can be aware that even in a democratic country like Canada injustice and intolerance have occurred in the past and will continue to occur unless people learn from the past and guard against such incidents.

Student writer Ruth Wax

(continued)

2. An argumentative essay

Topic: Government-funded cancer screening
Introduction:

Last month, the colour pink sprang up in store windows of retailers nationwide as part of the annual campaign to fund breast cancer research. Breast cancer takes the lives of 44,000 women in the United States every year. As a potential carrier of a gene predisposing me to breast cancer, I face the perpetual fear that one day I or my sister could become its victim. It would be almost unthinkable if the mammogram, the screening test for breast cancer, were not covered by our health-care plan. However, for men with a predisposition to prostate cancer, which has been linked to the gene associated with breast cancer, the cost of a blood test to screen for prostate cancer is not covered by the plan. Prevention and early intervention are critical for successful health care, and government-funded coverage for the $35 prostate cancer screening test is essential for men aged 45 and older.

Conclusion:

Today the best hope for a cure to prostate cancer lies in early intervention through the PSA screening test. Although the benefit of screening may be controversial, the evidence is hard to dispute: 80 per cent of patients with elevated PSA levels have prostate cancer. Surgical procedures are rapidly improving, and new options exist to treat complications of surgery or radiation therapy. Until proper medical coverage exists for early detection of prostate cancer, it will continue to cause the second-largest number of cancer-related deaths in men. Gender bias in government-funded cancer screening tests is unacceptable, and public pressure should be exerted for universal access to cancer screening.

Student writer Heather Dyble

3. An argumentative essay

Topic: Smoking and organ transplantation
Introduction:

The atmosphere grew tense in the cramped hospital room as eight-year-old Marla looked up through frightened eyes, trying to be strong for her mother. Everyone was trying to be hopeful, but Marla instinctively knew that she would not be getting a heart transplant in time; the waitlist was long, and an organ match was unlikely. Although Marla was an otherwise healthy girl, there were others on the transplant list who were ahead of her, though not all of them had as good a prognosis. Due to the scarcity of organ donations in comparison to many in need, serious debates have arisen concerning the suitability of some potential heart and lung recipients. Some feel that everyone should have equal right to a transplant and that there should be no pre-conditions relating to what they see as lifestyle choices, such as smoking. Others advocate that smokers should be refused transplants on medical or moral considerations since smokers are more likely to experience complications after surgery. Given the current crisis of long waitlists and variable success rates, lung and heart transplant candidates should be required to quit smoking at least six months prior to surgery in order to reduce smoking-related complications and maximize transplant success.

Conclusion:

The scarcity of organ donations and the length of waitlists have placed an increasing obligation on the part of health-care professionals to ensure the best outcome for their patients. Denying transplants to those who refuse to quit smoking may appear to discriminate against smokers and their lifestyle choice. However, doing so would result in better odds for post-transplant success and would involve the most efficient use of limited health-care services and resources. In short, health authorities should move to institute clear guidelines on pre-surgery smoking restrictions for the benefit of both individuals and the health-care system.

Student writer Annie Gentry

Exercise 7.9

Use one of the following topics to write an expanded thesis statement, introduction, and conclusion. Begin by brainstorming and creating an outline. Note that the topics are very general to allow you to choose the focus.

1. voting
2. funding for the arts
3. Canada's role on the world stage
4. travel as education
5. volunteerism
6. the effects of events around the world on Canadians
7. funding for intervention programs
8. reality TV shows
9. exercise and health
10. the role of education

The sample professional essay for this chapter is relatively short; therefore, the introduction and conclusion are brief. While reading, ask yourself how the author could have done more to help the reader understand her points.

Sample Professional Essay: Introduction and Conclusion

Alouette Anniversary

Hillary Windsor

[1] Fifty years ago this autumn, after many small steps, Canada took one giant leap into the future.

[2] The successful launch of the Alouette-I satellite on 29 September 1962 made Canada the third nation (after Russia and the United States) to design and build its own satellite and signalled to the world that our country was going to be a player in the space age.

> The author uses the transition *but* to link paragraphs.

[3] But it wasn't all smooth sailing straight into the stratosphere for the Ottawa-based research and design team, led by the late John Chapman under the auspices of Canada's Defence Research Telecommunications Establishment (later to become Communications Research Centre Canada). Although the team had world-class engineers and scientists working on the project and believed it would succeed, others weren't so sure.

> In an academic essay, a paragraph must include more than a quotation.

[4] "We were certainly confident," says Colin Franklin, chief electrical engineer of the Alouette-I. "But NASA considered the project too ambitious for the technology at the time. No one believed, outside of ourselves, that it would last."

[5] The public perception of the task facing the team was not much better. Franklin recalls reading an article published shortly before the Alouette's launch that stated all the possible things that could go awry during takeoff and highlighted the amount of money being "wasted" on the project. Still, the team was undeterred. "I remember looking at that article," says Franklin, "and it had absolutely no effect on us."

[6] Despite their assuredness, launch day at the US Pacific Missile Test Range in California was filled with a degree of uncertainty. Franklin, now 84, remembers the moment the team received word of the satellite's successful send-off into orbit aboard a Thor-Agena rocket. "There was a huge sigh of relief when it was working," he says. "And then there was jubilation."

[7] From start to finish, the entire Alouette-I project took only 3.5 years to complete, but it exceeded all expectations. Designed with a nominal lifespan of one year, it spent an impressive 10 active years collecting valuable data about the ionosphere before being decommissioned. Its immediate success kick-started the move to build and launch three more Canadian satellites over the next nine years—Alouette-II, ISIS I and ISIS II—and put Canada in the spotlight.

> While Windsor has written an expository essay, she also gives some opinion, which she indicates using words such as *only* and *exceeded all expectations*.

> The acronym ISIS stands for International Satellites for Ionospheric Studies. This acronym has been used since the 1960s in Canada.

[8] "The creation, launch and incredible success of the Alouette gave Canada an international reputation for excellence in satellite design and engineering," says Franklin, adding that at the time, no one on the team realized the long-term significance. "We were not aware that we were doing anything more than successfully building and launching the program. It was just a huge engineering challenge and an exciting program to be on."

[9] In 1987, Communications Research Centre Canada designated the Alouette-I as one of the 10 most outstanding achievements in the first 100 years of engineering in Canada—a notable tip of the hat that put the satellite in the same company as CPR's transcontinental railway network, the St Lawrence Seaway, and the CANDU nuclear power system.

[10] For many, the satellite's launch remains an iconic moment in Canadian history, shot through with personal meaning. Former astronaut Steve MacLean, the current president of the Canadian Space Agency, recalls hearing about it when he was just seven years old. "My dad worked at the National Research Council, so he made sure we remembered stuff like that," he says. "I collected stamps at the time, and a Canadian stamp with a picture of the Alouette on it came out. It's kind of a symbolic thing for me."

> The author skillfully switches from a focus on the past to the future possibilities for Canada.

[11] MacLean says that it's hard to predict what the next 50 years have in store for Canada's space industry but hopes that satellites will, in the next five years, provide communications parity for the country, especially in the North.

[12] For his part, Franklin—who's faced down naysayers before—doesn't like to set expectations or limits on what people can accomplish: "People have been spectacularly wrong about forecasting the future before."

[13] In other words, the sky's the limit.

Windsor, H. (2012, July/August). Alouette anniversary: Celebrating 50 years of Canada's role in space. *Canadian Geographic*. Retrieved from http://www.canadiangeographic.ca/magazine/ja12/canada_50_years_in_space.asp

Post-Reading Questions

1. Is the essay's thesis statement effective? How could it be improved?
2. How could Windsor have created a more effective introduction?
3. Does the author use effective topic sentences? Explain.
4. How do the paragraphs differ from what you learned in Chapter 3?
5. How could the conclusion be expanded into a full paragraph?

 # Chapter Review Questions

1. Why is a clear thesis important?
2. What is the difference between a simple thesis statement and an expanded thesis statement?
3. Why should you never start an introduction with an overly broad or obvious statement?
4. Why does an essay need a conclusion?
5. Why is a well-written conclusion as important as a well-written introduction?

8

Claims, Evidence, and the Analytical Model

In this chapter, you will learn

- the differences among three types of claims and when they are used;

- the kinds of evidence that can support a claim;

- ways to increase your credibility with your readers; and

- a generic model of the analytical essay.

No matter what type of essay you write, your thesis must be supported by solid, clearly linked evidence so that the reader can easily follow your logic. In this chapter, you will learn how to present a claim and to defend it with appropriate kinds of evidence. By choosing your support carefully, you increase your credibility with the audience, another important aspect of essay writing.

Kinds of Claims: Fact, Value, and Policy

There are two main elements to an essay, whether it is argumentative or expository:

- **claim**: a statement of fact, value or opinion, or policy (thesis statement)
- support for the claim: evidence and the writer's credibility in presenting that evidence

Whether you are reading or writing an essay, you often begin by identifying the claim about its topic.

Most topics can be explored through a claim of fact, value or opinion, or policy, depending on how it is presented. In an expository essay, the claim is presented as factual. In an argumentative essay, it is typically presented as value, opinion, or policy. If your essay topic was homelessness, your claim could be one of the following:

Factual claim:
Due to the unsettled economic climate, the prevalence of homelessness is increasing in most Canadian provinces.

Value or opinion claim:
In a society of excess, our indifference to the problem of the homeless is an indictment of our way of life.

Policy claim:
To solve the problem of homelessness in our city, council needs to increase the number of permanent shelters, erect temporary shelters in downtown parks, and educate the public about this escalating social problem.

Claim of Fact

A **factual claim** is usually **empirical**, meaning that it uses the evidence-gathering methods of observation and measurement. This type of claim can be proven by facts and figures or the findings of relevant studies.

Claim of Value

A **value** or **opinion claim** is an ethical claim that appeals to a principle or a moral system; values might be based on religion, a philosophical world view, or

A **claim** is an assertion about your topic that appears in your introduction, usually in the form of a thesis statement.

 Chapter 7 discusses effective and ineffective thesis statements.

A **factual claim** is proven by facts and figures or the results of relevant studies. The term *empirical* refers to a claim being based on observed or measured data.

A **value** or **opinion claim** is an ethical claim that appeals to the reader's principles or moral system. A **premise** is a statement assumed to be true.

social and cultural background. A claim of value is supported by a **premise** that a certain standard of good or bad, right or wrong, fair or unfair, is accepted.

Claim of Policy

A **policy claim** usually calls for some kind of action to fix a problem or improve a situation. Although this type does not need to be based on a claim of value, it often is. For example, a proposed change to a law that gives people more control over something in their lives may be rooted in a claim of value. The argument might be that the change will produce a more democratic society and greater individual freedom.

A **policy claim** is usually a call for action to fix a problem or improve a situation.

Exercise **8.1**

The 15 thesis statements listed here contain claims of fact, value or opinion, or policy. Identify the kind of claim, write thesis statements for the other types, and explain how each statement fits in its category. You may change the wording as long as the topic remains the same. Here is an example:

Cellphones are a wonderful modern convenience, but they can be dangerous in cars because they often distract the driver.

Claim of value: The statement asserts that cellphones can be dangerous (a bad thing).

Claim of fact: The recent use of smartphones in cars has increased the number of accidents in many urban centres—especially during rush hour. (The statement asserts that the number of accidents has increased.)

Claim of policy: Cellphones in cars should be prohibited as they are dangerous both for the user and for other drivers. (The statement advocates an action, though it is based on the value that cellphones in cars are dangerous.)

1. It is increasingly necessary to be bilingual in Canada.
2. Rap lyrics are inherently anti-social and encourage violence.
3. Women should not be allowed to serve in the military in anything but administrative roles.
4. Whatever one may think of same-sex marriages, it is evident that they are here to stay.
5. High school graduates should travel for at least a year before proceeding to college or university.

(continued)

6. We must provide more funding for technology in today's classroom and spend less on teachers' salaries.
7. The current practice of appointing Supreme Court judges in Canada is undemocratic.
8. With the number of sports teams, clubs, and cultural groups on campus, students who do not participate in extracurricular activities do not get good value for their education.
9. School uniforms provide many benefits to students and their parents.
10. The government should subsidize organically grown food.
11. Recreational use of steroids can cause physical and psychological damage to the user.
12. Before committing more resources to space exploration, we should work to solve global problems, such as poverty, that affect people every day.
13. The growing popularity of Eastern medicine shows that society is tending toward a more natural approach to health care.
14. Parents should have the right, within reason, to discipline their child as they see fit.
15. While advocates of a shorter work week believe that this measure will help our troubled economy, opponents say it will only weaken it and create social problems.

Evidence

Support in an essay is provided by the use of ample and credible evidence. **Evidence**, such as that gathered from books, journals, or personal experience, gives your claim more credibility.

A claim will not be accepted without **support**, or **evidence** to back it up. But evidence alone is not enough; you must also demonstrate your credibility (discussed later in this chapter). The effort of gathering and arranging evidence may be wasted if you do not seem credible.

Organization of Evidence

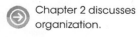
Chapter 2 discusses organization.

Evidence gathered from sources such as books, journals, and personal experience supports your claim and makes your reader more likely to believe it. Defend your claim in the essay's body paragraphs by using ample and sound evidence in your main points and subpoints. These points have the best impact when they are organized appropriately and ordered logically. Organizational methods include definition, division/classification, cause–effect, comparison and contrast, problem–solution, and chronology.

Kinds of Evidence

Depending on your topic, your discipline, and the assignment's instructions, you may use some kinds of evidence more than others. Writing in the humanities often relies on **primary**, or original, **sources**. If you write an English essay, for instance, your primary sources are literary works. The primary sources commonly used in historical research are biographies, newspapers, letters, and records from the era being studied.

Social sciences writing tends to focus on facts and figures, statistics and other numerical data, case studies, interviews, questionnaires, and personal observation. Scientific studies may use similar kinds of evidence, but they frequently rely on experimental methods. Examples are important in almost every discipline.

Using a variety of evidence will produce a stronger essay than relying solely on one kind. However, it is important to find **hard evidence**—facts, statistics, and statements from authorities (experts)—to support your key points. Hard evidence is essential in a factual claim and can be effective in a policy claim. It may be less important in a value or opinion claim, in which appeals to reason, emotion, and ethics and examples, analogies, brief narratives, description, or personal experience could produce an effective argument.

When you collect evidence for an essay, you must also analyze it, which includes evaluating the source (Is it credible?) and determining how best to use it (i.e., deciding where to put it so that it best supports your thesis). Once you decide placement, you need to link the particular point in your paragraph to the evidence. You must also decide whether to use a direct quotation, paraphrase, or summary. Always make sure you have created a verbal bridge between your own thoughts and the support you are using.

Original sources are known as **primary sources**.

Hard evidence provides direct support to a claim.

 Chapter 11 discusses paraphrasing and using direct quotations.

Facts and Statistics

Factual information is the strongest kind of evidence because facts can be proven to be true. For example, it is a fact that the United States has fifty states; it is an opinion that Canada is the fifty-first state.

Using facts effectively enhances your credibility as a knowledgeable writer. Facts are always relevant to a research essay, and they can provide support in other types if you are arguing a topic you know a lot about. However, you must use facts from reliable sources. In her in-class essay, student writer Lindsay Strummer uses several facts, including references to Internet piracy that she was apparently familiar with (see Chapter 6, pp. 138–40).

Statistics must come from reliable sources. Look out for possible bias or distortion and use caution with statistics cited by people or organizations promoting a specific cause or viewpoint. Imagine that your student union wants to use student funds to build an indoor pool and the campus newspaper reports that 94 per cent of those asked are in favour of the project. How many students were surveyed? How was the survey conducted? Perhaps only the students using the gym were asked. Reliable sources reveal their information-gathering methods, which you can evaluate.

An organization such as People for the Ethical Treatment of Animals (PETA) can be considered biased because it strongly opposes practices such as animal testing; however, statistics it publishes are reliable because they come from reputable sources. A PETA factsheet criticizing animal research cites a 1988 study that appeared in the refereed journal *Nature*, which "reports that 520 of 800 chemicals (65 per cent) tested on rats and mice caused cancer in the animals but not in humans (Lave et al. 631)." Bear in mind that such statistics and factual data are used for a specific purpose and that organizations may report on only those studies that agree with their mission or viewpoint. Evaluate evidence individually with the source's objective in mind. If you are not sure that a source is trustworthy, ask your instructors or librarians.

Authorities and Experts

An **authority** can be used for support if that person has direct knowledge of your subject. An authority who is not an **expert** carries less weight. For example, citing Albert Einstein in an essay that argues a mathematical point provides hard evidence. In an essay about vegetarianism, citing Einstein would provide **soft evidence**, as he is not considered an expert in this area. As you research your topic, you will discover who the experts are. You may also be able to interview an expert, asking questions related to your claim (see page 241).

Examples, Illustrations, Case Studies, Precedents

While hard evidence provides direct support, soft evidence indirectly supports your points and helps the reader understand them. Kinds of indirect support include examples, illustrations, case studies, and precedents.

We use **examples** in both speech and writing. Examples should always be relevant and representative. A teenager arguing for his independence might name several friends who live on their own. His parents might refute the argument by pointing out that the friends are not representative—one has a full-time job and another spent the summer travelling in Europe before moving out of her parents' house.

Examples often bring a point home by making it specific and concrete. They are especially useful if you are writing for a non-specialist reader, as they make it easier to grasp a difficult or an abstract point. Illustrations, case studies, and precedents are extended examples that can be used to explain or reinforce important points.

An **illustration** is a detailed example, usually an anecdote or a brief narrative. Student writer Graeme Verhulst uses an illustration to support his point in the following excerpt. Using logic, the reader can draw different conclusions from the premises:

Remember that special interest groups and similar organizations cite data for a specific purpose. Evaluate the facts and statistics with this purpose in mind.

 The essays in Chapters 9 and 11 use facts and statistics effectively.

An **authority** can be used for support if he or she is an expert, a specialist in your subject. An authority who is not an **expert** carries less weight.

Soft evidence indirectly supports your points and helps the reader understand them.

An **example** uses concrete details to translate an abstract claim into something the reader can more easily understand. An example is considered **soft evidence**.

Examples are especially useful if you are writing for a non-specialist reader, as they make it easier to grasp a difficult or abstract point.

An **illustration** is a detailed example that usually takes the form of an anecdote or a brief narrative.

Consider the example of the hydroelectric dam that the Urra company constructed in Colombia. The dam provides electricity to industry and profit to the companies and people who invest in it. The area flooded by the dam was inhabited by Indigenous peoples. The river was a source of fresh water and fish, and on the river's now flooded banks were food plants that sustained them. . . . If an analysis of this situation were based on the premise that all people should be treated equally and with respect, then through reason, the conclusion would be that this was a bad thing for the Indigenous peoples living along the river. If, however, the basic premise was that business interests are primary, then the logical conclusion would be that the hydroelectric dam was a good thing.

Case studies are often used as support, particularly in the social sciences, education, and business; they can also be the focus of research studies. Because case studies are practical, real-life examples, they can support a **hypothesis**. For example, to test the hypothesis that involving youth in decision-making could produce a safer school environment, a Vancouver school planned a series of student-led initiatives and activities. The results revealed that the students felt safer and had improved their pro-social and conflict resolution skills: the outcome supported the hypothesis.

A **precedent** is an example that refers to the way a particular situation was handled in the past. Legal judgments establish precedents that influence future court decisions. Once you have established an action as a precedent, you apply it to your argument. The successful use of precedents as evidence depends on your ability to convince the reader that both of the following are true:

1. Similar conditions apply to your topic.
2. Adhering to the precedent will produce a desirable result.

If you were arguing that Canada should offer free post-secondary studies to all academically qualified individuals, you could refer to the precedent of Denmark, one of the first countries to provide universal access to post-secondary schooling. You must make two points clear:

1. The situation in Denmark is comparable to the situation in Canada.
2. Denmark has profited from this system, so Canada will likely benefit from a similar course of action.

Analogies, Description, and Personal Experience

Some kinds of evidence are suggestive and indirect; they cannot in themselves prove a claim. These include analogy, description, and personal experience. You may use them in your essays if your instructor approves.

A **case study** is a carefully selected example that is closely analyzed in order to provide a testing ground for the writer's claim.

A **hypothesis** is a prediction or expected result of an experiment or other research investigation.

A **precedent** is an example that refers to the way a particular situation was handled in the past.

Chapter 4 discusses analogy, description, narration, and personal experience in detail.

Personal experience is a type of example that takes the form of direct experience or observation. It can often be effective in supporting a value claim.

Chapter 16 discusses objective language.

Three factors contribute to **credibility**: knowledge of the topic, reliability/trustworthiness, and fairness.

Breaking an essay into its essential elements enables you to analyze your own writing processes and those of other writers. It can show you how different elements of an essay contribute to the whole.

Chapter 9 discusses fairness in more detail.

Analogy (a kind of comparison) and description can help the reader understand and relate to a point. Like narration, description may also play a limited role in argument, perhaps to attract interest in the essay's introduction or to set up a main point.

Personal experience, which can take the form of direct experience or observation, can help the reader relate to your topic. You should keep your voice objective when using this kind of example; any bias will undermine your credibility. Personal experience can be effective in supporting a value claim. For example, if you had witnessed a dog fight, your observations could strongly support the claim that dog fighting is cruel. Similarly, if you have personal experience with homeless people by working in a food bank, you could use it to help support a related policy claim.

Credibility

As previously stated, demonstrating **credibility** as a writer will strengthen your claim. Three factors contribute to credibility: knowledge of the topic, reliability/trustworthiness, and fairness. Showing your knowledge isn't enough to make you credible. You must convince the reader that you also are reliable and fair.

You demonstrate knowledge through the points you make in the essay and the kinds of evidence you use to support them. But you can seem knowledgeable without seeming reliable. You show your reliability or trustworthiness by being able to answer "yes" to such questions as

- Is your essay well structured?
- Are your paragraphs unified, coherent, and well developed?
- Is your writing clear, your grammar correct, and your style effective?
- Have you used the rules and procedures of your discipline (if applicable)?
- Have you used critical thinking skills effectively? Are your conclusions logical and well founded?

In an expository essay, fairness is demonstrated by using evidence objectively. In an argumentative essay, it is shown by considering opposing views. While presenting a strong case for your views, you can pinpoint the shortcomings and limitations of the other positions. A fair writer is objective in addressing the other side, avoiding slanted language that reveals bias. You can demonstrate reliability by avoiding misuse of reason and you can demonstrate fairness by using emotional appeals selectively and without prejudice.

The Analytical Model

An effective essay is made up of interrelated parts, such as facts, organization, and word use, that make a whole. A successful essay has many connections among the concepts discussed so far and shown in Figure 8.1.

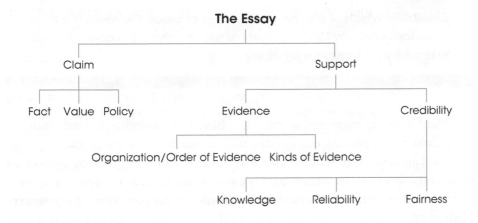

The Essay

| FIGURE 8.1 | The essay: An analytical model |

You need to think carefully about how everything fits together, both in the essays you write and the ones you read. In your own essays, you can ask these questions: Am I using the kinds of evidence favoured by my discipline? Am I organizing this evidence logically? Have I used enough sources? Is my essay well structured and my writing clear and grammatical? Have I used evidence fairly?

When reading an essay, you can ask similar questions to see if all the elements are connected. For example, grammatical errors will affect the writer's reliability, which will reduce credibility and weaken support for his or her claim. If you are aware of how the different elements relate in another's writing, you should be able to approach your own writing critically.

Exercise 8.2

Taking one of the claims for each statement in Exercise 8.1, determine how you would most effectively support it in the body of an essay. This exercise could take the form of a group discussion or a group strategic approach that specifically refers to the elements under "Support" in Figure 8.1. Consider the following:

Organization of evidence: Which patterns of organization/development would you likely use? What other patterns could be used? (See Chapter 4.)

Kinds of evidence: Which kinds of evidence would most effectively back up your claim? (See pp. 172–3.)

(continued)

Credibility: Which of the three categories of credibility seem the most important, and why? What general or specific strategies could you use to ensure your support is credible?

The following essay was posted as a blog (the underlined words indicate hyperlinks to supporting documents, such as journal articles, in the original). As you can see, even writers who use modern technology often follow the basic essay format. The author uses these patterns to help introduce evidence. While reading, think about how each element affects your view of the writer's credibility.

Sample Professional Essay: Basic Essay Format

Punishing Cheaters Promotes the Evolution of Cooperation

Eric Michael Johnson

> Johnson begins with a claim that will be supported later with research.

[1] Humans are one of the most cooperative species on the planet. Our ability to coordinate behaviour and work collaboratively with others has allowed us to create the natural world's largest and most densely populated societies, outside of deep sea microbial mats and a few *Hymenoptera* mega-colonies.

> He uses comparison to discuss cheaters and cooperators.

[2] However, a key problem when trying to understand the evolution of cooperation has been the issue of cheaters. Individuals in a social group, whether that group is composed of bacteria, cichlids, chimpanzees, or people, often benefit when cooperating with others who reciprocate the favour. But what about those individuals who take advantage of the generosity of others and provide nothing in return? These individuals could well thrive thanks to the group as a whole and end up with greater fitness than everyone else because they didn't have to pay the costs associated with cooperating. For decades the idea that cheaters may in fact prosper has been the greatest difficulty in understanding cooperation as an evolved trait.

[3] However, it turns out that cooperation could be a viable evolutionary strategy when individuals within the group collectively punish cheaters

who don't pull their weight. For example, Robert Boyd, Herbert Gintis, and Samuel Bowles published a paper in the journal *Science* in 2010 with a model showing how, so long as enough individuals work together to punish violators, each cooperative individual in the group can experience enhanced fitness as a result.

> When you write an academic essay, make sure you end with a concluding sentence. Do not end your paragraph with a quotation or paraphrase from other research.

[4] Before understanding how their model could explain the emergence of cooperative behaviour it is first important to look at the two leading explanations for the evolution of cooperation: William Hamilton's (1964) theory of kin selection and Robert Trivers's (1971) theory of reciprocal altruism.

> The author brings in secondary sources to support his earlier claims.

[5] Kin selection proposed that cooperation will emerge in groups that are made up of close relatives. Hamilton's rule, beautiful in its simplicity, proposed that cooperation occurs when the cost to the actor (c) is less than the benefit to the recipient (b) multiplied by the genetic relatedness between the two (r). This equation is written out simply as $rb > c$. Kin selection has been one of the most well-tested models that seeks to explain the evolution of cooperation and has held up among such diverse groups as primates, birds, and social insects (though Edward O. Wilson has recently challenged kin selection as an explanation in the latter).

[6] To put this into context: an alpha male lion and his brother share half of their genes, so have a genetic relatedness of 0.5. Suppose this brother recognizes that the alpha male is getting old and could easily be taken down. If so, the brother could potentially have eight additional cubs (just to pull out an arbitrary number). But, instead, that brother decides to help the alpha male to maintain his position in the pride and, as a result, the alpha ends up having the eight additional cubs himself while the brother only has five. The brother has lost out on three potential cubs. But, even so, because he assisted his brother he has still maximized his overall reproductive success from a genetic point of view: $0.5 \times 8 = 4 > 3$. He could have attempted to usurp his brother and, perhaps, had the eight cubs himself, but he wouldn't have been in any better of a position as far as his genes were concerned.

> Johnson gives a real-life example to illustrate the formula that he previously cited. This makes it easier for non-experts to understand the formula.

[7] Reciprocal altruism follows this same basic idea, but proposes a mechanism that could work for individuals that are unrelated. In this

scenario, cooperation occurs when the cost to the actor (c) is less than the benefit to the recipient (b) multiplied by the likelihood that the cooperation will be returned (w) or wb > c. This has been <u>demonstrated among vampire bats</u> who regurgitate blood into an unrelated bat's mouth if they weren't able to feed that night. Previous experience has shown the actor that they're likely to get repaid if they ever go hungry one night themselves.

> The author incorrectly uses a plural pronoun to refer to *bat* and *actor*. *They* should be *it* (*it wasn't able to feed*). It has become common to replace a singular noun with a plural pronoun in order to be non-sexist or gender neutral; however, grammatically, this is not acceptable.

[8] Whereas kin selection requires a community of closely related individuals for cooperation to be a successful strategy, reciprocal altruism requires that individuals be part of a single group, with low levels of immigration and emigration, so that group members will be likely to encounter each other on a regular basis. However, neither model can explain the emergence of cooperation in societies composed of unrelated individuals and where there is a constant influx of strangers. In other words, cooperation in human societies.

> The writer introduces recent research to show that earlier theories are supported even today.

[9] The more recent model proposed by Boyd et al. seeks to address this very problem. Their paper posits that fitness is enhanced, not by cooperating with close kin or reciprocating a previous act of generosity, but through the coordinated punishment of those who don't cooperate. In a social group individuals are able to choose whether they want to cooperate or defect. Suppose, for example, that a hunter returns from a successful hunt and must decide whether or not to share their gains with other members of the tribe. According to Boyd's model, the cost to the cooperator (c) is less than the overall benefit (b) but is still greater than the benefit to each member of the group (n): b > c > b/n. If the hunter chose to cooperate, the meat would be divided so that everyone benefits but the hunter still enjoys a slightly larger share. They would also receive a benefit in the future when other hunters had more success than they did (just as they would under reciprocal altruism).

> He provides support that the hypothetical model works in the real world but admits that further research is needed. This does not weaken the argument; it shows that Johnson did his research and is aware of the limitations of the studies he cites.

[10] However, if the hunter refuses to share with other members there are two stages to contend with. The first is the signalling stage in which individuals signal their intent to punish those who refuse to cooperate. This is a common occurrence not just in humans but in many animals, especially primates. Baboons, for example, <u>use threat signals</u> such as staring, eyebrow raising, or a canine display to warn others to change

their behaviour. In humans this can take a variety of forms, including angry looks, hand gestures, and/or harsh words. The cost of such signals are fairly low, but still high enough that it doesn't pay to signal and fail to back it up with action if necessary.

[11] If the warning doesn't provide the appropriate result the next stage is coordinated punishment. According to Boyd's model a quorum (τ) of punishers is required to work together to target an individual who refuses to cooperate. In such cases there will be a cost (p) to the target and an expected cost to each punisher of k/npa, where np is the number of punishers. Given that an outnumbered target is unlikely to inflict costs on the punishers, the model assumes that a > 1. What this means is that the higher the number of punishers, the lower the cost to each involved. Furthermore, the punishment doesn't necessarily involve physical attacks. The model allows for punishment to come in the form of gossip, group shunning, or any other nonaggressive action that brings a cost to the uncooperative target.

[12] According to this model a society would be made up of some combination of punishers Wp and nonpunishers Wn. If there were only a single punisher in the group ($\tau = 1$), what is known as the "Lone Ranger" condition, the fitness cost would outweigh the benefit and punishers

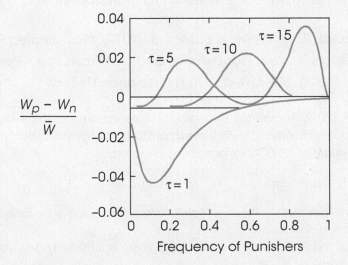

Punishment is an evolutionarily stable strategy when multiple punishers are involved. Source: Boyd, R., Gintis, H., & Bowles, S. (2010). Coordinated Punishment of Defectors Sustains Cooperation and Can Proliferate When Rare, *Science*, 328 (5978), 617–620

would decline in the population. However, for larger values of τ punishment does pay and therefore increasing the number of punishers increases their fitness.

[13] This model has had some empirical support. For example, last year Boyd and Sarah Matthew found that punishing desertion promoted cooperation in raiding parties among the Turkana pastoralists in East Africa. Likewise, Lauri Sääksvuori and colleagues published their results in *Proceedings of the Royal Society* suggesting that this form of enforced cooperation could emerge through competitive group selection. While further empirical tests are needed to confirm Boyd's model, it has the benefit of demonstrating how cooperation could evolve even in large societies where kinship is low and immigration is high: the very factors that were previously thought to confound the evolution of cooperation.

[14] However, given that many Indigenous systems are based on restorative justice (in which offenders are brought into a relationship with the victim and must make restitution to regain the society's trust) it's unclear how accurate a model focusing exclusively on punishment would be for understanding the evolution of human cooperation. Nevertheless, Coordinated Punishment now joins other recent approaches, such as Generalized Reciprocity, that seek to reexamine how the common good could emerge out of the selection for individual fitness.

Reference: Boyd, R., Gintis, H., & Bowles, S. (2010). Coordinated Punishment of Defectors Sustains Cooperation and Can Proliferate When Rare, *Science*, 328 (5978), 617–620. doi: 10.1126/science.1183665

Johnson, E. M. (2012, August 16). Punishing cheaters promotes the evolution of cooperation. *Scientific American*. Retrieved from http://blogs.scientificamerican.com/primate-diaries/2012/08/16/punishing-cheaters/

Post-Reading Questions

1. Is this an expository or argumentative paper? Support your answer with examples from the essay.
2. Identify the thesis statement. Which paragraph is it in? Why do you think it is placed here?
3. What type of claim does the author make? How would this essay be different if he had used a different type?

Side annotations:

Because *hunter* is singular, *their* should be *his or her*. When writing an academic essay, make sure your nouns and pronouns match (both singular or both plural).

Acknowledging that the research cited may be weak is a good strategy, as it shows the reader that the author is aware of what is happening in the research field and thereby increases the writer's credibility.

The author concludes with the shortcomings of the current research and an idea that the reader can ponder.

When composing an academic essay, reference all the sources you cited.

4. What type of audience is Johnson writing for? Support your answer with examples from the essay.
5. Are there any areas where you think the writer loses credibility? Where? Why?

 # Chapter Review Questions

1. What are the two main elements of an essay?
2. What are the advantages to using certain kinds of claims? When would these advantages occur?
3. What kinds of evidence can be used in an essay? What is the difference between hard and soft evidence?
4. Why is a writer's credibility important?
5. How can you establish your credibility in an essay?

9 The Argumentative Essay

In this chapter, you will learn

- how emotional and logical arguments differ;
- how to identify and avoid common errors of logic;
- what kinds of evidence can be used in an argumentative essay;
- why it is important to acknowledge the opposing point of view;
- how to create an outline for an argumentative essay; and
- how to create and deliver oral presentations.

Argument requires careful planning and critical thinking skills. Argumentative essays written at college and university rely on logic and reason supported by convincing evidence. You need to avoid errors in logic, as they can destroy your credibility. This chapter will introduce you to some of the most common errors in logic, discuss effective argumentative strategies, and include examples of well-argued essays.

Emotional versus Logical Arguments

People argue every day. Many arguments are emotionally based, such as when parents argue with their teenager about using the family car. Arguments can also be based on reason and moral standards. For example, letters to the editor tend to have the most impact when they use a combination of argumentative strategies and make **appeals** to reason, emotion, and ethics. Even résumé writing involves **argument**—you are convincing an employer to hire you. An argumentative essay requires the same logical and critical thinking skills that you use every day. Appeals to reason, emotion, and ethics all can be used in argument, as the following scenario suggests:

> You meet with your instructor to discuss a disappointing essay grade. By your effective use of reason, you try to convince her to change your mark, conceding the validity of some of her criticisms (**concessions** are used in many arguments). Going through the paper systematically, you focus on points that seem arguable, ask for clarification or elaboration, and present your counterclaims. As you do, you come across as a responsible, conscientious student: you make an ethical appeal. You appeal to her as being fair-minded, reiterating her helpfulness, your interest in the course, and your desire to do well. In this way, you succeed in establishing common ground, as you would try to do with the reader of your essay. If you argue with integrity, you will leave a good impression.

An **appeal** calls on reason, ethics, or emotion to persuade a reader that an argument is valid. An **argument** attempts to persuade your audience to change its mind or to see your point of view through claims of value or policy.

When you make a **concession**, or concede a point, you acknowledge its validity and show that you are fair and reasonable. Arguers often concede a minor point and follow with a strong point of their own.

Successful arguments at the college and university level make appeals to reason, ethics, and emotion. Of these, appeals to reason and logic are usually the strongest.

Exercise 9.1

There may not always be a firm line between exposition and argument, but you may be asked to write an essay that is either one or the other and your reader should recognize the type he or she is reading. Determine whether the statements below are most suited to argument or exposition by labelling them "A" or "E."

1. British Columbia's environmental policy is better than Alberta's policy.
2. Legislators should impose an outright ban on tablet computers in indoor public establishments and places of business.
3. Diplomacy and militarism are the two main approaches to foreign policy that, though sometimes used independently, are much more effective when used in combination.
4. While social media has become part of many people's lives, inappropriate posts can damage one's professional reputation.

(continued)

5. Genetically modified food has become a target of negative publicity, but without genetic modifications, farms would not be as productive as they are.

6. Hip-hop acts as a cultural bridge for widely diverse groups of young people to communicate across racial, class, religious, linguistic, and national divisions.

7. In spite of ethical concerns, can the human race afford to ignore the tremendous potential ability of embryonic stem-cell research to find cures for many diseases?

8. The government should take steps to regulate the monopolistic practices of airlines.

9. Probably nobody in the history of psychology has been as controversial—sometimes revered, sometimes despised—as Sigmund Freud.

10. What are the physical effects of artificial and natural tanning? What are the risks involved, and what can be done to educate the public about both?

In an argumentative essay, reason and logic appeals are strongest. Ethical appeals can play a vital secondary role in establishing your credibility for certain topics. Subtle emotional appeals can also be useful, depending on their placement in the essay, your topic, and your audience.

Some writers do not argue well because they use faulty logic or rely solely on emotional appeals. At the college and university level, you need to avoid these errors in an argumentative essay, as they affect your credibility.

Exercise **9.2**

In the following scenario, Ivannia Herrera summarizes an argument over what might seem a trivial issue; however, the underlying issues are important. In the course of the argument, some values are considered more significant than others. Although informal, the excerpt contains many features of a formal argument, such as a claim and supporting evidence. Rebuttals and concessions are also involved (see pp. 200–2). Read the argument carefully to find the appeals to reason, emotion, and ethics.

Tempest in a Teapot

Background: My roommate and I share a kitchen and utensils. Each day I make tea in a small stainless steel pot, which has a glass cover and a pouring spout with tiny holes that serve as a strainer. I pour two cups of water into the pot, let it boil, then add the leaves. When the tea is ready, I strain the tea water from the pot, leaving the tea leaves behind. I leave the pot on the counter until the next time I make tea.

The reason for the argument: My roommate has made it plain she does not enjoy seeing the pot with drenched tea leaves in the bottom.

This table lists the points that Ivannia and her roommate made during the argument. Which points seem the most convincing? Why? Are there any irrelevant points? Are points missing?

My Side	Roommate's Side
If I leave the pot with the tea leaves on the counter, I can reuse them three times. Since I make the same type of tea several times a day, it makes sense that I reuse the leaves rather than throw them out, which will cost me more money in the long run.	The pot is left on the counter for many hours. Though it's okay to reuse the leaves, the kitchen looks messy. I don't like the kitchen looking dirty with an unclean pot sitting there every day. Furthermore, I can't use this pot because it is always filled with tea leaves that I can't throw away.
I bought all the pots and pans in this household, and I am happy to share them; however, if you need a pot like this to use regularly, you should consider buying one yourself.	I also bought utensils for the household—and even the computer. I share these things and understand the concept of sharing. I think that having roommates means having to compromise.
I think of myself as a clean person, and I contribute greatly to the cleanliness of the household. I think that your having to look at a small pot is a small "defect," considering . . . Drinking tea is part of my daily life, and I enjoy it. As well, it costs me $6 per month; if I were to discard the tea each time, I would be spending $18 per month, and I can think of better ways to spend those extra $12!	I am not saying that you should throw away the tea leaves, but just find a better way to use them so they are not in sight and taking over the pot. I think that the cleanliness of my living space is a reflection on me, which is why I want a clean environment. I do not like seeing a messy pot, and this is my "defect." I also think I should be able to use the pot if I like, and I can't with the leaves in it.
We both agree on the need to compromise. I'm willing to compromise and buy a ball strainer that can hold the tea leaves inside for as long as need be. It is a small ball attached to a chain; the ball divides in half, the tea leaves are put in one half, the ball is closed, and it is placed inside a cup filled with boiling water. I suggest we compromise and each pay half for the ball strainer.	I'm happy to pay for half of it, as long as you keep the ball with the tea leaves in a cup in your own room. That way, you can bring it out anytime you want tea, but it will be out of my sight.

Argument, Opinion, and Facts

Ivannia's discussion in Exercise 9.2 contains the necessary elements of argument. However, the following sample paragraph is based solely on opinion and cannot be considered an argument. Although her topic can be argued, the writer oversimplifies and uses **generalizations** that are not backed up by evidence.

A **generalization** is a statement applied to all people or things in a large category. If there are many exceptions to the statement, the generalization is considered invalid.

Sports utility vehicles (SUVs) can also be called stupid useless vehicles.

They were designed for people who wanted to travel over different types of terrain in all kinds of weather. A Jeep is a perfect example of this type of vehicle.

If SUVs were used for their intended purpose, then they would be beneficial.

However, most people who purchase them seem to live in towns and cities, and the SUVs never seem to be dirty, which shows they are not used off-road.

Many of these vehicles are driven on highways with rarely more than one passenger, and these overly large vehicles use precious resources and pollute the environment.

Unless people can prove that the SUV is going to be used for the purpose for which it was designed, they should not be allowed to purchase one.

> The writer starts by abruptly stating an opinion that not all readers will share.

> The author uses a fact and an example but also introduces opinion with the adjective *perfect*, weakening the statement.

> The writer fails to support this point, which is based simply on moral high ground—she also uses flawed reasoning in assuming there is one "intended purpose" for these vehicles.

> The writer makes broad generalizations that cannot be argued against. Facts or statistics are more effective for showing a claim's validity.

> Again, the author uses a generalization and provides no support.

> The writer ends using opinion only, which is ineffective.

As the example demonstrates, being opinionated is not the same as arguing. The writer of the next paragraph makes it clear that he is opinionated; in doing so, he shows poor argumentative skills. A reader who is overwhelmed by an author's opinions may miss the essay's main points.

Institutions of higher learning are meant for people hoping to broaden their interests and knowledge in order to contribute to society. I, myself, agree with this principle, and I also agree that a degree can help me acquire a job and be good at it. Along with this, I do not doubt that these institutions facilitate higher cognitive functioning. What I do not agree with is the approach that these institutions have towards the sciences. In fact, I categorically oppose the favouritism that is always shown to the sciences whenever financial matters are considered.

Exercise **9.3**

Rewrite the paragraph on higher learning, eliminating the references to opinion and changing the pronouns *I*, *me*, etc., to *one* or a suitable noun. Does the revised paragraph sound more forceful? How is the writer's credibility enhanced?

Opinions are not the same as facts. The former can be challenged, but the latter can be verified by observation or research. Facts can be interpreted in different ways and used for different purposes; therefore, they can support the thesis of an argumentative essay. Effective arguers are always clear about when they are using facts and when they are using opinion. They also have an opposing view to argue against.

When reading, use your critical thinking skills to ask if the writer clearly separates facts from opinion. Some examples will help clarify the difference.

> Many arguments are based on opinion. Effective arguments are objective and use neutral language.

> In your argumentative essays, always separate fact from opinion. Support your opinions with logic and/or reliable evidence.

Fact (not challengeable):
According to moon landing conspiracy theories, the 1969 *Apollo* moon landing was faked.

Opinion (challengeable):
The *Apollo* moon landing was a hoax.

Fact:
On 13 November 2009 NASA announced that water had been found on the moon.

Opinion:
Now that water has been found on the moon, humans should set up colonies at the moon's poles by 2050.

Exercise 9.4

Consider the two pairs of statements about the moon. In groups, discuss the ways that fact differs from opinion in each case. Using other topics, write two statements for each, one representing a fact and the other an opinion.

Exercise 9.5

Briefly describe the circumstances of a recent argument. Divide a page in half vertically and summarize each point raised by your side and the other side (as in Exercise 9.2); simply report what was said. Analyze the strengths and weaknesses of each point. Does it make an appeal to reason, emotion, or ethics? Are the opinions supported with facts? Are the points logically related? Was the argument resolved? If so, how? Write a paragraph response to the argument, analyzing flaws such as simplifications and generalizations. Try to be as objective as possible to both sides.

Faulty Reasoning

It is easy to use faulty reasoning when writing an argumentative essay. If you know how to avoid it, you will be in a better position to point out flaws in your opponent's argument. Once you know some of the common problems, you can create arguable claims and support them with well-reasoned points and specific argumentative strategies.

Logical, Emotional, and Ethical Fallacies

Arguments that use logical, emotional, or ethical fallacies affect your credibility: we do not trust someone who misuses logic or reason. For example, we might mistrust a person who argues that all campus pubs should be closed because some students are underage.

Misuse of emotional or ethical appeals is unfair to the other side: emotional fallacies exploit emotions and are very different from valid appeals. People frequently misuse emotion. We have been told that larger vehicles are more harmful to the environment, but that doesn't mean that all drivers of pick-up trucks or SUVs in the city should be condemned, as stated in the excerpt on page 188. The vehicles have several uses within a city: for example, a landscaper might need a truck for work. By stating that all such drivers do not care about the environment, the writer is guilty of misusing emotional or ethical appeals.

Some fallacies are based on faulty inductive reasoning, such as cause–effect fallacies (e.g., "If I wash my car, it will rain."). Others are based on the faulty use of deductive reasoning, where general or universal statements that may not be true are made, such as "All people who ride bicycles are environmentalists."

Table 9.1 lists common argumentative fallacies that misuse reason, emotion, or ethics. Including them in your essays can weaken your position greatly, as a reader can easily think that your points don't make sense. When you use argument, you want your statements to be forceful and effective, not to arouse suspicion. Therefore, avoid them in your writing and look for examples in your opponent's arguments (more than one type of fallacy may be involved).

Writers need to look objectively at the way they argue and ensure that their arguments are always based on logic and that their appeals to emotion are always moderate. The writer who watches out for the first will appear reliable and trustworthy; the one who watches out for the last will appear fair.

Faulty reasoning can result from an invalid argument, a lack of proof for a claim, or an opinion that is not clearly separated from fact. A fallacy is a misleading or unsound argument.

Misuse of emotional or ethical appeals is unfair to the other side: emotional **fallacies** exploit emotions and are thus very different from valid appeals.

 See pages 198–9 for a discussion on inductive and deductive reasoning.

Writers need to look closely and objectively at the way they argue to ensure that their arguments are based on logic and that their emotional appeals are moderate.

TABLE 9.1 Argumentative Fallacies

Types	Term	Definition	Example
Irrelevant	Red herring	Attempts to distract the reader, often on an ethical matter. There may be some validity to the point, but it should not form the basis of an argument.	We need to accept higher tuition fees because education is important. (This argument makes a broad comment that distracts from the truth: higher tuition fees bring in more money and are unrelated to the quality of education.)
	Straw man	Misrepresents an opponent's main argument by substituting a false or minor argument in its place. The point is to get the audience to agree.	Thaddeus Tuttle points out that, while women have not achieved wage parity with men, they often take maternity leave, which means they don't work as much as men. (Among its flaws, this argument ignores the basic principle of equal pay for equal work.)
Emotional	Bandwagon	Argues in favour of something because it has become popular.	Everyone is using the latest iPhone. I have to get one too, even though my old one works just fine.
	Dogmatism	Common type of argument that asserts a point based on a firm, perhaps passionate, belief, without supporting evidence.	I believe that everyone should oppose whale hunting. (In argumentative essays, it's best to avoid the self-conscious reference to your opinion; instead, you should let your points talk for you.)
	Either/or	Suggests that there are only two available options.	You are either with me or against me. (These arguments often also lack logic.)
Logical	Circular	An argument that does not move forward or that continues in a circle. The main point is repeated but not expanded.	Applied degrees are now available at some community colleges in Canada. They are only offered there because community colleges teach applied skills.
Evidence	False analogy	Compares two things that are not alike. A true analogy can support a point, but you need to have a real basis for comparison.	How can people complain about circuses that use wild animals in their acts? We keep animals that were once wild, such as cats, in small spaces in our homes.

(Continued)

TABLE 9.1 Continued

Types	Term	Definition	Example
	False cause	Asserts that, simply because one event preceded another one, there must be a cause–effect relationship between them.	Tamara forgot to wear her lucky watch for the exam; consequently, she failed. (Superstitions can arise when people assume a causal relationship between two events. Of course, there are causal relationships between many events; for example, if Tamara walked in front of a car and was hit, her action obviously resulted in her injury. A false cause assumes a connection without valid evidence.)
	Hasty generalization	Forms a conclusion based on little or no evidence.	I talked to two people, both of whom said the text was useless, so I will not buy it. (If many people bought the text, two people may not be a good sample.)
	Prediction	Denies that an effect arises from a cause because it hasn't happened yet—therefore, it's not going to. The arguer projects into the future without considering probability or other evidence.	I did well on the last test and I didn't study much; therefore, I don't need to study much for the final exam.
	Tradition ("the way we have always done it")	Argues for a course of action because it has been followed before, even if the same conditions no longer apply.	You should not compose your essay on a computer. Handwriting is much better.

Exercise 9.6

For each of the following statements, indicate the type(s) of faulty reasoning used.

1. In our family, males have always been named "Harold" and females "Gertrude"; therefore, you should name your twins "Harry" and "Gerty."
2. If you don't get a degree in law, medicine, or business these days, you're never going to make any money.
3. When I serve you dinner, it's terrible not to eat all of it when you consider that one-third of the world's population goes to bed hungry.

4. The teacher hasn't called on me to answer a question for three consecutive days; it looks like I don't need to do the reading for tomorrow.
5. I know I went through the red light, officer, but the car in front of me did, too.

Using Slanted Language

A writer can also show a lack of objectivity by using slanted or loaded language. Such language detracts from his or her credibility. **Slanted language** can vary from extreme direct statements to qualifiers (adjectives or adverbs) that subtly convey a bias. If you use slanted language, readers could easily take offence and question your fairness.

Writers can use slanted language when words focus on the negative implications rather than on their literal meanings. A writer's careful and conscious use of a word's various meanings can be effective in an argument, but the writer's credibility will be at stake if the purpose is to distort the truth. In the following passage, "removed from office" has a more negative tone than "voted out of office" (a phrase the writer could have used instead). The italicized words indicate slanted language:

> In the recent election, the *reigning* political *regime was removed from office* as a result of the *atrocities they had committed* against the people of the province. The voters believed the new government would improve things, but when you achieve such easy victory there is a tendency to overlook the reason for your victory: the people who elected you. Today, the government is ignoring the middle class, *betraying* the very people who *naively* voted them into office.

> **Slanted language** reveals the writer's bias, affecting credibility. This language can take direct forms, such as accusation, or can be more indirect.

Exercise **9.7**

The following paragraphs use faulty logic, emotional appeals, and slanted language. Analyze the arguments, determine what makes them ineffective, and suggest improvements. Focus on identifying illogical statements and unfair appeals to emotion.

1. Genetically engineered foods are being sold in most supermarkets without anyone knowing that we are being used as guinea pigs for the corporations developing this technology. The general public is being kept in the dark entirely. The public is being told that genetically engineered foods are a safe and effective way to grow a lot of food faster. Though the proponents of genetically engineered foods attempt to convince the public that this technology will save lives, the reality is that major biotechnology companies are developing genetically engineered food crops to maximize their

(continued)

profits. Corporations would have us believe that the reason 19,000 children starve to death daily is because of inefficient agricultural practices, but the world currently produces enough food to provide a decent diet for every person on this planet. In spite of this fact, genetically engineered foods are being sold as the cure for Third-World starvation. This, however, is simply not true. The motives of the companies selling genetically engineered foods are not to save the lives of starving people but to line their own pockets by profiting from the biotechnological industry. As a society, we should move to force governments to ban the development of genetically engineered foods before it is too late.

2. The legalization of marijuana would destroy society as we know it. The typical Canadian would be exposed to many harsh drugs, such as coke, crack, and heroin, due to the increased acceptance of drugs within the community. Rehabilitation clinics for chronic drug users would be a huge drain on the economy. There would have to be new laws and screenings implemented to prevent people from working with heavy machinery or operating a motor vehicle while impaired by marijuana. Canadian business owners would be dissatisfied with many of their employees, and then discrimination would rear its ugly head. Firing someone for smoking marijuana and not being productive at work is not discrimination; however, the point would be made that it is. Clearly, our society would sink to a despicable level if this drug were legalized.

Creating Your Argument with Claims and Support

You can use a variety of strategies to create an effective argument, including

- making a claim of value (something is right or wrong);
- making a claim of policy (a policy or practice needs to be changed);
- interpreting facts, such as statistics, to support your claim;
- providing evidence from the experts;
- supporting your points with credible examples, such as case studies;
- supporting your points using soft evidence, such as analogy, description, or personal experience;
- defining a term or concept, especially if the term could be misunderstood; and
- comparing your ideas to others that the audience understands.

 See Chapter 8 for more about claims.

Using these strategies and avoiding fallacies will help you create an essay that builds your credibility.

Let's look at a few strategies more closely. As mentioned before, using analogy (comparison) or description makes a point easier to understand. However, you need to use one that the audience can relate to. Author Elizabeth Bowen used the following analogy in *The House in Paris*:

> Memory is to love what the saucer is to the cup.

Description may also play a limited role in argument, such as attracting interest in the essay's introduction or setting up a main point. Student writer Leslie Nelson begins her essay on adolescent depression this way:

> Imagine a deep, dark hole that stretches forever without end. There is no light at either end of this hole; there is nobody else in this hole except you. Imagine living in this hole for hours, days, weeks, years. Imagine believing that you will never escape. Most teenagers find themselves in this hole—depression—at least once in their adolescent life, a time when nothing seems to go right.

If you use personal experience, keep your tone objective. Check with your instructor before using this strategy.

> The limited use of personal experience is often effective in argument. However, simply using the pronoun *I* or *my*, as in "I believe . . ." or "My opinion is . . ." is not the same as using personal experience as evidence.

Definition can help readers understand how you are using a concept or term. If you are writing a paper about the value of post-secondary education, you might define what this concept means to you. Does it include university, community college, and private degree-granting institutions (such as the ones advertised on TV), or only university and community college?

 Chapter 4 provides more detail on analogy, description, and personal experience.

Comparison or contrast can help a reader visualize something by setting it alongside what he or she knows. In this example, the writer compares Japanese flooring with something she believes her readers are familiar with. (The excerpt also uses description.)

> Tatami, or rice mat, flooring is common in Japan. Tatami is similar to the rice mats that one can buy for use on the beach; however, tatami does not fold up. The rice matting is placed on large wooden frames and fastened securely to these frames. One mat is difficult for most adults to pick up alone. An average room can have six or eight mats on the floor.

Any of these strategies can be used to support your argumentative thesis. However, the beginning point for argument is in the introduction, where you state your thesis.

Arguable Claims

> A topic that can be argued is based on objective, not just subjective, standards and has an opposing viewpoint.

For a valid argument, you need an arguable topic. If you and a friend start debating whether Harvey's is better than A&W, who is right? If you use only subjective standards (such as what you think tastes better), neither of you is "right" because the topic is based on opinion, which cannot alone form a reason-based argument. On the other hand, you could base your argument on the respective nutritional values, fat content, or additives and preservatives.

The topic also needs an opposing viewpoint. You could not write an argumentative essay on the benefits of good health, as there is no opposing view. Obvious claims, such as "Computers have changed a great deal in the last decade," are unarguable. Just because a subject is controversial does not always mean that it is arguable. An argument that justifies computer hacking or the writing of viruses is likely invalid.

Specific, Interesting, and Manageable Claims

See Chapter 7 for more about thesis statements.

You must ensure that your claim is specific, interesting, and manageable. In this section, we focus on a sample argumentative claim, showing the kinds of questions you can ask to help you develop a strong and effective thesis for an argumentative essay.

Specific Claims

A specific claim must not be vague but state clearly and precisely what you will be arguing.

A specific claim states clearly and precisely what you will be arguing. The reader should know whether the claim is one of fact, value, or policy. Consider the following statement:

> Parents of children who play hockey would like to see fighting eliminated from the game at all levels.

Although this claim is arguable and has an opposing viewpoint, it is not specific enough to suggest the kind of argument to follow or even if the essay will be focused on argument rather than exposition: "parents," "would like to see," and "at all levels" are vague. Also, "eliminated from the game at all levels" seems unconnected to the rest of the claim. What does it have to do with the parents who presumably don't like seeing their children fight? An expanded thesis statement can help make the claim more specific. In the revised thesis statement, the claim is expressed more clearly through specific words as well as the inclusion of main points (*should* clearly reveals a policy claim):

> Fighting should be prohibited in hockey, since violent NHL players give young hockey players a negative role model and this reinforces a "win at all costs" mentality.

It is often a good idea to follow the claim by defining concepts central to your argument. In the previous example, the writer might define what she means by *fighting*. Does a fight start when the gloves are dropped, when there is excessive physical contact, or when a third player joins in? Definition enables you to make the topic more specific.

An "all or none" kind of claim is also non-specific. If your claim is too broad, use qualifiers such as *usually, often, sometimes, in part, many, some, several*, or *a few* to restrict its scope or reword your claim to make it more realistic. Alternatively, you can use verbs and verb phrases that qualify and limit, such as *contribute to, may, play a role in*, and *seems*.

Interesting Claims

To be interesting, a claim should be written for a specific audience. In the claim about fighting in hockey, the intended audience is hockey parents as well as people who can make changes. Many fans of professional hockey would not be interested in the main point of the argument, as it applies mostly to children. Those who never watch hockey or don't have children playing the sport probably would be even less interested. Similarly, an argument how best to prevent the growth of single-celled algae in China's lakes and reservoirs might be interesting to biologists but probably not to the average reader.

Along with audience interest, consider your audience's viewpoint. Are most people likely to agree with you, disagree, or be neutral? Will they possess general knowledge of the topic? Will most people have heard of the topic? These kinds of questions are extremely relevant when you write the body of the essay and support your claim. If your audience includes many who disagree with your claim, it may be important to establish **common ground** and to convince them that you have similar values and goals.

Manageable Claims

Manageable claims are determined partly by whether they are specific and interesting. They also depend on the essay's length, the support available, and the complexity of the issues raised by the claim.

Policy claims, which try to persuade people to take action, need to provide realistic solutions or at least suggestions that they exist. If the change you propose isn't practical, it may be best to reword the claim or change it to one of value. Your supporting points may be complex, but the thesis statement must be workable and clear to the reader.

The claim about hockey violence is arguable, specific, and interesting to the intended audience, but is it manageable? Remember that all claims need to focus on one main topic.

It would be too unmanageable to address banning fighting in hockey at both the professional and minor levels. Realistically, would the role model argument motivate NHL executives to ban fighting? To make the statement

To be interesting and specific, a claim should be written for a specific audience. Who might be interested in the topic but not share your viewpoint?

Establishing **common ground** is a strategy in argument that shows an opponent that you share similar concerns or basic values.

 See "Rebutting the Opposing View" on page 200 for specific audience strategies.

Factors in manageable claims include essay length, support available, complexity of the topic, and practicality of the claim.

manageable, the writer could focus either on the idea that NHL players who fight are poor role models or on the consequences of fighting in minor hockey.

Value claim:
Fighting in professional hockey gives young hockey players a negative role model because violence reinforces a "win at all costs" mentality.

Reworded policy claim:
Fighting should be prohibited in minor hockey below the midget level because violence reinforces a "win at all costs" mentality.

A Closer Look at Reason

Arguments use inductive and deductive reasoning. With inductive, you reach a general conclusion based on observable evidence. With deductive, you reach a conclusion by stating a general principle and applying it to a specific case.

Inductive reasoning, or scientific reasoning, relies on the collection and analysis of specific data to reach a conclusion. We use inductive reasoning daily; however, it can include logical fallacies. These can occur when there isn't enough evidence to generalize or the means for gathering the evidence are flawed or biased. Consider the following example.

Recorded observations of sunset in Halifax:

Date	Time of Sunset (p.m.)
5 June	9:16
6 June	9:16
7 June	9:17
8 June	9:17
9 June	9:18

Prediction/Claim:
On 10 June the sun will set at 9:18 p.m.

We can make this prediction because we have observed specific data about the setting sun. If we had simply recorded the times on 5 and 6 June, we might have concluded that the sun would set at the same time on 7 June, which would be incorrect: we would be drawing a conclusion without enough evidence. On the other hand, if we made our first set of observations in Edmonton and the second in Regina, the conclusions would also be incorrect because the evidence-gathering method would be flawed. A fallacy of this type can affect your credibility; it is important to always use sound reasoning and to consider the validity of every statement.

Inductive reasoning is sometimes called scientific reasoning because scientists and other researchers use it to answer questions about the natural world and make predictions about natural phenomena.

Two questions to ask yourself when using inductive reasoning are, "Have I provided enough support for each statement I make?" and "Have I been logical and consistent in the way I have used reason (my reasoning method)?"

 See Table 9.1 (pp. 191–2) for examples of faulty inductive and deductive reasoning.

Deductive Reasoning in Practice

The **deductive reasoning** process has three parts:

- *major premise*: a general statement of a principle
- *minor premise*: a specific statement about the topic
- *conclusion*: a statement that combines the major and minor premises

The following presents a logical argument based on the deductive method.

Major premise: It is wrong not to treat all people with respect.
Minor premise: In building the dam, the Urra company did not treat the indigenous peoples with respect.
Conclusion: The Urra company was wrong to build the dam.

We constantly see examples of faulty reasoning such as that in the next example, and they can have negative consequences. Many forms of stereotyping are based on faulty deductive reasoning.

Major premise: People who spend more than two hours a day at their computers are gamers.
Minor premise: Brandon spends more than two hours a day at his computer.
Conclusion: Brandon is a gamer.

Most logical arguments combine inductive and deductive reasoning. Arguing well is a challenge; to succeed, you need to test the logic of your own reasoning as you proceed from one point to the next.

In **deductive reasoning**, you use a general statement and a specific statement to arrive at a conclusion. Ask yourself two questions: Does the major premise (general statement) apply to the people or situation described? Is it a valid generalization? Faulty logic, like that used in the example about the sun, weakens your credibility.

Exercise **9.8**

Read the following scenarios and analyze how the police reached their decision (i.e., analyze their reasoning methods) or why the investigation failed. How might inductive methods have been involved? If they were flawed, was the problem related to a lack of evidence or faulty methods of evidence gathering? How might deductive methods have been involved? If they were, what generalization was used as a major premise?

1. The police settled on two possible suspects for a home robbery. One was seen near the house around the time of the robbery but has never previously been arrested. The second suspect, who has two prior robbery convictions, was not seen near the house but was unable to account for his movements that night. Police brought the second man in for questioning.

(continued)

2. Police believed they would easily be able to determine the suspect of an assault when they discovered blood samples at the crime scene. But the crime scene investigator, who was working on his first case, prepared the samples incorrectly and they deteriorated. Police were unable to come up with a suspect.

Rebutting the Opposing View

When you write an argumentative essay, you should present the opposing viewpoint. Addressing the other side shows the reader that you are aware of it and strengthens your argument by demonstrating that your points are strong enough to counter your opponent's. This part of the essay, called a **rebuttal**, may be determined by the topic, your audience, or your purpose.

> The **rebuttal** is the part of your argument in which you raise the other side's points, usually to strengthen your argument and to appear fair.

Topic-Based Rebuttal

If your reader is familiar with the topic and the major points of debate, raising and rubutting each one is a good strategy. If your reader knows little about the topic, it may be best to acknowledge only the major counterargument(s), ensuring that your points are stronger and more numerous. If the main arguments are obvious to everyone, however, there may be little point in giving them space in your essay.

Audience-Based Rebuttal

> Showing how opponents can benefit by agreeing with your thesis is a common argumentative strategy.

Two rebuttal strategies—acknowledgement and point-by-point—depend on your reader's opinion.

Acknowledgement

> A concise method of acknowledging your opponent is to summarize the argument in a phrase or dependent clause and follow with your summarized thesis in an independent clause. When you give background information or summarize the opposing view, make sure you use an objective tone and neutral language. Make your summary as concise as possible.

If your audience is mildly opposed to your topic or is undecided, you may simply acknowledge the other side and counter it with a strong argument. In such cases, you must decide how much space to devote to acknowledgement. Student writer Laura Benard briefly characterizes the opposing viewpoint by using only a prepositional phrase ("Despite their aesthetic value") ahead of her thesis statement. She presents no real rebuttal but treats the opposing argument, that people use pesticides to make their lawn look attractive, as obvious:

> Despite their aesthetic value, the negative impacts of maintaining lawns by means of pesticide, lawn mower, and water use are so great that lawn owners should adopt less intensive maintenance practices or consider lawn alternatives.

A writer will often put the acknowledgement in the form of a dependent clause that contains the less important (opposing) information, followed by his or her own claim expressed in an independent clause: "Although some may argue [major point of opposition argument], the fact is/I believe that [your thesis]."

It is often necessary to provide background for the reader or a brief summary of the opposing view. In such cases, the writer can begin with this position, then follow with his or her argument. To decide how much space to spend on the opposing view, consider how objective you want to appear versus the importance of presenting a strong argument of your own.

Point-by-Point

If your audience strongly opposes your thesis, analyzing these views should show that you find them inadequate. Address several of the strongest points on the other side if they have strong support or if your purpose is to arrive at a compromise or find common ground. In both cases, raise individual points, usually beginning with the opponent's, and then respond to the weaknesses in this position. If your purpose is to win the argument, stress the opposing views' inadequacies and inconsistencies and draw attention to any fallacies. If it is to find common ground, point out the weaknesses in the form of helpful, constructive criticism. In both cases, remain unbiased and objective.

In this excerpt, student writer Spencer Cleave addresses a common argument supporting the US embargo against Cuba. After a concession (italicized), he introduces two counterclaims that attempt to undercut the original claim:

> Many supporters of the maintenance of the trade embargo against Cuba contend that the Cuban government fails to uphold the human rights of its population. *It is true that Cuba has had a number of human rights violations in its past. Thus, it is conceded that Cuba is also morally at fault on certain issues.* However, many reforms have recently been made by the government in an attempt to remedy its human rights problems. These efforts show that the government has a desire to improve the conditions within its own nation. Furthermore, it would be in the best interest of the United States to applaud the Cuban government in any human rights improvements, thus giving the image of a cooperative partner.

You may choose to address the main points of your opponent's argument systematically, summarizing these points and refuting them with facts and statistics. You can also stress how readers can benefit from considering your view. If your topic is a highly charged one, such as providing safe injection sites for drug users, you may begin by arguing your weakest points and work up to your strongest points. This way, you address all types of opponents, from the

> You do not have to respond to all your opponent's views in a point-by-point rebuttal. In shorter essays, you may not have the space to rebut any more than one. The opposing side might have only one strong argument; you would not need to address weaker ones.

weaker to the stronger. However your reader feels, you should work to establish common ground. Making concessions shows that you're willing to compromise.

Purpose-Based Rebuttal

The primary goal of an argumentative essay is to engage readers who share your concern about the topic or to enable readers to see another side of an issue and view it with greater tolerance. Long-lasting change can often result when the arguer is open and flexible. This approach can be particularly effective with value-based claims.

When reading Sophia Lowe's essay, look for any places where the author introduces the opposing view. Try to imagine how you could oppose her points.

Sample Professional Essay: Argumentative Essay

Welcome to Canada? Immigration Incentives May Not Be Enough for International Students to Stay

Sophia Lowe

The author makes a claim of policy.

[1] Canada has intensified its competition to recruit and retain international students through direct marketing and immigration policy changes. Making it easier for international students to work and stay in Canada as skilled immigrants is indeed a sound policy objective. However, without investing in the settlement and integration supports to create welcoming communities for international students and their families, Canada may not be able to successfully retain international students as permanent residents. Equipped with relatively recognizable Canadian credentials and experience, international student migrants who are not adequately supported may choose to immigrate elsewhere. This is not only a lost investment for Canada's post-secondary institutions, but could result in a direct loss for Canada, where desirable skilled immigrants are increasingly needed to meet national labour market demands.

Lowe starts this paragraph with a fact that is easily confirmed. She then outlines her argument that she will support in the body of her essay.

PREFERRED IMMIGRANTS: INTERNATIONAL STUDENTS

[2] There have been significant changes in Canada's immigration policies vis-a-vis international students to better attract and retain

them as skilled immigrants and eventual citizens. It appears that these policies, in addition to an increase in global student mobility and a more unified Canadian marketing scheme, are increasing Canada's competitive edge in attracting students. In 2008–09, Canada ranked eighth as a destination country for international students in tertiary education, and at a post-secondary level, the number of international students increased by 97 per cent from 72,798 in 1999 to 143,826 in 2008 (CIC, 2009). In 2008, international students contributed approximately $6.5 billion to the Canadian economy, creating over 83,000 jobs and generating more than $291 million in government revenues (RKA Inc., July 2009).

[3] At the same time, intense competition for international students and skilled immigrants internationally means that attracting students and creating avenues for their permanent immigration may not be enough to make them stay. Permanent stay rates in Canada stand at about 18 per cent, compared to over 29 per cent in Germany and 27 per cent in France (OECD, 2010). In countries where immigration policies have catered increasingly to retaining international students as skilled immigrants, large numbers of economic migrants are now sourced within these countries, rather than offshore. For Australia, where the most rapid and aggressive immigration policies have been tailored to international students and changing labour market demands, 62 per cent of primary economic immigrant applicants were former international students in 2006–07 and by 2009, 66 per cent of all students from India transferred to permanent resident status (Hawthorne, 2010). For Canada, where stay rates are relatively low, there is a need to develop more incentives to encourage and support students to remain permanently.

> The author supports her argument with claims of fact.

> The writer takes the facts she presented and creates a logical argument.

POLICY CHANGES FOR INTERNATIONAL STUDENTS

[4] In order to increase its edge in attracting international students both as migrants and as immigrants, Canada has introduced significant reforms to allow international students easier access to Canadian work experience and to clear immigration pathways. In 2006, international students were given the right to work off-campus during their studies and in 2008, post-graduation work permits for international students allowed student graduates to work in a field unrelated to their education, anywhere in Canada for up to three years.

[5] For international students in Canada, immigration policy has also brought forth two major immigration pathways from within the country—the federal Canadian Experience Class (CEC) and the Provincial Nomination Programs (PNPS). Within each of these programs, international students generally transition through two distinct phases—first, as a student and second, as a temporary worker—before attaining permanent residency. These immigration changes have shifted Canada towards a "two-step" migration process (Hawthorne, 2010), changing the starting point for migrants from settling in their newly adopted country as permanent residents to proving themselves as worthy immigrants (through a period with temporary status) in order to gain permanent residency. These immigration streams may attract non-traditional international students whose primary intention is not to study temporarily but to immigrate and evidence from other jurisdictions where similar migration policy changes took place indicates that demand for education and permanent residence increased drastically.

[6] The number of former international students immigrating to Canada through all channels has almost doubled in the last five years, from 5,486 in 2003 to more than 10,000 in 2008 (CIC, 2009). Based on the preliminary CEC data available for 2009, 869 of 1,176 individuals were admitted through the international student stream of the program. The implication is that international students and their families are likely to make up the majority of applicants through the CEC, and this could amount to 18,500 new permanent residents a year. In turn, the volume admitted through the Federal Skilled Worker Program (FSWP) who are selected overseas by the federal government—Canada's main immigration program for skilled immigrants—will be decreased in proportion to migrants applying through the CEC if current immigration levels remain unchanged.

[7] International students—deemed "designer immigrants" by some—are the most sought-after immigrants, as they are able to avoid some of the hurdles faced by skilled immigrants such as the non-recognition of international credentials and foreign work experience and skills, and concerns over language and communication abilities (Simmons, 1999). For Canada, there is no conclusive evidence, but preliminary research does suggest that former international students have better economic outcomes, at least in the short-run (Sweetman & Warman, 2009).

[8] However, in Australia, which has a longer history of experimentation with shifting immigration policy to retain international students, it was revealed that former international students had annual salaries of $33,000 (compared with $52,500 for landed immigrants selected overseas, while both groups were employed within six months almost equally (Hawthorne, 2007). In a study by Khoo et al. (2008), about half of international students who did not apply to become permanent residents in Australia, did not do so for "employment-related reasons," implying there are better opportunities elsewhere. In fact, Australia has found that a significant number of international student graduates eventually leave Australia, despite policy efforts (Khoo et al., 2008).

[9] In Canada, the recent Canadian Bureau of International Education's (CBIE) 2009 Survey of International Students found that half of surveyed university students and three-quarters of college students choose to study in Canada because of post-graduate work opportunities (19). Another CBIE report explores the unique experiences of international students in attempting to enter the Canadian labour market, finding that due to real or perceived barriers, 68 per cent of the international student respondents did not plan to stay in Canada to work. For 80 per cent of the respondents, pessimism about career opportunities seemed to be the driving concern (2007: 18). From the students' perspective, it is clear that employment opportunities and successful entry into the labour market play a large role in their decision to immigrate.

> If a writer wants to use the acronym for an organization that is not well-known to the audience, he or she must include the complete name first and the acronym in parentheses. From this point forward, the acronym alone may be used.

[10] Connection to community is also critical to the success and retention of international students and permanent immigrants. Early intervention in settlement services and support has been shown to reduce the likelihood of poverty and underemployment (Statistics Canada, 2005; Picot & Hou, 2003). Ultimately, it has been found that "feeling more rooted in the new environment [in part achieved through settlement support services], newcomers are able to access their inherent skills to begin the climb back to independence and self-assurance—basic ingredients for integration into their new community" (Romberg, 1994). In Reitz's (1998) comparative study, he indicates how support for settlement is vital to migrants' economic success and inclusion in the community. Looking at early settlement support may have both short- and long-term

> The author assumes that many readers will not have a great deal of knowledge about the immigration issue, so she explains it in detail to help convince the reader that her claims are valid.

impacts on the success and integration of international students and their families into the labour market and society at large.

SUPPORT FOR SETTLEMENT: ESSENTIAL TO RETAINING INTERNATIONAL STUDENTS

[11] Successful immigration and settlement is not based solely on simplified and accelerated work permit procedures and permanent residency pathways. With the increased interest in recruiting and retaining international students, "the roles of universities are changing dramatically" to include "immigration related-issues" (Suter & Jandl, 2008: 403). Martin (2004) notes that universities play a vital role in providing support to migrants' settling permanently. However, many post-secondary institutions provide limited, if any, services to graduated students, and international students, while in school and on work permits, are ineligible for the majority of settlement services and supports in the community.

[12] International Student Offices (ISOS) are an invaluable resource for international students as they are generally their first and main point of institutional contact (CBIE, 2007). International students seek academic, community, and employment support through the ISO. According to the 2007 CBIE report, "for the most part . . . it is the staff at the ISO who carry the responsibility for institutional support" (25) and much of the time, they are not provided with the operational funding to do so. Highlighted in Gates-Gasse's 2010 literature review is how, for many post-secondary institutions, targeted international student services through the ISOs face funding and staffing challenges, despite the fact that international students pay more tuition than domestic students, but receive fewer investments to their education and supports. A 2010 study by Siddiq et al., which focused on all the Atlantic Provinces, found that international students spent $2.68 for every dollar spent on them by the four provincial governments.

[13] In order to fulfill its objectives to successfully integrate immigrants, the Canadian federal government funds a complex array of settlement services and supports. Unfortunately, federal settlement funds have strict eligibility criteria and international students and their families do

Lowe appeals to the reader's sense of fairness by showing that, while these students pay more for tuition, they do not receive more services, which she argues they need. This ties into her argument about making Canada more welcoming to immigrants.

not qualify for federal settlement services until they are granted permanent residency, which can take from 3 to 10 or more years as they transition from student to worker to immigrant. Even though international students applying through the CEC will have settlement needs—which will be unique to those of economic immigrants arriving from outside of Canada—the only settlement services accessible to international students (both as students and temporary workers) are provincially funded and have broader eligibility criteria. When considering all the settlement services provided within a province, both federally and provincially funded, overall there are fewer provincially funded settlement services. In Ontario, only about 20 per cent of settlement services are funded by the province and 80 per cent are funded by the federal government.

[14] For international students and their families, having access to settlement services may assist in a more effective transition for those pursuing permanent residency in Canada—and may indeed influence the choice of whether or not to remain in Canada. Other groups that do not have full access to settlement services have documented the difficulty they have integrating into the labour market. Since we know that labour market access and integration are critically important in international students' choice to immigrate, expanding access to settlement services for these migrants seems a logical policy move for retaining international students as skilled immigrants. A 2009 report by Chira on the internationalization of Halifax found that settlement agencies expressed interest in partnering with universities to support international students, but that the stringent eligibility criteria for services and the lack of provincial funds for international student settlement was a recurring issue that prevented successful partnerships.

> The author gives the reader the necessary background, and she can now make her claim of logic.

[15] We know that early support for newcomers in the community has strong labour market integration outcomes, as evidenced by the extra service supports and social networks that refugees and family class migrants have over other economic migrants in Canada. Due to these supports, these migrants do better than other immigrants in the economic class, especially in their first years in Canada (Zietsma, 2007). In Australia, where only humanitarian migrants qualify for publicly funded

settlement services, these services have been shown to increase early labour market entry and have a "strong and robust influence on employment 48 months later" (Liebig, 2007: 45). Looking at early settlement services and supports for international students may be the key to retaining them, and will certainly have both short- and long-term impacts on their success and integration into the labour market.

WELCOMING IMMIGRANTS: THE IMPORTANCE OF SETTLEMENT SERVICES

[16] In a 2005 study of 160 Chinese undergraduate international students at the University of Saskatchewan, the authors conclude that "social and emotional adaptations are [as] critical as economic adaptations in facilitating intentions to stay permanently" (Lu et al., 2009: 307). In the United States, a 2006 study revealed the same need for a welcoming and supportive environment for international students to choose to immigrate. Just over half of the respondents reported that "feelings of alienation from US culture" had influenced their decision to return home after their studies (Alberts & Hazen, 2006: 212). In Canada, for all immigrants, data shows that 13 per cent of skilled worker principal applicants leave Canada, but that early intervention in terms of services and supports makes a significant difference in helping retain and integrate permanent residents. For international students with families, the importance of settlement support and community ties are magnified. A 2009 Master's thesis by Mandal found that, of University of Manitoba students with high rates of family and friend social capital networks, 89 per cent indicated an intention to settle in Canada.

By now you have seen that Lowe believes Canada needs skilled immigrants and that we, as a country, need to do more to encourage international students to stay after graduating. Here, she claims that we are not doing enough to help these foreign students adjust, but she does not provide specific steps for assisting them. She seems to expect the reader to just agree with her point of view.

[17] There is some evidence to suggest that international students are not being adequately welcomed into Canadian communities. A 2006 survey of over 2,500 Montreal students found that 47 per cent were unsatisfied with their welcome by other students and 49 per cent were also unsatisfied with their success in establishing friendships with Canadian students (CROP, 2006). The 2009 CBIE Survey of International Students found that only about one in three respondents reported "lots of success" in making friends with Canadian students.

[18] However, there is a disconnect between CIC's policy objective of encouraging the immigration of international students as skilled immigrants to Canada and the lack of services to assist in their effective transition to the labour force. In addition to stringent eligibility criteria for accessing settlement services, the federal government has recently cut nearly $53 million from settlement agencies, mainly in Toronto. Given that Toronto will likely continue to receive the lion's share of new immigrants and already hosts the second largest share of international students in Canada—over 15,000—providing services to Canada's current migrants to help them get established will become increasingly difficult. For a country which is internationally applauded as welcoming to immigrants, recent cuts and disinvestment in Canada's current migrant population's settlement needs may be sending a message to potential skilled immigrants, propelling many of them to look for opportunities elsewhere.

> The author uses facts throughout the essay to support her point of view. However, she does not explain the rational for the changes being made. Does this affect the strength of her argument?

[19] In light of their current immigration objectives, the federal and provincial governments need to review the eligibility criteria for their settlement services, as well as the array of services available, which could be modelled on and adapted for international students' unique settlement needs. In addition, settlement supports and services should continue to be funded and prioritized as a part of an integrated strategy to attract and retain skilled immigrants. By providing the necessary settlement and labour market supports, Canada will maintain its reputation as a welcoming and inclusive society, and will ensure that it maintains its competitive edge in attracting and retaining international students as skilled and successful permanent immigrants.

> Lowe reiterates her main points from the essay in the concluding paragraph and brings the reader to her own logical conclusion.

References

Alberts, H., & H. Hazen. 2006. Visitors or Immigrants? International Students in the United States. *Population, Space and Place*, 12: 201–216.

Canadian Bureau of International Education (CBIE). 2007. "Canadian Universities and International Mobility of Students." Accessed at www.cbie.ca/data/media/policy/20080617_CanadianPanorama

Canadian Bureau of International Education (CBIE). 2009. "Canada First: The 2009 Survey of International Students." Accessed at www.cbie.ca/data/media/resources/20091110_SurveyInternationalStudents_e.pdf

Chira, S. 2009. From Internationalizing Atlantic University Campuses to Internationalizing Halifax, Nova Scotia? Commissioned by the Association of Atlantic Universities and the Atlantic Metropolis Centre.

Citizenship and Immigration Canada (CIC). 2009. Facts and Figures 2008. Government of Canada. Accessed at www.cic.gc.ca/english/resources/statistics/facts2008

CROP. 2006. Enquête auprès des étudiants internationaux de Montréal. CRÉ de Montréal. Accessed at www.credemontreal.qc.ca/Publications/Developpement%20Economique/Enquete%20-%20Etudiants%20Internationaux%20-%201006.pdf

Gates-Gasse, E. 2010. International Students as Immigrants: Literature Review and Good Practices. World Education Services.

Gribble, C. 2008. Policy Options for Managing International Student Migrations: The Sending Country's Perspective. *Journal of Higher Education Policy and Management,* 6(4): 25–39.

Hawthorne, L. 2010. Two-Step Migration: Australia's Experience. Policy Options. Institute for Research on Public Policy. Accessed at http://www.irpp.org/po/archive/jul10/hawthorne.pdf

Khoo, S-E., G. Hugo, & P. McDonald. 2008. Which Skilled Temporary Migrants Become Permanent Residents and Why? *International Migration Review,* 42(1).

Liebig, T. 2007. The Labour Market Integration of Immigrants in Australia. Organisation for Economic Co-operation and Development (OECD). Social, Employment and Migration Working Papers, 49.

Lu, Y., L. Zong, & B. Schissel. 2009. To Stay or Return: Migration Intentions of Students from People's Republic of China in Saskatchewan, Canada. *International Migration and Integration,* 10: 283–310.

Mandal, S. 2009. Settlement Intentions of Post-Secondary International Students in Manitoba. Masters of Arts Thesis, University of Manitoba.

Martin, P. 2004. Universities as Immigration Gatekeepers. Mimeographed Draft Paper.

Organization for Economic Co-operation and Development (OECD). 2010. Education at a Glance 2010: OECD Indicators. Paris, OECD. Accessed at www.oecd.org/document/52/0,3343,en_2649_39263238_45897844_1_1_1_1,00.html

Picot, G., & Hou, F. 2003. The Rise in Low-Income Rates among Immigrants in Canada. Statistics Canada, Analytical Branch research paper series. Catalogue no. 11F0019MIE.

Reitz, J. 1998. *Warmth of the Welcome: The Social Causes of Economic Success for Immigrants in Different Nations and Cities.* Boulder: Westview Press.

Romberg, P. 1994. Service Delivery to Refugees and Immigrants: Toward an Integrated Approach, *Refuge,* 13(9).

Roslyn Kunin & Associates, Inc. (RKA, Inc.). July 2009. Economic Impact of International Education in Canada: Final Report. Presented to Foreign Affairs and International Trade Canada. Accessed at http:// www.international. gc.ca/education/assets/pdfs/RKA_IntEd_Report_

Lowe, S. (2011, Winter). Welcome to Canada? Immigration incentives may not be enough for international students to stay. *Canadian Diversity, 8*(5), 20–24. Copyright of Canadian Diversity.

Post-Reading Questions

1. Consider your own position toward the issue discussed in the essay. Do you have any knowledge about this or similar issues relating to government decisions about education? How do government decisions about immigration affect you or other Canadians?
2. What are the sides of the debate? Which side do you support? How might your prior knowledge and opinions affect your response to this argument?
3. Is there anything that would have made the argument more effective? Be as specific as possible.
4. Are there any questionable appeals to emotion or ethics? Are there any logical fallacies? If so, give examples.
5. Why does the writer include information from other countries? Is this effective? Why or why not?

Organizing an Outline for Argument

Now that you know how to formulate an argument, you can begin to outline your essay. As noted earlier, ensure that you order your main points logically, in a way that suits your argument. You can use the climax, inverted, or mixed order.

Table 9.2 provides a template that you can follow. You do not have to include everything listed; for example, you might not need to include background if the issue is well known to most readers. You can also put the elements in a different order.

> The order of your points is often vital to argument. In the climax order, the weakest point appears first and the strongest point last. Inverted order does the opposite. The often-used mixed order begins with a moderately strong point, followed by a weaker one, and concludes with the strongest.

 Chapter 2 discusses the methods for ordering points in an essay.

TABLE 9.2 Argumentative Essay Template

Introduction	<ul><li>gain reader's attention and interest</li><li>include your claim</li><li>suggest the primary developmental method (if there is one)</li><li>establish your credibility (knowledge, reliability, and fairness)</li></ul>
Body paragraph 1: Background	<ul><li>present background information, if relevant</li></ul>
Body paragraph 2: Lines of argument	<ul><li>present good reasons (logical, emotional, and ethical appeals) in support of your thesis</li><li>use all relevant evidence—facts, statistics, examples, views of experts/authorities</li><li>present reasons in specific order related to argument</li></ul>
Body paragraph 3: Rebuttal	<ul><li>consider opposing points of view</li><li>note both advantages and disadvantages of opposing views; may use concessions or common ground</li><li>argue that your thesis is stronger than the opposing view and more beneficial to the reader</li></ul>
Conclusion	<ul><li>summarize your argument</li><li>elaborate on the implication of your thesis</li><li>make clear what you want the reader to think or do</li><li>possibly make a final strong ethical or emotional appeal</li></ul>

If you include a rebuttal, it may not need much space. Depending on the topic and other factors, you might choose to place it before your main points. You could include an acknowledgement in the introduction or background section or begin a point-by-point rebuttal in the first or second body paragraph.

Exercise 9.9

Choose one of the following topics and prepare an outline using the template in Table 9.2, narrowing the topic if necessary. Choose a position that you can argue with a value or policy claim; do not create an expository essay with a factual claim.

1. bullying
2. physical activity among teens
3. social networking sites
4. technology in schools
5. salaries of sports celebrities or CEOs

As you read the following essay, pay attention to how the author presents and supports her points. For each point, ask yourself whether she convinces you of her view or if you disagree.

Sample Student Essay: Argumentative Essay

Discrimination against Aboriginals in Canada: Bill C-45

Jane Freiburger

[1] Aboriginal people have been discriminated against for centuries. Many Aboriginals feel that land claims, which have been a major issue for well over two centuries, are a good illustration of this discrimination. This is true in many nations, and Canada is a perfect example. Aboriginals feel that obligations under the treaties and the Indian Act are not being met by the Canadian federal government.

> Freiburger uses a concrete example to show support for her opening statement, which could be based on opinion, not fact.

[2] On 18 October 2012, the Harper government introduced Bill C-45. This affects the Indian Act, the Navigation Protection Act, and the Environmental Assessment Act. These changes have angered many Aboriginal people as they believe that more laws and legislation will further erode treaty and Indigenous rights and the rights of all Canadians (CBC News, 9 questions about Idle No More, 2013). Many Aboriginals feel that this bill discriminates against them by taking the decision-making powers away from them, showing that non-Aboriginals know what was best for them, which is discrimination.

> The writer introduces a controversial issue to provide grounds for her claims.

[3] Bill C-45 alters the Indian Act, which includes changes to land management on reserves, making it easier for the federal government to control reserve land (Gotz, 2012). Bill C-45 also alters the Navigable Waters Protection Act. This Act was used to protect 2.5 million rivers and lakes and now only covers 97 lakes and 62 rivers. This leaves rivers, lakes, and oceans vulnerable to exploitation and it leads the way to mining and the controversial Enbridge Northern Gateways pipeline to move forward (Fotheringham, 2013). Again, this alteration is felt to be discrimination, as the people who live on these lands will not be consulted before their lives are disrupted.

> The author uses a fact to support her argument.

Again, Freiburger uses facts to support her argument.

[4] In order to protest this loss of rights, many Aboriginals and non-Aboriginals participated in the "Idle No More" campaign in order to bring awareness of the latest issue of discrimination to the Canadian public. Unfortunately, both Prime Minister Stephen Harper and the media added to the discrimination issue. During this protest, Prime Minister Stephen Harper typified Aboriginals as arrogant imperialists and denied that colonization exists. Minorities have always been a focus of the media, particularly framing them as the problem. It is part of the way the news is created rather than it being the people who carry personal prejudices. This type of structural discrimination is not intentional, but it is harmful (Kunz, 2013). In the Idle No More protest, this message was very apparent, supporting the Aboriginal claim of discrimination.

The writer begins with a controversial statement but quickly supports it with research.

[5] Among the non-Aboriginal population, there is a clear misunderstanding of what the Aboriginals are trying to attain. A recent poll from Ipsos Reid found that about two-thirds of Canadians believe Canada's Aboriginal peoples received too much support from federal taxpayers; they believe that Aboriginal peoples are treated well by the government and most of the problems Native people face are brought on by themselves. On the other hand the poll also found that two-thirds of Canadians believe the federal government must act now to improve life of Canada's Aboriginal peoples (Akin, 2013). This poll shows the ignorance on the part of most Canadians and adds to the discrimination that exists.

[6] Discrimination is an ugly aspect of any society, but it is even more disturbing when it is perpetuated by world leaders and the media. Aboriginal people in Canada have suffered through discrimination for far too long, and they have had far too many rights taken away. The Idle No More protest was their way of standing up and fighting back against the "others" in society who believe that they know better than the troublemakers in society. In order to stop this problem in society, people need to stop listening to those in authority and start studying the issues on their own.

References

Akin, D. (2013, January 15). Idle No More: Canadian public opinion set against First Nations protesters. Retrieved from *Toronto Sun*: http://www.torontosun

.com/2013/01/15/idle-no-more-canadian-public-opinion-set-against-first-nations-protesters

CBC News. (2013, January 5). 9 questions about Idle No More. Retrieved from CBC News Canada: http://www.cbc.ca/news/canada/story/2013/01/04/f-idlenomore-faq.html

Fotheringham, N. (2013, January 5). Canada's Bill C-45 reduces protected waterways from 2.5 million to 62 rivers and 97 lakes. Retrieved from GreenMoxie: http://www.greenmoxie.com/canadas-bill-c-45-reduces-protected-waterways-from-2-5-million-to-62-rivers-and-97-lakes/

Kunz, F. A. (2013). Newscasting: "Problematizing" minorities. In U. o. Waterloo, Centre For Extended Learning SOCWK 301 R (p. 38). Waterloo: The University of Waterloo Book Store and Media.doc.

Post-Reading Questions

1. How does the author of this piece establish her credibility?
2. What, if any, fallacies does this essay contain?
3. How does the author gain your attention in this essay?
4. Does the author argue a value claim or a policy claim in this essay? Give evidence to support your answer.
5. Which type of order does the author use for organizing this essay?

 # Oral Presentations

An oral presentation is often based on argument—you are trying to convince your audience that your point of view is a valid one. Therefore, you will use the organizational patterns of the argumentative essay. As with an essay, you must clearly state your thesis or main idea, your most convincing supportive points, and your findings. Visuals such as pie charts and graphs can make your evidence stand out and be easily understood by the audience.

Oral presentations are often used in the workplace, where proposals or reports are often delivered to a large audience face to face. For example, you may be asked to present a group of directors with a proposal to study a new method for increasing productivity. In this case, you would include your rationale, proposed timeline, and hypothesis. Usually, this information is accompanied by visuals, such as a PowerPoint presentation. Once you have finished your research, you may be asked to present your findings to the group.

> Oral presentations are often used in the workplace to present new ideas to a large audience.

Creating a Presentation

The most important consideration for any oral presentation is the time limit. You will often have a specific amount of time, such as 10 or 30 minutes. Make sure you use this time wisely. If your presentation is too short, your audience will wonder what you have left out or how much you really know about the topic. If the presentation is too long, you risk your audience becoming bored and tuning out before you make all your key points. You may need to allow time at the end for questions, so plan accordingly.

Oral presentations are unlike written documents. Listeners do not have the readers' luxury of going back over a point that they may have misread or misinterpreted. Therefore, make sure that your points are clear, precise, and logical. To help your audience understand your presentation, be sure to include transitions or markers to draw their attention to a point. When using an illustration, use a marker such as *for example*. When moving to new points, use words such as *additionally* or *on the other hand*. For the most important point, make sure you clearly indicate this to the audience with a marker such as *the most important aspect*. Successful use of these transitions or markers will help the audience clearly understand your movement from point to point.

When making a research-based oral presentation, less is more. Present only your most important information, with illustrations. If you are presenting a report on the rise of multi-tasking, explain the background (i.e., how the concept has evolved since the 1980s and the advent of the personal computer) but do not delve into details, such as listing all the articles you reviewed. Move on to discussing (again, without detail) some of your methods, such as how you chose a specific group to study. If you are studying students' ability to multi-task, you would give your basic criteria for choosing students—age, years of study, and perhaps their majors—but leave out other criteria such as cultural background or hobbies.

Focus most of your time on the findings of your study. Visuals are extremely helpful with this part. You can use charts and graphs to make your findings stand out. For example, you may want to include a pie chart showing the success rates of those who do and do not multi-task. Leave some time at the end to discuss possible ramifications of this study and where research can build on your findings. This is much like including a clincher in your conclusion.

If you base an oral presentation on an essay, help the audience orient to the topic by beginning with your thesis. Do not spend time leading up to your thesis, as the audience may not realize when you actually reach it. Next, present the main points from your essay with brief illustrations. If you have a relevant quotation, put it on a separate slide and pause briefly to give people time to read and absorb it. They are probably seeing it for the first time and will need to reflect on it to understand its importance. End your presentation by stating your conclusion clearly. Unlike essays, presentations can include such markers

Good presenters are well organized, and they make sure the audience can clearly follow their ideas.

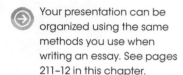 Your presentation can be organized using the same methods you use when writing an essay. See pages 211–12 in this chapter.

When presenting research, discuss only the most relevant parts.

Chapter 7 discusses conclusions and clinchers.

as *in conclusion*. This helps your audience understand that you are wrapping up. If you don't use a marker, people may not realize the importance of your closing remarks.

Visuals can add a great deal of impact but only if they are appropriate and not overwhelming. You want the audience to remember your information, so use graphics for only your most important points and keep the number to a minimum. As a general guideline, do not use more than one visual per minute, as the audience needs time to understand it and what you are saying. Don't overload your audience or cause "death by PowerPoint." In addition, do not use your visuals for your speaking prompts or read from them.

Keep your visuals simple. Each slide or screen shot should contain a minimal amount of information. For example, you can use the "five by five" rule: no more than five lines of text on each slide and no more than five words on each line. If you use graphs or pie charts, include only the most relevant data. Do not create a pie chart that has more than five segments, as the audience will not be able to differentiate the segments (see Figure 9.1 for a sample). Put only one chart or graph on each slide (with relevant documentation if the data are not from your own research).

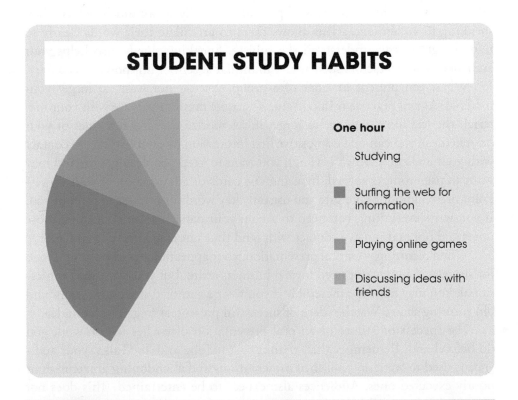

STUDENT STUDY HABITS

One hour

Studying

Surfing the web for information

Playing online games

Discussing ideas with friends

FIGURE 9.1   **Sample slide of a pie chart**
Sample source

When creating visuals, less is better.

Make sure you use colours that will be easy for the audience to read the slides. Light blue on a white background can be hard to see, as will light letters on a dark background. If you are using a PowerPoint template, use a simple one and avoid using unnecessary animations, such as text using Flyins or Blinds. Having points show one at a time is often effective if you want your audience to focus on each separately, but do not using rolling letters or other distracting animations. Using animations is wonderful for attracting attention, but many available on PowerPoint are not professional enough for the workplace or the classroom.

Delivering a Presentation

Many studies have shown that the people who communicate effectively in business are the ones who receive promotions. Use oral presentations as a stage for your abilities.

It is important to practise before making your presentation. When you practise, you are probably more relaxed than when standing in front of an audience. Therefore, you probably speak more slowly. Many a student has timed a presentation at home only to find it is much shorter when presented to the class. If you find you are speaking too quickly while presenting, pause, take a deep breath, and slow down. Successful presenters usually speak much slower when speaking to an audience. This allows them to articulate their words clearly so that the group can understand the subject. Speaking slowly also helps your audience adjust to factors such as an unfamiliar accent or unknown vocabulary.

When you present in front of a group, you do not want to forget your material. Again, practice is important. The more familiar you are with your material, the less likely you are to forget it. Memorize the first few lines of your presentation; you can make a positive first impression by establishing eye contact with your audience, which is vital if you want to keep people engaged. You may want to use prompts as well, by using cue cards or a hard copy of your PowerPoint presentation. Make sure you use only key words or phrases to prompt you. If you write everything you need to say on your papers, you risk reading those notes and not making eye contact with (and thus not engaging) the audience.

When planning your oral presentation, your appearance is important. Dress for success. You may not need formal business attire, but you must look professional. You may not appear credible if you wear a rumpled shirt, torn jeans, and old running shoes. Watch videos of successful presenters to give you an idea.

Knowing your material and being able to engage the audience are essential for success.

The success or failure of an oral presentation often lies in the work you do beforehand. Remember that, thanks to YouTube and TedTalks, your audience is used to watching polished presentations and abandoning amateurish or poorly executed ones. Audiences also expect to be entertained. This does not mean you have to tell jokes, but you need to present your material in a relevant, meaningful way. If you do so, and practise beforehand, you are well on your way to creating a presentation that will interest your audience.

Important Points to Consider When Making an Oral Presentation

Use the following list to help you prepare and deliver a successful oral presentation.

Preparation

- Know your material and practise a lot beforehand.
- Make notes to help you remember the key points and organizational structure of your topic.
- Create clear, easy-to-see visuals with necessary citations.
- Check your visuals for errors.
- Practise your presentation aloud and time it.
- Decide when you will address any questions. Will you encourage the audience to ask questions as they think of them or would you prefer them to ask at the end?
- Choose clothes that are appropriate for your audience.

Delivery

- Speak slowly and clearly. Make sure you are loud enough for everyone in the room to hear you.
- Let the audience know when you will address questions.
- Allow your audience time to read your visuals but do not read them.
- Discuss only relevant details.
- Watch your audience for signs of engagement and adjust to them. For example, if they did not seem to understand a point, expand on it. If they look bored, move on to a new point.
- Address all questions from the audience.
- Thank your audience for their time.
- Keep within your time limit.

Chapter Review Questions

1. Why is it important to understand your audience for an argumentative essay?
2. Why do you need to avoid fallacies when arguing?
3. What are the characteristics of an effective topic for an argumentative essay?
4. How do essays and oral presentations differ?
5. Why are good communication skills important?

PART THREE

Research

10 Conducting Research

In this chapter, you will learn

- how to conduct research for your essay topic;
- how to determine whether your sources are reliable;
- how to use the Internet for research; and
- what other types of resources are available.

At college and university, each essay you write needs a strong thesis that is supported by research. By adding relevant, reliable outside information, you demonstrate that you are familiar with the topic; if you research well, you show that you are becoming an expert in that field. This chapter is designed to help you develop your research skills so that you can defend your thesis using what experts, such as scientists and other theorists, have discovered about your topic. We will discuss how to explore what you know about a topic and address how to conduct research and where to find reliable sources. Much of this chapter focuses on expository essay writing, but the content can be applied to argumentative essays as well.

Developing Research Skills

It is often said that great thinkers stand on the shoulders of giants, meaning that they build on the knowledge of earlier researchers and thinkers. The Wright brothers did not just suddenly know how to build an airplane. They studied previous designs and ideas, such as Samuel Langley's aerodrome. Langley had no doubt studied gliders and other designs for flying machines. This is an example of progress in the sciences, the social sciences, and the humanities. The most knowledgeable experts depend on others' findings to help their own explorations; their research adds to the store of knowledge, enabling them to contribute to their chosen field.

Research is an important part of most expository and some argumentative essays. To use research effectively, you need to explore, check, and recheck what others have written. Once you have all the evidence you need from **primary sources** (literary texts, historical documents, surveys, questionnaires, and interviews) and **secondary sources** (authoritative books and journal articles, oral presentations, and conference papers), you **synthesize** it (i.e., put it together) to create your essay.

While a successful argumentative essay relies on the effectiveness of your argument, a successful expository essay relies on the presentation of your information. For example, you should find ways to make the essay interesting and appealing to the reader. Don't just assemble the facts and add transitions between ideas. Find out what someone else has discovered or thinks about the topic and then rewrite his or her points in your own words. Because an expository research essay generally uses claims of fact, you need to find reliable information, analyze what various researchers have discovered about the topic and, on the basis of their conclusions, come to a reasoned conclusion of your own. Put another way, exposition usually involves research.

Writing a research essay involves drafting an outline, adding and checking citations, and assembling and presenting the information you have found in the most effective way. When you draft your essay, you may begin with an outline,

Researching a topic involves finding out what others, especially experts, have written or said about it. **Primary sources** are original sources; **secondary sources** comment on primary ones. **Synthesis** is putting together ideas from different sources.

 Chapter 11 discusses the differences between quoting, paraphrasing, and summarizing. See Chapter 8 for more discussion of claims of fact.

When you write an essay for college or university, your instructor judges it not only on grammar and mechanics but also on your critical thinking. Therefore, your essay is not just a rewrite of what others have said but a combination of your thoughts and theirs.

While exposition implies research, research implies synthesis.

In-text citation requires acknowledging the source of your quotation, paraphrase, or summary.

but you will probably go back and add research and check citations. You will also need to ensure that you have accurately represented your research and focused on the most relevant and important aspects. The following section will help you proceed with greater confidence.

Research: Finding and Exploring

A research **proposal** announces the essay's topic, purpose, and research sources.

After choosing your topic (or being assigned one), your next step in writing a research paper involves finding possible sources. At this early stage, it is helpful to write a summary of your purpose as well as a tentative list of source material. Your instructor may even ask for a brief **proposal**, a document that tells him or her about the topic you want to study. You write the proposal after you have done sufficient background research to ensure there is enough information for you to proceed. You may be asked to provide relevant citations, to show that you have done the required preparation.

In the proposal, explain what the focus of your paper will be and perhaps include a working thesis. It may change as you begin to write, but it shows that you have a specific direction in mind. Providing the reason for writing about your topic is important. If the topic is not assigned, make sure to include why it is relevant to you. If the topic is assigned, do not simply state this as the reason but explain why your particular focus is of interest to you. Your proposal should be a few paragraphs in length so that you are able to expand on your topic fully.

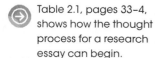 Table 2.1, pages 33–4, shows how the thought process for a research essay can begin.

The following proposal was created for the student essay "Computer Ergonomics" in Chapter 11.

By asking yourself key questions about the topic, you will discover what you already know and what you need to find out.

[1] When choosing a topic, one of immediate relevance was ergonomics, as the work force is getting older, and this is a relevant topic for both students and workers.

[2] Interest in ergonomics is personal, due to my own age, but also seeing a number of students in the hallways who use wheelchairs of various design, and also those who have been provided with special chairs due to various workplace injuries. Also, more desks at the school are being provided that are adjustable.

[3] Curiosity about the changes in ergonomics was a driving force for this essay, and also how people can protect themselves from injuries.

[4] Being a well-informed worker is important, so this essay will explore various aspects of the ergonomics issue, including prevention of injuries. The essay will be analytical and will include recommendations.

Such proposals help you in the "finding and exploring" stage of essay writing. Even if you are not asked to submit a proposal, you will have to think about the topic and use the pre-writing strategies you find the most effective. Some key questions can help you get started:

- What am I interested in?
- Do I know enough to explore a topic thoroughly?
- If I don't know very much, how can I obtain background information?
- What am I hoping to contribute to this subject area?
- Who is my audience?
- What kind of sources would be appropriate given my topic and my audience?
- Where will I find my source material?
- Do I know of the major authors in the field, or how can I find them?
- Have I given myself sufficient time to research, synthesize, organize, compose, document, and revise?

Synthesis I: Integrating

After you have found your sources, you begin to assimilate the information. By taking notes and summarizing where appropriate, you show that you can accurately represent another person's ideas and integrate them with your own. When you have finished taking notes and understand the information, you are ready to begin organizing your essay.

 Chapters 11 and 12 also discuss the integration stage.

Again, asking specific questions can help:

To assimilate means to take other people's ideas and incorporate them into your essay.

- Is my research geared toward supporting my points?
- Have I understood the results of the studies I've looked at and the positions of the experts whose works I have read?
- Are all my sources credible? Are there many recent ones?
- Have I summarized or quoted all sources adequately and accurately?
- Which sources are the most important?
- How do the different experts' views or conclusions fit together?
- Are there opposing positions? For example, do some findings challenge others?
- How does my research help me explore the topic?
- Has my research changed my view of my topic? If so, how? Do I need to change my thesis?

Organization: Arranging

Every essay needs a structure, which usually takes the form of an outline or template. Ask yourself these questions when you are ready to organize your essay:

Successful writers create outlines early in the writing process to help them organize their thoughts.

- Do I have enough support to begin an outline? If so, what kind of template should I use?
- Is there an organizational method I should use?
- Do my points thoroughly explore the topic?
- Are some points inadequately developed to produce substantial paragraphs?
- Are all areas of my research relevant to the points I want to make?
- What points are most essential and what sources are most relevant?
- Am I off-topic anywhere?
- Does the structure I chose reflect my purpose? Does it reflect my audience? Is it logical?

Chapters 7 and 9 discuss outlines for expository and argumentative essays, respectively; Chapter 11 includes an example of a student outline.

Synthesis II: Composing

During the first-draft stage, you integrate your sources into your essay. Here, synthesis takes place at the level of language. Thus, how you use summary and paraphrase and direct quotations will be important.

Questions to ask include

Chapter 9 examines summarizing; Chapter 11 discusses paraphrasing and using direct quotations.

- Am I over- or underusing my sources?
- Which sources should be summarized, which paraphrased, and which quoted directly? (Your answers will depend on various factors, including length, importance, and phrasing of the source.)
- Am I using my sources effectively? Have I used the best information from them? Have I represented this information correctly?
- Can I use ellipses to omit less important parts of the source?
- Am I providing smooth transitions between my sources and my own writing?
- Is the language level roughly the same throughout? Is it appropriate for my audience?
- Are direct quotations grammatically integrated and easy to read?
- Have I double-checked quotations for accuracy?
- Is my own writing clear, grammatical, and effective?

See Chapter 11 for instructions on using ellipses and Chapters 13–15 for help on grammar.

Whether you use MLA or APA, include a source only if you have used information from it in your essay.

In this stage of the research essay, you must document sources using an appropriate format, such as those of the Modern Language Association (MLA) or the American Psychological Association (APA). Manuals for both styles should be available in your college or university library or bookstore; information is also provided on each organization's website.

Use these questions when documenting your sources:

See Chapter 12 for instructions on using MLA and APA styles.

- What documentation style is expected for this essay?
- Where is information on documenting to be found?

- If I am using electronic sources, am I clear on acceptable methods for documenting them? (Has my instructor given me guidance or directed me to specific sites or sources?)
- Do I know what needs to be documented and what does not?
- Could the reader confuse my own ideas or observations with information taken from another source?
- Have I carefully documented other people's words and ideas without cluttering the essay with unnecessary citations?

Researching Your Topic

You have been conducting research informally for some time. For example, you probably didn't choose your school or program randomly. You might have read brochures or checked websites and talked to people (e.g., current students, graduates, or school counsellors). This information was no doubt helpful, but you likely also relied on factual evidence: programs, prerequisites, tuition fees, housing, and campus size. Perhaps you also consulted objective experts, such as people who have researched the different schools and ranked them according to various criteria.

This process of decision-making based on research is a life skill that includes the critical skills of analysis, judgment, and evaluation. College or university research assignments require similar skills but involve formal research, which entails analyzing, comparing, assessing, and/or synthesizing the work of experts in your subject area, generally by discussing multiple approaches to a problem. Simply rephrasing these sources or summarizing your own opinions or experiences is not necessarily research.

As discussed in previous chapters, one common approach to organizing a research paper is to compare and contrast the similarities and differences between two or more ideas. Another method is to evaluate the strengths and/or weaknesses of a point of view based on criteria that you create or borrow from experts. The following example involves both types.

> Formal research requires you to analyze, compare, assess, and/or synthesize the work of experts in your subject area, generally by discussing multiple approaches to a problem.

1. Identifying a problem:
   Many people use e-devices to read. Researchers claim that students do not understand material as well when using these devices.

2. Stating a claim or the thesis about this problem (what the writer will explore or prove):
   E-readers affect the way students understand material.

3. Describing the points made by one or more experts concerning the claim:

Researcher A claims that his study demonstrates that students do not understand material read with an e-device. He presents information gathered from a study comparing the reading comprehension levels between students who used an e-device and students who used paper.

Researcher B asserts that students comprehend material well regardless of whether they use e-devices or paper. She presents her study showing no significant difference in the reading comprehension levels between students who used e-devices and those who used paper. She goes on to claim that those using e-devices actually gained more knowledge through the use of hyperlinks embedded in the text and the ability to access online dictionaries.

4. Reaching a decision on the merits of these experts' approaches to the thesis:

Researcher B's arguments are more convincing than those of Researcher A. Researcher B is able to show that students gained a better understanding of the topic because of the additional features available when using e-devices.

5. Concluding with your judgment on the thesis, either by rating the experts' approaches or by suggesting a new way of thinking about the problem:

Researcher B has provided a strong argument that the use of e-devices for reading actually benefits students. While this is a relatively new field, this researcher created an additional parameter to study, which sheds light on how students use e-devices, rather than just testing reading comprehension, as Researcher A did.

Who Are These Experts—and Where Can You Find Them?

Experts are people who are experienced or well educated and have published or produced significant work about a subject.

Experts are experienced or well-educated people who have published or produced significant work about a subject. A documentary filmmaker may be an expert; his or her film may provide information for your essay. A journalist may also be an expert on a particular topic, and a person interviewed on radio or television could be very familiar with a topic through his or her research, knowledge, or personal experience. Library shelves are filled with the publications of experts, and the Internet may be another source of expertise. Since the number of experts on a topic can be enormous, you need standards for screening the quality of their information. In the case of the filmmaker, for example, you could consider the following criteria:

- An important part of research is to select sources whose work has been analyzed by others in the field. Is the film reviewed in any journals or other commentaries? These can show you what other filmmakers think about it.
- Is the film part of your institution's collection or available through a reputable organization such as the National Film Board?
- Since you are writing a research paper in an educational context, you may wish to consider the filmmaker's academic credentials.

Another criterion that measures the usefulness of research material is publication date. Since attitudes and analyses change over time, more recent information gives you the latest developments in your field. A further advantage to beginning with recent material is that the source often will refer to previous studies that might be useful. Sometimes just scanning the works cited or reference section at the end of a recent work will suggest other potential sources.

> When conducting research, ask your instructor about publication dates. Is there a limit to how far you can go back? Does an article have to be published after a certain year? Depending on the field, research conducted 10 years ago might be extremely dated or relatively new.

Exploring Your Topic

The first stage in research is to determine the major authors in your subject area and what they say about your topic. You also need to know where they provide this information so that you can quote or paraphrase and document them in your essay.

Finding important authors and works in your area may be easier if your instructor can recommend them. However, you will probably begin and narrow the search yourself, especially if you are free to choose your own topic. Looking for a general work, such as a textbook, in your subject area is a useful first step. As with recent publications, these works frequently include extensive bibliographies (alphabetical listings of works used or consulted), which you can scan for relevant titles and authors. Consult works in the library's reference section, such as indexes, encyclopedias, dictionaries, and comprehensive guides in your area. Most reference books can't be taken out of the library, but they can direct you to more specific sources that can be borrowed. Some may be available electronically, so check with the librarians.

> A useful first step when conducting research is to use a general work, such as a textbook.

Internet search engines and subject directories can also provide excellent starting points, providing you with general topics that you can narrow down. If you are having trouble finding information about your topic, use the glossary section of your textbook, which contains words relevant to your chosen topic.

When you find potentially useful sources, add them to your **working bibliography**, a list of books and articles you plan to look at. When you find a book on the list, scan the index and the table of contents to determine how helpful it will

> A **working bibliography** helps you keep track of the sources you have already looked at.

An **abstract** is a short summary that precedes most academic journal articles.

The term *bibliography* is not used in either APA or MLA, so change the title to References or Works Cited when writing your essay.

 Chapter 1 discusses reading strategies, such as scanning, that you can use when conducting research. Chapter 5 examines abstracts.

A **uniform resource locator (URL)** is the address of specific Internet content. A **digital object identifier (DOI)** is a number–letter sequence that begins with the number 10 and is often found on documents obtained electronically through databases. One or the other is used as the last element in a citation for articles found online.

be. If it looks promising, read the introduction, preface, or foreword. The author often summarizes his or her approach and sometimes provides chapter-by-chapter summaries in the introductory section. With articles, read the **abstract**.

Your working bibliography may not look much like the final list of works you actually use, but it often leads you to the most relevant sources. Remember to note the date of the work's publication (in books, found on the copyright page—the other side of the title page).

Note-Taking

Keeping clear records when conducting research allows you to read material efficiently as well as save time (and your sanity) when you write your paper. Make notes as you research your sources, ensuring that you record the following information:

1. A direct quotation, summary, or paraphrase of the writer's idea; if it is a direct quotation, make sure you put quotation marks around it.
2. The complete name(s) of the author(s).
3. The name(s) of editor(s) or translator(s), if applicable.
4. The title of the book, journal, magazine, newspaper, or website affiliation or sponsor.
5. The title of the specific article, chapter, section, or website.
6. Full publication details, including date, edition, or translation; for a journal article, these could be the volume and issue number; for Internet sites, the date the site was started or updated.
7. The name and location of the publisher (including province, state, or country) for books.
8. For Internet sites, the day you viewed the page and either the **uniform resource locator (URL)** or the **digital object identifier (DOI)**.
9. The call number of a library book or bound journal for later reference, if needed.
10. The page numbers you consulted, both those where you found specific ideas and the full page range you read (or some other marker for unnumbered online documents, such as paragraph numbers or section headings).

When making notes, don't forget to record your observations, comments, and queries. You need bibliographic details, of course, but you also need to synthesize the source's ideas with your own as your essay develops. In other words, you must relate the information to other sources and to your thesis statement. It's important, however, to keep source material separate from your own comments. Write your responses on another piece of paper or in a different colour. Always give yourself clear directions when you take notes and make comments.

Organizing Research Notes

Organizing your notes is an extremely important aspect of research. Being unable to find a key piece of information while working on a research paper is very frustrating. There are many organization methods: write your notes on index cards (remember to number them); record notes in a journal and use tabs to divide them into particular headings; or create a computerized record-keeping system, either by using a database program such as MS Access or by simply creating multiple document files in a folder.

> A **database** is a collection of related data organized for quick access.

A number of software programs can assist you in organizing your research. Programs such as Scribe (www.scribe.com) imitate the card file system, while others such as EndNote (www.endnote.com) and Nota Bene (www.notabene.com) are databases. RefWorks (www.refworks.com) creates a references or works cited page based on the information you enter into the system and the documentation style you specify. This document can help you retrieve information if you misplace your notes. However you keep track of your sources, review your final essay to ensure you have eliminated any you decided not to use.

Learning programs such as these take time, but they generally offer helpful extra features, such as automatic formatting of citations and references or bibliographies. Remember, though, that the program you use may not contain all the information you need when citing sources and there may be formatting errors. Make sure your in-text citations and references or bibliography sections are complete. If you choose to record your notes electronically, back up your work regularly in case of technical failure.

Cross-Referencing

> It is important to keep your research notes organized so that you can retrieve information quickly without having to reread material.

Cross-referencing your notes can make it easier to retrieve your information when you are writing your essay. You can create a list of central words, names, or themes and record where each occurs in your notes. You can cross-reference by writing notes in a margin or by using index cards or computer files. Some students draw a visual aid such as a mind map (graphic organizer) on a large sheet of paper to connect their main words or points. Some word-processing programs include a cross-referencing feature for single documents (e.g., in Word 2010, this is found under **Insert**). A few of the computer programs we mentioned have keyword-based cross-referencing systems.

Some Useful Research Strategies

Assimilating

- Begin the research by gathering definitions of the important words in your thesis statement.

- Read or view everything with the thesis statement in mind. Resist reading unconnected material, however interesting it might seem.
- Judge whether a book will be worth your time by checking your cross-referencing words in its index. Read the abstracts of journal articles to determine their usefulness.
- Consider how you can connect the information from different sources by using transitional words and phrases such as *because, as a result of, on the other hand*, or *in contrast*. This will help you select points that flow logically.
- Try to find an example to support every major statement you wish to make. An example can be a quotation, paraphrase, or larger concept that comments on or proposes a solution to your thesis statement.

Arranging

- When you finish your first round of research, write an outline with primary and secondary headings corresponding to the major elements of your thesis statement. Under the headings, list the lines of reasoning that support these points and the examples that support each of them.
- Decide how many pages to allot for each section of the paper, taking your instructor's requirements for paper length into serious account.
- Look over your outline. Do you have sufficient examples to support all your major statements? Do you have enough material to meet the required page or word count? If you have neither, perhaps you need to do more research. On the other hand, if you have too many key points and several examples for each, choose only the strongest ones in order to meet length requirements.
- Consider arranging your paper in a word-processing program according to the required length. If you use the manual "Page Break" option (under "Insert" in most programs) to create document sections that follow your outline, you'll easily be able to judge whether you're writing too much or too little for any portion of the paper.
- Design a timeline for each step in your paper if you haven't done so in a research proposal. This will help ensure that you don't spend too much time on any particular segment.

> Table 7.1, page 171, provides a template for arranging the information from research sources. You can either use this one or create your own electronically. Having a few copies on hand will make it easier if you rearrange material. Record changes on a clean copy, rather than erasing or crossing out information, to ensure nothing gets left out by mistake.

Using Contradictory Evidence

In the initial research stage, you need to find sources relevant to your topic; however, not all studies on a given topic reach the same conclusion. If your primary purpose is to explain or investigate a problem, assess the findings and try to discover why they are different, perhaps by analyzing their respective strengths and weaknesses. This process is a critical thinking skill and a fundamental part of the research process.

In the humanities, your thesis is often based on your interpretation of the findings—you must carefully show how other academics' interpretations differ from your own. An excellent strategy when discussing conflicting results is to acknowledge another interpretation and use it as a springboard into yours. Contradictory interpretations should not simply be dismissed without explanation; it is better to acknowledge and qualify them, possibly by briefly discussing their limitations. If you do not address contradictory studies, the reader may assume that you do not know enough about the topic, thus reducing your credibility. For example, many recent studies attempt to show the health benefits of vitamins. If you are investigating the benefits of vitamin E in preventing heart disease and find that credible evidence exists, you still need to acknowledge contradictory studies and explain how these findings fit into your claim.

> To write a well-researched paper, you must acknowledge findings that contradict your thesis, if any exist. If you ignore them, your instructor may tell you that you didn't research the topic adequately.

Researching a topic can be a challenging process—possibly a trial run for the kind of work you will do in your academic or professional career. If you experience doubts or uncertainties at any stage of the process, talk to your instructor as soon as possible. Don't wait until the day before your paper is due!

Sources of Research Material

Many different kinds of source materials exist. This section discusses most of the important ones.

Primary and Secondary Sources

The distinction between primary and secondary sources is crucial, as essay assignments frequently require that both be identified and referenced. To recap, primary sources are the original compositions of authors; personal documents, such as letters and diaries; and initial scientific articles reporting on a work. A secondary source is another writer's analysis of and commentary on a primary source. An article that cites someone else's research, a textbook that explains others' theories, and encyclopedia entries are examples of secondary sources.

> Check with your instructor before using online material as a primary source. Multiple translations/editions of a work are often available, and the online version may not be the most accurate or accepted one.

Start with Secondary Sources

An efficient way to construct a general framework of research from your thesis statement is to access reference sources such as indexes, almanacs, encyclopedias, dictionaries, and yearbooks. These can provide you with concise summaries of statistics, definitions, and biographies and a reading list of the principal primary and secondary sources. As mentioned, these books cannot be removed from the library; however, this type of information is widely available on the Internet. For instance, an online search of *black hole* and *encyclopedia* returns entries from the *Encyclopaedia Britannica*, *The Canadian Encyclopedia*, and numerous library-based sites offering further links to information on the subject. The *Britannica* entry includes a listing of relevant books, articles, websites, magazine articles, and videos on black holes. Remember that, at the college and university level, citing encyclopedias is not appropriate for research essays. They are a good place to start, but expand your sources.

Books

Continue your research by locating books that are mentioned in your preliminary search of reference materials and are relevant to your thesis statement. A book can cover a single topic; compile articles, essays, or chapters by a number of authors around a topic; or collect an author's individually pre-published pieces. Books can be located by searching a library's catalogue, the Internet, or a database. For instance, Project Gutenberg (http:// gutenberg.org) has digitally republished more than 30,000 e-books, ranging from the contemporary *Human Genome Project, Y Chromosome*, by the Human Genome Project, to the nineteenth-century novel *The Hunchback of Notre Dame*, by Victor Hugo.

Periodicals

Periodicals are published regularly—for instance, monthly, yearly, or daily. Examples include newspapers, magazines, journals, and yearbooks. Unless you are writing about an extremely current cultural aspect, you will probably concentrate on **journals**, which publish articles written by academics, scientists, and researchers. The most-respected journals are **peer reviewed** (other experts in that field have assessed the work prior to its being published).

Researchers publish their findings in scholarly journals in order to share their ideas—and advance their careers. Thousands of scholarly journals publish a wealth of research on just about any topic you can imagine. However, finding these articles online can be a challenge because the journals are generally distributed through expensive subscriptions only. College and university libraries subscribe to those that they consider most valuable and give access to students, faculty, and staff.

To find a journal article in your library's catalogue, you need a **citation**. Here is an example:

Zigler, E. F., & Gilman, E. (1993). Day care in America: What is needed? *Pediatrics*, *91*(1), 175–178.

As you can see, the citation includes the authors' names, publication date, article title, journal title, volume and issue numbers, and page numbers. You might not need the issue number, but record it just in case.

Periodicals are newspapers, magazines, journals, and yearbooks; a yearbook is a book of facts or statistics published every year.

A **journal** is a periodical that publishes the results of experts' research. Articles in **peer-reviewed** journals are assessed by other experts before publication.

A **citation** is needed after a quotation, paraphrase, or summary so that the reader knows the information is from another source. A citation includes the author name, publication date, title, publisher, location, and (in some cases) page numbers.

Most library catalogues allow you to search for journals only and then for the journal title (as opposed to the article title or author name). You will be given a call number that will direct you to the journal's location, where you can select the volume and issue and then use the page numbers to find the article. If you need help, ask the librarians or library technicians, who are trained and experienced in finding sources and can show you how to search quickly and efficiently.

Internet Searches

College and university libraries subscribe to databases and indexes that collect many journals and contain the full texts of their articles, which you can save directly onto your computer's hard drive. Databases may also house a blend of scholarly and non-scholarly information, including government-produced documents, popular magazines, newspapers, and non-peer-reviewed journals. In addition, databases supply links to the growing number of e-journals, which are available online only.

When you use journal articles, use only full-text articles; never cite from an abstract. If possible, indicate in your database searches that you want full-text articles, as searches can produce articles for which only the abstract is available. See Figure 10.1 for an example of a database search page.

Most databases let you search using **keywords** (including authors' names) and search options. **Boolean operators**, including the words AND, OR, and NOT, are used to customize your search. If you type AND between two or more search terms, your results will include both terms; if you type NOT between the terms, your results will omit what follows it. If you use OR as a search expander, each result will include at least one of the terms.

Let's say you are considering an essay on either caffeine or alcohol. An EBSCOhost search on "caffeine OR alcohol" turns up 27,388 entries. This is far too many to be useful, so you change it to "caffeine," which yields 1,658 entries. Thinking that you might want to compare caffeine and alcohol, you use the limiter AND, which produces 116 results. To exclude tobacco from your search, you add a second limiter, "NOT tobacco." Using the two limiters (caffeine AND alcohol NOT tobacco) produces 93 results—a more manageable start.

Some Popular Databases

This section lists several databases that can help you with your research. Some include various disciplines; others are more specific. Each academic discipline has specialized databases and indexes that concentrate on publications that

A **keyword** is a word identified by an author or a cataloguer as important in an article. **Boolean operators**, such as AND, OR, and NOT, customize your search.

Depending on your search engine, you can narrow or expand your search by using specific symbols. Putting words between quotation marks restricts the search to text that contains the words in the order you place them; for example, typing "fair trade coffee" with the quotation marks will return fewer results than if you don't use the marks because you will see only those articles that contain the exact phrase.

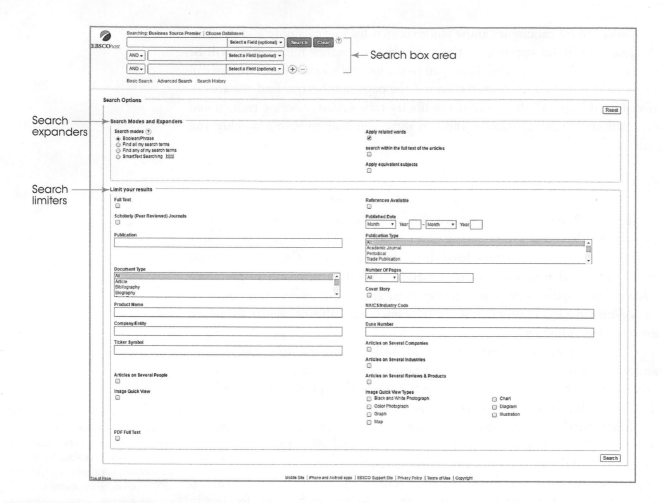

Search box area

Search expanders

Search limiters

Screenshot of EBSCOhost advanced search page

This screenshot shows how databases typically organize research information. By entering a word or phrase in one or more of the search boxes, you can retrieve any article that contains your keywords in the title or body of the thousands of periodicals available through EBSCOhost.

The list of article results can be enormous and overwhelming. For this reason, EBSCOhost allows you to limit your search to such factors as a specific date range or peer-reviewed journals only.

are particularly relevant to the field. You can ask your instructor to direct you to the most appropriate databases or search your library's website for discipline-related listings.

BioMed Central indexes hundreds of journals offering peer-reviewed research about biology and medicine. It is an open-access site that is free for everyone.

Business Source Elite is a database assembled for business schools and libraries; it incorporates scholarly journals and business periodicals relating to marketing, economics, and accounting.

Canadian Socioeconomic Information Management (CANSIM), a comprehensive database from Statistics Canada, contains nearly 18 million government documents.

EBSCOhost is a database service for more than 9,500 journals on a vast range of discipline areas that allows Internet-style (Boolean logic) searching. Widely available through college or university library sites, EBSCOhost is the academic database you should start with, and it might be the only one you need.

Education Resources Information Center (ERIC) is a large database that pertains to education and is best known for its expert summaries on educational topics (ERIC Digest Records). The ERIC Social Sciences Citation Index lists more than 1,725 social and behavioural sciences journals published after 1995.

Health Source: Nursing/Academic Edition offers full-text articles from more than 500 health and medical journals and indexes the abstracts of more than 850 publications.

IEEE/IEE Electronic Library contains full-text technical journals, conference proceedings, and active standards in engineering, physics, computer science, and materials sciences. Over 3 million full-text documents are available.

InfoTrac provides indexing and abstracts for 1,550 academic journals as well as news and general interest publications, along with full-text articles from more than 500 social sciences, technology, and humanities journals.

Ingenta Connect is an excellent source for journals in the humanities, sciences, social sciences, and education. It features full-text articles from almost 12,000 publications.

Lexis-Nexis Academic Universe contains full-text articles from nearly 2,000 sources, such as company reports, newspapers, transcripts of broadcasts, wire services, newsletters, journals, case law, government documents, and some valuable reference texts.

Newspaper Source allows access to a range of full-text articles from 40 international newspapers, including *The Christian Science Monitor*, transcripts from many news broadcasters, and 330 regional American newspapers.

Project MUSE offers full-text articles from more than 100 scholarly journals in the humanities, the social sciences, and mathematics. It also contains e-books. Articles are available from 1995.

ProQuest provides access to thousands of current periodicals and newspapers that are updated daily; it contains full-text articles from as early as 1986.

PsycINFO, operated by the APA, offers citations (not full-text articles) for reports, articles, dissertations, and book chapters relating to psychology in fields such as education, business, medicine/nursing, and sociology.

WorldCat, operated by a consortium of more than 9,000 universities, libraries, and colleges, allows users to view or borrow audiovisual materials, books, films, government documents, computer files, and research reports in 400 languages. This "database of databases" has thousands of full-text articles and an interlibrary loan service for non-digitized items.

Notes about the Internet

> Not all Internet sources are of equal value. Make sure you use credible online sources.

When assessing the credibility of a secondary source, especially an Internet source, consider the following line from George Orwell's *Animal Farm* (1945): "Some animals are more equal than others." Anyone with basic computer skills can publish online, which creates both new opportunities and new challenges for researchers. For instance, if you search for essay writing blogs, you will get many results; however, are the authors experts? Are they credible?

Searching the Internet for android device prices and using it for academic research require different criteria; for research you need to find trustworthy authors. The Internet has countless sites created by individuals, companies, and institutions, with few controls to guarantee the accuracy or fairness of the information. To retrieve quality information, you must assess the reputation of a site's creator and check the information in other sources.

Many thoughtful and well-respected authors use the Internet to reach others who share their interests; however, it is important to judge a website author's motivation carefully. Some information simply promotes the author's unsupported point of view or contains inaccurate details. Therefore, its usefulness is limited. Ask yourself, "Is the author providing a reasoned argument or just an opinion?" Be aware that personal blogs and listservs are largely designed for conversation and opinion rather than the promotion of academic research.

Using college or university library websites is an excellent strategy for beginning researchers because they provide a wealth of accurate scholarly information and appropriate online material. The final part of a website's URL indicates these websites. The addresses of degree-granting American educational institutions end with the domain .edu. Canadian schools' websites generally contain a shortened version of their name, followed by .ca.

Your instructor may require that all the sources in your essay must be peer reviewed. But if peer review is not a requirement, you may be able to use blogs, discussion boards, or even personal email correspondence. Credible blogs can provide you with interesting information. Many professionals publish regular blogs covering a variety of topics from vacation tips to psychological issues to "How to" guides. Use only those blogs that generally support what your other research has indicated, whether it supports your thesis or not. Avoid blogs that are inflammatory. For example, if you are writing about gaming, don't use a blog stating that gamers are introverts who are unable to function properly in social environments. This type of blog is designed to incite discussion based on the writer's opinion but is probably not focused on research.

Much like blogs, discussion boards can be a useful research source. Both professionals and laypeople can belong to any of these groups, and the opinions they post can help you understand what others consider important in the area you want to study. These sites can also guide you to relevant current research for your topic or introduce new areas that you hadn't considered. Again, be aware that anyone can post to discussion boards as long as he or she belongs to that particular group. Not all posts will be an appropriate research source.

> Blogs and discussion boards can be useful sources, as the authors can give you an idea about what is considered important in that particular field.

Personal email can also be used as a source for many essays. If you know of a person who is well respected in the field you are studying, you may decide to contact him or her about answering some questions. It is generally a good idea to do this only after you have thoroughly researched the topic. By doing the background work ahead of time, you can ask pointed questions that can be integrated into your essay (if the person agrees to participate). If you are writing about child development and are interested in Jean Piaget's theories, you can ask your source why he or she thinks these ideas have fallen out of favour. The answer can then be used as support for your argument.

> Personal email to a respected member of a particular field can also be used for research essays.

Do not leave contacting a source until the last minute, as it might take some time for your contact to respond and he or she may decline to answer your questions. You could provide a deadline for the response, but be reasonable, as your contact may be extremely busy.

Another very popular research source is Google Scholar. This site is geared more toward research than other, more commercially focused search engines, including Google and Yahoo. Some of the sources on Google Scholar are peer reviewed, which adds credibility. It allows you to search by keyword and to search related articles, giving you a broader view of your topic or providing a new direction for your research. Once again, remember that not all sources are equal. When you have done some research in the field, you will be able to discern which are acceptable and which are not.

One source to avoid citing is Wikipedia. This is a good source to start with if you are unsure about your topic and want some basic information. However, like all wikis, it is created by volunteers who add content. Most of the information is accurate, but not all of it is reliable. Sometimes Wikipedia provides links to scholarly papers that can be used in your research essay. However, make sure that the link leads to a credible source and not just further Wikipedia pages.

> While Wikipedia is a place to start, do not cite it in an essay.

Notes on Library Research

With the wealth of research information available electronically, it may seem unnecessary to go to a college or university library in person. In reality, libraries continue to be valuable resources for researchers at all levels of expertise, partly because they have books not available online. As well, they are staffed by professionals who understand how information is organized and interrelated. Most libraries have reference librarians who can save you time and direct you to sources you might never come across on your own. Reference librarians and library technicians have been specially trained and often know of different ways to retrieve information. The help desk staff will answer your questions and assist you with your searches.

> Reference librarians and library technicians have been specially trained and often know of different ways to retrieve information. The help desk staff will answer your questions and assist you in your searches.

Libraries often run courses to familiarize students with the specific systems the college or university uses; it is a good idea to sign up for a session or two. Participating in the same session more than once is often helpful, as the information can be overwhelming, and you can learn things you missed the first time.

Furthermore, libraries hold many important records, including the following:

- indexes for many periodicals, images, films, microfiche files, and videos
- theses and dissertations (book-length documents written by university students as part of their advanced degree requirements)
- historical documents, including maps and public records
- collections of textual and graphic material on special subjects, sometimes including original documents
- clipping files from newspapers and magazines
- bound volumes of journals
- collections of audio and film or video recordings

In addition, libraries store print information that has been gathered, sometimes over centuries, that is too expensive or fragile to digitize. A great deal of information created before 1985 is available in only paper form at a library. If your college or university library is small or if you are attending a newer school, ask about borrowing privileges at other schools close by. You may be able to access those libraries using only your student card, or you may be able to get special permission to use another school's library if they have information your own does not. Another option is the inter-library loan. If your college or university has this service, you can request that documents from another library be delivered to your school's library. However, you do need to plan ahead, as it can take several days or weeks to get the document.

> When searching for information, do not leave it to the last minute or you will be competing for help with other students who have the same deadline.

Using electronic sources to access journals that publish paper versions has another frustrating wrinkle: these publications often hold back their latest editions from databases in order to maintain their paid subscriptions. This means that it is still necessary to view the most current issues on paper. As we've stated earlier, accessing recent studies is vital, especially if your subject is a topical one.

Although the nature of research has changed dramatically with the increasing availability of online resources, it is best to think of the cyber–paper relationship as complementary. Relying on the Internet only is inadvisable, and some instructors may specify how much electronic research is allowed.

Alternative Sources

Although this section has emphasized written research information, many disciplines accept evidence from visual or audio media, such as television, film, video, works of art, performances, surveys or questionnaires, interviews, and observations. Using these alternative sources requires the same attention to detail in note-taking as when using traditional materials, and most citation styles provide instructions for citing and referencing non-textual research information. These approaches are more acceptable in some disciplines than in others—if your essay outline emphasizes alternative information sources, review it with your instructor early in the writing process.

Let's take a closer look at one alternative type of research: interviewing. If you have direct access to a noted authority in your field, interviewing can be effective. The main advantage of an interview, whether face to face, by telephone, or by email (as discussed earlier), is that you can ask questions specific to your research rather than searching many potential sources for this particular information. Interview subjects can be treated the same way as other experts; that is, their words can be summarized, paraphrased, or quoted directly. There are also specific methods for documenting interviewees. The college or university community—including, perhaps, one of your instructors—is an ideal place to look for experts.

Chapter Review Questions

1. What is the difference between primary and secondary sources?
2. Why is it important to know the experts in the field you are researching?
3. What is the difference between a database and the Internet?
4. What sources, other than books, can you find at a college or university library?
5. What is a Boolean operator?
6. What is the difference between a popular magazine and a journal?
7. What does it mean if an article is peer reviewed?

11

Using Your Research

Good writers use primary and/or secondary sources in their writing. But they do not mechanically insert the material: they integrate it seamlessly into their work, making the essay more readable. This chapter discusses several ways to incorporate sources. It also explains plagiarism, a serious academic offence, and outlines the steps for acknowledging others' work properly.

Outlines for Research Essays

> An outline for a research essay should include the sources you will use to support your main points.

 Chapter 10 examines methods for researching an essay topic.

An outline for a research paper should include the supporting material you intend to use in the essay. Your instructor may expect a specific or minimum number of sources. If not, you should probably have at least one source (direct quotation, paraphrase, or idea) to support each main point of your paragraph. Whereas an argumentative essay depends on effective reasoning and various kinds of evidence—including examples, illustrations, analogies, anecdotes, and perhaps the findings of secondary sources—an expository essay usually relies heavily on outside support. Including such sources in your outline will make it easier to write your first draft, when you will focus on integrating the sources with your own words. Moreover, researching your topic before proceeding to the outline can help you determine the topic's viability. Your research may even uncover interesting aspects of the topic you hadn't considered.

The following is student writer Sandy Crashley's outline for her essay on the cost of buying happiness (see pp. 254–8). This outline closely follows the template found in Chapter 4. (Following this template, which can also function as an essay outline, will help you produce a paper that is argued logically.) Although it is brief, the outline includes enough detail on both the main points and the relevant research for Crashley to elaborate on the former once she begins writing. When you read the essay, you'll see that she changed some of her sources as she wrote. Outlines do not have to be viewed as a complete reflection of the final product but can differ from the final essay.

Sample Student Essay: Research

Outline for "The Cost of Buying Happiness: Why Less is More"

Thesis and comment: Reducing the amount one consumes to be happier and healthier—the minimalist movement, the tiny house movement, and the locavore movement.

Topic sentence: Minimalist movement means fewer goods.

    A. Home less cluttered (Hancock)
    B. Less maintenance, more free time (Kondo)
    C. QUALITY VERSUS QUANTITY

Concluding sentence: Fewer goods of better quality will make one happier.

Topic sentence: Tiny houses mean fewer goods and also cost savings.

    A. Costs (The tiny life)
    B. Cost of house versus income (CMHC)
    C. Less cost, more money for other enjoyable activities (Mitchell)

Concluding sentence: Smaller space, fewer goods, more money.

Topic sentence: Locavore movement better for health and environment.

    A. Farmer's markets and local income
    B. Know where food comes from, so control pesticides and GMOs (Schindler)
    C. Savings overall

Concluding sentence: Locavore movement is better for you and cheaper in the long run.

Conclusion: Smaller means less debt and healthier, happier life.

Exercise **11.1**

In a small group, select a topic that you are all interested in. Go online or to the library and find some relevant sources. After skimming them, create an outline for a research essay.

 # Plagiarism

Much has been written recently about society's disregard for copyright laws. Millions of people download music or movies illegally. Studies have shown a rise in student cheating, and some say more than half of high school students have cheated on tests. File sharing is common, with sites such as YouTube making it possible to post videos directly from its site to your Facebook or Google+ account. The lines between what can be redistributed and what cannot are often unclear. However, this sort of "sharing" is not acceptable in academia. It is considered **plagiarism**, a serious academic crime that occurs when a writer

- fails to cite an idea, a paraphrase, or a summary;

Plagiarism is the intentional or unintentional use of someone else's work as if it were your own. All outside sources require parenthetical citations and an alphabetical listing in the paper's works cited or reference section. You must cite secondary sources—whether you quote from them directly, summarize them, paraphrase them, or just refer to them in passing—by using the appropriate style of your discipline.

- uses the exact language of the source without putting it in quotation marks; or
- uses the identical structure of the original.

Plagiarism can be intentional or unintentional, but both have equally serious consequences, from receiving a zero for that particular paper to failing the course to being expelled from the college or university. Intentional plagiarism includes using sections, sentences, or phrases from a website, book, newspaper article, magazine, etc., without acknowledgement. Buying an essay from the Internet or another person, submitting a friend's essay as your own, or reusing a paper you wrote for another class also falls under this crime. Unintentional or inadvertent plagiarism results from careless note-taking, improper documentation, or a lack of knowledge about plagiarism. Therefore, as we have stated throughout this book, it is important to take good notes and to cite all information taken from other sources, either primary or secondary.

An instructor can easily detect plagiarism from a shift in tone or word use. Many instructors do an Internet search for the questionable material to see if the exact wording appears in another publication. You may be required to provide an electronic copy to a service such as Turnitin before submitting your essay. Such sites compare your paper to thousands of documents and post any matching sources for you and your instructor to see.

The following examples demonstrate instances of plagiarism, as well as acceptable paraphrases.

Sample 1

Original:

Anybody who will look at the thing candidly will see that the evolutionary explanation of morals is meaningless, and presupposes the existence of the very thing it ought to prove. It starts from a misconception of the biological doctrine. Biology has nothing to say as to what ought to survive and what ought not to survive; it merely speaks of what does survive. —Stephen Leacock, "The Devil and the Deep Sea: A Discussion of Modern Morality"

Language of the source unchanged:

A person willing to see *the thing candidly* would realize that morals cannot be accounted for through evolution.

Sentence structure unchanged:

Biology does not distinguish between what should and should not survive; it simply tells us "what does survive."

Plagiarism does not apply just to the words of the source but also to the idea. You are plagiarizing if you use the language of the source without enclosing it in quotation marks or if you closely imitate the structure of the material cited—even if you change the words.

Plagiarism, whether intentional or unintentional, usually leads to the same harsh consequences, such as failing the course or being expelled from school.

 Chapter 12 provides detailed information on citing the most common sources used in research essays.

Acceptable paraphrase:

An honest appraisal can tell a person that morals cannot be accounted for through evolution. . . . Biology tells us only "what does survive," not what should and should not survive (Leacock 57).

Sample 2

Original:

Previous studies by the American Psychological Association show cheating is relatively infrequent in elementary school, but increases as children become adolescents and progress through grade levels. The increasing incidence of cheating correlates almost perfectly with increasing pressure from teachers to get good grades. —Minsky, A. (2009, August 9). Cheating stats getting out of control: Researcher. *CanWest News*. Retrieved from CBCA Current Events.

Language of the source unchanged:

As students progress to higher grades, cheating correlates almost perfectly with increasing pressure.

Language changed, but sentence structure unchanged:

Students cheat more because of mounting pressure to achieve high marks.

Acceptable paraphrase:

As students advance from one grade to the next at school, they often feel that they need to perform well, and this pressure seems tied to the frequency of cheating (Minksy, 2009).

Fortunately, you may not need to cite everything you include in your essay. Anything that falls under the categories of "general knowledge" or "easily obtainable" usually does not need to be cited, even if you obtained the information from a specific source. If you're writing an essay about the structure of the Canadian Government, you don't have to cite a statement that there are three main political parties because it is a well-known fact. You do, however, have to cite a source that explains how these parties formed, as many people do not know the specific dates of the parties' founding or the key players involved.

General knowledge can vary according to audience. If you are writing for an audience with a medical background, you may not need to cite the fact that the active ingredient in marijuana is tetrahydrocannabinol; if you are writing a paper for historians or political scientists, you may not need to cite the fact that British Columbia became a Canadian province in 1871. Your readers will either

> A good strategy for avoiding plagiarism (and for learning the information) is to study carefully the passage you want to use, close the text, and write out its points from memory completely in your own words. Finally, look at the passage again, ensuring that it is different from what you have written in both its structure and language—and that you have accurately restated the thought behind it.

> If a fact is general knowledge for your audience or is easily obtainable by the reader, you usually do not need to provide a citation.

already know this information or can easily obtain it from various sources. Your instructor may be able to tell you how many sources constitute easily obtainable information; a minimum number often given is three. If the general knowledge or the easily obtainable standards do not apply, make the citation.

 # Integrating Secondary Sources

Using secondary sources enables you to support your argument and to demonstrate your familiarity with source material. Your essay, interwoven with citations in the correct format, reveals your skills as a reader, researcher, and writer. As covered in Chapter 10, you can treat secondary sources in three major ways:

1. Summarize the source, or the section of it that is most directly relevant to your point.
2. Paraphrase the source.
3. Cite from the source directly.

Summary, Paraphrase, Direct Quotation, Mixed Quotation Format

> See pages 107–8 for a discussion of signal phrases and parenthetical citations.

Using a variety of methods to integrate secondary sources with your own ideas is usually best; however, there are general guidelines to help you choose a style. In all cases, remember that the source must be identified either in a signal phrase or in a parenthetical citation.

Summary

> For more about summaries and paraphrases, see Chapters 9 and 11.

Summarize if you want to use a source's main idea(s) to provide background information, to set up a point of your own (e.g., to show similarity or difference), or to explain a point relevant to your discussion. You can summarize passages of just about any length—from one sentence to several pages.

Paraphrase

Direct quotation is used when the source and the exact wording are important. This could be due to specialized vocabulary in the cited passage or the unique way that the source uses language or expresses the idea. **Block quotation** is a method of setting off a large quotation (4 or more lines or 40 or more words) from the rest of the essay's text.

Paraphrase when you want to cite a relatively small amount of material that is directly relevant to your point. Include all of the original thought but rephrase it.

Direct Quotation

Direct quotation is used when both the source and the exact wording are important. This could be due to specialized vocabulary in the cited passage or the unique way that the source uses language or expresses the idea. Used selectively, direct quotations are an essential part of most essays.

You can use direct quotations for small or (relatively) large amounts of text. If you choose to quote four or more consecutive lines, use the **block quotation** format, in which you indent the text one half-inch from the left margin and double-space it but do not use quotation marks. The usual procedure is to introduce the block quotation by a complete sentence followed by a colon (see the next section). If the original text includes quotation marks, you must retain them. Use double marks in a block quotation; otherwise, use single:

> Sarah said, "John told me to just 'walk away,' rather than argue with Peter."

The single quotation marks around *walk away* inform the reader that Sarah is quoting John directly.

Do not use direct quotes if

- the idea in the passage is obvious, well known, or could be easily accessed;
- the material is essentially factual and does not involve a particular interpretation of the facts; or
- the text can be easily paraphrased.

Avoid using large blocks of quoted material, especially as a way of meeting the essay's required length. Some instructors do not include direct quotations in your total word count.

These examples present unnecessary or ineffective direct quotations, followed by preferable alternatives:

Sample 1

"About one-third of infants are breastfed for three months or longer" (Statistics Canada).

Paraphrase:

Approximately 33 per cent of infants receive breast milk for at least three months (Statistics Canada).

Sample 2

"The greenhouse effect is the result of gases like carbon dioxide, nitrous oxide, and methane being trapped in earth's atmosphere" (Environment Canada).

Paraphrase:

The accumulation of such gases as carbon dioxide, nitrous oxide, and methane in the atmosphere has led to the greenhouse effect (Environment Canada).

> Use single quotation marks to indicate a word or passage in your source that is in quotation marks; use double quotation marks if these segments appear in a block quotation.

Many facts can be paraphrased rather than quoted directly. Avoid quoting long passages of statistical information that can easily distract the reader—paraphrasing the material is usually better.

The following direct quotations are effective:

Albert Einstein once said, "It always seems to me that man was not born to be a carnivore."

Direct quotation is a good—although not an essential—choice here because Einstein is a well-known person. In the next instance, precise wording matters and gives authority to the passage:

"Neither capital punishment nor life imprisonment without possibility of release shall be imposed for offenses committed by persons below 18 years of age" (UN Convention on the Rights of the Child).

Mixed Quotation Format

A **mixed quotation format** combines significant words of the source (direct quotation) with paraphrasing.

A **mixed quotation format** uses a combination of paraphrase and direct quotation to show a writer's familiarity with a source and confidence in integrating words and ideas smoothly. Here is an example:

In his tribute to Pierre Elliott Trudeau in *The Globe and Mail*, Mark Kingwell (2000) finds the "good citizen" behind "the fusion of reason and passion, the virility and playfulness, the daunting arrogance and wit, the politician as rock star."

Compare this statement with the original (the unused text is crossed out).

~~It's hard to say anything about Trudeau now that has not been said a thousand times before:~~ the fusion of reason and passion, the virility and playfulness, the daunting arrogance and wit, the politician as rock star. ~~All true; all banal.~~ But underneath all that I find ~~a more resonant identity, one which is at once simpler and more profound:~~ the good citizen.

Kingwell, M. (2000, September 30). Pierre Elliott Trudeau: 1919–2000. *The Globe and Mail*. Retrieved from http://v1.theglobeandmail.com/series/trudeau/mkingwellrefpol_sep30.html

When you use direct quotations, you must ensure that the quoted material is integrated with the surrounding text grammatically, clearly, and gracefully.

Sample 1

Ungrammatical:

Charles E. Taylor discusses the efforts of scientists "are defining a new area of research termed artificial life" (172).

Grammatical:

Charles E. Taylor discusses the efforts of scientists to "[define] a new area of research termed artificial life" (172).

Sample 2

Unclear:

Art critic John Ruskin believes that the highest art arises from sensations occurring to them only at particular times" (112).

Clear:

Art critic John Ruskin believes that artists produce the highest art from "sensations occurring to them only at particular times" (112).

Punctuate a direct quotation exactly as it is punctuated in the original but do not include any punctuation in the original that comes after the quoted material. Note the omission of the original comma after *recklessness*.

Original:

"Any accounting of male–female differences must include the male's superior recklessness, a drive, not, I think, towards death" (Updike, 1999, p. 31).

Direct quotation:

In his essay "The Disposable Rocket," John Updike (1999) states that "any accounting of male–female differences must include the male's superior recklessness (p. 31)."

> To test whether you've integrated a quotation properly, remove the quotation marks and make sure that the sentence is grammatical. Remember to put the quotation marks back in and to indicate any changes you made to the original with brackets or ellipses.

Exercise **11.2**

Choose five or six passages from a section of one of your textbooks. Using the techniques for integrating sources discussed in this chapter, create direct quotations, summaries, paraphrases, and examples of mixed quotation format for these passages.

Signal Phrases, Ellipses, and Brackets

Signal Phrases

> **Signal phrases** include the source's name and a signal verb; they "signal" an upcoming reference.

Signal phrases, such as those used on pages 107–8, introduce direct quotations. These phrases contain the source's name (Taylor, Ruskin) and a signal verb (*recalls,* *discusses*, or *believes*). They alert readers to exactly where the reference begins and can guide them through a complex issue that involves different findings or interpretations. The following paragraph, which uses MLA style, contains two citation formats: the first sentence contains a signal phrase; the second does not.

> *Richard Goldbloom states* that a surveillance video taken in Toronto showed that, in more than 20 per cent of incidents where bullying was involved, peers actively became part of the bullying (2). Furthermore, recent statistics show not only the pervasiveness of the problem but also that outsiders perceive bullying as a problem in schools today (Clifford 4).

The reader would easily be able to separate the two sources at the transition word *furthermore*, so a second signal phrase is unnecessary.

In APA style, the signal phrase includes the year of the work's publication after the author's name.

> *Asch and Wishart (2004) state* that the Slavey communities had grade schools by the 1960s, and people left their homes to live in communities so as to retain social benefits (p. 186). As children and parents were reminded, a half-dozen absences from school could result in fines and jail for the parents and the loss of family allowance payments (*The Catholic Voice*, 2000, p. 5).

Ellipses

Using direct quotation doesn't mean that you have to include full paragraphs or sentences from other texts. For example, if you find a passage that discusses two points and you want to discuss only one, you can leave out the irrelevant part. In fact, keeping it in might confuse the reader. However, make sure that leaving it out would not be misleading or create a bias that does not exist in the original.

Replace any omitted text in a direct quotation with an **ellipsis** (. . .). This punctuation mark informs the reader that you aren't quoting the entire sentence or paragraph. If the omitted text includes all the remaining words up to the period at the end of the sentence or you omit one or more complete sentences, add a fourth dot.

Keep the punctuation on either side of the ellipsis only if removing it makes the sentence ungrammatical.

> But some damage to the head occurs from fighting as a player's head is struck, . . . either by a fist or when he falls against the ice.

> As a general rule, do not use an ellipsis at the beginning or end of a direct quotation.

An **ellipsis** (. . .) indicates the omission of one or more words within a direct quotation. Add a fourth dot if you omit all the words up to and including the final period.

Brackets

Square brackets (or **brackets**), as opposed to **parentheses** (round brackets) indicate a change or an addition to a direct quotation, such as a stylistic change (e.g., upper- to lowercase), grammatical change (e.g., verb tense), or clarification (e.g., adding a word to make the context clearer). The following example illustrates these kinds of changes (although you would probably paraphrase a passage that contained this amount of brackets and ellipses):

> The text states that "all secondary sources require parenthetical citations and an alphabetical listing . . . at the end of [the] essay. . . . [Students] must cite secondary sources, whether [they] quote from them directly, summarize them, paraphrase them, or just refer to them in passing by using the [MLA or APA] style."

Original:

> All secondary sources require parenthetical citations and an alphabetical listing in the works cited section at the end of your essay (MLA) or the references section (APA). You must cite secondary sources, whether you quote from them directly, summarize them, paraphrase them, or just refer to them in passing by using the style preferred by your discipline.

You may occasionally use brackets to explain an unfamiliar term within a direct quotation:

> Emergency room nurse Judith McAllen said, "We triage [prioritize by severity of injury] patients if it's a non-emergency, and don't treat them on the basis of their arrival time."

Avoid using brackets any more than is strictly necessary.

Inserting *sic* (which means "thus") between square brackets tells the reader that what immediately precedes it occurs in the original exactly the way it appears in your quotation. One use is to call attention to an error in the original:

> As people often say, "Vive le [sic] différence!"

[Sic] here calls attention to the article error: *le* should be *la*. In APA documentation style, italicize *sic*.

Documentation: In-Text Citations

You now know what needs to be documented, but understanding where and when to document can also be confusing. If you document too much, your paper will not flow well; however, if you do not properly document your sources, you will be plagiarizing.

Parenthetical citations (the parentheses you see after a quotation, paraphrase, or summary that contain bibliographic information) are intended to convey as much information as possible about the source while interfering as little as possible with the essay's content and readability. The general rule is to cite enough to give the reader the information needed while avoiding unnecessary citations. If the specific source is clear without a citation, do not give one.

Do not cite every statement or fact from a source if you use that one source for consecutive references. In fact, you can sometimes combine a few references from the same source in one citation. For example, let's say you use three pages from a work by Jackson. When you finish drawing from that source, you could refer to a page range: (Jackson 87–89). This citation tells the reader that you used the source continuously—perhaps one idea came from page 87, two facts from page 88, and a paraphrased passage from page 89. However, if your own or another source's information intervenes, you need to cite Jackson more than once.

In the essay that follows, Sandy Crashley mainly uses paraphrasing to support her points. She uses the APA style for citation.

> Parenthetical citations are intended to convey as much information as possible about the source while interfering as little as possible with the essay's content and readability.

 For more on APA style, see Chapter 12.

Sample Student Essay: Research

The Cost of Buying Happiness: Why Less Is More

Sandy Crashley

[1] Society assigns status to people according to what they wear, what they own, what they drive, and what they do. This appears to be how to determine if one is successful in North America. A variety of "fads" or "movements" have crept into society recently which rail against this concept that people are defined by their "stuff," and an attempt is being made to redirect people's ever-consuming natures to view success with a less-is-more perspective. The minimalist movement, the tiny house movement, and the locavore movement are all centred on reduction, and the enrichment this reduction will then bring to one's life. The people who participate in these movements believe that money does not buy happiness.

[2] The minimalist movement is all about having fewer goods. The Dalai Lama has said, "If one's life is simple, contentment is sure to come" (Becker, 2014). Following this doctrine, people limit their possessions, which they then believe liberates them and allows them to be happy. This in turn frees people to invest in what they are truly passionate about, such as doing things that make one happy (Hancock, 2014, p. 141). Also, by removing the excess items, a home becomes less cluttered and requires less time to maintain. Also, by de-cluttering and maintaining a minimalist environment, people spend less time purchasing unnecessary goods. This savings in time can instead be spent on quality time with family or friends, or on hobbies that bring pleasure. Furthermore, people who follow the minimalist movement often realize that they don't need all of their belongings, and thus they can save money by not buying the latest gadget. The possessions that those who participate in the minimalist movement do keep or buy will actually come to mean something and be of value to them and make them happy (Kondo, 2014, p. 38). The focus is around need, not want, as well as quality over quantity. The minimalist approach to life is not without its obstacles. As with any habit, it takes conscious effort to adjust from the pursuit of material things to pursuits of a more enriching kind, such as spending time with family and friends. The memories and bonds forged through these times will dwarf the joy of a new iPod. So, while the minimalist movement requires life changes, in the end, the cost of happiness is much cheaper than trying to find happiness in the latest consumer trends.

> Crashley paraphrases her source.

> In the closing sentence, the writer links her paragraph to the thesis.

[3] All of the benefits of the minimalist movement can also be applied to the tiny house movement. The tiny house campaign continues to gain momentum through social media, advertising, and television shows, like FYI's *Tiny House Nation* and HGTV's *Tiny House Builders*. This movement advocates for a minimalist culture, as a smaller space means limited room to put things. Therefore, multiple possessions actually become a burden. Cost savings are also enhanced, as the average-sized 186-square foot "tiny house" costs only $23,000 when co-built by the owner (The Tiny Life, 2015, para. 2; PAD, 2012, para. 5). The modest expense will put the cost of housing below the 32 per cent of gross monthly income for most people, as is recommended by the Canada Mortgage and Housing Corporation (CMHC, 1996–2014, para. 7). One of the greatest

> Here the author paraphrases from two sources that provide the same information.

factors of the 2008 recession in Ontario, and the continued risks to the economy, is the inflated housing market. The average home price in Ontario in December 2014 was $437,601, according to the Canadian Real Estate Association (CBC, 2015). Couple that with current low interest rates that could increase significantly, and many people may find themselves in a position of finding their homes unaffordable. As tiny homes require fewer materials in order to build them and use less energy to heat and cool, there is also a large positive environmental impact to the movement. Those who participate in this movement do not require a burdensome mortgage, and they can, instead, focus on building a career and life that they love, rather than needing a job with high pay and long hours to pay high mortgage fees and utility bills. These people can also enrich their lives with travel and hobbies, and they have the ability to save for a secure retirement. Again, the tiny house movement, like the minimalist movement, is not without its own challenges. Obtaining land is not easy, with the majority of residential land being purchased in bulk by large house-building companies, leaving remnants expensive for the individual to purchase. As a "tiny house" does not provide collateral to secure, bank loans can often be difficult to obtain and many building laws do not support a "tiny house" in their definition of "minimum habitable structure" (Mitchell, 2012, para. 7). There is also the social pressure, as Ryan Mitchell (2012) states, "In our society today, bigger is better, more is better, we are conditioned to want more . . ." (para. 8). However, by living with less, these people are not burdened with the societal obsession of acquiring more just for the sake of appearances, and they have more time and energy for the pursuits that help one feel fulfilled.

[4] Owning a trailer-sized house in the closest vacant field or possessing fewer goods are not concepts that some are comfortable with. The minimalist and tiny house movements require some significant commitment. Another option to consider is the locavore movement. This movement, while sometimes more expensive than the other two, can provide happiness as well. Centred on local eating, this campaign aims to source food products from within a 100-mile radius. When people are able to eat whole foods and obtain them from known local farmers, people can attempt to safeguard against GMOs, pesticides, and other chemical enhancements that many do not want in mass-produced, over-processed

Crashley clearly links the two movements for the reader so that he or she does not lose sight of what was said in the first body paragraph.

Notice the use of the ellipsis. The rest of the quotation is not relevant to her point, so she omits it; however, the necessary information is in the essay.

Again, in the concluding sentence, Crashley links the paragraph to her thesis while also wrapping up the paragraph.

The writer links her three main ideas for the reader.

foods. The nutrient value is preserved in this food, and it usually tastes better, as it is not harvested early to survive long travel. This lack of travel, as well as a limitation on packaging, is also of great value to the preservation of the environment. This often creates a sense of well-being in those following the locavore movement. Additionally, the income to local farmers, vendors, and other businesses promotes sustainable communities and a balanced economy. Following this movement can be as simple as travelling to the local farmer's market on a weekly basis. Those who buy locally believe that what they are doing benefits many, which adds to their sense of satisfaction. They can also develop a close personal bond with the farmers and vendors, which adds to their happiness. However, depending on where people live, year-round local eating can pose a challenge. The solution to this chief obstacle is to plan: buy seasonal foodstuffs in bulk, then freeze or can items for use in the off-season. While the initial cost is high, there is significant savings over time. For some, the locavore movement may require as much commitment as the tiny house and minimalist movement do; however, the locavore movement is easier to moderately integrate into a family's natural rhythm and everyone can enjoy the nutritional, environmental, and social benefits.

> Note that there are no citations in this paragraph. Does this affect the paragraph's credibility when compared to the others?

[5] When it comes to happiness, many North Americans are raised to pursue "the dream." As soon as they are old enough to have a job, they join the consumer culture and often end up pursuing a job that can pay for future life "needs," instead of doing something they really love to do. Through this whole process, life becomes about working to pay for people's lives, instead of actually living them. What is it that people want to define their happiness or success? According to those who follow the above movements, people need not follow the path of others. These people have found that material goods do not buy happiness, but that a life of luxury means less. Perhaps money really does buy happiness, as long as one is not defined by possessions.

> The closing paragraph summarizes the body paragraphs.

> Note the rhetorical thought that the author leaves the reader with.

References

Canadian Mortgage and Housing Corporation. (1996–2014). *Step 2: Are you financially ready?* Retrieved from http://www.cmhc-schl.gc.ca/en/co/buho/hostst/hostst_002.cfm

CBC News. (2015). *Housing sales decline in December.* Retrieved from http://www.cbc.ca/news2/interactives/housing-canada/

Hancock, M. (2014). Buy less, live more. *Alive: Canada's Natural Health & Wellness Magazine.* Retrieved from http://www.alive.com/lifestyle/buy-less-live-more/

Kondo, M. (2014). *The life-changing magic of tidying up: The Japanese art of decluttering* (C. Hirano, Trans.). Berkeley, CA: Ten Speed Press.

Mitchell, R. (2012). *Top 5 biggest barriers to the tiny house movement.* Retrieved from http://thetinylife.com/top-5-biggest-barriers-to-the-tiny-house-movement

Portland Alternative Dwellings (PAD). (2012). *How much does a tiny house cost?* Retrieved from http://padtinyhouses.com/how-much-does-a-tiny-house-cost/

The Tiny Life. (2015). *Tiny houses and the people who live in them.* Retrieved from http://thetinylife.com/what-is-the-tiny-house-movement

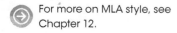

For more on MLA style, see Chapter 12.

Student writer Mike Butler uses some of the different methods we've discussed to integrate sources. He follows the MLA style in his essay.

Sample Student Essay: Research

Computer Ergonomics

Mike Butler

[1] In these technological times, many people are working at jobs that involve long hours sitting in front of a computer. In 1996 a study was done by Hanson that discovered 55 per cent of those studied had enough pain in their upper limbs to force them to get a professional medical opinion (Labeodan 66). As a result, working in an office setting at a computer for long durations can have serious negative effects on the body but fortunately there are many ways to avoid these strains and potential injuries.

STRAINS AND MUSCULOSKELETAL DISORDERS

[2] There are many types of strain and musculoskeletal disorders that can result from prolonged use of a computer. These can be

extremely painful and incapacitating and can affect the muscles, tendons, ligaments, joints, and nerves. Spacebar thumb and pop-up pinkie are nicknames given to computer specific strains to the body (Edwards 42). Carpal tunnel syndrome is a very common ailment and can be caused from leaning the wrists on the keyboard while typing (Edwards 42). Tendonitis develops because the pressure blocks the blood supply to the nerves in the hands. It can become such a problem that even small daily tasks like turning door knobs and opening jars are difficult to impossible without assistance (Linden 26). The wrists, back, neck, eyes, and shoulders can all become sore and damaged from improper posture while at the computer. Barbara Headley, an expert in her field of chronic muscle pain treatment, studied more than 700 patients for a period of time in regards to repetitive strain injuries (Taylor para. 4). She found that the body will rely on muscles not designed to do the job when the primary ones get tired. Initially, soreness from computer use will actually start at the back muscles, then move to the neck and only after that to the hands and arms (Taylor, para. 4). Most people won't complain or realize there is a problem until they feel it in their hands, which by then is a far greater problem because it has been going on for so long (Taylor, para. 4). All in all, there are many strains and disorders that can arise from working at a computer.

HOW TO PREVENT ONE'S OWN INJURIES

[3] The cheapest and easiest way to avoid problems is to take matters literally into one's hands. Exercise, stretching, and rest breaks are key to avoiding the physical ailments that come from using a computer excessively. Exercises and stretches that work the pectoral, shoulder, and neck will all help prevent repetitive strain injury (Taylor para. 4). To prevent injury, these exercises should be done daily, even stopping work throughout the day if there is pain (Taylor para. 4). People's bodies are meant for movement, so minibreaks of just a few minutes throughout the day will allow for a good stretch and will aid in the prevention of strain to the body (Edwards 42). It is easy to work this in by standing during phone calls, walking to a colleague's desk instead of emailing or standing to read long documents. If relief isn't found from stretching, then massage can be helpful to release trigger points

to regain normal movement (Linden 26). As important as all of these are, if people's work stations are not set up properly, it is a losing battle (Linden 26). Proper typing posture is obtained by sitting up with the spinal column directly above the pelvis and rolling the pelvis slightly forward. This uses deep core muscles for maintaining this proper seating position, which are very strong and efficient (Linden 26). By sliding a small rolled up towel under the tail bone, this position is achieved and easily maintained on any type of chair (Linden 26). Feet should be flat on the floor and the monitor directly in front of your body with the top of it at eye level and about an arm's length away. It is much more comfortable to place any work items within your reach zone. Arms should be at a 90-degree angle when on the keyboard and should not rest on the wrist pad when typing. At the very least, change positions and move throughout the day to improve circulation and reduce fatigue.

HOW TO PREVENT WITH EQUIPMENT

[4] If people are not able to keep pain at bay through their own means, then many assistive devices are currently on the market to help. Ergonomic chairs come in all shapes and sizes and can be adjusted to fit all different bodies. Split keyboards are basically cracked down the middle and split so that the wrists don't have to bend at odd angles to reach the keys. These can sit on keyboard trays that slide under the desk and are adjustable as to height, angle, and depth. Flat-screen monitors are much easier on the eyes than the older rounded variety (Edwards 42) and wireless mice are both easy to reach and built to conform to the shape of one's hand. Therefore, as this problem of computer ergonomics becomes more prevalent in an office environment, more and more ergonomic devices are developed to aid in this area.

[5] Most importantly, in order to avoid physical injury is to educate users about computer ergonomics and to use what is learned on a daily basis for the rest of one's working life. It is just not enough to have

the best chair and office equipment if posture is poor and a work-station improperly set up. Even a basic workstation can be appropriate if arranged well and the user pays attention to their body and takes minibreaks throughout the day (Linden, 26). Prevention is the best way to avoid long-term injury.

Works Cited

Edwards, Albert. "Beating Computer Strain." *Ergowise*, vol. 28, no. 2, 1997, pp. 42–49. File Master Elite database.

Labeodan, T. "Knowledge of Computer Ergonomics among Secretarial Staff in a Nigerian University Community." *International Journal of Health, Wellness & Society*, vol. 2, no. 3, 2012, pp. 65–74. CINAHL Complete database.

Linden, P. "Too Much of a Good Thing: Prevention of Computer-Related Repetitive Strain Injuries among Children." *The Journal*, vol. 26, no. 1, 1998, p. 26, http://eds.b.ebschost.com/eds/detail/detail?vid=5&sid=ae096823-f3d7-4fca-8cba-7bc1068.

Taylor, P. "Keyboard Grief." *The Globe and Mail*, 30 Dec. 1993, http://re.ocls.ca.rap.ocls.ca/ra/login.aspx?url=http://search.proquest.com/docview/385146459?accountid=40483.

Townsend, J. "Ergonomics at the PC: Raising Employee Comfort Levels through Training." *American Society of Safety Engineers*, vol. 43, no. 12, 1998, pp. 20–23, http://ra.ocls.ca.ocls.ca/ra/login.aspx?url=http://search.proquest.com/docview/200423522?ac counted=40483.

Post-Reading Questions

1. Examine both student essays and identify the different ways the writers incorporated their sources. Find examples of direct quotation, paraphrase, summary, and mixed format.
2. Does Butler rely too much on one particular method for integrating his sources? Give evidence to support your answer.
3. How effective is Butler's introductory paragraph? Why do you think he chose to use a quotation?
4. How much background information does Butler give about his topic? What does this tell you about his intended audience?
5. Look at the works cited list. Do you feel that Butler includes enough sources? Do they seem reliable? Give evidence to support your answers.

Chapter Review Questions

1. Why is outlining an important part of essay writing?
2. Why is it crucial to cite your sources?
3. What kind of information does not require a citation?
4. Summarize the section on plagiarism (pp. 245–8) in two or three sentences.
5. What are the three main ways of integrating information from a source? What are their differences?
6. When should you avoid direct quotations in essays? When should you use them?
7. What are signal phrases and why are they important?
8. What is the mixed quotation format method of source integration?
9. How could you indicate a grammatical change to a direct quotation in order to integrate it smoothly with your own writing?
10. What are ellipses and when should you use them?

12 APA and MLA Documentation Styles

In this chapter, you will learn

- how to cite sources according to APA and MLA styles;

- how to create references and works cited lists; and

- how to incorporate citations into your writing.

As you saw in Chapters 10 and 11, you must support the points in your research essays with information from outside sources. While the previous chapter dealt with how to integrate these sources into your essay, this chapter will introduce you to two major documentation methods, the American Psychological Association (APA) and Modern Language Association (MLA) styles, and enable you to give proper credit to your sources. We highlight common print and electronic formats, with examples of each style. APA and MLA sample essays are included to illustrate how to use these styles correctly.

 # Choosing Your Citation Style

Citations and references

A **citation** includes the author name, publication date, title, and publisher name and location. A **reference** gives complete retrieval information for a source used in an essay.

- give appropriate credit to others' work;
- establish your credibility as a researcher;
- show where your own work fits into other work in the field;
- avoid plagiarism, a form of theft and certainly one of the most serious academic crimes, and its severe penalties;
- enable readers (such as markers) to trace or verify your sources;
- find the reference if you need it for further research; and
- enlarge on a matter (in a footnote or an endnote) that would be disruptive if placed in the text.

Most styles require an abbreviated citation—placed in parentheses—in the sentence where the reference appears. Although there are many subtle differences among documentation styles, the main elements of a citation usually include

- the surname(s) of the author(s);
- the page number or a similar locator of the information;
- the year of publication; and, in some cases,
- other publication details.

Further details are given in an alphabetized list at the end of the essay under a heading such as "References" or "Works Cited."

Different areas of academia favour distinct styles. Business, education, psychology, social sciences, and some physical sciences use APA; literature, philosophy, and religion use MLA. Other major formats, which we will not discuss in this chapter, include the Council of Science Editors (CSE) and *The Chicago Manual of Style* (*CMS*). Subject areas such as chemistry, engineering, medicine, and music have their own style specifications. Your department or your instructor should be the final guide in your choice of citation style.

Each documentation format has a manual and/or website. If you are using the print version, which you can probably obtain at your school's library, ensure that it is the most current edition. The examples in this chapter are styled according to the following manuals:

American Psychological Association. (2010). *Publication manual of the American Psychological Association* (6th ed.). Washington, DC: Author.

Modern Language Association of America. (2016). *MLA Handbook* (8th ed.). New York, NY: Author.

The MLA also publishes the *MLA Style Manual and Guide to Scholarly Publishing*.

The following sections provide the basic standards for documenting sources in APA and MLA, with examples to illustrate each format. For more samples and updates, check the associations' respective websites (www.apastyle.org/ and https://style.mla.org/). If you use the websites for help, always double-check the information with at least one other site and take note of when the website was last updated, if possible. If you have run out of resources or simply don't have any more time to spend on finding citation rules, use common sense and adapt the rule closest to your particular case. You can also ask a reference librarian or your instructor for hard-to-find formats.

> APA and MLA are both parenthetical styles, meaning that parentheses are used to enclose brief bibliographical information about the source within the main text.

APA

APA style is parenthetical—whenever you directly quote or paraphrase an author in your essay or use an author's idea, you include a citation in parentheses in the sentence. You also provide a more complete description of all the sources in a reference list, which appears on the final page(s) of your essay.

APA In-Text Citations

Generally, APA in-text citations include the author's surname, the work's year of publication, and (for direct quotations or paraphrases) the relevant page number at the end of the sentence. Separate the items with commas and use the abbreviation *p.* or *pp.* for *page* or *pages* (do not italicize the abbreviations). In most cases, the end punctuation comes after the closing parentheses.

> APA in-text citations include the author's surname, year of publication, and page number(s).

(Ashton, 2008, p. 12).

If the sentence gives the author's name (i.e., uses a signal phrase) and does not include a direct quotation, do not repeat the name in the parenthetical citation. Include the publication year and page number(s) immediately after the author's name.

> Sandy Crashley's essay "The Cost of Buying Happiness: Why Less Is More" (see Chapter 11, pp. 254–7) uses the APA format.

Ashton (2008, p. 12) found that . . .

Here are more guidelines for APA in-text citations:

Citation after a direct quotation: Give the author's surname, year of publication, and page number. If there is no signal phrase (i.e., the author is not named in the sentence), include all the information at the end of the quotation.

> During both world wars, the Canadian government often employed masseuses because surgery and medical care were insufficient "to restore severely wounded men" (Cleather, 1995, p. ix).

If the author is named in the signal phrase, follow with the publication year; place the page number at the end of the quotation and before the punctuation.

> According to Stambouli and Traversa (2002), "each gallon of gasoline produced and used in an internal combustion engine releases roughly 12 kg of CO_2" (p. 299).

Block quotation: A quotation of 40 words or more begins on a new line and is indented one half-inch from the left margin. Quotation marks are not used, and the text is double-spaced. The author's surname, year of publication, and page number appear in parentheses at the end of the quotation and after the punctuation.

> . (Ellis & Bochner, 2000, pp. 81–82)

Citation for a specific reference (such as a paraphrase): State the author's surname, year of publication, and page number.

> Most of the profits from British Columbia's aquaculture industry go to Norwegians, who control 92 per cent of the industry (Macdonald, 2009, pp. 148–149).

Citation for a non-specific reference: A non-specific reference, such as an author's thesis statement or a study's main findings, applies to the work as a whole rather than to a specific page. Give only the author's surname and year of publication.

> Conservation biologists agree that protecting habitats is the most effective way to conserve biological diversity (Primack, 2000).

Citation referring to an indirect source: If it is necessary to refer to a source found in another work, include the original author's name in the sentence and cite the **indirect source**. Include the phrase *as cited in* (not italicized) before the author's surname. In the references section, list the details for the indirect source.

Do not include a page number in an in-text citation that refers to the work as a whole rather than to a specific page(s).

A paraphrase includes all the content of the source put entirely in your own words. When you paraphrase material, your citation must include the page number.

An **indirect source** is one that is cited in another work. Always use original sources whenever possible, but if you have to cite information from an indirect source, include the phrase *as cited in* before the citation.

Francis Bacon (as cited in Lindemann, 2001) observed that language affects our thinking when he said that "words·react on the under-standing" (p. 93).

Personal communication, including interviews: Give the author's surname and first initial(s), the phrase *personal communication* (not italicized), and the date of the conversation.

(J. Derrida, personal communication, September 20, 2000).

Personal communications are cited only in the text of your essay; they are not listed in the references section.

Multiple sources in one citation: You may include more than one relevant source in a single citation if your point applies to both. Order the sources alphabetically by last name and separate them with a semicolon.

> You may include more than one source in a single citation. Separate the sources with semicolons.

The practices of teaching composition in college have not radically changed in the last few decades (Bishop, 2005; Williams, 2007).

APA In-Text Citations by Format

Number or Kind of Authors

Work by one author: Give the author's surname, year of publication, and page number (if required). A book with both an author and an editor or translator is usually cited by the author.

(Bloom, 2002, p. xviii).

Work by two authors: State the surnames of both authors, with an ampersand (&) between them; year of publication; and page number (if required).

(Higgins & Wilson-Baptist, 1999, p. 44).

When naming the authors in the text of your essay, as in a signal phrase, use the word *and* instead of an ampersand.

> When you refer to a work with more than one author in a citation, use an ampersand (&) before the last author's surname. Use *and* when listing the author names in the main text.

Higgins and Wilson-Baptist (1999) argue that "a tourist exists out-side of experience. A traveller, though, submerges herself in the new" (p. 44).

Works by three, four, or five authors: List the surnames of all authors in the first citation. For later citations, include only the first author's surname followed by the abbreviation *et al.* (not italicized), which means "and others." Include the publication year and page number (if required) every time, unless the same authors are mentioned more than once in a paragraph.

(Higgins, Wilson-Baptist, & Krasny, 2001)
second citation in the paragraph: (Higgins et al.)

To cite six or more authors, give the surname of the first author followed by *et al.*

Work by six or more authors: State the first author's surname followed by the abbreviation *et al.*(not italicized) and the publication year and page number (if required).

(Terracciano et al., 2005)

Two or more works by the same author in the same year: Add lowercase letters alphabetically (*a*, *b*, *c*, etc.) to distinguish works published in the same year.

(Foucault, 1980a, p. 37)

The *a* in the example indicates that the writer has used at least two works written by Foucault and published in 1980. This citation must correspond with the entry for 1980a in the references list.

Two authors with the same last name: Include the authors' first initial(s) to distinguish the names.

(Sinkinson, S., 2001, p. 225; Sinkinson, B., 2001, p. 237)

If no author is given for a source, use the name of the group or organization.

Group or organization as author (corporate author): Documents published by companies and government departments may not list an author. In this case, use the group or organization's name. If the name is long or is well known by an acronym or abbreviation (for example, the United Nations Children's Fund is commonly known as UNICEF), include the full name in the first citation followed by the acronym in square brackets, the year of publication, and page number (if required). Use the abbreviation with the year throughout the rest of the paper. If the group name is not well known, use the full name with publication year each time.

(American Educational Research Association [AERA], 2001)
later citations: (AERA, 2001)

Work with an unknown author (including many dictionary and encyclopedia articles): When the author is unknown and there is no company name, use the first few words of the work's title followed with the year of publication and page number (if required).

> ("Plea to City Hall," 2003)

Anonymous or unnamed author: Cite in the same way as a named author, using *Anonymous* (not italicized).

> (Anonymous, 1887, p. 12)

Electronic Sources

The most challenging aspect of citing online documents is that they often lack page numbers. If the paragraphs are numbered, use these numbers in your citations, preceded by the abbreviation *para.* (not italicized). If neither page nor paragraph numbers are available but the document includes section headings, cite the heading title in quotation marks and include the paragraph number(s) in which the material occurs.

Sample in-text Internet citation: Include the author's surname, year the site was created or last updated, heading title (if applicable), and page or paragraph number.

> (Gregoire, 2000, "Bones and Teeth," para. 5)

Internet site without an author or without a date: Use the full or abbreviated title in quotation marks, the year the site was created or last updated, and page or paragraph number. Use the abbreviation *n.d.* (not italicized) if the site does not include a date.

> ("Muchinfo's Poll," 2002, para. 16)
> (Hannak, n.d., para. 2)

Non-Text Sources

Film, video, audio, TV broadcast, and musical recording: Use the most senior production person's name and the year of public release or broadcast.

> (Coppola, 1979)

Installation, event, performance, or work of art: Use the format followed by other non-text resources, such as the name of the artist(s) and date of presentation or creation.

> (Byrdmore, 2006)

Many articles retrieved from a database are viewed as Portable Document Format (PDF) files. In such cases, use the page numbers in the document, which are usually the same as those of the print version (if one exists).

If you cannot locate page or paragraph numbers in an electronic document, give the section heading in quotation marks and count by paragraphs from the heading to the relevant paragraph(s).

APA References

In APA style, the references section contains complete bibliographical information for a work's in-text citations. Follow these guidelines when creating a reference list:

- Begin the references on a new page at the end of the essay and number the section as part of the overall work.
- Centre the title ("References") an inch from the top of the page.
- Double-space the list, with 1-inch margins.
- Begin each entry flush with the left margin; use a hanging indent for subsequent lines. Do not number the entries.
- Alphabetize the list by author surname, usually the first item in each entry.
- Italicize titles of books, journals, plays, films, and other full-length works. Do not set titles of chapters or articles in quotation marks. Except for journals, capitalize only the first word, the first word after a colon, all proper nouns, and acronyms (e.g., NFB or CBC) regardless of how the original is capitalized.
- Capitalize each word in a journal title except for prepositions (*in, of, to,* etc.), articles (*a, an, the*), and conjunctions (*and, or*).
- Omit words such as *Publishers, Inc.,* and *Co.* in publishers' names. Include the full names of associations, corporations, and university presses.
- Use the following abbreviations where appropriate.

    - ed. (edition)
    - Ed. (Editor), Eds. (Editors)
    - No. (Number)
    - p. (page), pp. (pages)
    - para. (paragraph)
    - Pt. (Part)
    - Rev. ed. (Revised edition)
    - Trans. (Translator[s])
    - Vol. (Volume), Vols. (Volumes)

The standard APA reference begins with the author's surname followed by initial(s), not given name(s); publication date; title of work; and publication details. Here are two examples of specific types.

Sample book entry: Include the author's name, date of publication, title of book, place of publication, and publisher. Provide the city and province, state, or country in the location unless it is included in the publisher's name (e.g., University of Michigan Press).

Fries, C. C. (1962). *Linguistics and reading.* New York, NY: Holt, Rinehart & Winston.

Sample journal entry: Provide the author's name, date of publication, title of article, title of journal (italicized), volume number (italicized), issue number (if required), page range, and DOI or URL. Note that the comma after the journal title is also italicized and that there is no end punctuation after a DOI or URL. If you use an URL, introduce it with the phrase *Retrieved from* (not italicized).

> The order for most references is author's surname and initial(s); publication date; title of work; and publication details, which vary depending on whether the work is a book, journal article, or electronic document.

> Valkenburg, P. M., & Jochen, P. (2007). Who visits online dating sites? Exploring some characteristics of online daters. *CyberPsychology and Behavior, 10*, 849–852. doi:10.1089/cpb.2007.9941

 Chapter 10 discusses DOIS.

Number or Kind of Authors

Work by one author: See "Sample book entry."

Work by two authors: Invert both authors' names and separate them with an ampersand (&).

> For a work with two to seven authors, invert all authors' names and use an ampersand (&) between the second-last and the last name.

> Luckner, J., & Nadler, R. (1992). *Processing the experience*. Dubuque, IA: Kendall/Hunt.

Work by three to seven authors: See "Work by two authors"; list all the authors.

> Festial, L., Ian, H., & Gomez, S. (1956). *When economics fails*. Minneapolis: University of Minnesota Press.

Work by eight or more authors: Include the first six authors and the last author with an ellipsis (. . .) between the sixth and the final author.

> Unless there are more than seven authors in a work, include all authors' names in the reference.

> Terracciano, A., Abdel-Khalek, A. M., Ádám, N., Adamovová, L., Ahn, C. K., Ahn, H. N., . . . McCrae, R. R. (2005). National character does not reflect mean personality trait levels in 49 cultures. *Science, 310*, 96–100. doi:10.1126/science.1117199

Two or more works by the same author: Works by the same author are arranged chronologically, earliest to latest. Works with the same author(s) and publication year are arranged alphabetically by the first major word of the title. In the example, the earliest article is listed first; the *h* in *history* precedes the *P* in *Power*, justifying the order of the second and third items.

> Foucault, M. (1977). *Discipline and punish: The birth of the prison* (A. Sheridan, Trans.). New York, NY: Random House.

Foucault, M. (1980a). *The history of sexuality* (Vol. 1) (R. Hurley, Trans.). New York, NY: Random House.

Foucault, M. (1980b). *Power/Knowledge: Selected interviews and other writings 1972–1977* (C. Gordon, Ed.). Brighton, UK: Harvester Press.

Work by two authors with the same last name: The alphabetical order of authors' initials determines the sequence. If two works have the same first authors, the last names of the second authors determine the order.

Jason, L. A., & Klich, M. M. (1982). Use of feedback in reducing television watching. *Psychological Reports, 51,* 812–814.

Jason, L. A., & Rooney-Rebeck, P. (1984). Reducing excessive television viewing. *Child & Family Behavior Therapy, 6,* 61–69.

Group or organization as author (corporate author): Use the full group name in place of the author's name. If the name begins with an article (e.g., *The*), omit it. If the organization is also the publisher, use *Author* (not italicized) for the publisher's name.

Education International. (2008). *Guide to universities & colleges in Canada.* Victoria, BC: Author.

Work with an unknown author (non-electronic source): Alphabetize the entry by the first major word in the title. When an author is listed as "Anonymous," alphabetize by the letter *A*.

> When there is no author in a non-electronic source, alphabetize the entry by the first major word in the title. (Do not include words such as *The*.)

Interveners. (1993). In *Canadian Encyclopedia* (Vol. 11, pp. 344–348). Ottawa, ON: Smith Press.

No date: Use *n.d.* (not italicized) after the author's name.

Source Type

Edited work: Begin with the editor's name followed by *Ed.* (one editor) or *Eds.* (more than one editor; not italicized) in parentheses.

Corcoran, B., Hayhoe, M., & Pradl, G. M. (Eds.). (1994). *Knowledge in the making: Challenging the text in the classroom.* Portsmouth, NH: Boynton/Cook.

Chapter or other type of selection, such as an essay, in an edited volume: Begin with the author's name, year of publication, and chapter (or essay) title.

Follow with the name(s) of the book's editor(s), not inverted, preceded by *In* and followed by *Ed.* or *Eds.* (not italicized). The reference concludes with the book title, page range (in parentheses), and publication information.

> Sanders, D. E. (1984). Some current issues affecting Indian government. In L. Little Bear, M. Boldt, & J. A. Long (Eds.), *Pathways to self-determination: Canadian Indians and the Indian state* (pp. 113–121). Toronto, ON: University of Toronto Press.

Translated work: Place the translator's name and the abbreviation *Trans.* (not italicized) in parentheses after the work's title.

> Lacan, J. (1977). *Écrits: A selection* (A. Sheridan, Trans.). New York, NY: W. W. Norton. (Original work published 1966)

To cite a republished book in the text of your essay, use both the original and the current publication dates:

> (Lacan, 1966/1977)

Volume in a multivolume work: Include the volume number after the title.

> Bosworth, A. B. (Ed.). (1995). *A historical commentary on Arrian's history of Alexander* (Vol. 1). London, UK: Oxford University Press.

If referring to more than one volume, give the specific volumes or range (e.g., Vols. 1–3).

Second or subsequent edition of a work: Include the edition number after the title.

> Suzuki, D. T., Griffiths, A. J., & Lewontin, R. C. (1989). *An introduction to genetic analysis* (4th ed.). New York, NY: W. H. Freeman.

Article in a journal with continuous pagination: If a journal's pagination continues from one issue to the next, include the volume but not the issue number. Page numbers for journal articles are not preceded by *p.* or *pp.*

> Garner, R. (2003). Political ideologies and the moral status of animals. *Journal of Political Ideologies, 8,* 233–246.

> The usual order for an essay or other selection in an edited book is author name, year, essay title, book editor's name preceded by *In*, the abbreviation *Ed.*, book title, page range, and other publication details.

> For editions beyond the first, include the edition number in parentheses after the title.

Whether you include the issue number in a citation depends on whether each issue is numbered separately (include issue number) or the numbering continues from the previous issue (do not include issue number).

Article in a journal that is paginated by issue: If each issue of a journal is numbered separately, include both volume (italicized) and issue number (in parentheses and not italicized).

> Trew, J. D. (2002). Conflicting visions: Don Messier, Liberal nationalism, and the Canadian unity debate. *International Journal of Canadian Studies, 26*(2), 41–57.

Unlike journal and magazine articles, newspaper articles require the abbreviation *p.* or *pp.* with all page numbers included. References also include the exact publication date (i.e., year-month-day format).

Article in a magazine: Provide the complete date in the year-month-day format. Do not abbreviate month names. Include the volume and issue numbers if available.

> Knapp, L. (2007, September/October). Licensing music to the film and television industries. *Canadian Musician, 29*(5), 49–56.

Article in a newspaper: Include the author's name or, if none is given, the title of the article. Include abbreviation *p.* or *pp.* before the page number(s). If the article continues later in the work, give all page numbers and separate them with commas. A letter to the editor or an editorial follows the same format and includes specific information in square brackets after the title (e.g., [Letter to the editor]).

> Lawyer seeks mistrial for client accused of illegal midwifery. (2003, April 20). *National Post*, p. A8.

Book/movie review: Follow article format but include *Review of the*, the medium, title, and reviewer's name in square brackets (e.g., [Review of the DVD . . .]) after the title.

> Mihm, S. (2009). Swindled: The dark history of food fraud, from poisoned candy to counterfeit coffee [Review of the book *Swindled: The dark history of food fraud, from poisoned candy to counterfeit coffee*, by B. Wilson]. *Business History Review, 83*(2), 379–381.

Government document: If the author is unknown, begin with the name of the government followed by the agency (e.g., ministry, department, Crown corporation) and the document name.

> British Columbia. Office of the Auditor General. (2005). *Salmon forever: An assessment of the provincial role in sustaining wild salmon*. Victoria, BC: Author.

In cases or reports, such as government documents, the report number can be placed after the title (e.g., Research Report No. 09.171).

Indirect source: Give the work the citation comes from, not the original text.

 For more on indirect sources, see page 266.

Personal communication: Because they cannot be reproduced or verified, personal communications (including emails, phone calls, interviews, and conversations) are not included in the list of references.

> Do not include personal communications (including emails, phone calls, interviews, and conversations) in the reference list.

Electronic Sources

The APA manual recommends that electronic sources include the same elements of print sources in the same order, with exact location information added as needed. As we mentioned in "Sample journal entry," include a journal article's DOI if it is available (you'll find it with the other publication information, such as journal title and volume number, and/or on the first page of the article).

> APA encourages the use of a DOI where available, instead of an URL.

Not all publishers use this system. If the DOI is unavailable or your instructor tells you to do so, cite the URL of the journal's or publisher's home page. If the document would be hard to locate from the home page, provide the exact URL or as much as is needed for retrieval. APA does not require your date of access for Internet sources, but you should confirm electronic links before including them in your paper. More information on referencing electronic references in APA format is available at www.apastyle.org/manual/related/electronic-sources.pdf.

Sample electronic reference: Citation formats follow those of print sources with the title of the website included.

> Czekaj, L. (2014, May 23). Promises fulfilled: Looking at the legacy of thousands of black slaves who fled to Canada in the 1800s. Federation for the Humanities and Social Sciences. Retrieved from http://www.ideas-idees.ca/blog/promises-fulfilled

If it is necessary to break the URL over more than one line, break before punctuation, such as the slash before *blog* in the example; never use a hyphen unless it is part of the URL.

Group or organization (corporate or government) website: If there is no author, use the organization's name.

> Environment Canada. (2009, August 12). 10 things you should know about climate change. Retrieved from http://www.ec.gc.ca/cc/default.asp?lang=En&n=2F049262–1

The complete URL is given here because it would be hard to locate the document from the organization's home page.

Article in an online-only journal: Follow the format for a print article; add the URL at the end.

> Rye, B. J., Elmslie, P., & Chalmers, A. (2007). Meeting a transsexual person: Experience within a classroom setting. *Canadian On-Line Journal of Queer Studies in Education, 3*(1). Retrieved from http://jps.library.utoronto.ca/index.php/jqstudies/index

Article from a database (with a DOI): The name of the database is not usually required.

> The name of the database is not usually required in a reference, even if there is no DOI.

> Martel, M. (2009). "They smell bad, have diseases, and are lazy": RCMP officers reporting on hippies in the late sixties. *Canadian Historical Review, 90*, 215–245. doi:10.3138/chr.90.2.215

In this example, the quotation marks in the title indicate a direct quotation.

Article from a database (no DOI): The home page of the journal is used; the name of the database is not usually required.

> Barton, S. S. (2008). Discovering the literature on Aboriginal diabetes in Canada: A focus on holistic methodologies. *Canadian Journal of Nursing Research, 40*(4), 26–54. Retrieved from http://cjnr.mcgill.ca/

No date: Place *n.d.* (not italicized) where the date would normally go.

> Hegemony. (n.d.). In *Merriam-Webster online dictionary*. Retrieved from http://www.merriam-webster.com/dictionary/hegemony

E-book: Use *n.d.* (not italicized) for the date and include the URL.

> Radford, B. (n.d.). *Soil to social*. Retrieved from http://on-line-books.ora.com/mod-bin/books.mod/javaref/javanut/index.htm

Electronic version of a print book: Do not include the print version's publication details but include the reader version, if applicable, and either the DOI or the URL.

> Douglass, F. (1881). My escape from slavery [MS Reader version]. Retrieved from http://etext.lib.virginia.edu/ebooks/

Message posted to an online forum, discussion group, or blog post: Include the medium, such as *Web log message* or *Video file* (not italicized), after the title.

> Koolvedge. (2009, August 8). Reply to massacre in Peru [Web log message]. Retrieved from https://www.adbusters.org/blogs/ dispatches/massacre-peru.html#comments

Non-Text Sources

Lecture or other oral presentation: Include the name of the lecturer, the date (in year-month-day format), and the title (or topic) of the lecture, followed by *Lecture presented at* (not italicized) and location details, such as the sponsoring agency (or college or university department) and/or building name, school name, and school location.

> Armstrong, M. (2009, April 2). *Darwin's paradox.* Lecture presented at David Strong Building, University of Victoria, Victoria, BC.

Film or video: Use the following order: producer, director, year, and title of film followed by *Motion picture* (not italicized) in square brackets. Conclude by giving the country of origin and studio.

> Coppola, F. F. (Producer & Director). (1979). *Apocalypse now* [Motion picture]. USA: Zoetrope Studios.

Episode from a television series: Use the following order: writer, director, year, and title of episode followed by *Television series episode* (not italicized) in square brackets. Then give the producer's name and the title of the series. Conclude by giving the city and broadcasting company.

> Lindelof, D. (Writer), & Bender, J. (Director). (2005). Man of science, man of faith [Television series episode]. In J. J. Abrams (Executive producer), *Lost.* New York, NY: American Broadcasting.

Music: Use the following order: writer, copyright year, and title of song followed by the recording artist in square brackets (if different from the writer). Conclude by giving the album title preceded by *On* (not italicized), the medium of recording in square brackets, the city and country of origin, and the label. If the recording date is different from the copyright year, provide this information in parentheses.

> Morrison, V. (1993). Gloria. On *Too long in exile* [CD]. London, UK: Polydor.

The following student essay uses the APA documentation style.

Sample Student Essay: APA
Polar Bears: Bright Outlook or Grim Future
Adam Cook

INTRODUCTION

[1] The population of the polar bear (*Ursus maritimus*) species has been alarmingly decreasing throughout the years. The polar bear is classified as a vulnerable species, with approximately 8 of the 19 polar bear subspecies in decline. Polar bears have to continuously fight the extreme odds of man, machine, and the global environment just to keep their place on this planet. Everything from the human race overhunting and encroaching evermore on their territory, to the garbage and toxic pollution that is sweeping and growing over the Arctic, to the drastically changing weather and temperature fluctuations is unquestionably haunting and harming the future of the polar bear species, if indeed they even have one.

IMPACTS

[2] Humans: The human race is the number one cause for the dwindling population of the polar bear species. Every year, humans intrude further and further onto the polar bears' natural territory. Humans have almost pushed them right off of their land directly into the water with nowhere to go. Humans have so little regard for this species that we have intensely overhunted them for years to make carpets, coats, good luck charms, medicinal uses, head-trophies, etc. It is well known that the commercial hunting of polar bears almost drove them to extinction. Humans regularly disturb their breeding cycles, hibernation timeframes, and birthing den procedures, which causes immense stress to the mother polar bear. She can even lose her cubs if being disturbed during the developmental stages of the fetus in the mother's womb. American zoologist Dr Steven C. Armstrup conducted an 11-year study that proves the negative impacts that humans have on hibernating and prenatal polar bears. On top of that, humans have negative effects on the polar bears' food chain. Humans have hunted and also overhunted many of their own food sources to the point of depletion, which thus leave polar bears undernourished, stressed, and incredibly desperate

for food (Armstrup, 1993, p. 12). If polar bears are to survive, humans need to respect and maintain the natural habitat of these creatures.

[3] Garbage and Pollution: A major factor affecting the polar bear species is the ever-growing rate of garbage and pollution hitting their homeland. Every year, scientists are noticing the increasing trend of various amounts of garbage from all parts of the world making its way to the Arctic regions. Air and water pollution are negatively impacting the polar bears' natural territory and their species as a whole as time goes on. Over 80 per cent of marine pollution expels from land-based activities (WWF, n.d.). Everything from numerous types of deadly oils, varieties of virulent fertilizers, mounds and mounds of garbage, masses of sewage disposal, slews of toxic chemicals, and other contaminates affect the natural habitat of polar bears. Oil spills cause a great deal of damage to the marine environment. Fertilizer runoff has had severe negative impacts for coastal areas around the world. This runoff has some nutrients that can lead to eutrophication. Eutrophication is when algal blooms increase so significantly that it drains the water's dissolved oxygen, which horribly leads to the suffocation of the marine life (Walsh et al., 2011). Eutrophication has resulted in large "dead-zones" in many parts of the world such as the Bering Strait. Mounds of garbage also float their way throughout the oceans, containing copious amounts of plastic and non-decomposable garbage, glass items, packaging material, lumber, and toxic canisters. If people do not dispose of garbage correctly, just about every single item tossed incorrectly can orbit and grow in the seas and oceans. In many areas of the globe, man-made sewage typically flows substantially or completely untreated straight into the seas and oceans. Extensive research has shown that much of the urban sewage drained into the Atlantic Ocean from South America is completely untreated. This sewage can lead to eutrophication as well. Unfortunately, almost every single marine creature is contaminated by or with man-made chemicals. The human race once truly believed that the ocean was so vast that every single chemical, toxin, or bit of garbage would eventually dilute throughout the oceans and break down to the point that it vanished. The truth of the matter is that these dumped items have not simply disappeared. On top of that, certain dumped toxins and chemicals that have found their way into the food chain have become more concentrated and found at higher levels

> Note that many of the points in this paragraph are deemed general knowledge, so they do not need to be cited. See Chapter 11 for more on general knowledge.

compared to years past (WWF, n.d.). In order to protect polar bears from these toxins and the contaminants in their food sources, humans have to become responsible caretakers of the planet.

[4] Climate Change: The environment in which polar bears live in is extremely sensitive and can be easily disturbed. They typically live throughout the Arctic region, which is comprised of ice and snow. These natural elements that make up the Arctic are what the polar bears undeniably depend on for survival. Nowadays, such reductions in the thickness and length of the ice and extreme changes in the ice dynamics all negatively alter the condition and success of the polar bears' survival. Examples of this include Hudson Bay and James Bay in Canada. The ice is melting earlier in the spring and being formed later in the fall. The time polar bears spend on the ice is precious for hunting their prey. This is the time when they get to restore their body fat and fitness levels. Unfortunately, this crucial time for storing up fat and energy for the time when there is less ice and sparse food reserves is becoming dangerously finite. As the timeframe without food lengthens, their bodies start to decline quickly. This is certainly critical for mothers that are pregnant or nursing. Scientists have pointed to either lack of fat from the mother or lack of food to be number one causes for death in cubs. With such significant reductions in the ice length and thickness throughout the summer months, the open window for the polar bears' hunting time is ever more decreasing (Castro de la Guardia, Derocher, Myers, Terwisscha van Scheltinga, & Lunn, 2013, para. 4). Will this cause alone be the ultimate destruction of the polar bears' future?

> Cook assumes that people agree with the climate change evidence often spoken about in the media and with the fact that climate change exists. Would his argument be better with citations from outside sources?

CONCLUSION

[5] The polar bears are indeed an incredibly intelligent, strong, resourceful species that are truly the king of the food chain in the Arctic, but these admirable qualities are not enough for them to continue battling these ever-growing, negative effects moving forward into the future. Polar bears are directly threatened from how very little regard the human race has for them, other species, for the environment, and for the earth as a whole. From years and years of gathered, factual research, scientists have estimated that two-thirds

of the polar bear population could become extinct by 2050 (WWF, 2012). The way the human race continues to use and abuse the planet, undoubtedly the climate change supporting scientists will be correct about the polar bears' extinction unless immediate and corrective actions are engaged by people united. Can the human race pull it together, or are the polar bears' days truly numbered? Only time will tell.

References

Amstrup, A. C. (1993, April). Human disturbances of denning polar bears in Alaska. *Arctic Institute of North America, 46*(3), 246–250. Retrieved from http://arctic.journalhosting.ucalgary.ca/arctic/index.php/arctic/article/view/1349/1374

Castro de la Guardia, L., Derocher, A. E., Myers, P. G., Terwisscha van Scheltinga, A. D., Lunn, N. J. (2013, September). Future sea ice conditions in Western Hudson Bay and consequences for polar bears in the 21st century. *Global Change Biology, 19*(9), 2675–2687. doi:10.111/gcb.12272

Walsh, J. J., Dieterle, D. A., Chen, F. R., Lenes, J. M., Maslowski, W., Cassano, J. J. . . . Christensen, J. (2011). Trophic cascades and future harmful algal blooms within ice-free Arctic Seas north of Bering Strait: A simulation analysis. *Progress in Oceanography, 91*(3), 312–344.

World Wildlife Fund (2012). *Effects of climate change on polar bears.* Retrieved from http://assets.worldwildlife.org/publications/398/files/original/Effects_of_Climate_Change_on_Polar_Bears_fact_sheet.pdf

World Wildlife Fund. (n.d.). *Marine problems: Pollution.* Retrieved from http://wwf.panda.org/about_our_earth/blue_planet/problems/pollution/

APA requires that the references begin on a new page at the end of the essay.

 # MLA

Like APA, MLA style is parenthetical, meaning that it includes in-text citations. However, the reference list is replaced with a works cited list, and the information is presented differently.

MLA in-text citations include the author's surname and page or paragraph number(s).

MLA In-Text Citations

MLA in-text citations include the author's surname(s) and page number(s) in parentheses. Separate the items with a single space; do not use a comma unless you need to include both an author's name and title or separate the author's name from the paragraph number in an electronic source. Do not use the abbreviation *p.* or *pp.* before the page number. When including a page range, omit the repeated numbers over 100 (e.g., 212–47, not 212–247; but 34–37). In most cases, the end punctuation comes after the closing parentheses.

> (Ashton 12)

If the author is named in a signal phrase, only the page number appears in parentheses.

> Ashton found that . . . (12).

Here are more guidelines for MLA in-text citations:

Citation for a direct quotation, paraphrase, or summary: Give the author's surname and page number. The first example has no signal phrase; the second has one. When you use a signal phrase, place the citation at the end of the quotation, not after the author's name.

> During both world wars, the Canadian government often employed masseuses because surgery and medical care were insufficient "to restore severely wounded men" (Cleather ix).

> According to Stambouli and Traversa, "each gallon of gasoline produced and used in an internal combustion engine releases roughly 12 kg of CO_2" (299).

Block quotation: Begin any quotation longer than four typed lines on a new line; indent it half an inch from the left margin and set it double-spaced. Do not use quotation marks. Include the author's surname and page number after the final punctuation mark.

> . (Ellis and Bochner 81–82)

> If you have to cite information from an indirect source, include the phrase *qtd. in* (not italicized; *qtd.* is an abbreviation for *quoted*) before the citation.

Citation referring to an indirect source: If it is necessary to refer to a source found in another work, include the original author in the sentence but use the indirect source in the citation. Use the abbreviation *qtd. in* (not italicized) at the beginning of the citation.

> Francis Bacon observed that language affects our thinking when he said, "words react on the understanding" (qtd. in Lindemann 93).

In the works cited list, give the details for the indirect source (in this example, for Lindemann).

Personal communication, including interviews: Give the person's surname only.

(McWhirter)

Multiple sources in one citation: You may include more than one relevant source in a single citation if your point applies to both. Alphabetize the sources by last name and separate them with a semicolon.

The practices of teaching composition in college have not radically changed in the last few decades (Bishop 65; Williams 6).

 Page 294 discusses MLA notes.

However, if the citation is lengthy, consider moving the entire citation to a note. •——•

If you cite two sources in the same sentence, placing the citation after each one may help with clarity: "One study looked for correlations between GPA and listening to music (Cox and Stevens 757) while another related academic performance to three types of music (Roy 6)."

MLA In-Text Citations by Format

Number or Kind of Authors

Work by one author: Give the author's surname and page number. A book with an author and an editor will typically be cited by author.

(Bloom 112)

Work by two authors: Give the surnames of both authors, with the word *and* before the second name, and the page number:

(Higgins and Wilson-Baptist 44)

Work by three or more authors: Include the surname of the first author followed by the abbreviation *et al.* and page number.

(Terracciano et al. 96)

Two or more works by the same author: Give the author's surname, a shortened version of the work's title, and a page number. Separate the first two items with a comma.

(Foucault, *Power/Knowledge* 37)

Two authors with the same last name: Include the authors' first initials along with the page number. If the authors have the same initial, include their full names instead.

(S. Sinkinson 225; B. Sinkinson 237)

If no author is given, use the name of the group or organization—as a signal phrase, if possible.

Group or organization as author (corporate author): If a document does not have an individual as an author, use the group's or company's name. If possible, include the full name in the sentence to avoid long citations. It is also acceptable to shorten the organization's name and place it in parentheses, accompanied by the page number, in the same manner as a standard author citation.

The United Nations Children's Fund reports that indigenous children are at exceptional risk of becoming refugees (204).

or

Some child protection advocates suggest that indigenous children are at exceptional risk of becoming refugees (UNICEF 204).

Work by an unknown author (including many dictionary and encyclopedia entries): Give the title and the page number. Use the full title if it is short; condense long titles. Distinguish articles from complete works by placing the former in quotation marks.

("Plea to City Hall" 22).

Electronic Sources

The most challenging aspect of citing online documents is that they often lack page numbers. Use the following guidelines to determine how to cite this material.

If you are referring to a website as a whole rather than a specific part, include the author's name within the sentence and do not include a parenthetical citation.

Citation of an entire website: Give the author's surname or website name within the sentence and do not include a parenthetical citation.

In his article, Dillon compares reading practices for print media to those for electronic media.

For electronic documents without page numbers, use paragraph or section numbers if either is given. Insert a comma to separate the author's name from the number and use the abbreviation *par.* or *sec.* (not italicized), respectively.

Citation from a specific passage: Give the specific location of the material. If there are no page numbers, include the relevant paragraph or section numbers preceded by the appropriate abbreviation (*par./pars.* or *sec./secs.*; none are italicized). Insert a comma between the author's surname and the abbreviation. If the reference is specific but nothing in the document is numbered, cite it without a page, paragraph, or section reference.

One firmly entrenched belief is that reading screens will never replace reading books and other print media (Dillon, sec. 1).

Website without an author: Use the site's title (set in italics) to direct readers to the source of any information.

(*LHC Machine Outreach*)

Non-Text Sources

Film, video, audio, TV broadcast, musical recording, and other non-textual media: Give the name of the individual(s) most relevant to your discussion in the text. In the case of a film, this person could be the director, performer, screenwriter, or other contributor. If your focus is on the whole work, use the title. Do not include a parenthetical citation.

Francis Ford Coppola's film *The Conversation* explores the psychology of surveillance.

In the works cited section, the entry would be alphabetized under *C* for *Coppola*, the film's producer.

MLA Works Cited

In MLA style, the works cited section contains complete bibliographical information for a work's in-text citations. Follow these guidelines when creating a works cited list:

- Begin the list on a new page at the end of the essay and number the section as part of the overall work.
- Centre the title ("Works Cited") an inch from the top of the page. Do not underline or bold it.
- Double-space the list, with 1-inch margins.
- Begin each entry flush with the left margin; indent subsequent lines half an inch.
- Alphabetize the list by the first item in each entry, usually the author's surname.
- Capitalize the first letters of all major words in a work's title, even if the source does not.
- Omit words such as *Press, Inc.*, and *Co.* after the publisher's name and the articles (*The* or *A*) before it. Abbreviate *University Press* to *UP* (not italicized).
- Abbreviate months with more than four letters. Use the following abbreviations where appropriate.
  - ○ assn. (association)
  - ○ ch. (chapter)

o ed. (edition)
o P (Press)
o par. (paragraph), pars. (paragraphs)
o pt. (part)
o rev. (revised)
o rpt. (reprint)
o sec. (section)
o U (University)
o vol. (volume)

The standard works cited entry begins with the author's surname followed by his or her complete first name (unless the author has published only initial[s]). Italicize titles of complete works, such as book and journal titles, websites, plays, films, and artistic performances; place quotation marks around titles of articles, essays, book chapters, short stories, poems, web pages, and TV episodes.

Sample book entry: List the book (pamphlet or brochure) information in the following sequence: author, title (italicized), publisher, and year of publication.

> The order for most works cited entries is the author's full name, title of work, and publication details, which vary depending on whether the work is a book, journal article, or electronic document.

Fries, Charles C. *Linguistics and Reading.* Holt, Rinehart and Winston, 1962.

Sample journal entry: List the information in this order: author, title of article (in quotation marks), title of journal (italicized), volume number, issue number, year of publication, and page range.

Valkenburg, Patti M., and Peter Jochen. "Who Visits Online Dating Sites? Exploring Some Characteristics of Online Daters." *Cyber-Psychology and Behavior*, vol. 15, no. 1, 1996, pp. 41–50.

Number or Kind of Authors

Work by one author: See "Sample book entry."

> In a work by two authors, include all names with only the first author's inverted. Use a comma between the first author's first name and the word *and*. With three or more authors, include only the first author's name and use the abbreviation *et al.* to indicate that there are at least three more.

Work by two authors: Invert only the first author's name. Insert a comma before *and*.

Luckner, John, and Reldan Nadler. *Processing the Experience.* Kendall/Hunt, 1992.

Work by three or more authors: Give only the first author's name followed by *et al.* (not italicized).

Festial, Lawrence, et al. *When Economics Fails.* U of Minnesota P, 1956.

Two or more works by the same author: Arrange the works chronologically from earliest to most recent publication. The author's name appears in the first listing only, with three hyphens substituted for it in the additional citation(s).

> Foucault, Michel. *Discipline and Punish: The Birth of the Prison.* Translated by Alan Sheridan. Random House, 1977.
> —. *The History of Sexuality.* Trans. Robert Hurley. 3 vols. Random House, 1978.

Work by two authors with the same last name: Alphabetize by the authors' first names. If two works have the same first author, use the second authors' surnames.

> Srivastava, Sarita, and Margot Francis. "The Problem of 'Authentic Experience.'" *Critical Sociology,* vol. 32, no. 2–3, 2006, pp. 275–307.
> Srivastava, Sarita, and Mary-Jo Nadeau. "From the Inside: Anti-Racism in Social Movements." *New Socialist,* vol. 42, 2003.

Group or organization as author (corporate author): Use the full group name in place of the author's name. If the organization name begins with an article (e.g., *The*), omit it. When the group is both the author and publisher, begin with the document's title and include the organization's name only as the publisher.

> *Guide to Universities & Colleges in Canada.* 2000 ed. Education International, 2000.

When a work has a group rather than an individual as an author, use the group name.

Work without an author, publisher, or date (non-electronic): If the work does not provide an author's name, begin with the title. Use the following abbreviations for missing publication details: *n.p.* means "no publisher"; *n.d.* means "no date" (do not italicize the abbreviations in your citations). Use square brackets to identify any information that isn't from the source and add a question mark if the information may be unreliable.

No author name (unsigned encyclopedia entry):

> "Interveners." *Canadian Encyclopedia.* 1985 ed.

No publisher:

> Webb, Noah. *The Great Haileybury Forest Fire.* n.p. [1971?].

No publishing date:

> Case, Michael. *Opus Dei.* Slipshod P, n.d.

Source Type

Work by an author with an editor or a translator: Begin with the author's name unless you refer primarily to the editor's work (e.g., his or her introduction or notes), as shown in the second example. The original publication date can be included after the title.

> Hawthorne, Nathaniel. *The Scarlet Letter*. 1850. Edited by John Stephen Martin. Broadview, 1995.
>
> Martin, John Stephen, editor. *The Scarlet Letter*, by Nathaniel Hawthorne. 1850. Broadview, 1995.

Follow the same format for a translated work.

> Calvino, Italo. *Why Read the Classics?* Translated by Martin McLaughlin. Pantheon, 1999.

Chapter or other type of selection, such as an essay, in an edited volume: Begin with the author's name and chapter (or essay) title. Follow with the book title and book editor's name, not inverted and preceded by *edited by* (not italicized), the publication information, and the page range.

> The usual order for an essay or other selection in an edited book is author's name, essay title, book title, book editor's name preceded by *edited by*, publication details, and page range.

> Sanders, Douglas E. "Some Current Issues Affecting Indian Government." *Pathways to Self-Determination: Canadian Indians and the Indian State*, edited by Leroy Little Bear, Menno Boldt, and J. Anthony Long, U of Toronto P, 1984, pp. 113–21.

If you use more than one work from the same collection, you can economize by creating one entry for the work as a whole and abbreviated entries for specific works.

Main entry:

> Little Bear, Leroy, Menno Boldt, and J. Anthony Long, editors. *Pathways to Self-Determination: Canadian Indians and the Indian State*. U of Toronto P, 1984.

Specific entry:

> Sanders, Douglas E. "Some Current Issues Affecting Indian Government." Little Bear, Boldt, and Long. 113–21.

Introduction, preface, foreword, or afterword: Give the author of the part being cited followed by the section name (not in quotation marks). The title of the complete work comes next, then the work's author preceded by *by* (not italicized).

> Scholes, Robert. Foreword. *The Fantastic: A Structural Approach to a Literary Genre*, by Tzvetan Todorov, translated by Richard Howard, Cornell UP, 1975, pp. v–xi.

Volume in a multivolume work: State the volume number if you use one work; give the number of volumes used if you refer to more than one.

> Bosworth, A. B., ed. *A Historical Commentary on Arrian's History of Alexander.* Vol. 1. Oxford UP, 1980.

If you used two volumes, *2 vols.* would replace *Vol. 1* in the example. In your essay, the parenthetical reference includes the volume number after the author's name; separate the volume number from the page number with a colon.

Second or subsequent edition of a work: Include the edition number after the title (or editor, translator, etc.).

> Suzuki, David, Aaron Griffiths, and Rebecca Lewontin. *An Introduction to Genetic Analysis.* 4th ed. Freeman, 1989.

Book published before 1900: The publisher's name can be omitted.

> Baring Gould, S. *Old Country Life.* 5th ed. 1895.

Article in a journal: Whether the numbering of the journal continues with each succeeding issue (continuous pagination) or restarts with every new issue, include both the volume and issue numbers if they are available.

> Trew, Johanne Devlin. "Conflicting Visions: Don Messier, Liberal Nationalism, and the Canadian Unity Debate." *International Journal of Canadian Studies*, vol. 26, no. 2, 2002, pp. 41–57.

> Always include the journal's volume and issue numbers in your citation if they are available.

Article in a magazine: Cite the complete date (in day-month-year format) if the magazine is issued every week or every two weeks; include the month and year for magazines published monthly or every two months. If the article breaks off and continues later in the work, give the first page number followed by a plus sign, not the whole page range (e.g., 12+ indicates that the article begins on page 12 and continues somewhere after page 12).

Knapp, Lonny. "Licensing Music to the Film and Television Industries." *Canadian Musician*, Sept/Oct. 2007, pp. 49–56.

Article in a newspaper: Cite the author if given; if not, begin with the title. Give the day, month, and year and then the page number. Precede the page number with the section number or letter if the article is in more than one section. If the article breaks off and continues later in the work, cite the first page number followed by a plus sign, as for a magazine article. A letter to the editor follows the same format and includes *Letter* (not italicized) after the title.

"Lawyer seeks mistrial for client accused of illegal midwifery." *National Post*, 20 Apr. 2003: A8.

Book/movie review: Follow the reviewer's name by the review's title; if there is no title, continue with *Review of* and book/movie title followed by *by* and the author's (director's) name (do not italicize these terms). Conclude with the publication information.

Mihm, Stephen. Review of *Swindled: The Dark History of Food Fraud, from Poisoned Candy to Counterfeit Coffee*, by Bee Wilson. *Business History Review*, vol. 83, no. 2, 2006, pp. 379–81.

Government document: If the author is unknown, begin with the name of the government followed by the agency (e.g., ministry, department, Crown corporation) and document name.

British Columbia, Office of the Auditor General. *Salmon Forever: An Assessment of the Provincial Role in Sustaining Wild Salmon*. Office of the Auditor General of British Columbia, 2005.

Indirect source: Cite the work where you found the citation rather than the original text.

Lindemann, Erika. *A Rhetoric for Writing Teachers*. 4th ed. Oxford UP, 2001.

Personal communication, including interview: Include a description of the communication.

Carr, Emily. Letter to Lawren Harris. 12 December 1940.

Electronic Sources

As online sources often change or even disappear, the MLA recommends that you download or print research material that may become inaccessible. In cases where some relevant information is unavailable (such as page or paragraph numbers), cite what you can so that the reader is able to access the source. Note that an URL is used only if the source would be otherwise hard to locate. (If you need to divide the URL between two lines, break it after single or double slashes.) Including the date of access is optional but can be helpful to your reader.

> Make sure that none of the URLs in your essay, including the references or works cited page, are hyperlinked. They must be in plain text, not underlined or in a different colour.

Sample electronic citation: Include the title of the website after the work's title and then provide the site's publisher or sponsor (use *n.p.* if that name is unavailable). Give the date the website was created or last updated.

> Czekaj, Laura. "Promises Fulfilled: Looking at the Legacy of Thousands of Black Slaves Who Fled to Canada in the 1800s." *Federation for the Humanities and Social Sciences*, 23 May 2014, www.ideas-idees.ca/blog/promises-fulfilled. Accessed 12 Sept. 2016.

Group or organization (e.g., corporate or government) website: If there is no author, use the organization's name.

> Environment Canada. "10 Things You Should Know about Climate Change." 12 Aug. 2009, www.ec.gc.ca/cc/default.asp?lang=En&n= 2F049262–1.

The URL is included because the page would be hard to locate otherwise.

Article in an online-only journal: Online-only journals are cited in the same manner as print journals, except with a DOI or URL. The DOI is preferable if it is available; if using the URL, omit *http://* or *https.//*.

> Rye, B. J., Pamela Elmslie, and Amanda Chalmers. "Meeting a Transsexual Person: Experience within a Classroom Setting." *Canadian On-Line Journal of Queer Studies in Education*, vol. 3, no. 1, 2007, jqstudies.library.utoronto.ca/index.php/jqstudies/ article/view/3269/1444.

Internet article based on a print source and retrieved from a database: In addition to the information required for the print version of a journal article, include the name of the database.

> In addition to the information included in the print version, journal articles retrieved from a database require the database's name.

Barton, Sylvia S. "Discovering the Literature on Aboriginal Diabetes in Canada: A Focus on Holistic Methodologies." *Canadian Journal of Nursing Research*, vol. 40, no. 4, 2008, pp. 26–54. *Ingenta*, www.ingentaconnect.com/content/mcgill/cjnr/2008/00000040/00000004/art00003?crawler=true.

Work online that first appeared in print: Include details of the print source and follow with the title of the website and date of access.

Douglass, Frederick. "My Escape from Slavery." *The Century Illustrated Magazine*, Nov. 1881, pp. 125–31. Electronic Text Center, University of Virginia Library, xroads.virginia.edu/~drbr/douglas.html.

Letter or email: If the letter is published, cite it as you would a work in an edited volume, adding the date of the letter. If it is a personal letter or email, include a description, such as *Received by the author* (if you received it; not italicized) and date.

Barrett, Anthony. "Re: *Lives of the Caesars*." Received by the author, 15 Aug. 2008.

Message posted to an online forum, discussion group, or blog post: Follow the guidelines for "Sample electronic citation." If no title is given, include a generic label after the author's name.

Koolvedge. Comment on "Massacre in Peru." *Adbusters.org*, 8 Aug. 2009, 9:28 a.m., www.adbusters.org/blogs/dispatches/massacre-peru.html#comments.

Non-Text Sources

The general rule for citations of non-text sources is to feature the person(s) most relevant to your discussion, along with a description of their role. For example, if your paper is about actors, you can cite their contribution in a film either alongside or instead of naming the director.

Lecture or other oral presentation: Give the name of the speaker, the title of the presentation, the meeting and/or sponsor (if applicable), date, and location detail. Conclude with *Lecture, Reading*, etc. (not italicized).

Armstrong, Nancy. "Darwin's Paradox." Department of English. David Strong Building, 2 Apr. 2009, University of Victoria, Victoria. Lecture.

Film or video: Begin with the work's title unless you are referring mainly to one person's contribution (for example, a performer or writer). Follow with the name(s) of the most relevant individuals and conclude with the distributor's name and year of release.

Citing the film:

Apocalypse Now. Directed by Francis Ford Coppola. United Artists, 1979.

Citing a specific individual:

Brando, Marlon, performer. *Apocalypse Now*. United Artists, 1979.

Performance (e.g., play, concert): Begin with the title of the performance and follow with the relevant information, usually the writer, director, and main performers. Conclude with the company name, theatre, city, and date of performance.

Macbeth. By William Shakespeare. Directed by Des McAnuff. Performances by Colm Feore and Yanna McIntosh. Stratford Shakespeare Festival Company. Festival Theatre, Stratford, ON. 1 June 2009.

If you are citing one individual's contribution, begin with that person's name (see "Film or video").

Episode from a television or radio series: For a broadcasted episode, use the following order: title of episode (in quotation marks), title of program (italicized), network, call letters of local station, city, and date of broadcast.

"Man of Science, Man of Faith." *Lost*. CTV, CFTO, Toronto, 21 Sept. 2005.

If you watched the episode online, include the season and episode numbers, the site name, and URL.

"Smoke Gets in Your Eyes." *Mad Men*, season 1, episode 1, AMC, 19 July 2007. *Netflix*, www.netflix.com/watch/70143379?trackId=15036065&tctx=0%2C0%2Cefd6765f-0b19-42d1-9e97-f1e33c888817-16461049.

Information relevant to the episode (e.g., the writer or director) follows the episode title; information relevant to the series follows the series title. If you are citing one individual's contribution, begin with that person's name (see "Film or video").

Music: Use the following order: performer (or other most relevant individual), recording title, label, and year of issue.

> Morrison, Van. *Too Long in Exile*, Polydor, 1993.

If you are citing a specific song, place its name in quotation marks after the performer's name; use a period before and after the song's name.

Work of visual art: Use the following order: artist, title (italicized), date of composition (or *n.d.* if this is unavailable), name of institution that contains the work, and city.

> Escher, M. C. *Drawing Hands*. 1948, Cornelius Collection, National Gallery of Art, Washington.

Interview: Begin with the name of the interviewee and follow with *Interview by* (not italicized) and the interviewer's name. Conclude with the publication details.

> Murakami, Haruki. Interview by Maik Grossekathöfer. *Spiegel Online International*, 20 Feb. 2008.

If you are the interviewer, begin with the interviewee, followed by the type of interview (e.g., *Telephone Interview*; not italicized) and date of interview.

MLA Notes

MLA permits either footnotes (at the bottom of the page) or endnotes (at the end of the document) as a way of including information you feel is valuable but does not fit well within the text. You may use notes to explain a point further, to cite multiple sources or related points of interest, or to suggest additional reading. However, use notes sparingly; do not overwhelm or distract the reader from your main text. These notes are indicated by a superscript (raised) number directly to the right and above the word most related to the note or at the end of a phrase; they are numbered consecutively throughout the paper. Format the notes to match the rest of the document by double-spacing and indenting each note.

Exercise **12.1**

This exercise tests your ability to use summary, paraphrase, direct quotation, mixed quotation format, block format, signal phrases, ellipses, brackets, and APA and MLA in-text citations.

I

The excerpts in this part are from the online article "Comets May Have Led to Birth and Death of Dinosaur Era," written by Hillary Mayell and published in *National Geographic News* on 16 May 2002. They are from paragraphs 1–2, 4, and 3, respectively.

1. Paraphrase the following in one or two sentences. Do not use a signal phrase or any direct quotations. Use MLA style for the parenthetical citation.

    Comets slamming into the Earth may be responsible for both the birth and the death of the dinosaur era, an international group of researchers report. There is a considerable amount of evidence that a bolide [a comet or asteroid] collision with Earth triggered the end of the dinosaur era 65 million years ago.

2. Paraphrase the following sentence, but include one direct quotation that is no more than eight words (choose the most appropriate words for the quotation). Use a signal phrase to set up the paraphrase.

    "We have been able to show for the first time that the transition between Triassic life-forms to Jurassic life-forms occurred in a geological blink of an eye," said Paul Olsen, a geologist at the Lamont-Doherty Earth Observatory of Columbia University.

3. Using brackets, grammatically integrate the direct quotation into the complete sentence. Do not use a signal phrase.

    The cause of the end of the dinosaur age might have been "a giant ball of ice, rock, and gases smashed into the supercontinent Pangaea."

II

The following passage is from David Suzuki's article "Saving the Earth," which was published in the 14 June 1999 issue of *Maclean's*; the quotation appears on page 43. Integrate the text as if you planned to use it in an essay. Use a signal phrase and APA style followed by a direct quotation of the passage. In sentence three, omit "oral contraceptives, transoceanic phone calls" and "just to mention a few."

(continued)

In this century, our species has undergone explosive change. Not only are we adding a quarter of a million people to our numbers every day, we have vastly amplified our technological muscle power. When I was born, there were no computers, televisions, jet planes, oral contraceptives, transoceanic phone calls, satellites, transistors or xerography, just to mention a few. Children today look at typewriters, vinyl records and black-and-white televisions as ancient curiosities.

III

1. Paraphrase the following passage, which is from the same Suzuki essay (and the same page) as that quoted in the previous part, using APA style. Include one direct quotation no longer than three words; do not use a signal phrase.
2. Summarize the passage in one sentence of no more than 20 words (there are 54 words in the original); begin with a signal phrase and use APA style. Do not use any direct quotations.

In biological terms, the globe is experiencing an eco-holocaust, as more than 50,000 species vanish annually, and air, water and soil are poisoned with civilization's effluents. The great challenge to the millennium is recognizing the reality of impending ecological collapse, and the urgent need to get on with taking the steps to avoid it.

The following academic article is annotated to show some of the similarities and differences between academic essays and the kind of essays you will write. Academic essays, which usually appear in academic journals and can be accessed electronically through your school's databases, are longer and more complex than most student essays. Many of the challenges they present, however, can be overcome by knowing where to look for information. Following these steps will make the reading process easier:

1. Read the title and abstract to get an idea of the essay's purpose, topic, and results or findings. If the essay includes specific headings, they may also give useful information.
2. Read the introduction, especially the last paragraphs, where important information is placed.
3. Read the conclusion or discussion section (or, if it is not labelled as such, the last few paragraphs) in which the findings are summarized and made relevant, applying the reading strategies discussed on page 5.
4. If you know the essay will be crucial to your own research, go back and read the other sections closely.
5. Before reading the essay, review the questions on page 6.

Sample Professional Essay: MLA

What Lies Deep in the Unconscious:
A Psychoanalytical Scrutiny of Harry Potter
in J. K. Rowling's Harry Potter Series

Kaustav Chanda

ABSTRACT

Since the inception of its epical journey, Joanne Katherine Rowling's Harry Potter series has come a long way to become a phenomenon in the domain of children's literature, intriguing readers and critics alike, raising questions regarding its nature [and] its viability for children, and sparking debates among scholars around the world over the social, cultural, political, and psychological subtexts in the series. The paper intends to address the issues of sexuality and desire in J.K. Rowling's Harry Potter saga in the light of the psychoanalytical theories propounded by Sigmund Freud, focusing on the psychosexual development of Harry Potter in the series. The paper intends to unveil how his behavioural patterns and actions have, as their roots, the functioning of id, ego, and the superego, as well as how he copes . . . with unbearable impulses, or how he succumbs to them. The paper seeks to explore the Oedipal anxieties and desires inherent in the protagonist of the story, delving deeper into his unconscious, digging up his past, analyzing how his position in the several social strata or structures, his families, both at Hogwarts and the Dursleys, that are again microcosms of the larger structure of the wizarding and the non-magical worlds, his education and upbringing have impacted the formation of his identity.

Many academic essays and research papers begin with an abstract. Do not quote from the abstract but from the body of the essay.

[1] To read J.K. Rowling's Harry Potter series is a journey—a journey beyond the narrow periphery of reality, to embark on a joyride into the realms of the fantasia, with wizards and witches with their magical wands the waving of which makes the impossible look easy and achievable, dangerous quests into the unknown, into places where dragons, chimeras, griffins, and werewolves are no longer the stuffs of myths and legends. Paradoxically, having magical blood coursing through the veins of the characters in the world of Rowling does not make them anything else than human, and it is easily perceivable that the magical world operates on the same principles on which our world, the

non-magical, mundane, "normal" world runs. Their psychologies are in no way different from those of ours, and therefore, it will not be a sacrilege to subject the series to a psychological scrutiny, though definitely it will be an arduous task to see how desires are sublimated, or repressed, or denied, as in the words of Sigmund Freud himself:

> When I set myself the task of bringing to light what human beings keep hidden within them, . . . by what they say and what they show, I thought the task was a harder one than it really is. He that has eyes to see and ears to hear may convince himself that no mortal can keep a secret. If his lips are silent, he chatters with his fingertips; betrayal oozes out of him at every pore. And thus the task of making conscious the most hidden recesses of mind is one which is quite possible to accomplish. (Freud, *Dora* 23)

> Is this a quotation or a paraphrase? How do you know?

[2] When, in *Harry Potter and the Philosopher's Stone*, we meet Harry for the first time, Rowling describes her protagonist as a malnourished boy of 11, ill-treated by his only living relatives, a complete non-entity in the Dursley family:

> Perhaps it had something to do with living in a dark cupboard, but Harry had always been small and skinny for his age. He looked even smaller and skinnier than he really was because all he had to wear were old clothes of Dudley's, and Dudley was about four times bigger than he was. Harry had a thin face, knobbly knees, black hair, and bright green eyes. He wore round glasses held together with a lot of scotch tape because of all the times Dudley had punched him on the nose. The only thing Harry liked about his appearance was a very thin scar on his forehead that was shaped like a bolt of lightning. (14)

> How easy is it to see what Harry looks like based on this description? Writers often use a description like this so that the reader can visualize something and it becomes real.

[3] Therefore, from the very onset, we find him neglected and abused by his family. He is given a broom cupboard to use as a bedroom, hand-me-down [clothes] to wear, and leftovers to eat. He is treated no better than a dog that has strayed into the beautifully organized domestic domain of the Dursleys. He watches ruefully how his Aunt Petunia spoils her son, Dudley, and turns often deaf ears to Harry's complaints against him. On the other hand, he is subject to menial labour under constant

threats of physical punishment, especially from his uncle, Vernon Dursley, if he fails to carry out any task assigned to him. Maybe that is why he could fully understand the plight of Dobby the House-Elf and decides to help him gain his freedom from slavery in *Harry Potter and the Chamber of Secrets*. In fact, Vernon Dursley at one point of time blurts out that, when they took Harry into their family, he thought of squeezing magic out of him—an act that has similarities with the threats of castration. Also, the Dursleys let Dudley bully him, which he does with relish. Therefore, if we consider Petunia as Harry's mother-substitute, we see that Harry's libidinal drives directed towards her remain unsatisfied because of the fear of two physically greater rivals, Dudley and Uncle Vernon. The only time the wall between Harry and Petunia seems to breach is when the Dursleys depart with the wizards to a safe hideout: "She stopped and looked back. For a moment Harry had the strangest feeling that she wanted to say something to him; she gave him an odd, tremulous look and seemed to teeter on the edge of speech, but, then, with a little jerk of her head, she bustled out of the room after her husband and son" (*Deathly Hallows* 40–41).

By using direct quotations from Rowlings's books, the author supports his arguments and adds to the credibility of the essay.

[4] After Petunia, it is Molly Weasley who comes closest to replace Harry's mother. I have mentioned Petunia because, being Harry's maternal aunt, she is naturally expected to be a surrogate mother to Harry. Throughout the series we see Molly being extremely attentive towards Harry's needs, the way Petunia cares for Dudley. She, as a matter of fact, seems more caring and loving towards Harry than her own children. I wonder if that is because Harry is famous, and that she has always wanted to be acknowledged for taking care of him like his mother and have a share in his glory. I know that this argument may infuriate some of the avid fans of the series, but does she show such tenderness to the Weasley twins or even Ron? Is it only pity for Harry as he is an orphan? In *Harry Potter and the Deathly Hallows*, the horcrux echoes Ron's unconscious, which believes his mother to prefer [Harry] over him, by looking deep into his feelings. This may be discarded as Ron's imagination, but obviously he has seen how Harry is lavishly showered with attention from his mother. Sigmund Freud, in *Three Essays on the Theory of Sexuality*, argues that the [love the] mother holds for the child can also border on sexual desire:

Chandra acknowledges that his points may not be approved of by some readers, but he supports his argument with a question designed to encourage the reader to accept his point of view.

A mother's love for the infant she suckles and cares for is something far more profound than her later affection for the growing child. It is in the nature of a completely satisfying love-relation, which not only fulfils every mental wish but also every physical need; and if it represents one of the forms of attainable human happiness, that is in no little measure due to the possibility it offers of satisfying, without reproach, wishful impulses which have long been repressed and which must be called perverse. (*Essentials* 51–52)

As this is an essay written by someone with an advanced degree, paragraphs do not necessarily follow the structure you are taught. As you become a more proficient writer and you are aware of the rules governing writing, you may also be able to adapt essays according to your own style.

[5] Therefore, Molly Weasley's desire for Harry may be because of the fact that she is always infatuated with powerful and famous people, like the celebrated author, Gilderoy Lockhart, for whom she has always nursed a soft spot. In *Harry Potter and the Chamber of Secrets*, when her husband, Arthur Weasley, has a heated argument with Lucius Malfoy, she warns him: "You be careful, Arthur. The family's trouble, don't go biting off more than you can chew" (47), to which he snaps back: "So you don't think I'm a match for Lucius Malfoy?" (47). What I have noticed [is] that there is always a tendency in her to impose herself in the role of Harry's mother and undermine everybody else's affection and concern for him. When Sirius, Harry's godfather, tries to explain to Harry the modus operandi of the Order of the Phoenix, she gets impatient and forbids him to tell Harry more than he must know, despite the obvious fact that Harry has dealt with greater risks before, and that it is Sirius who is his guardian. In order to stop Sirius from giving Harry some classified information regarding the order, and to assert her presence in Harry's life, she accuses Sirius of being a reckless godfather who treats Harry as if he is Harry's father and his best friend, James, and not a young boy. She goes on until Lupin reminds her pointedly that she is not the only one who cares for Harry. When Harry is given a choice in this matter, he chooses to listen to Sirius. He feels inwardly guilty as she has said that he is as good as any of her sons. Harry's desire for her attention is reciprocated, but at the same time he feels impatient with her "mollycoddling." Molly Weasley's animosity towards Hermione is triggered when, in *Harry Potter and the Goblet of Fire*, Rita Skeeter, a journalist, spreads rumours about Hermione being an opportunist seductress of Harry. Her desire to be closest to Harry is

sublimated by her visible concern for him. There are numerous other instances when Molly Weasley appears inclined to keep treating Harry like a child. Even in the face of imminent danger, she feels it safer to conceal certain truths from him, like Sirius's escape from Azkaban, hardly heeding the fact that Harry must not be caught off guard by a mass murderer.

[6] Harry experiences his first relationship with Cho Chang. Although Harry has known and fancied her for years, it is in his fourth year at Hogwarts when he becomes aware of his longings for Cho. He asks her to be [his] partner at the Yule Ball and is politely turned down as she has already chosen Cedric Diggory as her partner. His desires get thwarted by Diggory whom he has so far liked, and admired. The boy whom he previously thought to have been more like a champion than himself, and of whom he was hardly ever jealous, becomes suddenly a rival. For Harry, Cedric becomes just a pretty boy with a bird's brain. Despite warming up to him and being distraught by his death, Harry's envy for Cedric's charisma never really leaves him. The fact that Cho actually chose Cedric over him hangs heavy on his mind even after Cedric's death, and after he and Cho become romantically involved with each other a year after Cedric's death. In *Harry Potter and the Order of the Phoenix*, when Cho wants to talk to him regarding Cedric's death, Harry gets irritated and refuses to talk about him. In another occasion, when they kiss each other, Harry realizes that she has been crying. He assumes quite childishly that maybe he is not competent enough. Also, he has to endure slights on his personal appearance when with Cho, from a group of Slytherins which obviously hurts his self-esteem, making him think that Cho was better off with Cedric: "Urgh, Chang, I don't think much of your taste . . . at least Diggory was good-looking" (*Order of the Phoenix* 614). At Madam Puddifoot's tea-shop, Harry watches Roger Davies kissing his girlfriend, with apprehension, feeling that Davies is setting a standard with which Cho may wish him to compete, and as if to confirm his fears, she informs Harry that she turned down Davies when he asked her out on a date. Harry interprets this to be Cho's consideration of him as an option, second to Roger Davies. The desire for the mother, according to Sigmund Freud, is diverted to other girls as the ego ideal

> Here Chandra inserts his opinion but does not support it with evidence. He assumes that adults who have read the book will agree with him.

prohibits the realization of the id. But despite that, a man looks for the qualities he admires in his mother, in his beloved. Harry's relationship with Cho does not last as she does not have qualities which Lily, Harry's mother, had—bravery, kindness, and a deep understanding of the human nature. Cho not only rages against Hermione after suspecting her to be the centre of affection for Harry, but also supports her friend, Marietta, who betrays every member of the secret group formed within Hogwarts, Dumbledore's Army, to Dolores Umbridge. She obviously lacks Hermione's patience and Ginny's strength, and Harry soon gets disillusioned with her.

[7] Harry meets Ginny Weasley for the first time at the King's Cross station. They meet again when, a year later, Harry visits the Burrow in *Harry Potter and the Chamber of Secrets*. We are told from the very beginning that Ginny fancies Harry. On the other hand, Harry seems to be oblivious [to the] truth, or he may simply have been indifferent. It is not until his sixth year at Hogwarts . . . that he [realizes he] is romantically inclined towards Ginny, a feeling that triggers when he comes across Ginny and Dean kissing [in] a deserted corridor and immediately wants to tear Dean limb from limb. He tries sublimation by trying hard to assume that his feelings for Ginny are simply older brotherly. In his dreams he sees himself replacing Dean in the act of kissing Ginny. After getting into a relationship with her, he ends it soon as he knows that the path ahead of him is dangerous. A boy, being jealous of his father, actually tries to emulate him, and imbibe his qualities, so that he can take his place in his mother's affections. Harry does what his father, James Potter, had done, that is, shield his family against danger, even at the cost of his own life and happiness. He ends the relationship to shield Ginny from any harm or disappointment. He never really gets out of it. He kisses Ginny on his seventeenth birthday, gets angry when Krum praises her beauty, and feels uncomfortable when he overhears Ginny's ex-boyfriend Dean expressing concern for her. At the wedding of Fleur and Bill, he imagines Ginny to be married to a tall, faceless man, and is overwhelmed with sadness. He sees the shadow of Molly Weasley in Ginny's eyes and is stunned by the likeness. With Ginny, . . . Harry's search to find a mother-substitute [ends].

[8] William Wordsworth, in his autobiographical poem, *The Prelude* speaks about the happiness and contentment of an infant at her mother's breast:

> No outcast he, bewildered and depress'd;
> Along his infant veins are interfused
> The gravitation and the filial bond
> Of nature, that connects him with the world. (lines 263–66)

[9] Not only Harry's, but also the behaviours, attitudes, outlooks, and tastes of all the characters in the Harry Potter series are rooted in the presence or the absence of the mother-figure in their lives. The series becomes a quest for love, and it is love, sexual or asexual, and the capability to love which defines their identities. Harry's messiah complex, Ron's volatile and insecure temperament, Voldemort's cruelty and narcissism, and Severus Snape's jealousies, all are deeply rooted in the role their mothers have played in their lives, as Sigmund Freud in his letter to Wilhelm Fliess emphasized on the universality of his notion of the Oedipus complex:

> A single idea of general value dawned on me. I have found, in my own case too [the phenomenon of] being in love with my mother and jealous of my father, and now I consider it a universal event in early childhood . . . if this is so, we can understand the gripping power of Oedipus Rex . . . the Greek legend seizes upon a compulsion which everyone recognizes because he senses its existence within himself. (Freud, "Letter")

Here the author clearly states his opinion. While people may not agree with it, he supports it with a paraphrase from Freud. Do you think this is an adequate closing?

Works Cited

Freud, Sigmund. *Dora: An Analysis of a Case of Hysteria.* Simon & Schuster, 1963.
—. *The Essentials of Psycho-Analysis: The Definitive Collection of Sigmund Freud's Writings.* Translated by James Stratchey, edited by Anna Freud. Penguin Books, 1991.
—. Letter to Wilhelm Fliess, 15 Oct. 1897. www.freudfile.org/psychoanalysis/arcvhive_4.html.
Rowling, J. K. *Harry Potter and the Chamber of Secrets.* Bloomsbury, 1998.
—. *Harry Potter and the Deathly Hallows.* Bloomsbury, 2007.

—. *Harry Potter and the Goblet of Fire*. Bloomsbury, 2000.

—. *Harry Potter and the Order of the Phoenix*. Bloomsbury, 2003.

—. *Harry Potter and the Philosopher's Stone*. Bloomsbury, 1997.

Wordsworth, William. *The Prelude* 1805. *William Wordsworth: The Major Works*, edited by Stephen Gill, Oxford UP, 2008.

Chandra, K. (2014). What lies deep in the unconscious: A psychoanalytical scrutiny of Harry Potter in J. K. Rowling's Harry Potter series. *International Journal of Multidisciplinary Approach and Studies*, 1(6), pp. 454–461.

 # Chapter Review Questions

1. Why are citations needed in an essay?
2. What are some of the different citation styles?
3. Can you combine different citation styles? Why or why not?
4. Why is it important to use the most current style guide when documenting your sources?
5. What is the difference between an in-text citation and a references/works cited entry?
6. What order is used in the references/works cited to list the sources used in your essay?
7. What are the basic elements of APA in-text citations? How does the use of a signal phrase affect this list?
8. What are the basic elements of MLA in-text citations? How does the use of a signal phrase affect this list?
9. When adding information to a references/works cited page, why do you need all the relevant information?
10. How can documentation add to the credibility of your essay?

PART FOUR
Grammar

13

Sentence Essentials

This chapter and the next two introduce the basic concepts for understanding and using English grammar and punctuation. We begin with the parts of speech and then sentences, phrases, and clauses. Chapter 14 offers guidelines for using certain punctuation marks, and Chapter 15 discusses how to craft grammatically correct sentences.

Grammatical Groundwork

Using correct grammar adds to your credibility as a writer and helps the reader understand exactly what you are saying, as you intended it. Grammar errors, on the other hand, make your work look unfinished. Many people love nothing more than to find grammatical errors in other people's work. Newspapers, magazines, and websites receive countless messages from irate consumers who are upset with these errors and feel the need to correct them. Most college and university instructors are not gleefully waiting to pounce on your grammar mistakes, but avoiding the most common ones leaves a very good impression.

To understand how bad grammar can affect your writing and hence your credibility (and increase your reader's annoyance metre), you need to know the building blocks used to create any written document. Unfortunately, in Canada, many of us are taught only the very basics of grammar. We are taught rules such as "Don't start a sentence with *because*" and "Do not say *me and Jenny* but *Jenny and I*." However, most grammar rules are more advanced than that. To delve into the more complex rules, we need to revisit the parts of speech.

Parts of Speech

Nouns

We all remember that **nouns** are people (*Brad*), places (*St John, New Brunswick*), and things (*desk*). However, nouns also include qualities (*honour*), concepts (*terabytes*), and the categories in Table 13.1.

> A **noun** is the name of a person, place, thing, or idea.

Exercise 13.1

Add your own examples for each type of noun in Table 13.1. If you are unsure what type your example is, look it up in a dictionary.

Some nouns can be proper or common, depending on how they are used in a sentence. For example, *dad* is a common noun in the following sentence because it is not used as a person's name.

My dad is an engineer.

However, it is a proper noun (as is *Clair*) in the following sentence:

Dad, I would like to introduce you to Clair.

TABLE 13.1 Noun Types and Functions

Type	Function	Example
Proper	A name; usually begins with a capital letter.	*Bob; Lambton College*
Common	Refers to a general group; is not capitalized.	*dog; orange; air*
Concrete	A physical object or something experienced with the senses.	*house; cement; lamp*
Abstract	Concept, idea, or abstraction.	*Wi-Fi; terabyte; charitable*
Count	Items that can be counted; often written with an –s or –es. Sometimes the word forms change. Sometimes requires a number to indicate the amount because the form does not change.	*boat/boats; cat/cats* *person/people; child/children 1 shrimp/5 shrimp; 1 moose/10 moose*
Non-count	Items that can't be counted, such as liquids.	*air (molecules of air,* not *airs); water (drops/bottles/glasses of water,* not *waters)*
	Can be singular or plural.	*scissors; mail*
Collective	Groups that can either be identified as singular or plural; if the individuals in the group are acting as one unit, use the singular verb; if they are acting separately, use a plural verb.	*jury; staff; team*

Subject–verb agreement is the principle that a sentence's verb must match its subject in number (i.e., a singular subject requires a singular verb, and a plural subject requires a plural verb).

Subject–verb agreement with collective nouns can be challenging. Consider these sentences (the verb is underlined).

The jury <u>is</u> unanimous.

The jury members have decided one verdict and are acting together. Therefore, the singular verb *is* is used.

The jury <u>are</u> divided in their opinions.

The plural verb *are* is used in this sentence because the members cannot agree on one verdict; they are referred to as individuals.

 For more on subject–verb agreement with collective nouns, see page 367.

Exercise **13.2**

Identify the nouns and noun types in the following sentences.

1. The children built a large snow fort.
2. The doors were slammed closed by the wind.
3. The women present were all wearing hats.
4. I would like five glasses of water, please.
5. I bought a hard drive that has five terabytes of memory.
6. I went to Niagara Falls yesterday.
7. I graduated from Red River College last summer.
8. My job as assistant manager is very challenging.
9. King Arthur's Knights of the Round Table were loyal and chivalrous.
10. Learning a new language is difficult. Learning to speak Chinese is especially so for English speakers.

Pronouns

Using too many nouns in a sentence can be repetitive and confusing for the reader. Consider this sentence:

> Tom said that Tom was going to Tom's mother's house to give Tom's mother a present.

There are so many Toms that the reader may wonder how many people are involved. **Pronouns**, which replace nouns, make the sentence much clearer:

> Tom said that he was going to his mother's house to give her a present.

Writers have to ensure that the use of pronouns does not baffle the reader. Here is an unclear pronoun reference.

> Sarah told Jill that she failed the exam.

Who failed the exam, Sarah or Jill? In this case, you need to use a name rather than a pronoun, such as

> Sarah told Jill that Sarah failed the exam.

Pronouns can be found at the beginning of sentences (subject pronouns) or near the end of a sentence (object pronouns). They can indicate ownership (possessive pronouns) or refer to the person already discussed (**reflexive pronouns**; see Table 13.2). Here are some examples:

A **pronoun** is a word that takes the place of a noun (in this case, also called the antecedent) in a sentence.

A **reflexive pronoun** ends with–*self* (e.g., *himself*). This type of pronoun can be used only if the person has been referred to earlier in the sentence.

TABLE 13.2 Types of Pronouns

Subject	Object	Possessive	Reflexive
I	me	my, mine	myself
you	you	your, yours	yourself
he	him	his	himself
she	her	her, hers	herself
it	it	its	itself
we	us	our, ours	ourselves
you	you	your, yours	yourselves
they	them	their, theirs	themselves

Yuko and I went to the store.
This is her book. This book is hers.

(Notice there is no apostrophe with possessive pronouns.)

Ahmed drove himself to the hospital.
My grandmother gave my husband and me a wedding present.

To determine whether to use *I* or *me* in the above sentence, eliminate "my husband and." You will then see that *me* is the correct pronoun here.

My grandmother gave me a wedding present.

Indefinite Pronouns

An **indefinite pronoun** (i.e., *each, either, one, everyone*) refers to an unspecified individual or group. Most are considered singular and therefore take a singular verb.

Indefinite pronouns, such as *everybody*, *someone*, and *each*, are often used to indicate people in general. As Table 13.3 shows, some are always singular, some are always plural, and some can be both.

Exercise 13.3

Determine whether the underlined pronoun is correct or incorrect in the following sentences.

1. Abiha and me are going to the movies tonight.
2. Greg and myself believe that the test results are inaccurate.
3. Can you deliver this to Lara and her?
4. We need to buy the dog it's own water dish.
5. This car belongs to ourselves.

TABLE 13.3 Common Indefinite Pronouns

Singular	Plural	Both
everyone	all	none (not one or not any)
everybody	more	
someone	most	
each	some	
anyone	any	
anybody		
no one		
nobody		
either		
neither		

When you write sentences using nouns and pronouns, you must make sure that the pronouns agree in number and gender with the nouns that are being replaced (the **antecedents**). If a noun is singular, the pronoun must be as well. For example, in the sentence

> A student left <u>his</u> or <u>her</u> textbook in the classroom.

the noun *student* is singular, so you must use a singular pronoun to replace it. Because you don't know whether the student is male or female, use *his or her*.

There is some debate about whether to use the pronoun *their* in this case. The "singular *their*" is gradually becoming accepted in informal situations, but it is still best to use the singular pronouns to replace singular nouns in academic writing. It is always best to check with your instructors to ensure you meet their expectations.

The **antecedent** in a sentence is the noun that the pronoun replaces.

 The pronouns *his* or *her* are often used to make language gender-inclusive; see pages 371–2.

Exercise 13.4

Fill in the blanks with the correct pronouns.

1. All students must submit _____ assignments on time.
2. Both Kenji and Thomas gave _____ approval.
3. A police officer must understand the laws _____.
4. An employee must sign _____ contract before beginning to work at this company.
5. The members must cast _____ ballots before the deadline.

Verbs

Most children are taught that **verbs** are action words. These include *run*, *jump*, *drive*, *eat*, and *sing*. Some kinds of action are not necessarily visible but are interior or mental (e.g., *think*, *imagine*, and *suggest*). The verbs in the examples are italicized:

> The chauffeur *drove* us to the movie premiere.

Verbs such as *feel*, *sound*, and *appear* are states of being.

> The conductor *feels* that the concert should be postponed.

Verbs also link the subject of a sentence to a description of it. These **linking verbs** include all forms of the *to be* verb (*is*, *are*, *was*, *were*, *seems*, etc.) and words such as *look*.

> Phillipe *is* very articulate.

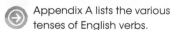

Verbs may be modified by adverbs or adverbial phrases (an adverb with two or more words). Compare these two sentences (the adverbs are in bold):

> He *acted* the part of Hamlet **splendidly**.
> He *acted* **sick** by staying home from school.

See page 314 for more on adverbs.

In the first sentence, *acted* is an action verb and is modified by the adverb *splendidly*. In the second sentence, *acted* is a linking verb—he acted [behaved as one who is] sick and thus is followed by a **subject complement**, the adjective *sick*.

Sometimes verbs are composed of more than one word, called **helping** or **auxiliary verbs**. The most common helping verbs are forms of *to be* (*am, are, is, was, were, will be*, etc.) and *to have* (*have, has, had*, etc.).

> Sukhdeep *will be* going home for the holidays.
> You *have* had ample time to complete the assignment.

A **modal verb** is placed before the main verb to express necessity, obligation, possibility, or probability. These modal verbs are *can, could, may, might, ought to, shall, should, will,* and *would*.

> You *should* wash your car before winter comes.

Exercise **13.5**

Read the following sentences and determine whether the verb (which is italicized) is an action word, state of being, or linking verb.

1.   She *is* beautiful.
2.   The music *sounds* wonderful.
3.   He *drives* to the fairgrounds every weekend.
4.   It *seems* as if he were floating on air.
5.   She *ran* the race in record time.

Modifiers: Adjectives and Adverbs

Adjectives, Articles, and Determiners

An **adjective** modifies, or describes, a noun or a pronoun. It can come before or after the noun or pronoun and be more than one word. **Articles** (*a*, *an*, and *the*) and determiners (such as *this* and *her*) also act as adjectives. An adjective answers the following questions: Which? What kind? How many?

> An **adjective** describes a noun or pronoun and usually precedes the noun it modifies, but it can also follow a linking verb, where it modifies the subject. An **article** (*a*, *an*, or *the*) precedes and modifies a noun.

Let's look at a few examples.

The tall woman is beautiful.

The, *tall*, and *beautiful* tell us about the woman.

The dusty, old sports car sat in the broken-down barn.

The, *dusty*, *old*, and *sports* describe the noun *car*; *the* and *broken-down* describe the noun *barn*.

He is an expert.

The adjectives *an* and *expert* describe the pronoun *he*.

Nouns can also become adjectives when they are used to modify other nouns.

The CN Tower was the world's highest freestanding structure for many years.

CN is normally a noun—as in "CN is a prosperous company"—but is an adjective in this sentence because it tells us which tower. *World's* modifies the noun *structure* and is thus also an adjective here.

Adverbs

An **adverb** modifies a verb, adjective, adverb, or sentence.

An **adverb** describes verbs, adjectives, other adverbs, and even complete sentences. Adverbs often end in *–ly*, such as *really, quickly,* and *sharply.* They answer these questions: When? Where? Why? How? To what degree? How much?

> Usain Bolt runs <u>quickly</u>.

The adverb *quickly* modifies the verb *runs.*

> Usain Bolt runs <u>very quickly</u>.

In this sentence, both *very* and *quickly* are adverbs. *Quickly* modifies the verb *runs,* and *very* modifies the adverb *quickly.*

> Some NBA players look <u>very</u> short on court.

See the next section for more information on conjunctions.

In this sentence, *very* modifies the adjective *short.*

Some adverbs can also act as conjunctions to connect two **independent clauses** or two complete thoughts. These are most commonly called **conjunctive adverbs.**

An **independent clause** is a group of words that has a subject and a predicate and can therefore stand alone as a complete sentence. A **conjunctive adverb** (e.g., *however, therefore,* or *thus*) joins two independent clauses. It is preceded by a semicolon and usually followed by a comma.

> Richard was hired on Monday; <u>however</u>, he was fired on Tuesday.

Note the semicolon separating the **clauses** and the comma after *however.*

Be careful not to confuse adverbs with regular conjunctions (such as *and, or,* and *but*), which join words, phrases, and clauses. A conjunctive adverb joins two independent clauses.

A **clause** is a group of words containing both a subject and a predicate. A clause may be independent or dependent.

Joiners: Prepositions and Conjunctions

Prepositions

 Pages 320-2 discuss phrases and clauses in more detail.

A **preposition** is a small word or short phrase that often refers to place or time, such as *before, after, between, in front, except,* and *over.* It joins the noun or pronoun that follows to the rest of the sentence. Table 13.4 contains common prepositions.

A **preposition** joins a noun or pronoun to the rest of the sentence, adding information.

Prepositions introduce prepositional phrases, which function as adjectives or adverbs depending on what part of speech they modify. A prepositional phrase never contains the simple subject of the sentence. In the following examples, the preposition is italicized and the prepositional phrase is underlined.

 See pages 320-1 for more on prepositional phrases.

> The letters are *in* <u>the attic</u>.
> *During* <u>the summer vacation</u>, she planted trees.
> They laughed *at* <u>him</u>.

TABLE 13.4 Common Prepositions

about	beside(s)	like	since
above	between	near	than
across	beyond	next (to)	through
after	by	of	throughout
against	despite	off	to
along	down	on	toward(s)
among	during	onto	under
around	except	opposite	until
as	for	out	up
at	from	outside (of)	upon
before	in	over	with
behind	inside	past	within
below	into	regarding	without

Conjunctions

A **conjunction** is a word or phrase that connects words, phrases, and clauses of equal or unequal weight or importance. In other words, conjunctions can join two complete thoughts, an incomplete thought and a complete thought, or groups of words.

A **coordinating conjunction** joins equal units—word to word, phrase to phrase, clause to clause. An important use of these words is to join independent clauses in compound sentences. *For, and, nor, but, or, yet,* and *so* (collectively known as FANBOYS) are coordinating conjunctions.

Bob is planning to go skiing this weekend, <u>but</u> Susie is going to a spa.

In this compound sentence, there are two complete thoughts: "Bob is planning to go skiing this weekend." and "Susie is going to the spa." The coordinating conjunction we use depends on whether we are adding ideas (*and*), contrasting them (*but, yet*), or showing a contrary relationship (*so*). Note the comma before the conjunction.

A **subordinating conjunction** joins unequal units. You can join a **dependent clause** (meaning that the thought is unclear unless you join it to a complete one) to an independent clause (a complete thought). In the following examples, the subordinating conjunction is italicized and the dependent clause

A **conjunction** is a word that joins words, phrases, or clauses. A **coordinating conjunction** joins equal units, such as two independent clauses. A **subordinating conjunction** joins a dependent clause, which contains less important information, to an independent clause, which contains more important information.

 See page 320 for a discussion of compound sentences.

A **dependent clause** is a group of words that contains a subject and a predicate but expresses an incomplete thought. It needs more information to form a complete sentence.

For a list of common subordinating conjunctions, see page 326.

is underlined. When a dependent clause is placed before an independent clause, as in the second example, a comma needs to separate the two.

> I went to the store *because* I needed milk.
> *Because* I needed milk, I went to the store.

Notice that the second sentence begins with *because*. As long as you complete your thought, you can begin a sentence with *because, while, since,* or *although*. However, if you don't include an independent clause, your reader will wonder what the rest of the idea is.

Correlative conjunctions occur in pairs and require parallel structure.

> She will <u>either</u> go to college <u>or</u> take a year off to travel.
> <u>Both</u> Nicola and Dimitri enjoy opera.

A **correlative conjunction** is a two-part grammatical unit that joins parts of a sentence; both must be used to complete the sentence.

Exercise **13.6**

This exercise is a take on the game Mad Libs. Your instructor divides the class into four or eight groups and assigns each a part of speech (noun, verb, adjective, or adverb). Each group comes up with 10 examples of its respective part. Try to think of unusual or funny words. Keeping your textbook closed, decide the order you will use your words. Choose one member of the class to read the following sentences. As the blanks come up, one member of the part of speech group will read the group's chosen word. For example, in the first sentence, the "verb group" provides its chosen word at the first blank, then the "adjective group" at the second, and so on until the sentence is complete. The idea isn't to try to make sense but to create strange sentences that are grammatical.

1. If you do not ____ your ____ ____, someone might ____ ____ your ____.
                   verb   adj noun   adv verb   noun
2. We all occasionally ____ ____, but some ____ ____ ____their ____ every day.
                       verb adv   noun (pl) adv verb   noun
3. The ____ ____ looked ready to ____ ____ into the ____ ____.
       adj noun   verb adv   adj noun
4. Before you ____ your ____ ____, it's best to ____ your ____ ____.
              verb   adj noun   verb   noun adv
5. The ____ ____ that ____ on the ____ ____ ____.
       adj noun   verb   noun verb adv

Exercise **13.7**

In the following article, identify
   five nouns
   two pronouns
   six verbs

three adjectives
two adverbs
four prepositions
two conjunctions

Justin Trudeau, Canada's newly elected prime minister, must be the only 43-year-old who is ecstatic to be returning to the house he grew up in.

Canada's new premier has had to shake off his privileged background. The son of the country's iconic 16-year PM Pierre Trudeau, Justin was born in the Canadian prime minister's residence at 24 Sussex Drive. However, there are some aspects of his evolving personality, after a lifetime in the media spotlight, that are just now coming to the fore.

As ever, ahead of the zeitgeist, British comedian John Oliver lampooned Trudeau's changing image on the eve of Canada's federal election.

"If you do a Google image search on him you can find every poor fashion choice that he has ever made. From a 90's boyband member one week before entering rehab, to an LL Bean sweater model who just underwent a lobotomy to Johnny Depp's evil twin," Oliver said on his late-night comedy show *Last Week Tonight*.

In March 2012, Trudeau entered the Canadian psyche not as the son of a much-loved former prime minister but as a fighter, literally. He beat Conservative senator Patrick Brazeau in a charity boxing match, giving his opponent a bloody nose in the final round.

Paton, C. (2015, October 21). Justin Trudeau: Boxer, practical joker, "evil Johnny Depp" and now Liberal Canadian prime minister. *International Business Times*. Retrieved from http://www.ibtimes.co.uk/justin-trudeau-boxer-practical-joker-evil-johnny-depp-now-liberal-canadian-prime-minister-1525057

Sentences

In academic writing, you must always use full sentences. Knowing the parts of speech is necessary, as sentences are built from them, but you must also know the elements of sentences (see Table 13.5). For example, one way to examine a sentence is to identify the **complete subject** and the complete predicate. "I ran" has the subject *I* and the predicate *ran*. Therefore, it is a **complete sentence**. It is also an example of a simple sentence, as it contains one subject and one predicate. (Note that nouns and pronouns can be both the subject of a sentence

A **complete subject** is the subject of a sentence plus its modifiers. A **complete sentence** contains at least one subject and one predicate and expresses a complete thought.

TABLE 13.5   Definitions of Sentence Components

Element	Definition	Example
Simple subject (SS)	The noun or pronoun that performs the action of the verb (the "doer" of the action).	The hungry <u>twins</u> ate all the sandwiches. (The noun *twins* is the simple subject. We ignore the adjectives *the* and *hungry*.)
Complete subject (S)	The simple subject of the sentence, plus its modifiers. It answers the reader's question, "Who or what is this about?"	<u>The hungry twins</u> ate all the sandwiches. (For the complete subject, we include both the adjectives and the noun.)
Simple predicate (SP)	The complete verb of the sentence.	The hungry twins <u>ate</u> all the sandwiches. (The verb *ate* is the simple predicate. Everything else is left out.)
Complete predicate (P)	The complete verb of the sentence, plus its modifiers, objects, etc. It tells us something the subject is doing or what is being observed about it.	The hungry twins <u>ate all the sandwiches</u>. (For the complete predicate, we include the verb *ate* and all the modifiers.)
Direct object (DO)	It receives the action of the verb.	I gave the <u>ball</u> to him. (The noun *ball* receives the action, so it is the direct object.)
Indirect object (IO)	It is usually preceded by a preposition (such as *in*, *between*, *with*); it is also called the object of the preposition.	I gave the ball to <u>him</u>. (Note that *him* follows a preposition, so it is the indirect object.)
Subject complement (SC)	It follows a linking verb (often a form of *to be*, such as *is, are, was, were*) and can be linked to the subject.	Shelley is <u>happy</u>. (The adjective *happy* describes Shelley, so it is a subject complement.)

Pages 319–20 explain sentence patterns.

and part of the predicate.) Your instructor may also ask you to identify **direct objects (DO)**, **indirect objects (IO)**, and **subject complements (SC)**. Understanding these will help you identify errors in your sentence structure.

A **direct object (DO)** receives the action of the verb; an **indirect object (LO)** is part of a prepositional phrase and usually tells for whom the action in the sentence is done. A **subject complement (SC)** is a noun or adjective following the verb that gives more information about the subject.

Exercise **13.8**

For the following sentences, identify the parts of speech and sentence elements.

1. I slept.
2. Henry bought a ball.
3. Mr Safi gave the test to Joshua.
4. Stacey is homesick.

Exercise **13.9**

For each of the following sentences, identify the complete subject and the complete predicate.

1. Bob and Yan went to the movies.
2. They really enjoyed the new superhero movie.
3. However, they ate too much popcorn and drank too much pop.
4. They also spent too much money.
5. Bob and Yan are now poor.

Exercise **13.10**

Identify the simple subject and simple predicate in the sentences in Exercise 13.9.

As you can see, a complete sentence contains at least one subject and one predicate. Grammatically, it needs nothing else to complete the thought, although more detail might be required for clarity. For example, the following sentence is complete because it has both a subject (*Peter*) and a predicate (*drove*).

> Peter drove.

However, you could add more information so that the reader doesn't wonder where to or whom.

> Peter drove Alice to the train station.

The subject and predicate are the same, but we have added a direct object (the noun *Alice*) and a prepositional phrase (*to the station*). The phrase contains a preposition (*to*), two adjectives (*the* and *train*), and a noun (*station*).

Sentence Patterns

Complete sentences come in four basic patterns: **simple**, **compound**, **complex**, and **compound-complex**. In each of the following examples, the subject is underlined once and the predicate twice.

Simple sentence: Subject + Predicate

A **simple sentence** contains one subject and one predicate. Two or more independent clauses joined by a coordinating conjunction make a **compound sentence**; an independent clause joined to a dependent clause by a subordinating conjunction creates a **complex sentence**. A **compound-complex sentence** is a compound sentence joined with a complex one.

> Peter <u>drove</u>.
> Peter and Gill <u>drove</u>.

Compound sentence: Subject + Predicate, + FANBOYS + Subject + Predicate

> Peter <u>went sailing</u>, and Layla <u>went horseback riding</u>.
> Peter and Gill <u>went on a picnic</u>, but Alice and Layla <u>went sightseeing</u>.

Put another way, a compound sentence is two simple sentences joined by one of the FANBOYS.

Complex sentence: Subject + Predicate + Subordinating Conjunction + Subject + Predicate
or
Subordinating Conjunction, + Subject + Predicate + Subject + Predicate

This type of sentence uses a subordinating conjunction to join an independent and dependent clause. In the following examples, the independent clause is italicized and the dependent clause is bolded.

> *Spring is often muddy in Canada* **while summer is not.**
> **While summer is not always muddy in Canada,** *spring is.*

Compound-complex sentence: Subject + Predicate + FANBOYS + Subject + Predicate + Subordinating Conjunction + Subject + Predicate

> *Spring is my favourite season* and *summer is my second favourite* **because I love warm temperatures.**

Prepositional Phrases

A **phrase** is a group of grammatically linked words that lacks a subject, predicate, or both. It functions as a single part of speech.

A **prepositional phrase** consists of a preposition and a noun or pronoun (the object of the preposition). The phrase can act as an adverb to modify a verb or as an adjective to modify a noun or pronoun.

A **phrase** is a grammatical unit that often acts as a part of speech and lacks a subject, predicate, or both. A **prepositional phrase** acts as either an adverb or an adjective. As you've seen earlier in this chapter, a group of words that includes more than one part of speech can modify a verb. In this case, it functions as an adverbial phrase.

> She drove me <u>into town</u> so I could do my laundry.

The prepositional phrase *into town* begins with the preposition *into* and is followed by the noun *town*, the object of the preposition. As a unit, however, the phrase functions as an adverb modifying the verb *drove* by explaining where the action took place: Drove where? Into town.

Similarly, a group of words can modify a noun or pronoun, in which case it functions as an adjective. Consider the prepositional phrases (which are underlined) in this sentence:

An obsession <u>with *Star Wars*</u> led to her career <u>as an astronomer</u>.

> An adjectival phrase usually follows the noun or pronoun it modifies. This order is different from that of a one-word adjective, which usually precedes the noun it modifies.

The first phrase contains a preposition (*with*) and proper noun (*Star Wars*). It functions as an adjective because it gives us more information about the noun *obsession*.

The second phrase, *as an astronomer*, also functions as an adjective; it modifies the noun *career*.

Prepositional phrases do not contain the sentence's subject. In the following sentence, *at the start of class* does not contain the actual subject even though it begins the sentence.

<u>At the start of class</u>, students in Japan bow to their teacher.

The subject here is *students*, and *at the start of class* is a prepositional phrase answering when they bow. Thus, it acts adverbially.

Noun and Verb Phrases

In the following example, the combination of the indefinite pronoun *some* and its modifier, *of the injured*, makes a **noun phrase**. The entire phrase, *some of the injured passengers*, is the sentence's subject because it tells us who had to be hospitalized.

> A **noun phrase** is a group of words that acts as a noun in a sentence and can be either the subject or an object.

<u>Some of the injured passengers</u> had to be hospitalized.

A phrase, then, can function as a noun subject or object.

Finally, consider the next example, in which the **verb phrase** *we will be looking* acts as a unit in the sentence, conveying the action of the subject *we*:

> A **verb phrase** is a group of words that acts as the verb in a sentence.

<u>We will be looking</u> carefully for the person with a red flag on her backpack.

Verb phrases are very common because you will often need helping verbs to create different tenses beyond the one-word simple tenses (verb phrases are italicized):

Simple present: I think, you say, she takes
Simple past: I thought, you said, she took
Present progressive: I *am thinking*, you *are saying*, she *is taking*
Past perfect: I *had thought*, you *had said*, she *had taken*

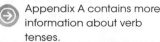

Appendix A contains more information about verb tenses.

In addition to forms of *to be* and *to have*, verb phrases occur when modals combine with main verbs to convey ability (*can, could*), possibility (*may, might*), necessity (*must, have*), and other meanings.

Exercise **13.11**

Identify the word groups in parentheses as adverbial, adjectival, noun, or verb phrases and then indicate the subject of each sentence.

1. Tomorrow, (the class time) will be changed (for the rest)(of the semester).
2. (Some of the food) (in the fridge) (has spoiled).
3. The store (in the mall) (with the latest fashions) (has closed).
4. A search (of the abandoned house) (turned up) several cartons (of stolen goods).
5. (The 2018 hockey season) (will belong) (to the Leafs).

Exercise **13.12**

Identify the different clauses in each of the following sentences.

1. I will meet you at the airport before the flight.
2. Because Stan likes ginger ale, I bought two flats of it.
3. Yesterday, while I was reviewing my finances, I noticed that I forgot to pay my electric bill.
4. I had to pay the bill with my credit card and I am now at my credit limit.
5. I need to go to the bank to apply for a loan, and I need to visit my parents because I need more money this month.

Exercise **13.13**

Identify the phrases in the sentences of Exercise 13.12.

Imperative Sentences

An **imperative sentence** issues a command. Its subject, *you*, is always understood even though it is not expressed.

There is one situation when you do not need to write the subject of the sentence: an **imperative sentence**, or a command. In this case, the subject is silent and the context of the sentence makes it clear. In many cases, this subject is often the pronoun *you*.

Close the door!
Put your pencils down.
Go to your room.

In each of these sentences, we can imagine the word *you* at the beginning.

Exercise **13.14**

Indicate which of the following are complete sentences. Mark with an *S* those that contain only a subject and a *P* those that contain only a predicate. Use an *N* if there is neither subject nor predicate.

1. The empty cup on the bench.
2. Signed his name to the bottom of the petition.
3. Faith heals.
4. Can grammar rules be bent?
5. Eat your Brussels sprouts!

Sentence Errors

Sentence Fragments

There are four types of **sentence fragments**: missing subject or predicate, add-on, *–ing*, and dependent clause.

A **sentence fragment** is a major grammatical error that consists of an incomplete clause or a dependent clause on its own.

Missing Subject or Predicate

In this type of fragment, either a subject or predicate is missing. The following sentence is incomplete because it consists only of a subject and a phrase that expands on it; the subject isn't doing anything.

A driver who never stops at a red light.

Who never stops at a red light tells us what kind of driver he or she is but goes no further. The sentence needs a predicate, such as *is dangerous*, to be complete.

A driver who never stops at red lights is dangerous.

Similarly, *thousands of tourists around the world* is a fragment. Something essential is missing: What about the tourists? Do they exist? Are the tourists doing something? What do they look like? Who saw them? To answer any of these questions is to complete a thought—and the sentence.

Thousands of tourists around the world experience jet lag.

The Taj Mahal is seen by thousands of tourists from around the world.

The first example adds a predicate (*experience jet lag*); the second adds a subject (*the Taj Mahal*), introduces a verb (*is seen*), adds a preposition (*from*), and turns the fragment into part of the predicate.

Exercise **13.15**

Complete the fragment *thousands of tourists around the world* in two ways other than those discussed. Then, complete the following fragments by adding predicates.

1. The store that I missed.
2. The brilliant idea that came to me in the middle of the night.
3. A marching band that is able to rouse everyone.
4. The kind of doughnut that doesn't have a hole in the middle.
5. The rugby towel that was on the ground.

Add-on Fragment

> Add-on fragments lack a subject and a predicate. They may begin with a word (e.g., *especially*), a phrase (e.g., *such as*), a transition word or phrase (*also, as well as, besides, especially, except (for), for example, including, like*), a preposition (*on, in, to*), or a prepositional phrase.

Add-on fragments contain neither a complete subject nor a complete predicate. Writers can mistake them for complete sentences because there is usually a pause between them and the preceding sentence in speech; you may mistakenly associate a pause or drawn breath with a new sentence. The easiest way to fix these kinds of fragments is to make them part of the previous sentence or to supply the missing essentials. Punctuation may not be needed; at other times, you can use a comma or a dash.

Fragment: Exaggerated images of fitness are everywhere. Especially in teen-oriented magazines.
Corrections: Exaggerated images of fitness are everywhere, especially in teen-oriented magazines.
or
Exaggerated images of fitness are everywhere—especially in teen-oriented magazines.
Fragment: Sewage contains more than 200 toxic chemicals that are flushed down sinks or toilets. Not to mention the runoff from roads.
Correction: Sewage contains more than 200 toxic chemicals that are flushed down sinks or toilets, not to mention the runoff from roads.

When you begin a sentence with a preposition, check that the sentence expresses a complete thought and includes both a subject and a predicate.

Fragment: On top of the biggest sundae.

Who or what is there and what is taking place?

Correction: The cherry was on top of the biggest sundae.

-ing Fragment

A third kind of fragment occurs when an **incomplete verb form**, or **base verb form**—a verb from ending in *–ing* or *–ed/en*—is mistaken for a complete verb. To avoid sentence fragments, always ensure you write a complete verb form.
Here are some examples of incomplete verb forms:

- *listening, studying, thinking, being* (present participle form of verb)
- *given, thought, written, taken* (past participle form of verb)
- *to begin, to tell, to be, to look* (infinitive form of verb)

While complete verb forms can be joined to a subject by adding a helping verb, incomplete verb forms can't.

Incomplete: She listening, they given
Complete: She was listening, they are given

The following are examples of fragments with incomplete verb forms:

Dogs running around the fenced-in play area.

What are the dogs doing? If you said "They are running," you have changed the fragment into a complete sentence by adding the helping verb *are*:

Dogs <u>are running</u> around the fenced-in play area.

Fragment: As a new doctor fascinated by innovative surgery procedures.
Correction: As a new doctor, he was fascinated by innovative surgery procedures.

The first three fragment types can act as nouns, adjectives, and adverbs in a sentence but not as verbs.

Incomplete verb form as noun: Eating sensibly is the best way to lose weight.

> An *-ing* fragment occurs when an **incomplete verb form** (or **base verb form**) is mistaken for a complete verb.

> Learn how to recognize incomplete verb forms in your writing. Doing so will help you avoid this kind of sentence fragment.

Eating is the noun subject of this sentence.

> Incomplete verb form as adjective: My growling stomach told me it was time to eat.

Growling is an adjective modifying *stomach*, the noun subject. Note that there is another incomplete verb form in this sentence—*to eat*—which acts as an adjective modifying *time*.

Exercise **13.16**

Add a subject and/or predicate to the fragments in Exercise 13.14, making them complete sentences.

Dependent Clause Fragment

A dependent clause fragment is the most common type of fragment because, at first glance, a dependent clause looks a lot like a grammatical sentence. You can identify a dependent clause by the word it begins with—a subordinating conjunction or a relative pronoun (see Table 13.6).

A dependent clause fragment sounds incomplete and leaves us wondering about the missing part. Consider this fragment:

> Because he was late.

TABLE 13.6   Common Subordinating Conjunctions and Relative Pronouns

after	ever since	unless	which
although	if	until	whichever
as	if only	what	while
as if	in case	whatever	who
as long as	in order that	when	whoever
as soon as	once	whenever	whom
as though	since	where	whose
because	so that	whereas	why
before	that	wherever	
even though	though	whether	

You can think of a dependent clause as searching for an answer to a question—in this case, "What happened because he was late?" When you provide that information in an independent clause, you will have a complete sentence. You can also test a sentence for completeness by asking whether it is true or false. *Because he was late* can be neither due to missing information.

Because he was late for work, he lost some pay.

The subordinating conjunction that introduces the dependent clause indicates the relationship between the dependent and independent clauses, such as one of cause–effect (*as*, *because*), time (*before*, *since*, *when*, *while*), or contrast (*although*, *though*, *whereas*). If you take away the subordinating conjunction, you are left with a subject and a predicate and a sentence that expresses a complete thought. Another way to fix a dependent clause fragment, then, is to remove the subordinating conjunction; you will have a simple sentence expressing one idea. However, it may not be the idea you intended to convey:

He was late for work.

This is a complete sentence, but it does not explain the consequences of his being late.

See page 315 for more information about subordinating conjunctions.

To test whether you have written a dependent clause fragment, answer these questions: Does the idea sound complete? Can you answer "true" or "false" to it? Does it begin with one of the words in Table 13.6? If the answer to question 1 or 2 is "no," it is probably a fragment.

Exercise 13.17

The following may or may not be complete sentences. For each one that is a fragment, identify the type and make it into a simple sentence.

1. Completing the test on time.
2. Huge tears rolled down his cheeks.
3. Being that she worked late.
4. He promised to call her tomorrow. To see if she was still all right.
5. A murder of crows, along with a flock of sheep.
6. He must be guilty. Since he's already confessed.
7. Walking beside the tracks, he eventually reached the town.
8. Introducing our next prime minister.
9. For example, the reboot of the famous TV show *The X-Files*.
10. Swimming on her back.

Check your answers in Appendix D and then do questions 11–20.

11. Because trips create memories.
12. Stress can make us victims of illnesses. Including mild to life-threatening ones.

(continued)

13. Which is an example of a dependent clause.
14. The objection was overruled. As the judge felt that the jury needs to hear the statement.
15. Learning about people from different ethnic groups.
16. Painting is a good hobby and helps people see the world more clearly. Such as the increased perception of shadows.
17. Golf courses always include obstacles. These being water hazards and sand traps.
18. Although there are options in today's schools for Indigenous students to learn about their culture.
19. Sounds and textures are common features of dreams. While smell and taste are usually absent.
20. The horse is my favourite animal. Which is a Chinese Zodiac symbol.

Exercise 13.18

Find the four sentence fragments in the following passage; correct them by joining them to complete sentences or by adding information.

When considering college or university. Many students must decide where to live. If they are going to school close to home, they may decide to continue living with their families. Listening to their parent's advice. However, if the school is far away and commuting is not possible, students must decide whether to live in the school residence or in an apartment. Residences are convenient. Especially if there is a meal plan available. Meal plans that are nutritious. Apartments might be a better idea though, especially if students need to work. Not all residences are close to where jobs are. Privacy might be an issue in residence. Not all students can get their own rooms. Apartments may provide privacy, but only if there is no need for roommates. Many factors need to be considered when choosing where to live.

Exercise 13.19

Construct compound, complex, and compound-complex sentences from these independent clauses (simple sentences). After you have joined the clauses in the most logical way, identify the sentence type, ensuring that you have at least one example of each. You can make small changes to the clauses and sentence order.

1. They intended to eat at Benny's Bistro.
    They saw a long line-up outside Benny's.
    They went to Kenny's Kitchen instead.
2. There may be nearly two million kinds of plants in the world.
    There are likely at least as many different kinds of animals.
    No one can know how many species have evolved, flourished, and become extinct.
3. Timothy Findley's story "Stones" takes place in Toronto.
    Norman Levine's "Something Happened Here" takes place in northern France.
    Both stories describe the tragic assault by Canadian troops on Dieppe during the Second World War.
4. We may suspect that earth is not unique as a life-bearing planet.
    We do not as yet have any compelling evidence that life exists anywhere else.
    We must restrict our discussion of the presence of life to our own planet.
5. Cooking has become a popular hobby.
    Many celebrities have cooking shows.
    These celebrities have written cookbooks that promote their shows.

Sentence Errors

Run-On Sentence

A sentence may contain one or more subject–predicate clauses, but they must be joined correctly with commas and conjunctions so that the reader can distinguish the ideas. Otherwise, they must be separated by a period to form separate sentences. A **run-on sentence** occurs when a writer joins two sentences without including any punctuation between them. The writer charges through the end of the first complete thought and into the second one, like a driver running a stop sign. However, a run-on sentence is not the same as a long sentence with FANBOYS or other conjunctions.

> A **run-on sentence** isn't just a long sentence: it's a major grammatical error in which two sentences are not properly separated.

Incorrect:

The cruise to Alaska was full Tom and Yumi decided to fly to Jamaica instead.
The Dene peoples live in Northern Canada they speak different languages.

Once you determine where the first clause ends and the second one begins, make them into two simple sentences or use a comma and the appropriate co-ordinating conjunction to join them.

Correct:

The cruise to Alaska was full. Tom and Yumi decided to fly to Jamaica instead.

The cruise to Alaska was full, <u>so</u> Tom and Yumi decided to fly to Jamaica instead.

The Dene peoples live in Northern Canada. They speak different languages.

The Dene peoples live in Northern Canada, <u>and</u> they speak different languages.

The following run-on sentences contain two complete thoughts or two main ideas. Lines indicate the division between subject and predicate; diagonal lines show where the first sentence ends and the second begins and where a period or a comma and coordinating conjunction should be placed.

Incorrect:

Many people | have smartphones // smartphones | are very practical devices.

The poverty line | is very low in Canada // many people | live below the poverty line.

Correct:

Many people have smartphones. Smartphones are practical devices.
Many people have smartphones, as they are practical devices.
The poverty line is very low in Canada. Many people live below the poverty line.
The poverty line is very low in Canada, but many people live below it.

Comma Splice

An error more common than the run-on sentence is the **comma splice**, which is the joining of two complete sentences by only a comma. This error is like slowing down at a stop sign before charging through. The comma has many uses within the sentence, but it alone cannot connect two sentences.

Comma splices sometimes occur when two clauses are very closely related or the second clause seems a continuation of the first one. It's important to be able to separate two independent clauses. The simplest way to avoid comma splices is to find where one complete thought (independent clause) ends and the next begins and place either a period or a comma and a coordinating conjunction between them.

A **comma splice** isn't just a problem in comma usage; it's a major grammatical error in which a comma alone is used to separate two complete thoughts.

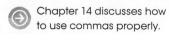 Chapter 14 discusses how to use commas properly.

Incorrect:

Models today are very thin, they look ill.
The population is rising, some think the earth cannot sustain itself.

Although the second clauses in these sentences are closely related in meaning to the first, they are not part of those clauses and must be separated from them by something stronger than just a comma. A "stop" form of punctuation, such as a semicolon or colon, may be a good choice in these cases:

Correct:

Models today are very thin. They look ill.
Models today are very thin; they look ill.
The population is rising. Some think the earth cannot sustain itself.
The population is rising; therefore, some think the earth cannot sustain itself.

 Chapter 14 contains instructions on using stop punctuation.

Remember that a pronoun generally replaces a noun that precedes it in a sentence. Like a noun, a pronoun can act as the subject of a clause. In the following sentences, a pronoun is the subject of the second clause. Lines indicate the division between subject and predicate; diagonal lines show where the first sentence ends and the second begins and where a period or a comma and coordinating conjunction should be placed.

Incorrect:

Working in a busy office environment | was completely new to her, // she | had always worked at home.
Censorship | does not just mean getting rid of swearing and nudity, // it | can also mean blocking an idea or a viewpoint.

Correct:

Working in a busy office environment was completely new to her. She had always worked at home.
Working in a busy office environment was completely new to her, for she had always worked at home.
Censorship does not just mean getting rid of swearing and nudity. It can also mean blocking an idea or a viewpoint.
Censorship does not just mean getting rid of swearing and nudity, but it can also mean blocking an idea or a viewpoint.

If you wish to use a comma to connect two independent clauses, you must also use one of the seven coordinating conjunctions (FANBOYS). Use a semi-colon before words such as *however*, *therefore*, or *thus* to join two independent clauses.

Exercise **13.20**

Indicate whether each sentence is run-on or contains a comma splice. Fix the errors by using a period to make two separate sentences or, if you already know the rules for using them, other forms of punctuation to join independent clauses.

1. I read two books in two days I did nothing else but read.
2. I couldn't use my laptop today, I forgot to plug it in before the battery was dead.
3. I was frightened during my first driving lesson the instructor yelled at me.
4. It's easy to punctuate sentences, just put a comma whenever you pause.
5. She finished watching the movie then took the bus home.
6. Magazines are available for digital download, this is better for the environment.
7. Technology continues to evolve, but we can't always predict whether this is good or bad.
8. Humans are imitators, conforming is something they are good at.
9. Many immigrants want to learn about Canadian culture they take courses about it.
10. Binge drinking is a serious problem, many students engage in this behaviour.

Exercise **13.21**

Correct the errors in the following sentences.

1. He managed to pass the year though he seldom did his homework, what will happen to him next year is anyone's guess.
2. The opening ceremonies were delayed. On account of rain.
3. She has decided to work at a fast-food restaurant. Not a great place for tips.
4. Movies provide entertainment for people, different people prefer different genres such as horror.
5. Since she bought the new tablet.
6. The only way a person can learn. To pay attention to what is going on in class.
7. He was too tall and thin to excel at sports. Except basketball, of course.

8. The concept that "bigger is better" is part of our culture, it is promoted by both advertisers and the media these days.
9. Understanding the theory of relativity and its impact on our daily lives.
10. Justin Trudeau may eventually be as well known as his father, Pierre had charisma and charm.

Check Appendix D for the correct answers before doing questions 11–25.

11. The Romans were willing to change their religious beliefs quite easily, the Greeks, however, were less willing to do this.
12. Although video games can eat up your time if you are not careful.
13. The computer is not the only way to access email today, telephones and tablets may come equipped with email capability.
14. It seems that the North American mass media prescribes two roles for women, they can be sex objects or passive housewives.
15. Martial arts are attracting more people than ever before. Especially those who want to gain self-control and self-awareness.
16. We can no longer turn our backs to what is happening in the north it is time to take action.
17. BlackBerry is located in Waterloo, Ontario, it employs people from around the world.
18. Her message about crime was lost on the audience, they wanted to hear about terrorism.
19. Part of a long line of police officers.
20. Speaking in public is distressing for some, the most common fear is that people will laugh even if the presentation is serious.
21. Speakers in the House of Commons need to speak loudly, their message will not be heard otherwise.
22. One of the most tragic events of the twentieth century. The detonation of the atomic bomb over Hiroshima.
23. Podcasts are current, up to date, and appear automatically, thus they can be enjoyed anywhere at any time.
24. I have been to London and Paris neither city is in Europe though.
25. Many factors contribute to poverty. Including geographic factors, disease, and lack of education or health care.

Exercise **13.22**

Identify and correct the sentence errors in the following paragraph.

The "Freshmen 15" is not a recent phenomenon this refers to the weight students typically gain during their first year at college or university. What concerns doctors now is the amount of weight gained during this time. In the 1970s and 1980s, students typically gained 5 pounds,

(continued)

now it is up to 15. This is a very unhealthy weight gain. Once the weight is gained. It is very hard to lose. Because of this. Cafeterias are starting to offer more nutritional meals with fewer calories. Student councils are beginning to be proactive and inform students of the dangers of excess weight gain. School gyms are offering more classes to help students battle this weight gain. In the future, many hope that the "Freshman 15" becomes non-existent.

 # Chapter Review Questions

1. What is a noun? A noun phrase?
2. What is a verb? A verb phrase?
3. What is an adjective?
4. What is an adverb?
5. What is a preposition? Prepositional phrase?
6. What is the difference between a coordinating and subordinating conjunction?
7. What are the different types of sentence patterns?
8. What are the two essential parts of a sentence?
9. What are the different types of sentence fragments?
10. What is the difference between a run-on sentence and a comma splice?

14 Punctuation

In this chapter, you will learn

- how to use commas;
- how to use semicolons;
- how to use colons;
- how to use dashes and parentheses;
- how to use apostrophes; and
- how to avoid common punctuation errors.

While some punctuation rules change, some of the uses we see every day are incorrect. This chapter will introduce you to the current standards for properly using punctuation and ways to avoid some common errors. Once you have studied the rules, you may notice other people's mistakes in using commas, semicolons, colons, dashes, parentheses, and apostrophes. Various exercises will help reinforce the punctuation rules you need to know in order to write error-free documents.

Do Commas Matter?

The short answer to this question is "yes" because readers look for commas in specific places to help them read. When a comma is missing or misplaced, the reader might have to reread the sentence, looking for another cue to its meaning. Furthermore, comma errors make your writing appear unreliable. The following examples labelled as incorrect are missing commas and therefore could confuse a reader. The correct version is much easier to follow.

> Incorrect: The year before a deadly virus ravaged much of the countryside.
> Correct: The year before, a deadly virus ravaged much of the countryside.
> Incorrect: Although dating services may ask you for a photo appearance is less important than personality.
> Correct: Although dating services may ask you for a photo, appearance is less important than personality.

Correct comma use guides the reader through the sentence, clarifying the relationships among its parts.

Myths about comma use abound. For example, the "one breath rule" states that you should insert a comma wherever you naturally pause. However, commas assist the typical silent reader more than the one who reads aloud. If you are writing a speech, you may want to place commas where you plan to pause for breath, but this rule is simply too vague to be of use in formal writing; it can even lead you astray.

In general, commas separate the smaller or less important units in a sentence. Working with coordinating conjunctions, they also separate large units, or independent clauses. In a sentence, commas separate

- items in a series;
- independent clauses;
- parenthetical (types of non-essential) information; and
- adjectives, dates, addresses, titles, and the like.

See Chapter 13 for more on independent clauses.

Commas separate the smaller or less important units in a sentence. Working with coordinating conjunctions, they also separate independent clauses.

Rule Category 1: Items in a Series

Commas separate three or more items (words, phrases, or clauses) in a series.

This rule category applies to three or more grammatically parallel items, whether single words—such as nouns, verbs, or adjectives—phrases, or clauses. Here are some examples.

A series of three nouns:

> It doesn't matter whether the items in the series are words, phrases, or clauses.

A series of three predicates:

Every Saturday, Davina gets up, drowns herself with coffee, and stumbles to the door before she realizes what day it is.

A series of three clauses:

Flowering plants produce seeds, ferns produce spores, and coniferous trees produce cones.

The comma before the last item in a series, referred to as the serial (or Oxford) comma, is often omitted in informal writing.

> A list or series contains three items separated by commas. Do not use a comma to separate two items unless they are two independent clauses with a word such as *and*, *or*, or *but* in between.

Informal: My three favourite months are May, June and September.
Formal: My three favourite months are May, June, and September.

However, the serial comma often makes a sentence much easier to follow. It should not be omitted if the last element or the one that precedes it contains two items. In this example, the last item in the list is a compound (*toast and jam* is a single thing consisting of two elements):

> Always include the serial comma in a list of three or more items unless your instructor tells you otherwise.

She ordered orange juice, an omelette with cheese, and toast and jam.

The serial comma is especially helpful to the reader when the second-last or the last item is significantly longer than the other items.

The two-year specialization includes 10 half-courses, 2 full courses that involve internships in health-care facilities, and a research paper.

Rule Category 2: Independent Clauses

This comma rule applies to three related situations: (2a) two independent clauses joined by a coordinating conjunction; (2b) introductory words, phrases, or clauses when an independent clause follows; and (2c) some conclusions when an independent clause precedes them.

2a: Use a comma to separate two independent clauses with a coordinating conjunction in between. In other words, use a comma before the coordinating conjunction in a compound sentence.

> Use a comma before the coordinating conjunction in a compound sentence.

 See Chapter 13 for descriptions and examples of sentence patterns.

The course was supposed to be offered in the fall, *but* it was cancelled.
The grocery store is two kilometres away, *so* he never walks.
Dyana was the best dancer on the cruise ship, *and* she won an award to prove it.

Exceptions to this rule may be made if the second clause is very short or if the clauses are so closely related that they could be considered compounds (i.e., the ideas are hard to separate). In the following sentence, there is no comma between *dress* and *and* because the clauses are short:

"She wore the dress and I stayed home," sang Danny Kaye in the movie *White Christmas*.

2b: Use a comma after an introductory word, phrase, or clause when an independent clause follows it.

> After six years as committee chair, it was time for her to retire.
> To get the maximum enjoyment from his stereo equipment, Curtis put it in a room where the acoustics were excellent.

The one-word introduction in the next sentence is a **sentence adverb**, which modifies the independent clause that follows it:

> Unfortunately, we have run out of mineral water.

Insert a comma after a dependent clause that introduces an independent clause. The former are italicized in the examples.

> *While the drinking age is 19 in most provinces*, it is only 18 in Alberta.
> *When she first encountered the Canadian education system*, she was surprised by the many differences between the North American and Japanese systems.

2c: In general, use a comma before a concluding word or phrase when an independent clause precedes it.

> W.J. Prince wrote to his client Larry Drucker, asking direction in the case.

This rule applies when a statement is followed by a reference to the person or group that made the statement:

> "We still think of a powerful man as a born leader and a powerful woman as an anomaly," Margaret Atwood once said.
> Students who participate in sports or social activities are more likely to consider themselves satisfied with their lives than those who do not, according to a recent study.

A **sentence adverb** is an adverb that modifies the complete independent clause that follows it.

Use a comma after an introductory word, phrase, or clause when an independent clause follows it.

Combining rules: The following sentence illustrates rules 2a and 2b.

In America, [2b] 20 per cent of homeless children repeat a grade in school, [2a] and another 16 per cent of these children are enrolled in special education classes.

In general, use a comma before a concluding word or phrase when an independent clause precedes it.

Combining rules: The following sentence illustrates rules 2b and 2c.

By banning the use of cellphones, [2b] Newfoundland and Labrador encouraged its drivers to focus on the road, [2c] reducing the number of collisions.

Rule 2c does not usually apply when an independent clause is followed by a dependent clause. If you begin with a dependent clause and follow with an independent one, follow rule 2b. If you begin with an independent clause and conclude with a dependent, you do not generally use a comma. However, a dependent clause that begins with *although, though, even though,* or *whereas* suggests a contrast with the independent clause and should usually be preceded by a comma.

> In general, use a comma when you begin a sentence with a dependent clause and follow with an independent clause, but do not use a comma if you begin with an independent clause and follow with a dependent clause.

No comma required: The sleek Siamese cat lay on the sofa *where it was sunny.*

Comma required (use of *whereas* suggests contrast): The sleek Siamese cat lay on the sofa, whereas the old Labrador retriever curled up by the fire.

Rule Category 3: Parenthetical Information

> A **non-restrictive clause** contains information that can be left out of the sentence without affecting the meaning. A **restrictive clause** contains information that is necessary for the reader to understand the sentence.
>
> **Relative pronouns** introduce dependent (adjectival) clauses.

When you place information in parentheses, you signal to the reader that it is less important than the other parts of the sentence. Commas operate similarly, indicating whether a clause is **non-restrictive** (additional/non-essential) or **restrictive** (essential). Both types modify and follow nouns and often begin with the **relative pronouns** *who*, *whom*, *which*, or *that*. Three rules help you decide on the importance of a clause and thus punctuate accordingly.

3a: Use commas before and after non-restrictive phrases or clauses. Although the information in such a clause may be important, it can be left out without changing the main point of the sentence. A restrictive clause is essential to the meaning of the sentence. If you left it out, the sentence would mean something different or would be ungrammatical. Consider these examples:

Tony, who often wears a leather jacket, was identified as one of the rescue team.
A man who wore a leather jacket was identified as one of the rescue team.

The main idea in the first sentence is that Tony was identified as part of the rescue team. Tony's leather jacket may be important elsewhere in a larger narrative, but it is not part of the main idea here; therefore, this information is enclosed by commas. Note that two commas are required, just as two parentheses would be.

> Use two commas around a non-restrictive clause to separate it from the rest of the sentence, just as you would use parentheses.

In the second sentence, the information about the jacket is essential to the person's identification. Without the clause *who wore a leather jacket*, the sentence would mean simply that a man, not a woman, was on the rescue team. This is how you can test whether information in clauses beginning with *who*, *which*, or *that* is restrictive: if you omit the clause and the sentence says something different, the information is essential. Try omitting the *who* clause in this example:

> Many students, who take out loans, have a heavy debt burden after graduation.

Removing the clause leaves you with a sentence that says simply, "Many students have a heavy debt burden on graduation." That's different from the more specific statement about those students with loans. Therefore, *who take out loans* is a restrictive clause and no commas should be used.

When writing clauses, whether non-restrictive or restrictive, use *who* to refer to people. Use *which* to refer to non-humans in non-restrictive clauses and *that* to refer to non-humans in restrictive clauses.

> The actor *who* appeared in the movie *that* we saw last night also starred in *The Avengers*.

3b: Use commas to set off appositives—nouns that are grammatically parallel to a preceding noun or phrase. They name, rephrase, specify, or explain the noun or noun phrase that comes just before. The appositives in the following sentences are underlined.

> Her first work, <u>a short story collection called *Drying the Bones*</u>, received outstanding reviews.

> Seal hunting, <u>a traditional means of livelihood among Inuit</u>, has been criticized by some environmentalists.

Use commas around true appositives. Sometimes, however, the second noun completes the first, giving essential information. In this case, do not set off the second noun with a comma. If in doubt, remove the second noun or noun phrase and see if the sentence is still complete and makes grammatical sense.

> The lion, king of the beasts, is the subject of many fables by the ancient Greek writer Aesop.

Why are there commas around *king of the beasts* but not before *Aesop*? Which is the true appositive?

You can use the appositive rule for words and phrases that can be considered subsets of a larger set—for instance, examples in phrases beginning with *such as* and *including*—even though they are not strictly appositives.

Sidebar notes:

Use *who* to refer to people in restrictive and non-restrictive clauses. Use *which* to refer to non-humans in non-restrictive clauses and *that* to refer to non-humans in restrictive clauses.

Use commas around nouns that (re)name the previous noun and are grammatically parallel with each other.

Combining rules: The following sentence illustrates appositive rule 3b and independent clause rule 2a.

His first purchase, [3b] the painting of the Northern Ontario landscape by Tom Thomson, [3b] is now worth thousands of dollars, [2a] but he says he will never sell it.

The celebration of certain holidays, such as Christmas and Halloween, has been banned by several local school boards.

3c: Use commas to set off adverbs and adverbial phrases that interrupt the flow of the sentence from subject to predicate and from verb to object or subject complement. Such words or phrases—including *after all, for example, however, in fact, indeed, needless to say,* and *therefore*—often emphasize or qualify a thought.

> I must say that your performance on the aptitude test demonstrates, beyond a doubt, that you would make an excellent engineer.

Sometimes, especially in informal or semi-formal writing, using two commas around a small word or phrase that interrupts the sentence may produce clutter. Except in the most formal writing, commas around adverbial interruptions can be omitted if they directly follow a coordinating conjunction, such as *but,* to avoid three commas in close proximity.

> Commas can be omitted: Leslie worried about her driver's test, but in fact she aced it.
> Correct but cluttered: Leslie worried about her driver's test, but, in fact, she aced it.

Use commas around words and phrases that interrupt the flow of the sentence.

 See pages 312–14 for more examples of adverbs and adverbial phrases.

Rule Category 4: Conventional and "Comma Sense" Uses

A number of other comma rules don't often fit into a neat category but must be followed.

4a: Use commas to set off the name of the person being addressed directly:

> I can tell, Naomi, that you really do understand the math concepts taught last week.

Stylistic convention more than grammar dictates that you use commas between coordinate adjectives before a noun; with dates, addresses, and titles; and before and after direct quotations.

4b: Adjectives modify a noun and usually precede it. When a series of adjectives is **coordinate**, or equal and interchangeable, separate them by a comma. When the series is **non-coordinate**, or unequal and not interchangeable, do not use a comma.

Coordinate adjectives can be placed in a different order within a list without changing the meaning of the sentence. **Non-coordinate adjectives** cannot be moved around because the meaning will change. Use a comma between two coordinate adjectives, not between two non-coordinate.

Coordinate adjectives: big, friendly dog; tall, white tower; proud, condescending man
Non-coordinate adjectives: white bull terrier; welcome second opinion; incredible lucky break

One way to confirm that adjectives are coordinate is to mentally place the word *and* between the adjectives, such as *big (and) friendly dog*. If the phrase makes sense, the adjectives are coordinate and require commas. Applying this test to *white (and) bull terrier* does not work, as the phrase contains non-coordinate adjectives; therefore, commas are not used.

4c: Use a comma to separate a quotation from the rest of the sentence, as in attributions (i.e., where a source is named):

The sign says, "Trespassers will be prosecuted."
"I am not a crook," said Richard Nixon.

4d: Use a comma to distinguish names and locations in addresses:

The Prime Minister of Canada, 24 Sussex Drive, Ottawa, Ontario, Canada

Convention also dictates that you place a comma after the name of a province, territory, state, or country if the sentence continues:

I lived in Calgary, Alberta, until I moved back to Quebec.

4e: Use a comma to separate the day and year in a date. Do not use a comma in day-month-year or month-year format:

October 7, 1951
but
7 October 1951 and October 1951

4f: Use commas to separate degrees, titles, and similar designations:

Sabrina Yao, MD, PhD, FRCPS

4g: Use commas to separate groups of three digits in non-metric numbers:

The output of chemical waste was 13,890,457 tons per day for that factory.

In 2006, the population of Nunavut was 29,474, according to Statistics Canada.

The US Defense Department listed 2,356 casualties earlier in the year.

In the metric system, insert a space rather than a comma between every three digits in a number of more than four digits (the space is optional with four-digit numbers):

13 890 457; 29 474; 2356

4h: Place commas and periods inside quotation marks and most other punctuation outside. (In the UK, the convention is to place commas and periods outside quotation marks).

The new topic, "Where Ecological Ends Meet," has been posted.
We have been told that our meals "are not gratis"; however, the company has paid for our transportation.

4i: In some cases, you will have to apply "comma sense." If a sentence seems confusing when you read it, you might need to insert a comma to clarify it. Commas in the following sentences ensure the sense intended.

In 1971, 773 people were killed in an earthquake in Peru.
He told the student to come now, and again the following week.

> Your instructor can tell you whether to use metric when writing. Otherwise, use the industry standard for your profession.

> Commas are used between some elements in addresses, dates, degrees, and numbers and between quotations and their source.

> Place commas and periods inside quotation marks and most other punctuation outside.

> Combining rules: The following sentence illustrates the rule for comma use with quotations (4h) and the independent clause rule 2c.

> "You should always put periods and commas inside quotation marks," [4h] said Professor LeGuin, [2c] "though this system is predominant in North America and may not apply in other countries."

Exercise **14.1**

Add commas to the following sentences where required and name the rule category you use (each sentence reflects one rule).

1. After her inaugural speech several members of the House rose to congratulate her.
2. The optional package includes bucket seats dual speakers and air conditioning.
3. We have collected more than $20,000 and there is a week remaining in our campaign.
4. Metaphors similes and personification all are examples of figurative language.
5. As one can see the tower is leaning 4.5 metres to the south.

(continued)

6. Hardly daring to breathe Nelson took a quick look at the valley far below him.
7. Although many are called few are chosen.
8. The magnificent country estate is hidden behind a long elegant row of silver birches.
9. "We can't achieve peace in our time if we assume war is inevitable" he said.
10. Her house was a newer one with dark wood trim and large open rooms.

After you've checked your answers in Appendix D, complete questions 11–25.

11. As well as the Irish many Africans were forced to leave their families behind during times of famine.
12. Because of the humidity levels it feels hotter than the actual temperature.
13. Joe Clark the former prime minister has a famous wife.
14. Even though many people are aware of global warming and climate change fewer are aware of the term *carbon footprint*.
15. James Earl Jones who is the voice of Darth Vader in *Star Wars* is a well-known actor.
16. *The Globe and Mail* is a popular paper across Canada whereas the *Toronto Star* was created for the Toronto and area market.
17. Trust is important in any relationship and it always takes time to develop.
18. The types of RNA required for protein synthesis are messenger RNA transfer RNA and ribosomal RNA.
19. People have immigrated to Canada from countries in Asia Europe the Middle East and Central and South America.
20. The committee studying the proposal is a mixture of health officials journalists and politicians.
21. Caffeine a stimulant is unregulated and completely legal.
22. Since climate change is a global problem it requires global solutions.
23. Diesel-powered cars have long been on the North American market yet they have never been widely accepted by the typical motorist.
24. The aggression effect of a video game depends on the type of game the way it is played and the person playing it.
25. Now a widely accepted theory evolution was discounted when Charles Darwin published *On the Origin of Species* in 1859.

Exercise 14.2

Add commas to the following sentences where required. More than one comma rule applies in most sentences.

1. I had planned to go to Calgary but my bus was delayed for more than four hours so I decided to go back home.
2. Juliet studied medicine at Dalhousie University in Halifax Nova Scotia before setting up her practice near Prince Albert Saskatchewan.

3. Like Jane Austen's character Emma the heroine of *Clueless* Cher is less superficial than she first appears.

4. Nick and Nicole were married on 20 April 1995 but they separated two years later.

5. Jessica Julep the mayor of Anytown Nova Scotia provided inspirational leadership.

6. The simple sentence as we've seen is easily mastered by students but compound sentences necessitate an understanding of various forms of punctuation.

7. The waste of our resources including the most precious resource water is the major environmental problem that Canada is facing today.

8. British general Sir Frederick Morgan established an American–British headquarters which was known as COSSAC.

9. The book with the fine red binding on the highest shelf is the particular one I want.

10. Agnes Campbell Macphail the first woman elected to Canadian Parliament served for 19 years beginning her career in 1921.

After you've checked your answers in Appendix D, complete questions 11–20.

11. The first steam-powered motorcycle known as the bone-shaker led to the bikes we use today.

12. Following successful completion of the English test another skills test is taken which is in a written format.

13. He combed through directories of professional associations business and trade associations and unions looking for possible contributors to his campaign.

14. Oliver Wendell Holmes an American was known as a master essayist but Canadian Barry Callaghan is also internationally respected as an essayist.

15. After visiting her ancestral homeland China and meeting her sisters from her mother's first marriage Amy Tan wrote the novel *The Joy Luck Club*.

16. The soldier with the red coat in the picture fought on the side of our enemies the Americans.

17. In 1885 the Canadian government introduced a racist bill the Chinese "head tax" which forced every Chinese person entering the country to pay a $50 fee.

18. Currently ranked fourth behind heart disease stroke and respiratory infections AIDS is set to become number three say researchers in a new report.

19. Leslie Hornby known as "Twiggy" became a supermodel overnight and was identified by her skinny 90-pound body.

20. Jeff Deffenbacher PhD a specialist in anger management thinks that some people have a low tolerance for everyday annoyances.

When Commas Are Not Required

Do not use a comma to separate simple compounds (two words, phrases, or clauses joined by a conjunction such as *and*). Recall that only a series of three or more items requires commas. A separate rule applies to compound sentences, where a comma is required before the coordinating conjunction.

Incorrect:

Some of the heaviest damage from steroid use occurs to the heart, and the liver. [two nouns]
Logging reduces the number of old-growth forests, and destroys these habitats. [two predicates: *reduces* . . . and *destroys* . . .]

Do not use a comma to separate the subject and the predicate. This error is probably the result of writers mistakenly applying the "pause" non-rule.

Incorrect:

The only way our society is going to be fixed, is if we change our laws.
One advantage in using helicopters to fight fires, is the accuracy of their drops over the scene of the fire.

It is easy to be distracted by parentheses and mistakenly insert a comma between a subject and a predicate. In the following example, another option is to add a comma after *Medicine* and remove the parentheses:

 Page 354 discusses parentheses.

Incorrect:

The American College of Sports Medicine (a body that advances research into exercise and sports), considers all physically active females at risk for developing eating disorders.

Do not use a comma alone to join independent clauses or with a word other than a coordinating conjunction. This produces a comma splice, a serious grammatical error.

Incorrect:

Chapter 13 provides more information on comma splices.

Football is one of the most popular sports in North America, it is also one of the most brutal of all sports.
You must use the buttons provided at the bottom of the pages to navigate through the application, otherwise, you could lose your connection.

Exercise **14.3**

Add commas in these paragraphs, following the rule categories discussed in this chapter and avoiding comma splices. A few commas have been included to help with comprehension, but they may be incorrect.

1. If you asked people to name the most gruelling and challenging race in the world most of them would probably say that it was an auto race such as the Indianapolis 500, few people would name the Tour de France which is a bicycle race. Thousands of cyclists however vie for an elite position in this annual event. Even with the modern advances in bicycle technology cyclists still find the course very challenging, it offers a variety of climbs including slight inclines hills and steep grades. The Tour de France has a history that dates back about a hundred years, in the years to come the race will continue to challenge inspire and glorify new riders.

2. Autism is a much misunderstood problem, often children with autism are viewed as a "handful" and "hyperactive." Very little is known of its causes and characteristics can vary making a diagnosis difficult. In children it is even harder because other children can exhibit some of the characteristics associated with autism. Although autism can cause many behavioural difficulties autistic children can still live near-normal lives if they are surrounded by understanding caregivers. Working with autistic children can change a person and make one realize the need for better understanding and education. Treating autism can be difficult because often there is no feedback from the patient. Over the years there have been many ideas of how to treat autism but not all were correct and have at times made treatment problematic.

Other Forms of Punctuation

The careful use of semicolons, colons, dashes, and parentheses gives your writing polish and precision. The semicolon and colon are stronger, more emphatic marks of punctuation than the comparatively mild-mannered comma. Learn how to use these marks to implement stronger breaks, longer pauses, and emphasis in your writing.

Semicolons

As discussed, one of the major functions of commas is to separate independent clauses in a compound sentence. Two rules for semicolons also involve independent clauses; the third rule is to separate items in a series that contains commas.

1. To join independent clauses: You may use a semicolon rather than a comma and a coordinating conjunction to join independent clauses if there is a close relationship between them. A semicolon alerts the reader to this connection. Consider the following examples:

> Strong economies usually have strong school systems, and investment in education is inevitably an investment in a country's economic future.
>
> Strong economies usually have strong school systems; weak economies generally have weak school systems.

In the first sentence, the second clause is logically related to the preceding one; however, they have different subjects and are not so closely related that a semicolon is called for. In the second sentence, both clauses are concerned primarily with the relationship between economic strength and school systems. That shared focus justifies the use of a semicolon.

A semicolon is often used if you want to stress a contrast between two independent clauses, as in these examples:

> Scott was impatient to get married; Salome wanted to wait until they were financially secure.
>
> Japanese food is generally good for you; fast food is not healthy.

Note that the semicolons in both sentences could be replaced by a comma and the coordinating conjunction *but*—they could not be replaced by a comma alone.

Here are other examples where a semicolon stresses the close relationship between independent clauses:

> Gymnastics is not just any sport; it's one of the most challenging and physically taxing of all sports.
>
> Some children may have lost a parent due to illness or divorce; others may have been cared for by grandparents or other relatives.

2. To join independent clauses by using a conjunctive adverb: The second rule involves using a semicolon with a conjunctive adverb/transitional phrase followed by an independent clause. Table 14.1 lists the most common conjunctive adverbs and transitional phrases. In the following examples, these terms are italicized.

> My roommate lacks charm, friendliness, and humour; *still*, he is an excellent cook.

Use a semicolon to replace a comma + a coordinating conjunction in closely related independent clauses.

Do not use a semicolon to separate an independent clause from a dependent clause.

 Pages 337–9 provide the rules for punctuating independent and dependent clauses.

TABLE 14.1 Common Conjunctive Adverbs/Transitional Phrases

accordingly	likewise
afterward	meanwhile
also	moreover
as a result	namely
besides	nevertheless
certainly	next
consequently	nonetheless
finally	on the contrary
for example	on the other hand
further(more)	otherwise
hence	similarly
however	still
if not	subsequently
in addition	that is
indeed	then
in fact	therefore
instead	thus
in the meantime	undoubtedly
later	

 See Chapter 13 for conjunctions.

A recent study has found a surprising correlation between a rare form of sleeping disorder and those with telephone numbers that include the number six; *however*, the conclusion is being challenged by several researchers.

> Use a semicolon before words such as *however* and *therefore* if they are joining independent clauses. Follow the joining word/phrase by a comma.

Adverbs such as *however* and *therefore* can act as ordinary adverbs (interrupters) or as conjunctive adverbs (joiners). A common error is to confuse these uses. The following sentences illustrate this distinction. The first requires commas because the adverb occurs in the clause as an interruption between the subject *he* and most of its predicate. In the second, a semicolon is required before the conjunctive adverb because *however* is joining two independent clauses:

Dr Suzuki will not be in his office this week; he will, *however*, be making his rounds at the hospital.

Dr Suzuki will not be in his office this week; *however*, he will be making his rounds at the hospital.

In the following sentences, *therefore* changes its function from interrupter to joiner:

The CEO has been called away for an emergency briefing; her secretary, *therefore*, will have to cancel her appointments.

The CEO has been called away for an emergency briefing; *therefore*, her secretary will have to cancel her appointments.

At first, it seems that the only difference between these sentences is *therefore*'s placement. If you look closely, though, you can see that changing the word's position can change its function. In the second sentence, an independent clause precedes and follows *therefore*, requiring the semicolon before and the comma after. (The comma is required because *therefore* introduces an independent clause.)

Be careful not to confuse the words and phrases in Table 14.1 with subordinating conjunctions, another large group of joiners that connect dependent to independent clauses. *Although* and *whereas* are sometimes mistaken for conjunctive adverbs, but they are subordinating conjunctions and cannot be used to join two independent clauses.

> See pages 314–15 for more on dependent and independent clauses.

> Don't put a semicolon before or a comma after subordinating conjunctions (e.g., *although* or *whereas*). They do not join independent clauses but introduce dependent ones.

3. To separate items in a series (the serial semicolon): A semicolon can be used between items in a series if one or more of the elements contain commas. Without semicolons, these sentences would be confusing:

Her company included Alex Duffy, president; Marie Tremble, vice-president; John van der Wart, secretary; and Chris Denfield, treasurer.

Bus number 1614 makes scheduled stops in Kamloops, British Columbia; Valemont, British Columbia; Jasper, Alberta; and Drayton Valley, Alberta, before arriving in Edmonton.

> A semicolon can be used between items in a series if one or more of the elements contain commas or if one of the elements is much longer than the others.

You may also use semicolons to separate items in a list where each piece is a long phrase or clause, especially if there is internal punctuation. Using semicolons to separate the items makes this sentence easier to read:

The role of the vice-president will be to enhance the school's external relations; strengthen its relationship with alumni, donors, and business and community leaders; implement a fundraising program; and increase the school's involvement in the community.

Exercise **14.4**

The following sentences are punctuated correctly. The italicized word or phrase is either an ordinary adverb (interrupter) or a conjunctive adverb (joiner). Rewrite the sentence by moving this word/phrase and giving it a different function. Punctuate accordingly.

Example:

Original: The weather this summer was very wet; *however*, it did not make up for the drought we have experienced.

Rewritten: The weather this summer was very wet. It did not, *however*, make up for the drought we have experienced.

or

The weather this summer was very wet; it did not, *however*, make up for the drought we have experienced.

1. One of my roommates rode her bicycle to school most of the time; she was more physically fit, *as a result*, than my other roommate, who didn't even own a bicycle.
2. SPCA officers work for but are not paid by the government. It is donations, *in fact*, that provide their salary.
3. If homelessness continues to increase, it will be costly for taxpayers; *moreover*, homelessness affects downtown businesses.
4. Many professional golfers use the same caddy for years; *for example*, Steve Williams caddied for Tiger Woods from 1999 to 2011.
5. Scientists tend to strongly support stem-cell research. Most evangelical Christians, *however*, just as strongly oppose it.

Do not use a semicolon if what follows it is a fragment. In the first two examples, an incomplete verb form (an *–ing*) follows the punctuation. In the third sentence, a prepositional phrase (*such as* and two nouns) follows. In all three cases, a comma should replace the incorrect semicolon to separate the independent clause from the concluding phrase.

> A semicolon should be preceded and followed by an independent clause unless it is being used to separate items in a series.

Incorrect:

When the media portrays minorities, it often stereotypes them; leading audiences to reinforce the stereotype through their behaviour.

Valuable land is destroyed when it is cleared for grazing; reducing habitats for other animals.
For many years, Canada has been a leader in multiculturalism, along with a few other countries; such as the United States and England.

Do not use a semicolon to introduce a list or series; a colon is correct.

Incorrect:

Shakespeare's last plays are sometimes called romances and include the following; *Cymbeline, A Winter's Tale,* and *The Tempest.*

Colons

It is often said that a semicolon brings the reader to a brief stop, but the colon leads the reader on. The colon has three main uses: to set up a quotation, to set up or introduce a list or series, and to separate an independent clause from a word, phrase, or clause that answers, completes, or expands on what precedes it.

> You may use a colon to set up a direct quotation if the preceding thought is complete and fully expressed.

1. To set up a quotation: When you use direct quotations in your essays, you can set them up formally with a colon:

The *Oxford English Dictionary* defines the word *rhetoric* this way: "The art of using language so as to persuade or influence others."
Health Canada has made the following recommendation for dentists: "Non-mercury filling materials should be considered for restoring the primary teeth of children where the mechanical properties of the material are safe."

Direct quotations can also be set up less formally with a comma or no punctuation. To determine which is appropriate, treat the complete sentence as if it contained no quotation and see if one of the rules for using commas applies:

According to the American Academy of Dermatology, "a tan is the skin's response to an injury, and every time you tan, you accumulate damage to the skin."
The most general definition of evolution is "any non-miraculous process by which new forms of life are produced" (Bowler 2).

In the first sentence, a comma rule dictates the use of a comma before the quotation; in the second, there is no rule that necessitates a comma. A comma after *is* would be incorrect.

2. To set up or introduce a list or series: The most formal way to set up a list or series is to make a complete statement followed by a colon and the list of items:

> In 1998, the CBC outlined three challenges for the future: to attract more viewers to Canadian programming, to increase the availability of "under-represented" categories, and to direct its resources toward this kind of programming.

Avoid the temptation to insert a colon before you start the list unless what precedes it is a complete sentence. Normally, you would not use a colon after *including* or *such as* or right after a linking verb (e.g., *is* or *are*), though these words are often used to set up a list or series.

Incorrect:

> Caffeine withdrawal can have many negative effects, such as: severe headaches, drowsiness, irritability, and poor concentration.
> One of the questions the committee will attempt to answer is: Does our current public health system work?

3. To separate an independent clause from a word, phrase, or clause that answers, completes, or expands on what precedes it: What follows a colon may answer, complete, or expand on what is asked or implied in the preceding independent clause. This could be as little as a word or as much as an independent clause. Like the comma and semicolon, then, the colon can be used to separate independent clauses; however, what follows the colon must answer the question asked in the previous clause:

> There is only one quality you omitted from the list of my most endearing characteristics: my modesty. [answers "What quality?"]
> David's driving test was a memorable experience: he backed over a curb, sailed through two stop signs, and forgot to signal a left turn. [answers "Why was the test memorable?"]
> The New Testament of the Bible gives the ultimate rule for Christians: to treat others the way you want them to treat you. [answers "What rule?"]

You may use a colon to separate an independent clause from a word, phrase, or clause that answers or completes what precedes it.

Unless you are using semicolons to separate items in a series, what precedes and follows a semicolon must be an independent clause. What precedes a colon must be an independent clause that makes a complete statement.

If what follows the colon is at least the equivalent of an independent clause, it may begin with a capital letter. It is perfectly acceptable to begin with a lower-case letter, however, as in the examples.

Dashes and Parentheses

Although some people use em dashes (named because they are the width of the letter *m*) and parentheses interchangeably, their functions are different. Imagine that you are in a crowded room where everyone is talking. Somebody takes you aside and begins speaking in an unnaturally loud voice about the latest rumour; other people are listening, which is the design of the person talking. A couple of minutes later, somebody else approaches and very discreetly whispers the same information in your ear. Using em dashes is like giving information that is meant to be overheard, to be stressed. But parentheses are more like asides. They convey additional information that is not important enough to be included in the main part of the sentence.

Em dashes, then, emphasize a word or phrase or convey a break in thought. You can find em dashes in Word by choosing **Insert**, then **Symbol**, **More Symbols**, and **Special Characters**. Another option is to type two hyphens—if you don't leave a space after the second one, your computer may automatically convert them to an em dash.

> Don't use one hyphen if you want to set off a word or phrase. Hyphens are a mark of spelling—not punctuation.

Where dashes emphasize, parentheses de-emphasize. Use the latter sparingly to include a word or phrase, or occasionally a sentence, that isn't important enough to be included as part of the main text. You may also use parentheses to refer to a source in a research essay:

> "Crayolas plus imagination (the ability to create images) make for happiness if you are a child" (Robert Fulghum).

Punctuating parenthetical insertions depends on whether the statement in parentheses is complete or part of the larger sentence. In the first instance, place the end punctuation inside the closing parenthesis, as the information pertains only to what is between parentheses. (For example, the period in this sentence goes inside.)

In the second case, punctuate the sentence just as you would if there were no parentheses. The following sentence illustrates punctuation that has nothing to do with the parenthetical insertion but is required to separate independent clauses. Notice the lowercasing of *both*:

> Cassandra wanted to be an actor (both her parents were actors), but she always trembled violently as soon as she stepped on a stage.

Use dashes and parentheses sparingly in your writing.

Chapter 12 offers more information on parenthetical documentation methods.

You may use em dashes occasionally to set off words from the rest of the sentence.

You may use parentheses to include less important information of the sentence.

Exercise **14.5**

Using the rule categories discussed, replace commas in the following sentences with the most appropriate form of punctuation (semicolon, colon, dash, parentheses). In some cases, the commas are correct and should not be replaced.

1. April showers bring May flowers, May flowers bring on my asthma.
2. A developing salmon goes through four stages, the alevin, the fry, the smolt, and the adult.
3. Every essay needs three parts, an introduction, a body, and a conclusion.
4. He paused to admire the splendid sight before his eyes, the ruins of Montgomery Castle.
5. Mayumi tended to look on the good side of things, Glenn usually saw the bad side.
6. The following is not a rule for comma use, put a comma wherever you pause.
7. It is probable, though not certain, that she will be promoted to the rank of corporal next year.
8. It was the best of times, it was the worst of times.
9. Marselina has a fine ear for music, unfortunately she can't sing a note.
10. In my health sciences class, we studied the four main food groups, dairy products, meats, carbohydrates, and fruits and vegetables.
11. Whenever I order designer clothing for my boutique, I shop in Toronto, Ontario, Buffalo, New York, and London, England.
12. The Online Dictionary defines animal cruelty this way, "treatment or standards of care that cause unwarranted or unnecessary suffering or harm to animals."
13. The tuition increase has affected many lower income families, therefore, there is an even greater demand for student loans.
14. Brian never tired of misquoting Shakespeare, "The quality of mercy is not stained."
15. Virginia Woolf had this to say about the essay, "Of all forms of literature it is the one which least calls for the use of long words."

After you've checked your answers in Appendix D, complete questions 16–30.

16. First advice to those about to write a novel is the same as Punch's to those about to wed, don't (Victor Jones).
17. The Romans were willing to change their religious beliefs quite easily, however, the Greeks were less willing.
18. In compound sentences, use a comma to join independent clauses where there is a coordinating conjunction, use a semicolon where two such clauses are not joined by a coordinating conjunction.
19. His plans for the new development included the following, an apartment complex, single-family residences, a 60-store mall, and a multi-use recreation centre.

(continued)

20. Oil, electricity, and solar power are popular sources for heating homes, however, the most popular is natural gas.

21. The tour includes visits to the following museums, the Prado in Madrid, Spain, the Louvre in Paris, France, and the Rijksmuseum in Amsterdam, the Netherlands.

22. It was the ideal summer job, you were outdoors in lovely weather, you were active, and the pay was more than reasonable.

23. School cafeterias often offer unhealthy options, such as hot dogs, which have virtually no nutritional value, hamburgers, which have a high fat content, and poutine, known as "heart attack in a bowl."

24. The zero emissions of a battery-electric vehicle come with a drawback, the emissions are only as clean as the means used to generate the power.

25. This year's conference on the environment is intended to focus on three main areas, global warming, pollution, and the destruction of natural habitat.

26. The art of writing the news lead is to answer as many of the following five questions as possible, Who?, What?, Where?, When?, and How?

27. The current figures of mercury absorption have been announced by the ADA, however, the group's review has been criticized as misleading.

28. A lack of essential nutrients can result in deficiencies, for example, a vegetarian may have iron deficiency.

29. As rainwater travels downward through the soil, it may collect a number of pollutants, furthermore, an extended period of time may elapse before this pollution is discovered.

30. Freewriting can be a useful means of overcoming blocks, it can help you write when you're not in the mood, it can generate ideas, even if you are the kind of writer who has a hard time coming up with main points, and it can energize your writing.

Exercise 14.6

Correct or add commas in the following passages. Among your changes and additions, include at least one semicolon and one colon in each passage. Some commas have been included to help with reading; however, they may not be correct.

1. Cocaine an alkaloid obtained from coca leaves is a stimulant to the nervous system, unfortunately it is one of the most addictive drugs and it is possible to overdose and die on first use. Among the 3 million users today 500,000 are highly addicted. Cocaine users describe the high as a euphoric feeling, they feel energetic and mentally alert, however this feeling wears off in as little as 20 minutes. User responses to the drug vary but may include the following, hyperactivity elevated blood pressure and heart rate

and increased sexual interest. Large amounts of cocaine such as more than 100 milligrams can cause bizarre erratic and violent behaviours.

2. Labour shortages during the late nineteenth century in Canada became an impediment to progress and something had to be done to fix this problem. For white politicians and business owners the solution seemed obvious, exploit cheap labour. Chinese immigrants provided exactly what was needed to boost the labour scene, they were male unskilled and cheap. Between 1881 and 1885 approximately 17,000 Chinese immigrants arrived in Canada, Chinese men were employed in masses, their jobs included those in mining forestry canning and above all railroad construction. Sir Matthew Begbie the chief justice of British Columbia said "Chinese labourers do well what white women cannot do and what white men will not do."

Apostrophes

The apostrophe is a mark of spelling that indicates the possessive and shows where letters have been omitted in a contraction.

Technically, the **apostrophe** isn't a mark of punctuation; it is a mark of spelling that indicates the possessive case of nouns and some indefinite pronouns. It is also used in contractions, to show the omission of one or more letters.

Apostrophes for Possession in Nouns

The **possessive** case indicates ownership and similar relationships between nouns and pronouns, such as association, authorship, duration, description, and source of origin. The possessive indicates that the second noun belongs to or is associated with the first. When an apostrophe and *s* are added to a noun to show the possessive, the noun functions adjectivally and can be replaced by the corresponding possessive adjective. Most pronouns, however, do not show the possessive through an apostrophe.

The **possessive** case indicates relationships such as ownership.

the hard drive of the computer/the computer's hard drive/its hard drive [ownership]
the landlady's apartment/her apartment [ownership]
the tenants' rights/their rights [association]
Dvorak's *New World Symphony*/his symphony [authorship]

Singular Nouns

Singular nouns take an apostrophe + s to indicate the possessive.

The usual rule with a singular noun, including proper nouns ending in *s*, *ss*, or the *s* sound, is to add *'s* to make it possessive.

the attorney's portfolio; Mr Price's car; the week's lesson

Because it may look and sound awkward to add an apostrophe + *s* to a singular proper noun ending in *s*, some authorities add only the apostrophe (e.g., *Tracy Jarvis' book*, meaning *the book of Tracy Jarvis*). Others follow the rule for singular nouns (*Tracy Jarvis's book*). Either treatment is acceptable, but choose one and apply it consistently in your essay.

Plural Nouns

With a plural noun, an apostrophe is added after the *s* to make it possessive.

> the islands' inhabitants; the Hansons' children; the Gibbses' marriage certificate; two weeks' lessons; the readers' perceptions

Make sure you carefully distinguish between singular and plural nouns when applying the rules for possessives:

> company + *'s* → the company's profits [one company]
> companies + *'* → the companies' profits [more than one company]
> society + *'s* → our society's attitude toward war [one society]
> societies + *'* → past societies' attitudes toward war [many societies]

A few plural nouns do not end in *s*: *children, women, men, people*. They are treated as singular nouns for the possessive.

> the popular children's book; the women's group

Joint Ownership

In the case of joint ownership, where both nouns share or are equal parties in something, only the last noun shows the possessive. Ensure from the context that both nouns reflect a truly equal, shared relationship. In the following sentences, the assumption is that Salem and Sheena shared hosting duties at one party but that the general manager and the district manager received separate wages.

> I attended Salem and Sheena's party.
> Morana raised the general manager's and the district manager's wages.

Piaget and Montessori did not share the same belief or theory:

> Incorrect: Piaget and Montessori's beliefs about how children learn were similar in many ways.

Correct: Piaget's and Montessori's beliefs about how children learn were similar in many ways.

Apostrophes are sometimes misused with plural nouns. Avoid the following incorrect uses:

Incorrect:

I have 6 CD's.
The 1990's were a decade of extravagant spending.
The lemon's are on sale this week.

Exception: Apostrophes can be used for clarity with numbers, letters, or symbols to indicate the plural:

Adrian got two A's and three B's this semester.

Apostrophes with Indefinite Pronouns

Like nouns, but unlike other kinds of pronouns, many **indefinite pronouns** take an apostrophe + *s* to show the possessive:

In times of stress, it is not in *one's* best interest to act quickly or reflexively. [i.e., the best interest of one]

> **Indefinite pronouns**, unlike personal pronouns, take an apostrophe + *s* to indicate the possessive (e.g., *one's beliefs*).

Contractions

The second main use of the apostrophe is to show missing letters. People often confuse the contraction *it's* (*it is*) with the possessive form *its* (as in *I gave the dog its bone*). The contraction *who's* (*who is*) is sometimes confused with the possessive form *whose* (*the man whose house I'm renting*). Contractions are not generally used in formal writing. You should check with your instructor to see if they are acceptable in your assignment.

> Don't confuse *its*, the possessive pronoun, with *it's*, the contraction for *it is*.

Exercise **14.7**

For the following sentences, add apostrophes and make any other necessary changes to the nouns requiring the possessive.

1. In South Africa, the current crime rate is using up much of the countrys GDP.
2. Parents and teachers often complain about televisions influence in todays society.
3. The Crosses house is up for sale, and its list price is $179,000. (The last name is Cross.)

(continued)

4. Ones education should not depend on the financial resources of ones parents.
5. The schools biggest draw for new students was the brand new recreation complex.
6. The course I took required two hours homework a day.
7. The mayors biggest asset is her commitment to the citys future growth.
8. In anorexia nervosa, a patients fingernails and teeth may be damaged due to a lack of calcium.
9. Ryans and Jessicas birthday is on the same day.
10. Apples, oranges, mangoes, and tomatoes are the stores specials today.

After you've checked your answers in Appendix D, complete questions 11–25.

11. Its a shame that Lennys parents werent able to attend their sons graduation ceremonies. (Lenny is an only child.)
12. I dont know whether this etching is his or hers, but theres no doubt its worth a lot in todays market.
13. Its true there are four *ss* and four *is* in the word *Mississippi*, but there are only two *ps*.
14. This weeks classifieds had several jobs for legal secretaries, all requiring three years experience in solicitors work.
15. Zebra stripes always make me homesick for my Uncle Filbert, whos in jail for stealing his brothers life savings. (one brother)
16. The instructor found Bens copy of Shakespeares play *The Winters Tale* in the recycle bin after the last class.
17. As a child whose parents were relatively well off, I thought all my relatives lives were as easy as mine.
18. Our societys fascination with celebrities lives is a product of the medias daily obsession.
19. Books, music, and DVDs can be found on Amazon, one of the Internets most popular sites.
20. The young man stated his churchs mission is to spread Jesus message to people throughout the world.
21. Drugs called immunosuppressants can interfere with the bodys ability to fight infection.
22. Nowadays, rap is used to express a persons experiences, feelings, and opinions.
23. Climate change is caused by harmful chemicals that trap the suns energy in the earths atmosphere.
24. The Smiths and the O'Neils won the trip to see the Seattle Mariners play the Blue Jays in the Mariners home town.
25. The introductory paragraph should capture the readers interest while developing the writers credibility.

Exercise **14.8**

The following passage concerns responses to the article "Spin Doctors," posted on the Canoe website. Punctuate the text for correctness and effectiveness, ensuring that all punctuation is used properly. Minimal punctuation has been provided in places to aid in understanding; however, some may be incorrect.

Reader reaction was swift and impassioned. The sites traffic which averages 65 to 70 million views each month experienced an additional 50,000 page views within the first 10 days of the posting. The investigation drew more than 400 letters to the editor hundred's of emails to the message boards and more than 16,000 responses to an online poll.

The intensity of the response surprised veteran investigative journalist Wayne MacPhail the articles author. Although the sheer volume of letters was unexpected it proved to him that there was an audience for online journalism in Canada. MacPhail has experimented with hypertext reporting since the late 1980s but outside of "Spin Doctors" he believes that by and large newspapers have done a "woeful job" of building an audience for Web-based investigative reporting. . . .

Unlike it's media rivals Canoe has never made journalism it's only or even its most important focus. A headline announcing the top story of the day appears underneath the Canoe banner but there are so many other things to do, shopping email contests Web utilities and lifestyle tips all compete with the news.

The CNEWS section isnt necessarily the first place people are expected to go on the network though it is usually at the top of the highlighted sections. It is also part of the site that changes the most during daylight hours. In other words when CNEWS changes the entire home page changes. A "This Just In" feature was recently added but theres no set schedule for posting stories. Despite this expansion of the news section Canoes promotional material drives home the message that the site is about much more than current events. One recent ad reads, "shop chat email read, in that order."

Chapter Review Questions

1. What are the comma rules?
2. When should you not use a comma?
3. Identify at least one comma use that you did not know or that you had previously learned incorrectly.
4. When do you use semicolons?
5. When should you not use a semicolon?
6. When do you use colons?
7. When should you not use a colon?
8. Why do you use dashes or parentheses?
9. What are the rules for apostrophe use?
10. Provide examples of incorrect apostrophe use that you have seen outside the classroom.

15 Agreement, Pronoun, and Sentence Structure Errors

In this chapter, you will learn

- how to ensure subject–verb agreement;
- how to fix pronoun errors;
- how the incorrect use of pronouns can show gender bias;
- how modifiers can affect clarity; and
- how to use parallelism to create clear sentences.

The grammar rules discussed in this chapter are easily missed when writing an essay draft. Mastering these rules will increase your credibility as a writer and help you create documents that are easy to understand.

Agreement

A verb must agree in number with its subject: they must be both singular or both plural. Similarly, a pronoun must agree in number, person, and gender with its antecedent (the noun it replaces). These forms of agreement reinforce the close connection between a subject and the verb it governs, along with the close connection between a noun and the pronoun that replaces it.

Subject–Verb Agreement

You will not usually have to stop and think about whether a verb agrees in number with its subject, especially if English is your first language. However, determining whether a subject is singular or plural is not always straightforward. The specific rules explained here help you apply the important principle of **subject–verb agreement**.

Usually, the subject of a sentence or clause is the noun or pronoun that performs the action of the verb (or that exists in the state expressed by the subject complement). In most cases, the subject precedes the verb and is easy to find.

Kevin and Nigel are happy that they passed the exam.

Sometimes the subject is harder to spot for one of the following reasons.

1. The sentence begins with *Here is/are, There is/are, There has/have been*, etc. Because the subject follows the verb, you have to look ahead to the first noun/pronoun to determine whether the subject is singular or plural. The following examples underline the noun and italicize the verb.

    There *are* many reasons to support the legalization of marijuana.
    Here *is* one person who supports raising the drinking age.

2. The sentence is phrased as a question. You may need to look ahead to determine the number of the subject.

    What *is* the main reason for legalizing marijuana?
    Where *are* all the people who are in favour of raising the drinking age?

3. The subject is delayed. Because the sentence begins with a prepositional phrase, the noun(s) may seem to form the subject, which is actually later in the sentence. You can always rearrange these kinds of sentences to confirm that they use a **delayed subject** construction.

Agreement is the principle that a verb must agree with its subject, and a pronoun must agree with its antecedent.

 Chapter 13 discusses pronouns and antecedents.

Subject-verb agreement is the principle that a verb must agree with (i.e., match) its subject in number—that is, a singular subject requires a singular verb, and a plural subject requires a plural verb.

If a sentence begins with a phrase such as *Here/There is*, is a question, or uses a delayed subject construction, look ahead to find the subject.

 Chapter 13 discusses prepositional phrases.

A **delayed subject** appears after a prepositional phrase and the verb.

After watching *Downton Abbey*, <u>I</u> decided to travel to England.

Sentence rearranged with subject first:

<u>I</u> decided to travel to England after watching *Downton Abbey*.
Among Graham's favourites was <u>the last album</u> by David Bowie.

Sentence rearranged:

<u>The last album</u> by David Bowie was among Graham's favourites.

4. The subject governs a linking verb that has a plural complement. Don't be distracted by what follows the verb; the subject alone determines whether the verb is singular or plural.

   Tanning <u>salons</u> *are* not the safest way to get a tan.
   The <u>topic</u> for discussion tomorrow *is* the pros and cons of indoor tanning.

5. The subject is followed by one or more prepositional phrases containing nouns and/or pronouns. A noun or pronoun that directly follows a preposition (e.g., *of*) cannot act as a subject; it is the object of the preposition. If there are several nouns before the verb, backtrack carefully to find the noun or pronoun that governs it. You can put parentheses around the distracting words:

   > If several nouns precede the verb, identify the true noun/pronoun subject before deciding whether the verb should be singular or plural.

   A long <u>list</u> (of items, including vegetables, fruits, meats, and several kinds of bread,) *was* handed to Tao.
   The <u>roots</u> (of his dissatisfaction with the course) *go* very deep.

   A related problem occurs when a writer mistakes a prepositional phrase or even a dependent clause for a subject. The following sentences can be fixed by omitting the preposition and beginning the sentence with the noun subject:

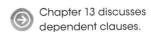 Chapter 13 discusses dependent clauses.

Incorrect: By choosing to take a few correspondence courses may afford a student athlete greater flexibility in meeting academic requirements.

By choosing has been mistaken for the subject.

Correct: <u>Choosing</u> to take a few correspondence courses may afford a student athlete greater flexibility.

Incorrect: With the development of the computer led to automated robots on the production line.

With the development of the computer has been mistaken for the subject.

Correct: The <u>development</u> of the computer led to automated robots on the production line.
Incorrect: Edna thinks of her children at the last moment before her death does not change the fact she is still willing to leave them.

Although Edna thinks of her children at the last moment before her death, a dependent clause, has been mistaken for the subject. A dependent clause contains its own subject.

Correct: Although Edna thinks of her children at the last moment before her death, <u>she</u> is still willing to leave them.

Edna thinks of her children at the last moment before her death, though this does not change the fact that she is willing to leave them.

Rules for Subject–Verb Agreement

The section "Precision and Logic" (pages 428-9) also discusses subject-verb agreement.

A **compound subject** contains two nouns, two pronouns, or a noun and a pronoun acting as one subject.

1. A **compound subject** joined by the conjunction *and* usually requires a plural verb form.

   Thanh <u>and</u> his friend *are* visiting Ottawa.

   Occasionally, a compound subject expresses a single idea.

   <u>Rhythm and blues</u> *was* always popular with younger audiences.
   <u>To compare and contrast</u> the roles of setting in the novels *is* sure to be a question on the exam.

   In both examples, the compound subject can be treated as a singular subject since the elements are so closely connected that separating them changes their meaning.

2. When the nouns or pronouns in a compound subject are linked by a correlative conjunction (*either . . . or* or *neither . . . nor*), the noun or pronoun nearest the verb determines its form. These conjunctions suggest a choice between one thing or the other much more than *and*.

   The chairs <u>or the table</u> *is* going to auction.

Neither famine <u>nor floods</u> *are* going to force the people to leave their homes.

If you changed the order of the nouns making up the compound subject in these sentences, you would need to change the number of the verb as well.

3. A prepositional phrase can also be used to join two nouns in a compound subject. *As well as, along with, in addition to, together with,* and *combined with* are examples of such phrases, which do not have the strength of *and.* When you use one of these joiners, you stress the first element more than the second one. Logically, then, the verb form agrees with the first element.

> When using a compound subject, look at the joining word(s) to determine whether the subject is singular or plural.

The <u>instructor, as well as her students,</u> *is* going to attend the symposium on the environment.
The Australian <u>prime minister, along with his ministers for education and foreign affairs,</u> *is* set to arrive tomorrow.

As you can see, the prepositional phrase is set off with commas, which may help you determine the correct verb form. To stress equality, the sentences would be changed to

The <u>instructor and her students</u> *are* going to attend the symposium on the environment.
The Australian <u>prime minister, minister for education, and minister for foreign affairs</u> *are* set to arrive tomorrow.

4. A **collective noun** refers to a group. It is singular in form but may be either singular or plural in meaning, depending on context. If the context suggests singular, the verb form is singular; if plural, the verb is plural. Examples of collective nouns include *audience, band, class, committee, congregation, family, gang, group, jury, staff,* and *team.*
    Whenever the context suggests that the members of the group are considered *one unit,* all doing the same thing or acting together, the verb form is *singular;* when the members are considered *individuals acting independently,* the corresponding verb form is *plural.*

> A **collective noun** may be singular or plural, depending on context. If in doubt, consider it singular.

 See Chapter 13 for a discussion of nouns.

The <u>jury</u> *is* out to consider the evidence.
After the lecture, the <u>class</u> *are* going to be able to ask questions.

Most often, a collective noun is considered singular; if in doubt, choose this form. If a plural verb with a collective noun sounds odd, rephrase the subject so that the collective noun functions adjectivally before an appropriate plural noun.

After the lecture, <u>class members</u> *are* going to be able to ask questions.

5. In these phrases, the verb form is singular, even though the noun or pronoun that follows is plural: *each of, either/neither of, every one of, one of, the only one of,* and *which one of.*

    <u>One of</u> our 115 students *has* written an A+ essay.
    Alec <u>is the only one of</u> those attending who *has* difficulty speaking before a large group.

6. An **indefinite pronoun** refers to non-specific individuals or objects. Most indefinite pronouns are considered singular and take a singular form in agreement. *Anybody, anyone, anything, each, either, everybody, everyone, everything, neither, nobody, no one, nothing, one, somebody,* and *someone* are singular indefinite pronouns. Unlike other pronouns, many indefinite pronouns use the apostrophe to express the possessive:

<u>Everybody's</u> opinion *is* welcome.

Compare with

<u>His or her</u> opinion *is* welcome; <u>their</u> opinions *are* welcome.

Some experts believe that, when context clearly warrants the use of plural agreement with the antecedents *everyone* and *everybody*, as in the next example, you may use the plural pronoun.

When the pepper was spilled, <u>everyone</u> rubbed <u>their</u> noses.

7. There is a separate rule for phrases involving portions and fractions + *of,* such as *all, any, a lot, a variety, a number, (one-)half, more, most, much, none, part, plenty, some,* and *the majority/minority.* The form of the verb depends on whether the noun or pronoun following *of* is singular or plural.

In these examples, the verb agrees with the bolded word:

<u>None of the missing **pieces**</u> *have* been found yet.
<u>Some of the **losses**</u> incurred with the companies' merger *are* being absorbed by the shareholders.
<u>Half of the **pie**</u> *is* gone.
<u>One-third of the **employees**</u> *are* out on strike.

8. Subjects referring to distance, time, money, weight, or mass are usually *singular.* When the subject is *the number of,* the verb is *singular* (in contrast with rule 7).

<u>Twelve miles</u> *is* not a great distance to an experienced hiker.
<u>The number of</u> people attending the courses *has* dropped in the last two years.

9. Some nouns ending in *s* refer to a singular concept or subject; therefore, they require a singular verb. Examples include *athletics*, *billiards*, *darts*, *economics*, *gymnastics*, *mathematics*, *measles*, *mumps*, *news*, *physics*, *politics*, and *statistics*.

<u>Statistics</u> *is* an inexact science.
No <u>news</u> *is* good news.

Depending on their context, many of these nouns can be considered plural and should take a plural verb form. For example, *statistics* could refer to a set of facts rather than to one subject:

The <u>statistics</u> on global warming *are* alerting politicians to the need for worldwide action.

Whether the titles of artistic works or the names of companies are singular or plural does not affect the verb. A singular verb needs to agree with the subject.

<u>*Montreal Stories*</u> is a collection of Mavis Gallant's fiction; <u>McClelland & Stewart</u> *is* the publisher.

10. The following terms are plural and require the plural form of the verb: *both*, *few*, *many*, *parts of*, *several*.

A well-educated <u>few</u> *seem* to care about correct grammar and punctuation these days, but <u>both</u> *are* essential parts of the writing process.

> Most errors in subject–verb agreement occur in one of three situations: use of a compound subject, use of an indefinite pronoun as the subject, or use of intervening words between the subject and the verb.

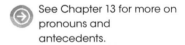

See Chapter 13 for more on pronouns and antecedents.

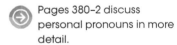

Pages 380–2 discuss personal pronouns in more detail.

 # Pronouns at Work

Pronoun-Antecedent Agreement

Most problems in **pronoun–antecedent agreement** apply to personal pronouns, such as *she*, *he*, *they*, and *them*, as well as to the possessive form of pronouns, *its* and *their*. A pronoun must agree with its antecedent noun in number. If you have difficulty finding the antecedent, see which noun in the sentence can be substituted for the pronoun:

The first thing that usually strikes us about <u>a person</u> is <u>his or her</u> [a person's] physical appearance.

> A pronoun's antecedent is the noun it replaces, and a pronoun must agree with its antecedeqnt in number.

The rule for **pronoun-antecedent agreement** also applies to possessive adjectives, such as *their*, which are formed from pronouns.

Dieters should realize that a diet only works when they [dieters] restrict their [dieters'] caloric intake.

Most of the rules for subject–verb agreement also apply to pronoun–antecedent agreement. For example, a compound antecedent requires the plural form of the pronoun or possessive pronoun.

Connie and Steve *have* invited me to their cottage.

If the compound subject includes the word *each* or *every*, the singular form should be used.

Each book and magazine in the library *has* its own entry.

When two antecedents are joined by *or* or *nor*, the pronoun agrees with the closest antecedent.

Neither the prime minister nor his advisors *were* certain how to implement their proposal.

As with subject–verb agreement, a collective noun antecedent requires the singular pronoun form if it is thought of as a unit; if the context suggests that individuals are being referred to, the pronoun takes a plural form.

Our hockey team *will play* its final game against its archrivals. [The team will be playing as a unit.]
The team *will be receiving* their new jerseys Friday. [Each individual team member will be given a jersey.]

With a pronoun referring to a portion or fraction, agreement depends on whether the noun following *of* is singular or plural.

Studies show that a large number of college and university students *are* cheating on their exams and essays; however, a much larger number are not.

If the pronoun has an indefinite pronoun antecedent such as *anybody*, *one*, or *someone*, the singular form applies, as it does with subject–verb agreement.

One should be careful about pronoun agreement, or one's teacher will certainly point out the error to one.

Although grammatically correct, this sentence could be improved by replacing the indefinite pronoun *one* with a personal pronoun. However, you must be careful to use a *singular* pronoun, which the writer of the following failed to do:

Incorrect: <u>One</u> should be careful about pronoun agreement, or <u>their</u> teacher will certainly point out the error to <u>them</u>.

In the next example, a singular pronoun replaces the singular antecedent *one*—but the sentence is incorrect because the possessive adjective *his* and the personal pronoun *him* refer to only one gender.

 The next section discusses gender bias and inclusive language.

Incorrect: <u>One</u> should be careful about pronoun agreement, or <u>his</u> teacher will certainly point out the error to <u>him</u>.

Problematic Pronouns: Inclusive Language

In recent years, efforts to avoid gender bias led to a neutral or **gender-inclusive**, but grammatically incorrect, use of the plural personal pronouns *they*, *them*, and *their*. Using correct pronouns in the form of *him or her* or *his or her* is awkward compared to the inclusive *him*, but it is preferable to an incorrect *their* and better than a form that may appear sexist. The following sentence includes both singular forms to replace the antecedent *student*.

A <u>student</u> must footnote <u>his or her</u> references, or the teacher will expect <u>him or her</u> to correct the oversight.

The problem of pronoun–antecedent agreement is especially common when the antecedent noun is either an indefinite pronoun or a singular noun that is not gender-specific—a generic noun such as *reader*, *writer*, *student*, *teacher*, *individual*, *character*, or *person*. Here are three options to consider in this situation.

Gender-inclusive language is the careful use of terms and grammatical forms that include both genders. When an antecedent is either a generic singular noun or an indefinite pronoun, the personal pronoun that follows must be both singular *and* gender-inclusive. This often means using two personal pronouns, such as *he or she*. Certain organizations are now adopting the pronoun *they* to refer to gender-neutral people. This practice is not yet standard; discuss it with your instructor before you use it.

1. Replace the plural pronoun with *both* singular personal pronouns (or possessive adjectives). This option is nearly always acceptable in academic writing but can be awkward and repetitive in journalistic and business writing.

   Incorrect: <u>Anybody</u> not willing to put in long hours for little pay should give up <u>their</u> idea of becoming a writer.
   Correct: <u>Anybody</u> not willing to put in long hours for little pay should give up <u>his or her</u> idea of becoming a writer.

2. Change the singular antecedent into the equivalent plural form and use the plural pronoun.

   <u>Those</u> not willing to put in long hours for little pay should give up <u>their</u> ideas of becoming writers.

   Note the plural *ideas* to agree with *those* and *their*.

3. Revise the sentence to use the gender-neutral pronoun *you*. This option is not always possible and may occasionally sound too informal for academic writing.

If <u>you</u> are not willing to put in long hours for little pay, <u>you</u> should give up <u>the idea</u> of becoming a writer.

Exercise 15.1

Using all the options presented in the last section, fix the pronoun–antecedent agreement errors in the following paragraph.

If a child begins to perform poorly at school nowadays, they will likely be sent to a school counsellor to deal with the situation. Everyone assumes that attention deficit disorder is the culprit, and they just as automatically assume that drugs are the answer. On the other hand, perhaps the child is just not interested in a particular subject, or they do not understand the material. Parents, in turn, treat the child as if he is the problem instead of listening to him to find out how he can be helped.

Exercise 15.2

Choose the correct form of the verb and/or pronoun for these sentences and make any other necessary changes in agreement. Rewrite the sentence where required.

1. Everybody who supported the motion raised (his/her/their) hand.
2. Neither the film's director nor its producers (was/were) on hand to receive (his/her/their) prestigious award.
3. The instructor, as well as the students, (thinks/think) the room is too small.
4. It is unfortunate when a person no longer cares what others think about (him/her/them).
5. One should never expect to succeed unless (one/they) (is/are) willing to persist—even against the odds.
6. It is the tried and true that (provides/provide) the ultimate refuge in mediocrity.
7. Everyone who works during the year (is/are) obliged to file (his/her/their) income tax return.
8. Her set of baby teeth (was/were) complete when she was only 18 months old.
9. He was one of those few candidates who (was/were) able to win re-election.
10. None of the company's products (requires/require) testing on animals.

11. Lining the side of the highway (is/are) a lot of billboards advertising fast-food restaurants.
12. Every specimen of the horned grebe (has/have) a distinctive tuft on each side of (its/their) head.
13. Media and information technology training (provides/provide) students today with important communication skills.
14. Neither team members nor their coach (expects/expect) the season to last another game.
15. The maximum number of people allowed on this elevator (is/are) 30.

Exercise 15.3

Correct the subject–verb agreement and/or pronoun–antecedent agreement errors in the following sentences. Some contain no errors; others contain more than one.

1. Every person in the community should have the right to attend university and create new opportunities for themselves.
2. Especially unique to adolescent depression are physical symptoms, such as headaches.
3. The tonal quality of Amati's violins are excellent but not perfect.
4. Over the past week, there has been some unexplained occurrences on the girls' floor of the residence.
5. Small class sizes and a low student population means few opportunities to meet new people.
6. A typical poem by Emily Dickinson leaves the reader searching for another line or even another stanza to satisfy their craving for closure.
7. Use of the leaves of the coca plant for its stimulant effects dates back thousands of years.
8. A coalition of neighbourhood organizations, students, and unions are currently forming to oppose the university's proposed plan.
9. Everyone who has purchased tickets is eligible for the grand prize, but they must be residents of Canada to claim their prize.
10. If a child is denied the opportunity to play, how can they develop emotionally and physically?

After you've checked your answers in Appendix D, complete questions 11–25.

11. Participation and public education is necessary in a true democracy.
12. When a person contracts jaundice, their skin as well as the white part of their eyes turn yellow.
13. Another round of intense labour negotiations have not produced a settlement, so each union member has been told to do his duty on the strike line.
14. Before rendering its unanimous verdict, the jury was polled individually.
15. Almost nothing shapes a person's true character as much as their home.

(continued)

16. The nature and role of human resources in organizations have undergone tremendous change in the last two decades.
17. In P.K. Page's poem, it is apparent that the landlady's prying nature and lonely life has made her forget her place.
18. Stereotyping and the use of degrading language in the book serves to reinforce its theme.
19. His overriding concern with rules and regulations, together with his excessive neatness and demand for order, suggests a mild obsessive-compulsive complex.
20. A person who continually disregards others' feelings will pay for their neglect sooner or later.
21. The encouragement of curiosity, questioning, and discussion is vital to the success of today's school environment.
22. In Japanese culture, a person's reputation along with their social standing depend on the concept of "saving face."
23. Medieval universities established a system of education and academic credentials that continue to function in today's universities.
24. The give and take in any relationship is the most important factor in sustaining it.
25. Although the Canadian Forces is still one of the best-trained military in the world, the training standards and morale of the forces is declining, according to some people.

Other Problems with Pronouns

Other pronoun pitfalls are errors in *pronoun reference*, *pronoun case*, and *pronoun consistency*.

Pronoun Reference

Consider life without pronouns.

A Lost Loonie Leads to a Lesson Learned

Alex and Alex's lawyer, Alan, left in Alex's limousine for Loonies Unlimited to buy Alex's landlady, Alice, a litre of light lemonade. Alice told Alex and Alan to also buy a litre of light lemonade for Alice's long-time lodger, Alison. When Alex and Alan alighted at Loonies Unlimited, Alex and Alan were alarmed that Alex had left Alex's loonie in Alex's loft. So Alphonse, of Loonies Unlimited, allowed Alex and Alan only one litre of lemonade, along with a length of limp licorice, and Alphonse loudly lamented Alex's and Alan's laxness.

Exercise **15.4**

Rewrite "A Lost Loonie Leads to a Lesson Learned," replacing as many nouns as possible with pronouns and ensuring that the antecedents are clear. If in doubt about the clarity of antecedents, refer to the section on pronoun reference.

As discussed earlier, the relationship between pronoun and antecedent must always be clear—this principle is called **pronoun reference**. You can test for pronoun reference errors by seeing whether you can replace a pronoun with a specific noun that appears earlier in the sentence (i.e., its antecedent).

> As reality shows have become more popular, <u>they</u> [reality shows] have become more and more bizarre.

In the next example, the antecedent is unclear:

> Reality shows have become more popular while their participants have become more and more bizarre; consequently, <u>they</u> [reality shows? participants?] can no longer be believed.

There are four kinds of pronoun reference errors, which can be repaired in different ways.

1. **No reference (missing antecedent):** This error occurs when the pronoun has no apparent noun antecedent. Consider this sentence:

   > Following the prime minister's speech, he took several questions from reporters.

   The personal pronoun *he* apparently replaces *prime minister's*, which is a possessive adjective. Pronouns replace nouns, not adjectives. In the following sentence, the noun antecedent is implied but not actually stated; grammatically, the reference is missing.

   > One thing that Canadians are especially proud of is <u>its</u> national health-care system.

   Where there is no antecedent, one must be provided or the pronoun replaced with an appropriate noun.

   > After the <u>prime minister</u> spoke, <u>he</u> took several questions from reporters.

   or

   > After speaking, the <u>prime minister</u> took several questions from reporters.

The principle for **pronoun reference** is simple: each pronoun should refer clearly to a specific antecedent.

If the antecedent is missing, revise the sentence by adding an antecedent that agrees with the pronoun.

One thing that <u>Canadians</u> are especially proud of is <u>their</u> national health-care system.

A tendency in speaking, and sometimes in informal writing, is to use the impersonal third-person pronoun *it* or *they* to refer vaguely to some unmentioned authority. Avoid this habit in your formal writing.

<u>They say</u> there's nothing like a nice car to make you popular.

If a sentence begins with a prepositional phrase, the noun that is the object of the preposition cannot be an antecedent. These examples illustrate this problem and its solutions:

Incorrect: With the new Formula One scoring system, <u>it</u> keeps fans excited throughout the season.
Correct: The new Formula One scoring system keeps <u>fans</u> excited throughout the season.

or

With the new Formula One scoring system, <u>fans</u> remain excited throughout the season.

2. **Remote reference:** A reader should not be expected to connect a pronoun to a noun when they are separated by more than one sentence.

In George Orwell's prophetic book *1984*, people's lives were watched over by television screens. These screens, along with brainwashing techniques, enabled people to be kept under firm control. <u>It</u> is an example of dystopian fiction.

> If the pronoun and its antecedent are far from each other in a sentence or paragraph, repeating the noun is often the best way to fix the problem.

The pronoun *it* takes up the thread too late. Many nouns have intervened, making the reader hunt for the antecedent. Repeating the noun is often the best solution when the antecedent is far away from the pronoun.

> If the antecedent could grammatically be more than one noun, you may need to rewrite the sentence so the antecedent is clear.

3. **Ambiguous (squinting) reference:** This error occurs when the pronoun seems to refer to two or more nouns, either of which could be the antecedent.

When <u>Peter</u> gave <u>Paul</u> <u>his</u> driver's licence, <u>he</u> was very surprised to see that it had expired.

Who was surprised in this sentence? The pronoun *he* could refer to either *Peter* or *Paul*.

The problem for readers aspiring to look like the models in women's magazines is that <u>their</u> photos have been airbrushed. [*Their* has two grammatical antecedents: *readers* and *models*.]

In 1916, a member of the Russian parliament denounced Rasputin before <u>his</u> colleagues. [Does *his* refer to the member's colleagues or to Rasputin's?]

While it is sometimes possible to correct ambiguous reference by repeating the noun intended to act as the antecedent, the result is not always pleasing:

When <u>Peter</u> gave <u>Paul</u> his driver's license, <u>Peter</u> was surprised to see that it had expired.

Rewriting may be the better solution:

On giving <u>his</u> driver's license to Paul, <u>Peter</u> was surprised to see that it had expired.

The problem for <u>readers</u> aspiring to look like the models in women's magazines is that the <u>models'</u> photographs have been airbrushed.

In 1916, a <u>member</u> of the Russian parliament denounced Rasputin before <u>the House</u>.

4. **Broad reference (vague reference):** A reference is broad or vague when the pronoun (often *this*, *that*, or *which*) refers to a group of words, an idea, or a concept rather than to *one specific noun*.

    > If the antecedent appears to be an idea rather than a specific noun, add a noun that sums up the idea to the part of the sentence where the error occurs.

    Incorrect: Children these days are too prone to lazy habits, such as watching television. <u>This</u> shows we have become too permissive.

    This replaces too much text—in effect, the whole preceding clause. The next example is quite acceptable in anything but the most formal writing, even though the pronoun *which* replaces *received top marks* rather than a specific noun. The meaning of the sentence, however, is clear.

    She received top marks for her final dive, <u>which</u> gave her the gold medal in that competition.

    In the following sentence, the pronoun *this* refers to an idea rather than a noun antecedent, making the meaning of the second independent clause unclear.

    Incorrect: Many older drivers are retested if they have had medical problems, but <u>this</u> needs to go further.

A **demonstrative pronoun** makes the reference to a noun clearer (e.g., *this book* vs. *that book*).

Broad reference often requires a sentence rewrite. Sometimes, the easiest way is to provide a noun and change the **demonstrative pronoun** into a demonstrative adjective. (A demonstrative adjective has the same form as a demonstrative pronoun—*this*, *that*, *these*, *those*—but it precedes a noun as a modifier rather than taking its place.)

Correct: Children these days are too prone to lazy habits, such as watching television. <u>This tendency</u> shows that we have become too permissive.
Correct: Many older drivers are retested if they have had medical problems, but <u>this retesting</u> needs to go further.

While there is perhaps a "broad" allowance for broad reference error, depending on the level of formality required, *it* is a personal pronoun and, like all personal pronouns, should always have a clear noun referent. In some cases, you may need to use a noun instead.

Poor: We try not to mention specific businesses by name in our article; however, <u>it</u> can't be avoided in some situations.
Better: We try not to mention specific businesses by name in our article; however, we can't avoid <u>names</u> in all situations.

Exercise **15.5**

Fix the broad pronoun references in the following paragraph.

Genetically modified foods have been engineered to flourish in harsh environments. *This* will help alleviate the need for usable farmland as *this* will enable farming to occur on lands once considered unsuitable for growing crops. *This* will be a major benefit to many nations in Africa, Asia, and South America where there is a shortage of food and available land.

Exercise **15.6**

For each of the following statements, construct a sentence or clause that contains the antecedent to the pronoun.

Example:

He just shrugged off all she had to say in her defence.

Preceding sentence:

Lucinda explained her behaviour to Ted, but he just shrugged off all she had to say in her defence.

1. She had long, brown hair down to her waist.
2. He found him sleeping soundly on the kitchen floor the next morning.
3. They lived as if nobody else mattered but themselves.
4. This will be her chance to prove whether she is good enough to make the team.
5. They have a responsibility to educate the public.
6. His attorney decided on a not guilty plea.
7. She awoke suddenly to the sound of gunfire.
8. They make a delightfully odd couple.
9. She will eat only the most expensive kind of deluxe cat food.
10. After hearing their protests for a long time, he finally agreed to take them along.

Exercise 15.7

Identify the kind of pronoun reference errors in the following sentences; then, make the necessary revisions.

1. *It* says in my textbook that pronouns should always have a clear referent.
2. Whenever a staff meeting is called, *they* are required to attend.
3. Racism is a disease that will continue to plague society until *it* is non-existent.
4. Sixty per cent of our pesticides are used on cotton, and *this* is our major ground water pollutant.
5. During Roosevelt's Pearl Harbor speech, *he* identified the United States as a peaceful and tolerant nation.
6. I know it said "*No Parking*," but I went ahead and parked there anyway. They gave me a $20 fine.
7. Her second novel was far different from her first. It was set in the remote Hebrides.
8. Previous Afghan successes were significant victories; for example, they last waged war against the powerful Soviet Union.
9. Some psychologists and researchers believe in the "innate" theory of prejudice. According to this theory, ingrained prejudice is cross-cultural and awareness of race is one of the earliest social characteristics to develop in children. These findings may help account for its popularity.
10. During the dinosaur age, they lived in a rapidly changing environment.

After you've checked your answers in Appendix D, complete questions 11–20.

11. It is the right of everybody to have access to knowledge, and this means access to the education of choice.

(*continued*)

12. In Chapter 21 of my textbook, it analyzes the success of the Liberal Party in Canada.
13. Supervisors may discourage workers from reporting injuries since they receive annual bonuses for low injury rates.
14. Children often hide their compulsive behaviours from friends and family due to feelings of shame, causing them to remain undiagnosed.
15. To experienced gamers, the quality of the video card is crucial; this is because the latest games require a high standard of video card.
16. The Catholic kings of Spain rallied the country to fight their enemies, the Moors. This became known as the Reconquista.
17. Huck Finn was the physically abused son of Pap, who harasses Judge Thatcher when he is drunk. This creates sympathy in the reader, which makes him more likeable.
18. By teaching today's youth safe and healthy approaches to sexuality, it will elevate their self-esteem.
19. Part of the appeal of driving an SUV is that they are big and look impressive beside the "merely mortal" car.
20. Japanese smokers consume more than twice the number of cigarettes as American smokers do, and it continues to increase steadily.

Pronoun Case

Pronoun case is the principle that a pronoun changes its form depending on its function in the sentence (e.g., *I/me, she/her, they/them*). **Personal pronouns** refer to persons. The *first person* refers to the one *doing* the speaking or writing; *second person* refers to the one *spoken to; third person* refers to the one *spoken about.*

Some personal, relative, and interrogative pronouns change their form to reflect their function in the sentence. You must be aware of **pronoun case** in order to use the correct form.

Personal Pronouns

Personal pronouns refer to persons. The first person refers to the one doing the speaking or writing; the second person refers to the one spoken to; and the third person refers to the one spoken about. Most nouns can be considered third person and can be replaced by third-person pronouns. Table 15.1 lists the different groups. These distinctions are important because the personal pronoun's role in a sentence determines whether the pronoun is subjective or objective. (Notice that the second-person pronoun *you* doesn't change its case.)

Consider the pronoun forms under "Subjective–Singular and Subjective–Plural" in Table 15.1:

> <u>He</u> was swimming in the pool.

He, the third-person singular masculine form of the pronoun, is the subject of this clause/sentence; therefore, it is in the subjective case.

TABLE 15.1 Personal Pronouns

Pronoun Person	Subjective-Singular	Subjective-Plural	Objective-Singular	Objective-Plural
First	*I*	we	me	Us
Second	You	you	you	You
Third	he, she, it	they	him, her, it	Them

I was swimming in the pool with her.

The subject *I* is first-person singular, but *her* acts as the object of the preposition *with*. When a personal pronoun acts as the object of a verb or of a preposition, it is in the objective case.

> She spoke so softly to the teacher that it was difficult for him to understand her.

She is the subject of the verb *spoke*; *him* is the object of the preposition *for*; *her* is the object of the infinitive *to understand*.

Notice the different pronouns in these two sentences:

> Anna, the king, and I are going out for Chinese food tonight. [*I* is part of the subject.]
> Anna arrived late for her dinner with the king and me. [*Me* is part of a prepositional phrase; it is the object of the preposition *with*.]

There are two steps to deciding which form to use:

1. Determine the grammatical relationship involved. Is the pronoun the subject of a clause/sentence or the object of a verb, preposition, or infinitive?
2. Choose the appropriate form (subjective or objective). Until the forms become familiar, you can refer to Table 15.1.

Although the principle of pronoun case with personal pronouns is quite straightforward, it can be tricky with compounds.

> Tina and [*I? me?*] plan to attend Mavis's wedding on 15 May.

Isolate the pronoun from the noun to determine the correct form:

> ~~Tina and~~ I plan to attend Mavis's wedding on 15 May.

<aside>
The first and third forms of the personal pronoun and the pronouns *who* and *whom* change *case* (i.e., *form*) to express their grammatical function in the sentence.

 Chapter 13 has more on pronoun categories.
</aside>

Mavis's wedding will be a joyous occasion for ~~Tina and~~ me.

We ~~students~~ believe firmly that our rights should be given back to us. Our rights should be given back to us ~~students~~.

Possessive Pronouns

Possessive (adjectival) pronouns also change their case (e.g., my *uncle's* pet alligator; *his* pet alligator).

The book doesn't belong to Anthony but to Kristy; it is <u>hers</u>.

Never use an apostrophe with a form such as *hers* ("belonging to her") or *theirs* ("belonging to them").

Hers is the noun form of the possessive pronoun replacing the antecedent *Kristy*. The adjectival form is seen in the following sentence:

The book doesn't belong to Anthony but to Kristy; it is <u>her</u> book.

Table 15.2 lists the possessive forms of pronouns and the noun (complement) forms.

Relative Pronouns

A **relative pronoun** introduces a dependent clause and usually functions adjectivally, modifying the preceding noun. A clause that begins with a relative pronoun is called a **relative clause**.

A **relative pronoun** *relates* the dependent clause it introduces to the noun that it follows. A **relative clause**, then, usually functions as an adjective, modifying the preceding noun. Of the major relative pronouns (*who, whoever, which, whichever, that*), only *who* and *whoever* change their form depending on whether they are the subject of the clause or the object of either the verb or a preposition in the clause.

To determine the case of a relative pronoun, look at *the role the relative pronoun plays within the clause*; in other words, the answer to whether you use *who* or *whom* lies *in the clause that the relative pronoun introduces*.

If *who* or *whoever* is the subject of the clause or is the subjective completion, use the subjective form. If the pronoun acts as an object of the verb or of a

If the pronoun *who* is the subject of the clause, use *who*; if it is the object of the verb or of the preposition in the clause, use *whom*.

TABLE (15.2) Possessive Pronouns with Adjectival and Noun Forms

Pronoun Person	Adjectival-Singular	Adjectival-Plural	Subject Complements-Singular	Subject Complements-Plural
First	*My*	*our*	*mine*	*ours*
Second	*Your*	*your*	*yours*	*yours*
Third	*his, her, its*	*their*	*his, hers, its*	*theirs*

preposition in the clause, use the objective form: *whom* or *whomever*. Consider these two sentences (italics indicate the dependent, or relative, clause):

> The old man shouted at *whoever happened to be within listening distance*.
> The old man should be free to shout at *whomever he chooses*.

In the first sentence, *whoever* is the subject of the clause it introduces. In the second, *he* is the subject of the clause, and the relative pronoun is in the objective case. If the relative clause has a subject, the relative pronoun will *not* be the subject of the clause. *He* does the choosing and is the subject of the verb; *whomever* is the object of the verb.

One test for case is to substitute the third-person form of the personal pronoun for the relative pronoun in the relative clause. *Whoever* (relative pronoun) *happened to be within listening distance* becomes *he/she* (personal pronoun) *happened to be within listening distance*. In the second sentence, the relative clause would be *he chooses he*, which is incorrect.

Determining pronoun case with relative pronouns always involves determining the function of the relative pronoun that begins the clause. Which of the following is correct?

> Jeong-Gyu is someone who, we firmly believe, will go far.
> Jeong-Gyu is someone whom, we firmly believe, will go far.

The first example is correct. *Who* is the subject of the relative clause *who will go far*. *We firmly believe* is not part of the relative clause but part of another clause (with another subject) that interrupts the relative clause.

> Jeong-Gyu is someone who, ~~we firmly believe~~, will go far.

Interrogative Pronouns

The **interrogative pronouns** (*who/whoever*, *which/whichever*, *what*) always ask questions. Once you know how to determine the case of the relative pronouns *who* and *whom*, the interrogatives shouldn't give you much trouble. Again, you need to establish their function to determine pronoun case. The exception is *what*, which does not change.

> With whom did you go out on Saturday night? [object of the preposition]
> Who says you should never reveal your feelings? [subject of the verb]
> Whom would you recommend for the new opening? [object of the verb]

The **Interrogative pronouns**— *who*, *which*, and *what*— introduce questions.

> The function of the interrogative pronoun in a sentence determines whether *who* (subjective form) or *whom* (objective form) is used.

If a pronoun is part of a prepositional phrase, it will normally follow the preposition. However, it's possible to structure the sentence so the pronoun precedes the preposition (e.g., *"Whom is the note for?"*). You can rearrange a sentence that ends with a preposition so that the preposition comes before the pronoun. It is then clear that the pronoun's objective case should be used.

<u>Whom</u> did Professor LeGuin direct the question to?

The more formal usage makes it easier to determine case:

<u>To whom</u> did Professor LeGuin direct the question?

It is now clear that *whom* is the object of the preposition *to*.

Exercise 15.8

Choose the correct form of the pronoun.

1. Management often forgets about the needs of (we/us) wage earners.
2. (Who/whom) should run for office this election?
3. I have no intention of speaking to (they/them).
4. The person (who/whom) finishes first will be rewarded.
5. You recommend (who/whom) for the position?
6. As she entered the room, a mysterious feeling came over (she/her).
7. Margaret Laurence was a novelist (who/whom) entertained her readers with well-developed plots and realistic characters.
8. People (who/whom) use memory aids tend to be better spellers.
9. The instructor explained the different pronoun cases to Gail and (I/me).
10. Hey, (who/whom) did you mean to refer to when you used that insulting term?

After you've checked your answers in Appendix D, complete questions 11–25.

11. (Whoever/whomever) fails to address the most important issue—unemployment—will find themselves among the unemployed.
12. The last person (who/whom) she wanted to see at the track meet was her former coach.
13. My fifth-grade teacher always let her favourite students—Mallory, Cindy, and (I/me)—help her with clean-up.
14. I wanted to ask her (who/whom) the note should be addressed to.
15. The young narrator's goal is to bring back a present for his friend's sister (who/whom) he admires from afar.
16. Chris's rival, Mike, lasted longer in the ring than (he/him).
17. We were allowed to invite (whoever/whomever) we wanted to the party.
18. I proposed that Geordie and (I/me) would stack chairs after the meeting.

19. The only "mother" (who/whom) the kitten has known is Madeline, (who/whom) rescued it from traffic.
20. The newly renovated house is a very pleasant place for my brother and (I/me) to live.
21. During his career, Jackie Robinson was subjected to racial hatred from many people (who/whom) he came in contact with.
22. Prejudices decrease when children observe non-prejudiced behaviour by peers (who/whom) children associate with during their pre-teen years.
23. Christy so drastically changed his personality that his own father can barely believe it is (he/him).
24. "[I]n these fits I leave them, while I visit / young Ferdinand, (who/whom) they suppose is drowned." —Shakespeare
25. Choose the grammatical poem:

    a. Roses are red,   b. Roses are red,
       Butterflies are free;   Birds can fly;
       You must choose   You must choose
       Between him and me.   Between he and I.

Pronoun Consistency

A pronoun must agree in number, gender, and person with its antecedent—this rule is called **pronoun consistency**. Referring to different people in the same sentence is acceptable as long as the change isn't arbitrary. If you want to replace a preceding noun with a pronoun, the latter should be the same *person* as its antecedent.

> **Incorrect:** During final exams, if students must go to the washroom, raise your hand so you can be escorted there. [Students is third person; your and you are second person.]
> **Correct:** During final exams, if students must go to the washroom, they should raise their hands so they can be escorted there.

Or, more informally,

During final exams, if <u>you</u> need to go to the washroom, raise <u>your</u> hand so <u>you</u> can be escorted there.

Incorrect: It is possible that <u>our</u> desire to make life easier for <u>ourselves</u> will, in fact, make <u>humans</u> redundant.

Our and *ourselves* are first person; *humans* is third person.

Pronoun consistency is the principle that a pronoun must agree in number, gender, and person with its antecedent. Do not needlessly switch from one person of pronoun to another. If an antecedent is a noun, use the third-person form to replace it.

Correct: It is possible that <u>our</u> desire to make life easier for <u>ourselves</u> will, in fact, make <u>us</u> redundant.

or

It is possible that the desire to make life easier for <u>humans</u> will, in fact, make <u>them</u> redundant.

Incorrect: Educators today should teach <u>students</u> learning skills, such as how to manage <u>your</u> money.

Correct: Educators today should teach <u>students</u> learning skills, such as how to manage <u>their</u> money.

Exercise 15.9

The following paragraph contains errors in pronoun consistency, along with some awkward use of third-person pronouns. Rewrite the paragraph, striving for correctness and effectiveness. Decide which person you want to refer to consistently: this decision might be based on the level of formality you want to use (first- and second-person pronouns, such as *I/me* and *you*, are considered more informal than third-person pronouns, such as *he/she* and *him/her*).

You can definitely learn a lot from educational TV; we can learn things that we cannot learn from written texts. If one is a major in commerce, for example, and if he or she watches the business news, he or she can understand the commerce textbook better by applying what he or she learns from the news. Similarly, I think that watching sports programs can provide people with excitement. Watching sports can also give us a better understanding of the game. On the other hand, if one chooses to watch comedy all the time, people are not going to gain any real benefits. I feel comedies are generally meaningless.

 # Sentence Construction Errors

Sentence construction errors result from forgetting two basic principles in English grammar: a modifier should be placed as close as possible to the word it is intended to modify, and coordinate (equal) elements in a sentence must be grammatically parallel and complete. Misplaced and dangling modifiers are examples of errors that result when writers do not adhere to the first principle. Faulty parallelism and comparisons occur when the second principle is not followed.

Misplaced Modifiers

The main function of adjectives is to modify nouns, while the main function of adverbs is to modify verbs. Prepositional phrases can also function as adjectives or adverbs. A **misplaced modifier**, then, can be an adjective, adjectival phrase, adverb, or adverbial phrase. It is mistakenly placed next to a part of speech that it is not intended to modify.

The meaning of a sentence in English heavily depends on word order, or **syntax**; it is partly through syntax that writers communicate their meaning and that the reader understands the message.

Adjectival Modifiers

A one-word adjective usually appears immediately before the noun it is intended to modify, but an adjectival phrase or clause usually follows the noun it modifies. Most misplaced **adjectival modifiers** are phrases or clauses. Consider the following examples of misplaced modifiers (the modifiers are underlined):

Incorrect: They headed for a child in the front row <u>with a long overcoat</u>.

The child, not the front row, is wearing the long overcoat. The adjectival phrase should follow the noun *child*.

Correct: They headed for a child <u>with a long overcoat</u> in the front row.
Incorrect: The furnace thermostat is located upstairs, <u>which displays the temperature settings</u>.

In this sentence, the adjectival (relative) clause, *which displays the temperature settings*, is placed next to the adverb *upstairs* instead of the noun *thermostat*.

Correct: The furnace thermostat, <u>which displays the temperature settings</u>, is located upstairs.

Adverbial Modifiers

Misplaced adverbs and adverbial phrases are more common than their adjective counterparts because adverbs can often be moved in a sentence without affecting meaning. However, it is safest to place **adverbial modifiers** right before or after the word or phrase they are supposed to modify.

The meaning of the following sentence could be misconstrued:

Incorrect: Students should buy this book because it will give them all the information they need to know about writing <u>in a convenient form</u>.

A **misplaced modifier** is an adjective, adjectival phrase, adverb, or adverbial phrase that is too far away in the sentence from the word it should modify, possibly giving the sentence an unintended meaning. **Syntax** means the way words are put together into sentences in a language.

Chapter 13 discusses adjectives and adverbs.

An **adjectival modifier** is a word or phrase that functions as an *adjective*.

An **adverbial modifier** is a word or phrase that functions as an *adverb*.

Presumably, the writer did not mean "convenience in writing" but that the book "will give them . . . information . . . in a convenient form."

> Correct: Students should buy this book because it will give them, <u>in a convenient form</u>, all the information they will need to know about writing.
> Incorrect: The conviction carries a penalty of 8 to 10 years in <u>two provinces</u>.

Because of the misplaced prepositional phrase, the writer seems to be saying that, on being convicted, the criminal will have to serve time in two provinces. Either of the following rephrased sentences is correct:

> <u>In two provinces</u>, the conviction carries a penalty of 8 to 10 years.
> The conviction carries a penalty <u>in two provinces</u> of 8 to 10 years.

Fixing Misplaced Modifiers

The solution to misplaced modifiers, whether an entire clause, phrase, or single word, is simple: move them. The following misplaced modifier makes the sentence awkward or misleading:

> Incorrect: The instructor marked the essay I wrote <u>unfairly</u>.
> Correct: The instructor <u>unfairly</u> marked the essay I wrote.
> or
> I thought the instructor marked my essay <u>unfairly</u>.

A misplaced modifier can occur anywhere in a sentence; however, they often occur at the end, almost as an afterthought.

> A misplaced modifier should be placed as close as possible to the word(s) it is intended to modify.

> Incorrect: Cars today produce large amounts of toxic chemicals that can damage human cells <u>if inhaled</u>.
> Correct: Cars today produce large amounts of toxic chemicals that, <u>if inhaled</u>, can damage human cells.

One-Word Modifiers

You need to be especially careful in placing one-word modifiers in a sentence, especially with limiting adverbs such as *only*, *almost*, *just*, *even*, *nearly*, *barely*, and *merely*.

Does one little word out of place *really* affect the meaning of the sentence? Consider how the meaning of the following statement changes, depending on where *only* appears.

Only Jared didn't do *his homework* yesterday.

Everyone but Jared did his or her homework; *only* is an adjective modifying *Jared*.

Jared only didn't do his homework.

The meaning of this sentence is unclear. It could mean the same as the first sentence, that Jared did other things but not his homework, or that the fact Jared didn't do his homework isn't important.

Jared didn't only *do his homework* yesterday.

Now *only* is an adverb modifying the verb *do* and suggests that Jared did his homework and other things.

Jared didn't do *only his homework* yesterday.

Placing *only* before *his homework* means that Jared definitely did his homework and other things as well. It might also mean that Jared was involved in doing someone else's homework in addition to his own.

Jared didn't do his *only homework* yesterday.

Placing *only* between *his* and *homework* implies that Jared didn't have much homework, but he didn't do it.

Jared didn't do his homework *yesterday only*.

Perhaps Jared is not such a lazy student after all: the only day he didn't do his homework was yesterday!

Dangling Modifiers

Misplaced and **dangling modifiers** can be the grammatical equivalent of life's most embarrassing moments: a modifier that is misplaced or dangling can give the communication a quite different, sometimes humorous, meaning from the intended one. The next example seems to refer to precocious parents:

> Incorrect: <u>When only seven years old</u>, my parents decided to enroll me in a Highland dancing course.

Consider the following sentence from a résumé, which doesn't mention the applicant:

Grammatically, a **dangling modifier** modifies the closest noun, often giving the sentence an unintended meaning.

Incorrect: <u>When not working or attending classes</u>, my hobbies are gardening, doing macramé, and bungee jumping.

A **dangling participle** modifies nothing in the sentence, as the noun or noun phrase it should modify is absent.

As dangling modifiers are often *–ing* participle (adjectival) phrases, they are sometimes called **dangling participles**. These adjectival phrases are dangling because the intended noun or noun phrase is not in the sentence. That's why it doesn't help to move the modifier.

Correct dangling modifiers by providing the noun or noun phrase in the independent clause to give the modifier something to modify or by turning the dangling phrase into a dependent clause with a subject.

Correct: When only seven years old, <u>I</u> was enrolled by my parents in a Highland dancing course. [method 1]

Correct: When <u>I</u> was only seven years old, my parents decided to enroll me in a Highland dancing course. [method 2]

Correct: When not working or attending classes, <u>I</u> enjoy several hobbies, including gardening, doing macramé, and bungee jumping. [method 1]

Correct: When <u>I</u> am not working or attending classes, my hobbies include gardening, doing macramé, and bungee jumping. [method 2]

While a misplaced modifier frequently appears at the end of a sentence, a dangling modifier usually is found at the beginning of a sentence, though occasionally in the middle or at the end. These examples show you how to identify dangling modifiers by asking the appropriate questions.

Incorrect: <u>When arriving in Calgary</u>, the clouds had scattered, and the sky was aglow with bands of pink and red.

Incorrect: <u>Though a well-known writer</u>, his latest book failed to make the bestseller's list.

Who is arriving in Calgary? Who is the well-known writer? The answers are not in the sentences; therefore, the modifiers are dangling. In each case, the missing information needs to be provided in the independent clause, or the dangling phrase needs to be turned into a dependent clause that can modify the independent one that follows.

Correct: When arriving in Calgary, <u>I saw that</u> the clouds had scattered, and the sky was aglow with bands of pink and red. [method 1]

<u>When I arrived in Calgary</u>, the clouds had scattered, and the sky was aglow with bands of pink and red. [method 2]

Correct: Though a well-known writer, <u>he</u> failed to make the best-seller's list with his latest book. [method 1]
Though <u>he was</u> a well-known writer, his latest book failed to make the bestseller's list. [method 2]

In the following example, the dangling modifier is at the end of the sentence:

Incorrect: Verbal and non-verbal skills are greatly enhanced <u>when living in a foreign country</u>.

Who is living in a foreign country? This information is missing, so the participial phrase *when living* is dangling. To correct it, add information:

Correct: <u>When living in a foreign country, you</u> are able to enhance your verbal and non-verbal skills. [method 1]
Verbal and non-verbal skills are greatly enhanced when <u>you live</u> in a foreign country. [method 2]

Exercise 15.10

Working in groups, identify the misplaced or dangling modifiers in the following sentences. Determine whether the meaning is incorrect or ambiguous and then fix the problem using one of the methods discussed in the previous sections.

1. A striped hat was on his head that came to a point.
2. As we were leaving, he promised to visit us with tears in his eyes.
3. Although unambitious and downright lazy, I have never known Sam to break his word.
4. His ego was further inflated by being awarded first prize in the Ben Affleck look-alike contest.
5. Every character has a purpose in Shakespeare's play, big or small.
6. When asked what my favourite sport is, I usually say that it is running without any hesitation.
7. Stepping out of the airplane, the fresh air was most invigorating.
8. Gabriel Kolko describes peace in Vietnam after the war in his book.
9. Opening the door unexpectedly, his eyes fell upon two of his employees sleeping in front of their computers.
10. Teacher Laurie McNamara posed for the photographer with Principal Dan Saunders, who gave her a kidney last month, in the Cloverdale Elementary School hallway.

Exercise **15.11**

Correct the following sentences, each of which contains a modifier error. In some instances, you will need to reword the sentence for clarity and correctness.

1. In our city, shady characters lurk on quiet corners that offer a variety of drugs.
2. Over the years, several world-class cyclists have had spectacular careers, such as Eddy Merckx and Greg LeMond.
3. Running down the street without a care in the world, two pedestrians had to quickly move out of his way.
4. Being a member of the Sikh community, my paper will be given a strong personal focus.
5. Built in mere minutes, you will have a fully interactive website for your business or for your personal use.
6. Benefits will only result from a smoke-free environment.
7. Germany has built an extensive network of highways through its countryside, known as the Autobahn.
8. Trying to find a job today, employers are stressing verbal and written communication skills more than ever before.
9. People's rights to privacy should be forfeited when caught in criminal behaviour.
10. This species of snake will eat frogs, mice, and small pieces of meat in captivity.

After you've checked your answers in Appendix D, complete questions 11–25.

11. Walking through the streets of Srinigar, devastation and fear are immediately evident.
12. As a beginner, my instructor taught me about the respect one karate student must show to another.
13. Tylenol and Aspirin effectively reduce pain when experiencing a fever.
14. Speaking from experience, tans that dye the top layer of the skin last for about one week.
15. Moving to Nebraska at the age of 10, Jim Burden's narrative reveals the reflections of a child.
16. Being an Elizabethan playwright, I am certain that Shakespeare would have been a major influence on Marlowe.
17. Adolescents essentially experience the same depressive symptoms as adults do.
18. As a serious snowboarder, it is exciting to observe the growth of this sport.
19. In John Donne's "Death, Be Not Proud," Death has a personality that is usually only given to a human being.
20. The boy in *Araby* returns home empty-handed without the highly valued object, in this case, a gift for Mangan's sister that most quests require.
21. Darwin's theory of evolution may be contested on the grounds that species may cease to appear abruptly.

22. Another example of imagery of light and dark in *Heart of Darkness* occurs when Marlow encounters an African dying in a clearing with a white scarf.
23. Based primarily on the work of Karl Marx, socialists see the creation of profit as a complex process.
24. Having an emotional personality, Beethoven's music identified him as a nineteenth-century Romantic.
25. A mother and her daughter were recently reunited after 18 years in a checkout line.

The Parallelism Principle

Balanced constructions give a sentence grace and strength, while unbalanced constructions make a sentence weak and unstable. A sentence must be constructed so that coordinate words and phrases are treated the same grammatically. **Parallelism** ensures that the elements in a sentence that have the *same grammatical function* are expressed in parallel structures. Learning the fundamentals of parallelism will help you make your writing grammatically correct and easy to read.

Experienced writers have mastered the principles of parallel structures and use them routinely in their writing; such balanced structures are rhetorically effective. Consider, for example, the following excerpt from Francis Bacon's (1601) essay "Of Youth and Age," which consists almost entirely of parallel words, phrases, and clauses (shown in italics). Without parallel elements, this paragraph would be very hard to follow:

> A man that is *young in years*, may be *old in hours*, if he have lost no time. But that happeneth rarely. Generally, youth is like the *first cogitations*, not so wise as *the second*. For there is a youth *in thoughts*, as well as *in ages*. . . . Young men, in the conduct and manage of actions, *embrace* more than they can hold; *stir* more than they can quiet; *fly* to the end, without consideration of the means and degrees; *pursue* some few principles, which they have chanced upon absurdly; *care not* to innovate, which draws unknown inconveniences; *use* extreme remedies at first; and, that which doubleth all errors, *will not acknowledge or retract* them; like an unready horse, that will neither *stop* nor *turn*. Men of age *object too much, consult too long, adventure too little, repent too soon*, and seldom *drive* business home to the full period, but *content* themselves with a mediocrity of success.

Student writer Allison McClymont was able to use parallel structures to create a dramatic opening for her essay on school uniforms.

Parallelism is the principle that the elements in a sentence that have the *same grammatical function* are expressed in parallel structures.

 Chapter 3 contains more information on using repetition and creating balanced structures.

In the hallways of today's high school, students congregate in various cliques, using their dress as an indicator of their conformity: there are the "jocks" in their letterman jackets, the "nerds" in their high pants and suspenders, the "cheerleaders" in their short skirts and sweaters, and the "arties" in their paint-covered hippie clothes. Other easily identifiable cliques include the "gangsters," the "preppies," the "mods," the "punks," the "weirdos," and "the band geeks."

Identifying and Fixing Parallelism Problems

Use a two-stage approach to identify and fix non-parallel structures in your writing.

In the first stage, identify structures that should be parallel: *lists, compounds, correlative conjunctions*, and *comparisons*. For example, the following sentence contains a compound object of the verb *prefer*:

> You should check to see whether all the elements are parallel whenever you use a list (three or more items), a compound (two items), correlative (paired) conjunctions, or a comparison (two parts).

> Ian would prefer *to snack* on some chips rather than *eating* a regular dinner.

In the second stage, make the identified parts parallel. Using our example, the two objects of the verb *prefer*, *to snack* and *eating*, must be expressed in parallel form. Either the verbal noun (infinitive form of the verb acting as a noun) or the gerund can function as an object, so either of these changes is correct:

> Correct: Ian would prefer *to snack* on some chips than *to eat* a regular dinner.
> or
> Ian would prefer *snacking* on chips to *eating* a regular dinner.

The next example needs four nouns to make it grammatically parallel.

> Incorrect: The basic human needs are *food, clothes, shelter*, and *having a good job*.
> Correct: The basic human needs are *food, clothes, shelter*, and *a good job*.

Three predicate adjectives or three independent clauses in the following sentence make the list parallel:

> Incorrect: After her 10-kilometre run, she felt *weak, tired*, and *she badly needed water*.
> Correct: After her 10-kilometre run, she felt *weak, tired*, and *very thirsty*.

or

After her 10-kilometre run, *she felt weak, she was tired*, and *she badly needed water*.

There are also two options for the following sentence: change *to sleep* to a gerund or *watching* and *looking* to infinitives.

Incorrect: Our cat enjoys *watching* TV, *looking* out the window, and *to sleep* at the foot of our bed.
Correct: Our cat enjoys *watching* TV, *looking* out the window, and *sleeping* at the foot of our bed.
or
Our cat likes *to watch* TV, *to look* out the window, and *to sleep* at the foot of our bed.

Finally, this sentence is fixed by using two verbs after the correlative conjunction *neither . . . nor*:

Incorrect: Neither a *borrower* be, nor *lend* to others.
Correct: Neither *borrow* from nor *lend* to others.

You could also follow Shakespeare's example in his play *Hamlet* and use two nouns after the conjunctions:

Correct: Neither a *borrower* nor a *lender* be.

When checking for parallel structure, consider first the structurally essential words, such as nouns and verbs (not their modifiers). If adjectives or adverbs appear in a list without words to modify, ensure they are in parallel form. Look at any larger grammatical units, such as prepositional phrases, which should be parallel to each other. Similarly, dependent clauses should be parallel with other dependent clauses and independent with other independent.

Parallelism in a List or Series

As noted earlier, the items in a list or series must be parallel. For example, if you use an expanded thesis statement that lists your essay's main points, you need to ensure that all the elements are grammatically parallel.

Incorrect: Research into cloning should be encouraged as it could lead to *cures* for diseases, successful organ *transplants*, and *put an end to infertility problems*.

Correct: Research into cloning should be legalized as it could lead to *cures* for diseases, successful organ *transplants*, and *solutions* to infertility problems.

The elements are now parallel. Notice that, to avoid repeating the word *cures*, a word with a similar meaning has replaced it.

Length is not necessarily a factor in parallelism. For example, a simple noun is normally considered parallel with a noun phrase (but not with a prepositional phrase) because they have the same grammatical function.

The following sentence contains two nouns preceded by adjectives and a noun followed by an adjectival (prepositional) phrase. The important words here are the nouns:

Discipline in single-sex schools has been shown to directly affect regular *attendance*, good *grades*, and *standards* for dress and behaviour.

The incorrect versions of the following thesis statements include unparallel lists:

Incorrect: The major forms of eating disorders involve the compulsion *to count calories*, *to constantly exercise*, and *the need to alter one's appearance*.
Correct: The major forms of eating disorders involve the compulsion *to count* calories, *to constantly exercise*, and *to alter* one's appearance.
Incorrect: Buddhism teaches that one's karma can be affected by many things: *your generosity to* those less fortunate, *your behaviour to* strangers, and *if you treat* even your enemies with respect.
Correct: Buddhism teaches that one's karma can be affected by many things: *your generosity to* those less fortunate, *your behaviour to* strangers, and *your respect* even *for* your enemies.

You also need to be careful that items in a list are *logically* parallel. The following list contains five nouns/noun phrases, but not all of the items are logically parallel.

Incorrect: Common injuries in the meat-packing industry include *chemical burns*, *broken bones*, *lacerations*, *amputations*, and *even death*.
Correct: Common injuries in the meat-packing industry include *chemical burns*, *broken bones*, *lacerations*, and *amputations*. Some accidents even result in *death*.

More informal lists that use bullets or numbers also require parallel structure. Choose a set-up or starting point; then, ensure that each item has the same grammatical function and, if necessary, form.

Incorrect:
Before choosing a graduate program, a student should investigate

- the number of graduate students who receive financial support;
- the expertise of faculty in the student's desired specialty;
- course work required; and
- *do research opportunities exist for graduate students?*

Starting all items in the list with a noun or noun phrase makes the list grammatically parallel:

Correct:
Before choosing a graduate program, a student should investigate

- the number of graduate students who receive financial support;
- the expertise of faculty in the student's desired specialty;
- the course work required; and
- *the research opportunities available.*

Compounds

You must apply the principle of parallel structure to **compounds**. A coordinating conjunction, such as *or, and*, or *but*, can signal a compound, as can a prepositional phrase joiner such as *as well as*; in a comparison, *than* or *as* may join the two elements of a comparison.

> A **compound** consists of two of the same parts of speech acting as a grammatical unit.

Once you've identified a compound, look at the important word or phrase in the first element and ensure that the second, which follows the joiner, uses the parallel grammatical structure. Several examples of compounds follow.

> Incorrect: It is actually cheaper *to convert* a used vehicle into an electric vehicle than *buying* a new gas-powered model.
> Correct: It is actually cheaper *to convert* a used vehicle into an electric vehicle than *to buy* a new gas-powered model.

Some compounds with helping verbs cause trouble. In these cases, it may be helpful to draw a line where the first element begins and another where the second begins (after the conjunction). Then, see if both parts line up with the main verb that follows; you can draw a line there too. The main verb in the sentence below is *worked*:

> Incorrect: The prohibition of marijuana and the laws in place for it | *do not* and | *have never* | worked.

Test: The prohibition of marijuana and the laws in place for it | *do not . . .* worked and *have never* worked.
Correct: The prohibition of marijuana and the laws in place for it *do not work* and *have never worked.*

Sometimes a compound phrase ending in a preposition doesn't line up with what follows. Here are examples of a compound in which the words following the verbs don't fit with the object. Again, the presence of a coordinating conjunction can alert you to these tricky kinds of compounds:

Incorrect: Most people under 30 *are familiar or have heard of* the rapper Eminem.
Correct: Most people under 30 | *are familiar with or* | *have heard of* | the rapper Eminem.
Incorrect: "We have to change our production methods to make sure the products we sell are *as good* or *better as* any in the world," said the Minister of Agriculture.
Correct: "We have to change our production methods to make sure the products we sell are | *as good as* | or *better than* | any in the world," said the Minister of Agriculture.

Correlative Conjunctions

A specific kind of compound involves correlative conjunctions, joiners that work in pairs (*either . . . or, neither . . . nor, both . . . and, not . . . but, not only . . . but also*). Logically, the part of speech that follows the first half of the compound should also follow the second half. It might be helpful to draw a line after each conjunction:

Incorrect: A college diploma today is an investment *not only* in students' financial resources *but also* | their time.

What follows *not only* is a prepositional phrase that begins with *in*; therefore, a prepositional phrase, not just a noun (*time*), must follow the second member of the pair:

Correct: A college diploma today is an investment *not only in* students' financial resources *but also in* their time.
Incorrect: The lack of classroom availability means *either* constructing new buildings *or* lower the number of students accepted into programs.

Correct: The lack of classroom availability means *either constructing* new buildings *or lowering* the number of students accepted into programs.

Comparisons

Faulty comparisons sometimes have less to do with grammar than with logic. Because comparisons are always made between two things, both elements must be fully expressed for the comparison to be complete. Often either the comparison is left incomplete or the terms being compared are incompatible; that is, they cannot be compared because there is no basis for comparison.

> *Than* is the word for comparisons, not the adverb related to time, *then*. Other words and phrases can also signal comparisons: *compared to, similar (to), different (from), as, like,* etc.

You need to ask if the two parts of a comparison are grammatically parallel, if both parts of the comparison are fully expressed, and if the two objects of the comparison can logically be compared. In the next sentence, the reader is left to assume whom males are being compared to.

Incomplete: An unfortunate stereotype is that males are more scientific and less intuitive.
Complete: An unfortunate stereotype is that males are more scientific and less intuitive *than females*.
Incompatible: I have found that students are less judgmental at university compared to high school.

You can ask what precisely is being compared and if the comparison is logical; grammatically, the writer is comparing a perceived trait of *students* at university to high school. People must be compared to people.

Correct: I have found that *people* are less judgmental at university *than they are* at high school.

The two sides of the comparison are now complete and compatible.

Incompatible: In the study, men's running times were recorded for 30 more years than women.

What is being compared here? Are the terms comparable? The writer is comparing running times (for men) to women.

Compatible: In the study, men's running times were recorded for 30 more years than *women's times*.

Exercise **15.12**

Each of the following word groups contains three or four main points related to a topic. Using these lists, write a thesis statement for each topic, making sure that the sentences are parallel. Put the points in whatever order you like.

1. Why I like toe socks:
    - warm and comfortable
    - they are the latest fashion in socks
    - come in many colours and designs

2. The advantages of yoga:
    - to relax and reduce stress
    - to exercise
    - also can meet people in yoga classes

3. The importance of computers to students:
    - they provide entertainment
    - cutting down on homework time is important
    - you can obtain a wealth of information quickly

4. Living with roommates:
    - they can create a lot of mess
    - invade your personal space
    - you can talk to them about your problems

5. The benefits of coffee:
    - coffee helps you wake up
    - it improves your mood
    - it improves your concentration

After you've checked your answers in Appendix D, complete questions 6–10.

6. The comparison of two recreational drugs:
    - their possible dangerous side effects
    - who uses them
    - the effects they produce in the user

7. The facts about organically grown food:
    - the way organically grown food is farmed
    - the cost of these kinds of foods
    - their nutritional value

8. The advantages of home birthing:
    - allows the parents to maintain control over their surroundings
    - a positive and friendly place for the child to be born
    - is as safe as a hospital birth if common sense is used

9. School uniforms are beneficial:
   * promote school identity and school pride
   * they save parents money and hassle
   * reduce the pressure of students to conform to the latest fashions
   * to make it easier for school authorities to enforce discipline

10. The legalization of marijuana:
   * it is less addictive than some other illegal drugs
   * the Canadian government has already made it legal under certain circumstances
   * governments could increase their revenue by selling it
   * making it legal would reduce crime since people wouldn't have to obtain it illegally

Exercise 15.13

These sentences contain parallelism errors. Identify the kind of error (series, compounds, correlative conjunctions, or comparisons) and fix it.

1. A good journalist is inquisitive, persistent, and must be a good listener.
2. Music can directly affect your thoughts, emotions, and how you feel.
3. In this essay, I will be looking and writing about the role of women in the military.
4. Tiddlywinks is not only a game of considerable skill but also strategy.
5. Television can affect children in a variety of negative ways since children often lack judgment, are naturally curious, and easily influenced.
6. There are three main qualities that a leader must possess: a leader must be enthusiastic, organized, and have creativity.
7. Aman never has and never will be good at golf.
8. She was not only the best teacher I have ever had, but also I was impressed by her modesty.
9. Tremors may occur on either or both sides of the body.
10. There are many reasons why people choose to or enjoy watching television.

After you've checked your answers in Appendix D, complete questions 11–25.

11. A recent study has found that Caucasian children acquire self-awareness at an earlier age than other ethnic groups.
12. Alyssa's trip to London involved such pleasures as Buckingham Palace, feeding the pigeons, visiting her relatives, and those quaint London accents.

(continued)

13. I enjoyed watching *The Last Samurai*, *The Last of the Mohicans*, and *Braveheart* was also enjoyable.
14. I want to emphasize that my work as MP in this riding has not, and will not, be affected by political developments.
15. When Jim has the choice of either jumping or to stay on the doomed ship, he chooses to jump.
16. Physical education teaches children not only to work well together but also patience and discipline.
17. Smoking should be banned because it raises health-care costs, physically harms both smokers and non-smokers, and because cigarette production damages the environment.
18. Users of ecstasy report feeling euphoric, energized, intensified pleasure, and increased sensory awareness.
19. What made Beethoven's music different from other composers was his expressive style.
20. Recent studies suggest that wellness depends on three main factors: feeling good about yourself, your everyday eating habits, and being comfortably active.
21. Although two very different American writers, Nathaniel Hawthorne's and Mark Twain's works are nevertheless similar in many ways.
22. Differing viewpoints in a work of fiction not only add conflict, but they can also reveal differences in characters' ages, genders, and upbringings.
23. Those who exercise regularly show a decrease in anxiety, depression, fatigue, and elevated vigour.
24. In Sonnet 130, Shakespeare stresses the reality of his mistress rather than portraying her as something she is not.
25. According to a recent poll, the premier has more support among college students than the general public.

Passive Constructions: The Lazy Subject

Ordinarily, the subject of a sentence is acting, as in this example:

Ezra placed the book on the table.

A **passive construction** displaces the subject. In other words, the subject of the sentence is not doing the action:

The book was placed on the table by Ezra.

In a **passive construction**, the subject of the sentence does not perform the action. Instead, the noun that receives the action is the subject and is placed at the beginning of the sentence.

The direct object, *book*, has become the subject, and the original subject, *Ezra*, is now the object of the preposition *by*. The verb form has also changed. This sentence has a subject that is acted on rather than acting. Further, the passive construction requires more words than the active to provide the same information. Effective, direct English is geared toward the *active voice*.

Exercise 15.14

Use your school's database to find some corporate annual reports. Search the documents for examples of passive voice constructions.

The passive voice uses a form of the verb *to be* followed by a past participle. If the actor is named, it is the object of a prepositional phrase that begins with *by*. Don't confuse the identifying verb forms with a construction in which the *to be* verb is used with the past participle as a predicate adjective. For example, in the following sentence, the subjects are clearly the actors; you can't add the preposition *by* after *determined* or after *pleased*. This sentence uses an active construction:

Dana *was determined* to succeed at any cost; I *am pleased* to see him succeed.

The following sentence contains three indicators of a passive construction:

The *door was opened by* a tall, sinister *man*.

The subject (*door*) is not doing the action expressed by the verb *open*; the preposition *by* precedes the actor (*man*); and the simple past of *to be* combines with the past participle of the main verb to form the passive voice of the verb.

Here's how to change a passive to an active construction:

1. Move the subject so that it follows the verb as the direct object.
2. Move the object of the preposition *by*, the actor, to the beginning of the sentence/clause to replace the passive subject.
3. Remove the identifying passive forms of the verb and the preposition *by*.

> A fast way to change a passive into an active construction is to move the noun or pronoun that follows *by* to the beginning of the sentence. Then, the other required changes will be easier to see.

A tall, sinister man ~~was~~ opened the door ~~by~~.

Here's a slightly more complicated example:

Passive: The special commission *was informed* of its mandate *by* a superior court judge last Monday.

Active: A superior court judge informed the special commission of its mandate last Monday.

In its active form, the sentence contains fewer words, and the thought is expressed more directly.

As a general rule, *don't use the passive voice if the active will serve*. However, there are times when the passive is acceptable or is even the better choice:

1. When the subject isn't known or is so well known it doesn't matter.

    Pierre Trudeau *was first elected* prime minister in 1968.

    It is unnecessary to mention that the voters or the electorate elected him.

2. When passivity is implied or if the context makes it seem natural to stress the receiver of the action.

    When a cyclist completes a hard workout, massages *are usually performed* on the affected muscles.

    In this sentence, the massages are more important than the person giving them.

    Acceptable passive: The woman *was kidnapped and held* hostage by a band of thugs.
    Questionable passive: Several of the thugs *were picked out* of a line-up *by* the woman.

    In the first sentence, the woman obviously is the passive recipient of the thugs' action. In the second sentence, she is doing the action; therefore, the active voice is preferred:

    Active: The woman *picked* several of the thugs out of a line-up.

3. When the rhythm of the sentence requires it or because it is rhetorically effective.

    The books obviously *had been arranged* by a near-sighted librarian.

    In this sentence, the librarian's near-sightedness is important; the placement of the adjective near the end of the sentence gives it emphasis.

4. When, in academic writing, it is unnecessary to mention the author of a study or the researcher; the passive may be used to stress the object of the study or the method of research.

> Don't use the passive unless you want to de-emphasize the actor (active subject).

Through case studies, a comparison of two common methods for treating depression *will be made*.

In the following examples from academic writing, the passive is preferred either because the actor doesn't matter or because the writer wants to stress the receiver of the action:

In 1891 the science of embryology *was shaken by* the work of the cosmopolitan German biologist and vitalist philosopher Hans Driesch (Bowring, 2004, p. 401).

The emergence of second-hand smoke (SHS) [as a cancer hazard] *has been offered* as a viable explanation for the increased enactment of local smoking restrictions (Asbridge, 2003, p. 13).

Exercise 15.15

The following sentences use passive constructions. Change unnecessary uses of the passive voice to form active constructions. You may have to add the actor, or "active" subject (see the example). Be prepared to justify your decision to keep any passive constructions.

Example:

Passive:

The suspect's behaviour had been watched for more than one month.

The suspect's behaviour had been watched [by the police] for more than one month.

Active:

The police had watched the suspect's behaviour for more than one month.

(continued)

Decision:

Leave as passive because *suspect's behaviour* is more important to the meaning than *the police*.

1. I was given two choices by my landlord: pay up or get out.
2. It was reported that more than a thousand people were left homeless by recent flooding.
3. The manager's protest was heard by the fairness committee.
4. The tree was buffeted by the wind, which tore off one of its lower branches.
5. Beethoven's Third Symphony, *The Eroica*, originally was dedicated to Napoleon, but the dedication was erased after Napoleon proclaimed himself emperor.
6. Education needs to be seen by the government as the number one priority.
7. Many acts of self-deception were committed by Bertha, the protagonist of "Bliss."
8. The belief in a powerful and infallible Creator is commonly held today.
9. Poverty in First Nations communities must be addressed by the federal, provincial, and First Nations' governments.
10. There are two ways of looking at rights-based ethics that were put forward by Immanuel Kant.

Exercise **15.16**

The following five paragraphs contain various errors discussed in Chapters 13–15.

1. Identify and correct the following:

   a. comma splice
   b. comma error
   c. pronoun case error
   d. broad pronoun reference
   e. missing pronoun antecedent
   f. two pronoun–antecedent agreement errors
   g. omitted apostrophe
   h. ambiguous pronoun reference
   i. failure to use gender-neutral language

   In my family, my father and sister play video games as much as me. They have become very complex, and can even improve problem-solving in children. By progressing through increasing difficulty levels, it can help childrens thought processes. On the one hand, if the child goes straight to the hardest setting, they may feel discouraged, on the other, if the child tries to systematically progress through increasing levels, they can learn the mechanics of the game step by step. This can help in the study of math, as the child may learn to persevere until he finds the solution.

2. Identify and correct the following:

    a. comma error
    b. subject–verb agreement error
    c. sentence fragment
    d. two parallelism errors
    e. misplaced modifier
    f. dangling modifier
    g. pronoun inconsistency
    h. comma splice

Having a job and earning one's livelihood is a necessary goal in life, it is one of the reasons you acquire an education. At the place where I work however, many people come in expecting to find a job lacking presentation skills. Many are poorly dressed, do not know how to behave, and they may not speak grammatically. Untidy, disorganized, and unprepared, I still have to match them with a prospective employer. They lack the skills to present themselves to others and knowing what to do in public. Although they may be highly intelligent people.

After you've checked your answers in Appendix D, complete questions 3–5.

3. Identify and correct the following:

    a. comma splice
    b. misplaced comma
    c. parallelism error
    d. two omitted apostrophes
    e. sentence fragment
    f. two pronoun–antecedent agreement errors

Logic can be defined as "the science of the formation and application of a general notion." Meaning that logic is apt to vary according to ones way of seeing certain things as important. A vegetarians logic, asserts that it is completely unnecessary—not to mention cruel—to eat animals in our day and age. Today's meat eater also has their logic. For them, meat is to be enjoyed, the taste of the food and the social interaction involved is to be cherished. We need to allow time in our busy lives to eat more and feeling guilty about it less.

(continued)

4.   Identify and correct the following:

   a.   four comma errors
   b.   semicolon error
   c.   comma splice
   d.   pronoun case error
   e.   apostrophe error
   f.   dangling modifier

The Myers–Briggs personality test is based on the work of Swiss psychologist, Carl Jung, and two Americans; Isabel Briggs Myers, and her mother Katharine C. Briggs. Myers developed the tests, and tried them out on thousands of schoolchildren; she wanted to see how the test results would correlate with vocation. Consisting of a series of questions requiring a yes or no response, she tested a group of medical students, who she followed up on 12 years later and who confirmed the test's validity. Variations of Myer's test are sometimes given by employers today, however, the results should not be the sole means for a hiring decision.

5.   Identify and correct the following:

   a.   comma splice
   b.   comma error
   c.   punctuation error other than comma
   d.   parallelism error
   e.   two apostrophe errors
   f.   subject–verb agreement error
   g.   pronoun–antecedent agreement error
   h.   broad pronoun reference

According to the principle's of Buddhism, neither sensual pleasures nor self-mortification bring about enlightenment, instead, the "Middle Way" is the path between these extremes; this can be understood through the "Four Noble Truths." These truths are: the truths of suffering, of the origins of suffering, of the cessation of suffering, and finding the path to end suffering. The Buddhas teaching asks each individual to examine their own conscience, and to come to a conclusion about the nature of truth.

Exercise **15.17**

Identify and then correct the error(s) in each sentence.

1. Written through the eyes of a young boy, one can see the perspective of the Indigenous peoples.

   a. dangling modifier
   b. misplaced modifier
   c. pronoun–antecedent agreement error
   d. comma error

2. The daily stresses of students, such as project or assignment due dates, teaches you to manage your time wisely.

   a. subject–verb agreement error
   b. pronoun inconsistency
   c. more than one error
   d. parallelism error

3. Parents sometimes push their children so hard to excel that they lose interest altogether.

   a. colon error
   b. pronoun reference error
   c. more than one error
   d. subject–verb agreement error

4. My roommate thinks it would be better for society, if all drugs were decriminalized.

   a. dangling modifier
   b. comma error
   c. subject–verb agreement error
   d. none of the above

5. Contributors to homelessness include the lack of good-paying jobs, increasingly large families and, probably the most important factor, which is the cost of living in a large city.

   a. dangling modifier
   b. more than one error
   c. comma error
   d. parallelism error

(continued)

6. One of the most tragic events of the twentieth century. The detonation of the atomic bomb over Hiroshima.

    a. sentence fragment
    b. comma splice
    c. pronoun reference error
    d. none of the above

7. With the increasing media focus in the 1980s on the plight of homeless women, came the need for more research, unfortunately, this research was not comprehensive.

    a. comma splice
    b. more than one error
    c. pronoun–antecedent agreement error
    d. parallelism error

8. Optometrists have been reshaping the cornea in order to correct vision for 50 years.

    a. parallelism error
    b. comma error
    c. misplaced modifier
    d. subject–verb agreement error

9. Information on airlines, currency exchange, and other passenger services are available on this website.

    a. subject–verb agreement error
    b. comma error
    c. more than one error
    d. run-on sentence

10. Many people are intrigued by the lives movie and TV heroes seem to live; these viewers tending to be teenagers.

    a. more than one error
    b. semicolon error
    c. parallelism error
    d. sentence fragment

Exercise 15.18

Identify the error (a, b, c, or d) and correct it in the sentence (there is one error in each sentence).

1. Anorexia <u>starts</u> when <u>a person</u> decides to take control over <u>their</u> <u>body</u> weight.

                   a   b   c   d

2. There <u>are</u> three types of turbine engines used in aircraft<u>;</u> the <u>turbojet</u>, the
      a   b   c

   turbofan<u>,</u> and the turboprop.
         d

3. Work <u>songs</u> and street <u>vendors</u> <u>cries</u> <u>are</u> examples of traditional
        a   b   c   d

   African-American music styles.

4. <u>Reforms</u> of the UN Security Council <u>include</u> abolishing the veto or <u>to extend</u>
    a   b   c

   the Council beyond the <u>current five</u> members.
                          d

5. Results from a recent study <u>showed that</u> patients <u>suffering from</u>
                              a   b

   osteoarthritis, <u>who listened to music for 20 minutes each day,</u> reported
                               c

   <u>a 66 per cent</u> reduction in their perception of pain.
       d

After you've checked your answers in Appendix D, complete questions 6–10.

6. As a <u>known</u> anarchist<u>,</u> <u>Chomsky's views</u> <u>have been</u> much debated.
        a   b   c   d

7. The brain of <u>a drug addict</u> <u>is</u> physically <u>different from</u> <u>a non-addict</u>.
             a   b   c   d

8. The tobacco in cigarettes is not <u>the only</u> problem<u>,</u> <u>cigarettes</u> contain many
                                    a   b   c

   dangerous chemicals <u>as well</u>.
                   d

9. By teaching <u>today's</u> youth safe and healthy approaches to sexuality<u>,</u> <u>it</u> will
              a   b c

   elevate <u>their</u> self-esteem.
          d

10. Holly Hunter, the actress <u>who</u> <u>I</u> most admire<u>,</u> appeared in several
                         a b   c

   <u>award-winning</u> movies.
      ·d

Chapter Review Questions

1. How do you find the subject of a sentence?
2. Does a prepositional phrase that follows a subject affect the verb form? If so, how?
3. What is a compound subject? How is a verb form affected by a compound subject?

4. When is a collective noun followed by a plural verb form?

5. Are most indefinite pronouns considered singular or plural? Why?

6. What are the three situations that cause most subject–verb agreement errors?

7. Why is the sentence *"One should always finish their homework"* incorrect?

8. How can you check for pronoun–antecedent errors?

9. What are the four kinds of pronoun reference errors?

10. When is it correct to use *who* in a sentence or clause? When would the use of *whom* be correct?

11. What are misplaced modifiers? Give an example.

12. What are dangling modifiers? Give an example.

13. What is parallelism and why is it important?

14. What is a compound?

15. When should you use passive sentence constructions?

16 Achieving Clarity and Depth in Your Writing

In this chapter, you will learn

- the importance of clarity in all your writing;
- strategies for cutting unneeded words and phrases;
- ways to avoid weak sentence constructions;
- the value of using direct and forceful language;
- the difference between formal and informal diction;
- the correct usage of confusing words;
- strategies for variety and emphasis;
- successful proofreading techniques; and
- a format for presenting your essay.

Many beginning writers believe that their essay is ready to submit once they have completed their first draft. Unfortunately, they forget about a crucial stage of essay writing—revision. Papers can always be revised for clarity, precision, and conciseness. This chapter will help you create clear, direct, and reader-focused essays.

Effective Style: Clarity

Style is the way that one writes.

Clear writing, or **clarity**, is grammatical, concise, direct, precise, and specific.

Chapter 12 addresses MLA and APA styles.

Revising involves editing to achieve a polished final version.

Clear writing is the result of hard work and attention to detail. Few writers—experienced or inexperienced—write clearly without making several revisions, which largely consist of making the language reflect the thought behind it.

When you write for an audience, it is not enough that you understand your ideas; your readers must also understand them. Revise with your audience in mind.

Chapters 13–15 provide most of the information you need to write grammatically correct sentences. See page 432 for a discussion of clichés.

What is **style**? If you have written a research essay, you know that the word is applied to documentation formats, such as MLA or APA. *Style* is also a term applied to individual writers, as in a dense, sophisticated style or a spare, terse style. Although every writer has a unique writing style, he or she must make **clarity**, or clear writing, the priority when writing with a specific purpose for a specific audience.

Clarity depends on various factors. If you were writing about a specialized topic and used words unfamiliar to your general audience, you would not be writing clearly, though a specialist might understand you. Word choice and level of language, then, are important factors in clear and effective writing.

Writing clearly is the result of hard work and attention to detail. Few writers—experienced or inexperienced—write clearly without making several revisions. Much of the **revising** process consists of making the language reflect the thought behind it.

One of the differences between experienced and inexperienced writers is that the former expect to spend much of their time revising their work; they ask, "Can this be clearer?" Student writers should also ask themselves this question. If the answer is "yes" or "maybe," try paraphrasing the content. Can you do so easily? Does your paraphrase express the point more clearly? Rewording a phrase or sentence often brings you closer to your intended meaning. However, it is not enough that you understand your ideas—your readers also need to understand them. Revise your work with this thought in mind.

Ask yourself the following questions when revising your work:

- *Is it grammatical?* Do your sentences and paragraphs use proper grammar? Have you checked for errors?
- *Is it concise?* Do you use only as many words as you need? Have you used basic words and simple constructions that reflect what you want to say? Do not use slang and clichés, as they are not concise.
- *Is it direct?* Have you used straightforward language? Are your sentence structures as simple as possible given the complexity of your points?
- *Is it precise?* Does it say exactly what you want it to say? Remember, "almost" or "close enough" is not sufficient. Would another word or phrase more accurately reflect your thought?

- *Is it specific?* Is it as detailed as it needs to be? Is it definitive and concrete, not vague or abstract? Do not use adjectives such as *big* or *huge*. Use concrete numbers, if possible, or other words to help the reader understand your point. For example, say "Many people believe this is a problem" instead of "It is a huge problem."

Writers who carefully work to make their writing more grammatical, concise, direct, precise, and specific will likely produce a clear essay. However, experienced writers aim for forceful writing as well; therefore, they may introduce variety and emphasis in their writing.

> Do not use more words than necessary to express an idea.

Exercise 16.1

The following paragraph is from an argumentative essay. Find examples that illustrate the stylistic problems discussed to this point. How could the paragraph be clearer?

> Foie gras is considered a delicious delicacy by some, yet it is viewed with disdain by others. Foie gras is duck or goose liver pâté, which is very fatty. It is created by force-feeding the ducks or geese with a corn-based food. Tubes are forced down the animal's throat and then it is forced to consume more food than it would normally, either in the wild or in captivity. Many organizations in both Europe and North America are calling for a ban on the sale of foie gras in order to encourage the immediate cessation of this form of animal cruelty. In some states, such as the glorious state of California, this force-feeding has been outlawed by the courts. Some chefs, including celebrity chefs, refuse to use foie gras, as they firmly believe that the force-feeding practice is unnecessarily cruel and a terrible thing. If more people were aware of the cruel and inhumane treatment of the poor ducks and geese, then maybe they would stop supporting this cruel and inhumane industry. It is our necessary duty to inform the uninformed population.

Exercise 16.2

Choose one of the student essays in this textbook. Find examples of how the writer addresses the audience and note any places where he or she uses variety in the sentences or paragraphs to make the essay more interesting and the points more forceful.

Why should so much effort be devoted to concise and direct writing? Such work is easy to follow and keeps the reader's interest. Unnecessary repetition and other clutter may dull a writer's points. Have you ever read a novel filled with pointless details? How interested were you in the book? If you are like most readers, you probably stopped reading. Redundancy and excessive detail create the same reaction in your readers.

Just as concise and direct writing makes you seem reliable, indirect writing may give the sense that you lack confidence in what you're saying, that you are trying to impress the reader, or that you are using unnecessary words to reach a word limit. Finally, when you use more words than you have to or express yourself in a round-about way, you increase the odds of making grammatical and mechanical errors.

> When you use unnecessary words or express yourself in a meandering way, you increase the odds of making grammatical and mechanical errors.

Cutting for Conciseness

To achieve conciseness, cut what is inessential. The simplest way to determine if something is unnecessary is to remove it and see if the meaning and effectiveness of the statement changes. If not, you don't need it. Your instructor may indicate problems with conciseness by putting parentheses around what is unneeded or by writing *wordy* or *verbose* in the margin. Don't think of it as criticism but as advice on how to be a better writer.

The following sections describe many common stylistic patterns that student writers adopt, especially in their early drafts. Consider the strategies to avoid them as you revise your essay.

Doubling Up: The Noah's Ark Syndrome

Writers sometimes suffer from "double vision," where two words sometimes automatically pop up: two verbs, two nouns, two adjectives, or two adverbs. Experienced editors offer this formula: one + one = one-half. Put another way, using two words when one is enough halves the impact of the one word.

> The administrative officer came up with an *original*, innovative suggestion for cost-cutting. [Anything innovative is bound to be original.]
> The event will be held at *various* different venues. [*Various* and *different* mean the same thing.]

> If a second noun, verb, adjective, or adverb doesn't make your meaning clearer, delete it.

Although it is not always wrong to use two of the same parts of speech consecutively, the terms cannot convey the same thing. Be especially wary of verb–adverb combinations; ensure that the adverb is necessary.

> The airport was *intentionally* designed for larger aircraft. [Can a design be unintentional?]
> She *successfully* accomplished what she had set out to do. [The word *accomplished* implies success.]

Here are some common verb–adverb pairings and other combinations that are usually redundant. The unneeded words are in parentheses.

(anxiously) fear	gaze (steadily)
(better/further) enhance	(harshly) condemn
(carefully) consider	hurry (quickly)
(clearly) articulate	plan (ahead)
climb (up)	ponder (thoughtfully)
combine/join (together)	praise (in favour of)
(completely) surround	progress (forward/onwards)
descend (down)	protest (against)
dominate (over)	refer/return/revert/reply (back) to
drawl (lazily)	rely/depend (heavily) on
dwindle (down)	sob (uncontrollably)
emphasize/stress (strongly)	(strictly) forbid
estimate/approximate (roughly)	(successfully) prove
(eventually) evolve (over time)	(suddenly) interrupt
examine (closely)	(symbolically) represent
fill (completely)	(totally) eradicate/devastate
finish (entirely)	unite (as one)
gather/assemble (together)	vanish (without a trace)

Be wary of repetitive adjective–noun pairings such as the following:

(advance) warning	(past) memory
(brief) encapsulation	(positive) benefits
(dead) carcass	(powerful) blast
(fiery) blaze	(sharp) needle
(future) plan	(terrible) tragedy
(knowledgeable) specialist	(timeless) classic
(mutual) agreement	(total) abstinence
(new) beginning	

Redundancies are also evident in such familiar phrases as *consensus of opinion*, *end result*, *end product*, *in actual fact*, *this point in time*, *time frame*, *time period*, *time span*, *years of age*, etc. Finally, unnecessary nouns are redundant. These words steal the thunder from other parts of speech, including other nouns and verbs.

Exercise 16.3

Listen to your favourite radio station or podcast or watch one of your favourite TV shows. Pay attention to the language used by the advertisers, announcers, and actors. Write down some of the most frequent examples of doubling up and be prepared to share them with the class.

The *world* of politics demands that you kowtow to the ineptitude of others.
The efforts of conservationists in the *fields of* ecology and biodiversity are leading to renewed efforts to save old-growth forests.

In each of these examples, a weaker noun displaces the most important noun. In the first sentence, we are not talking about a world, but about politics. In the second, the noun *fields* is redundant because ecology and biodiversity are fields of study.

Phony Phrases

Phony phrases are redundant prepositional phrases. Look for them after verbs and nouns.

> Unnecessary: For now, the patient's kidneys are functioning *at a normal level*.
> Better: For now, the patient's kidneys are functioning *normally*.

Here, the preposition *for* introduces the phony phrase:

> Unnecessary: The bill was legislated in 1995 *for a brief period of time*.
> Better: The bill was *briefly* legislated in 1995.

> If you can sum up a prepositional phrase with a one-word adverb or adjective, use the one-word modifier.

A cluster of non-specific nouns, such as *level, scale, basis, degree*, and *extent*, are connected to phony phrases beginning with *on, to*, or other prepositions. Watch for these prepositional phrases: *on/at the international level, on a regular basis, on the larger scale, to a great/considerable degree/extent*. Such phrases can likely be replaced by an appropriate adverb.

> Unnecessary: Jindra checks her voicemail *on a regular basis*.
> Better: Jindra checks her voicemail *regularly*.

A relative clause is adjectival and may sometimes be replaced by a corresponding adjective preceding the noun. In the following sentence, the relative clause *that is high in protein* modifies *diet*:

> Unnecessary: Most bodybuilders follow a strict diet *that is high in protein*.
> Better: Most bodybuilders follow a strict, *high-protein* diet.

The Small but Not-So-Beautiful

Writers may think that small words, such as prepositions and articles, make an ordinary phrase sound more impressive. But these terms can be omitted from many sentences. In these examples, parentheses indicate words that can be omitted:

> He was (the) last out (of) the door.
> (The) taking (of) life can never be condoned.

The word *that* can be used as a pronoun (demonstrative or relative), adjective, or subordinating conjunction. It can often be omitted if the subject of the second clause is different from the subject of the preceding clause. By methodically checking your first draft for unnecessary *that*s, you can often improve sentence flow.

> I thought (that) Silas was going to attend the same school (that) his brother went to.

Unravel the meaning of the following statement:

> It's certain that that *that* that that person used was wrong.

> **If possible, delete "clutter words" such as *of* or *that*.**

Unintensives

An intensive is a word or phrase that emphasizes the word or expression it modifies but has little meaning on its own. Intensives should be avoided in all levels of formal writing unless they truly add emphasis. The intensives in the following sentence are unneeded:

> She is *certainly* a *very* impressive speaker.

Words such as *certainly* and *very* are overused and may add nothing to the sentence.

Many intensives are adverbs modifying verbs or adjectives. In some instances, you can simply replace a weak verb and an intensive with a stronger verb or use a stronger adjective instead of an intensive plus a weak adjective. A better option may be to get rid of the intensive.

> **Unnecessary:** He was *very grateful* for his warm reception.
> **Better:** He was *gratified by* his warm reception.
> or
> He *appreciated* his warm reception.

> **Instead of using adverbs such as *very, highly, really,* or *extremely* before adjectives, use a stronger adjective or simply delete the adverb.**

Overused intensives:

absolutely	indeed
actually	inevitably
assuredly	in fact
certainly	interestingly
clearly	markedly
completely	naturally
considerably	of course
definitely	particularly
effectively	significantly
extremely	surely
fundamentally	totally
highly	utterly
incredibly	very

Other overused qualifiers:

apparently	overall
arguably	perhaps
basically	quite
essentially	rather
generally	relatively
hopefully	seemingly
in effect	somewhat
in general	sort of
kind of	virtually

Here are some intensives that may clutter your sentences:

aforementioned	in regard(s) to
amidst	in terms of
amongst	in the final analysis
analogous to	in view of the fact that
as a result of	irregardless
as to	notwithstanding the fact that
at this point in time	oftentimes
cognizant of	pertaining to
consequent to	so as to
despite the fact that	subsequent to
due to the fact that	that
each and every	the majority of
in accordance with	thusly
in as much as	whether or not
in comparison to	whilst
in conjunction with	with regard(s) to
in connection with	with respect to
in reference to	

Writing Directly

Writing should get straight to the point. Indirect writing stresses the less important parts of the sentence.

Black Hole Constructions

Whenever possible, avoid starting sentences with *it is* or *there are* constructions. Using these weak beginnings may make your reader lose interest.

Banishing all passive constructions would unreasonably limit writers. However, inappropriately passive constructions not only use too many words but also place the stress where it doesn't belong, weakening the entire sentence. Other indirect constructions can also weaken a sentence. Think of them as the black holes of writing: they swallow up the substance of the sentence.

1. ***It was***

    It was Mary Shelley who wrote *Frankenstein* in 1816.

    As simple as this sentence is, it begins weakly by displacing the logical subject, *Mary Shelley*, and substituting *it was*. The sentence is stronger and more direct when the most important noun is the subject:

    Mary Shelley wrote *Frankenstein* in 1816.

If a relative pronoun (*who*, *which*, or *that*) follows the displaced subject, consider getting rid of it and the "empty" subject (*it was*, *there is*, *here is*) to make the statement more direct and concise.

Occasionally, you may want to use the *It was* and similar constructions for rhetorical effect. In such cases, emphasis, rather than directness, may determine your choice.

> Notice how many sentences in the sample paragraph in Exercise 16.1 contain weak openings. They affect the entire paragraph, making it hard to read.

Unnecessary: *There are* a variety of strategies that you can use to reduce excess verbiage in your writing.
Better: *You can use* various strategies to reduce verbiage in your writing.

2. **One of**
Avoid the phrase *one of* in your sentences.

Poor: The path you have chosen is *one of* danger and uncertainty.
Better: The path you have chosen *is dangerous and uncertain.*
or
You have chosen *a dangerous, uncertain* path.

3. **The reason . . . is because**
This phrase is both illogical and redundant.

Incorrect: *The reason* Jessica is lucky *is because* she has a horseshoe on her door.
Correct: Jessica is lucky *because* she has a horseshoe on her door.

Numbing Nouns

Writers sometimes fall into the habit of using a weak verb and a corresponding noun rather than a verb that directly expresses the meaning. In each of these cases, a direct verb replaces a weak verb phrase:

> Weak verb + noun constructions begin with common verbs such as *have*, *make*, or *take* and follow with a noun object, which can usually be made into a strong verb.

Weak Constructions	**Strong Constructions**
I *had a meeting* with my staff, and I am now asking you to *provide a list of* all your clients.	I met with my staff and now ask you *to list* all your clients.
Inexperienced writers *have a tendency* to be wordy.	Inexperienced writers *tend* to be wordy.
She *made changes* to the document, *making clear* what was ambiguous.	She *changed* the document, *clarifying* ambiguities.

| Sam *offered comfort* to Amanda, who *received a failing grade* on her essay. | Sam *comforted* Amanda, who *had failed* her essay. |
| Canada *made a significant contribution* to the war effort in France and Belgium. | Canada *contributed significantly* to the war effort in France and Belgium. |

For the weak phrase *has an effect on*, where *has* is the verb and *effect* is the noun, *affect* is the corresponding verb form.

> Global warming *affects* shifting major weather patterns. Its *effects* are widely felt throughout the globe.

Nouns that pile up in a sentence can create a numbing effect. This situation is common with nominals, nouns formed from verbs (see Table 16.1). You can use a polysyllabic noun formed from a verb, unless a more concise and direct alternative exists.

> The conflict between Billy and Claggart ultimately serves as a device in the interruption of the reader's attempts at a coherent interpretation of the novel as an ideological message. In addition to problematizing

Avoid a succession of long words if shorter, basic words are just as effective.

TABLE 16.1   Nominals

Verb	Nominal	Example
accumulate	Accumulation	Nominal: The accumulation of evidence is overwhelming. The nominal *accumulation of* can be deleted: The evidence is overwhelming.
classify	Classification	We will now proceed with the classification of Vertebrata. Verb: We will now classify Vertebrata.
intend; install	*intention; installation*	Nominal: Our intention is to complete the installation of the new system this month. Verb: We intend to finish installing the new system this month.

definitive interpretations, this technique effectively secures a lasting relevance for the novel.

The thought in these sentences can be expressed more directly and clearly by omitting words and reducing the number of nominals.

The conflict between Billy and Claggart challenges a coherent ideological reading of the novel, making definitive readings difficult and ensuring the novel's relevance.

Euphemisms

The term *euphemism* comes from the Greek word that means "to use words for good omen." Many ancient cultures used euphemisms to avoid naming their enemies directly, thereby refusing to give those they feared power. Today, we use such words out of kindness to those who may be suffering, as a way of speaking about taboo subjects and objects, or as a form of satire or irony. For example, *to pass away* or *pass on* are the most common euphemisms for *die*.

Along with protecting us from the unpleasant, euphemisms give us false assurance. For example, *urban renewal* avoids the implications of *slum clearance*, *revenue enhancement* has a more positive ring than *tax increase*, and *collateral losses* attempts to sidestep the fact that civilians have been killed during military action. We also sometimes use euphemisms to give something more dignity or a sense of importance: *pre-owned automobile* for *used car* and *job action* for *strike*. The Plain English Campaign once gave a Golden Bull Award to writers who described the act of laying bricks as "install[ing] a component into the structural fabric."

The following classified ad uses some wordy and euphemistic language:

We are seeking an individual who possesses demonstrated skills and abilities, a sound knowledge base coupled with the experience to provide service to mentally challenged teenagers with "unique" and significant challenging behaviours.

The position's requirements can be expressed with half the words:

Applicants need proven skills, knowledge, and experience to serve mentally challenged teenagers with challenging behaviours.

A special category of "acceptable euphemisms" are those that society agrees should be substituted for expressions that have acquired inappropriate or offensive connotations. For example, to refer to someone in a wheelchair as a *cripple* inappropriately stresses the disability and its limitations. A more sensitive and

A **euphemism** is a word or phrase substituted for the actual name of something, usually to make it more acceptable or to give it dignity. It is an example of indirect writing.

accurate description is *a person with a physical disability* (or *a physical challenge*). The person is not the disability.

Exercise 16.4

In groups, think of or make up 10 euphemisms. Read the list to your other class-mates and have them guess what each describes.

Exercise 16.5

The following sentences can be revised for conciseness and directness. Make the necessary changes and be prepared to justify them.

1. Tanya has been invited to provide us with a summary of the significant main points of her findings.
2. The totally unexpected tsunami turned the fields into either a large waste land or a large junk yard.
3. Gretta was decidedly overjoyed after being the unexpected recipient of an income tax refund in excess of $1,000.
4. The protagonist of *Life of Pi* is confronted with the necessity of making the decision about whether he wanted to continue on living or not.
5. It was because of her clear, beautiful voice that she was made the winner of the singing contest.
6. The disappearance of even one single species at the lower end of the food chain can have dire adverse effects in many instances on the survival of various other species.
7. Although Copernicus's radical idea that the earth made revolutions around the sun was once considered an extreme heresy and was ridiculed mercilessly by his peers, the idea eventually gained gradual acceptance.
8. The fact is that for many students of above-average intelligence, school can seem tedious and dull so they begin to act up in class and cause other students who are not as smart to miss the important and salient points of the lesson in question.
9. Perhaps in the heat of emotion the act of capital punishment would seem to be a feasible idea, but when you come to think of it rationally, this act would accomplish virtually next to nothing at all.
10. In protest of their salary freeze, all of the teachers who teach at the high school in Oak Bay have made the unanimous decision not to undertake any tasks of a supervisory nature until the school board has conducted a fair and impartial salary review.
11. Vehicles that have the four-way drive feature option are an extremely prac-tical and pragmatic form of transportation for the majority of the Canadian population in this day and age.

12. There are many people in our society today who have serious drug addictions that take complete and utter control over their lives.

13. From the beginning of its conception, Canada has been a country concerned with promoting an active multicultural society, although the reality of unity within the country is still a large, unanswered question in the minds of most of the people of Canada.

14. A French scientist by the name of Louis Pasteur was the first individual to make the discovery that microbes were harmful menaces to the well-being and healthy functioning of the human body.

15. The reason yoga allows us to live a healthy lifestyle is due to the fact that it provides a strong basis for the efficient functioning of the body's endocrine system.

Exercise **16.6**

Rewrite the following passage, aiming for concise, direct writing.

Dear Employers,

The Youth Resource Centre, in conjunction with the Federal Human Resource Department of Canada, has opened the Hire-A-Student office once again this summer, staffing summer employment officers working towards finding the best possible student employees for any jobs that you may have available to post with us at the centre.

Our service, conveniently situated at 147 High Street, is a totally free service to both employers posting jobs in the centre and to students and youths trying to secure employment opportunities throughout the community. The service is a means for you the employer to help advertise any positions you may have available, and is additionally a way to assist students who are showing initiative in finding possible long-term or limited-term seasonal employment.

We are not a solicitation firm, and this is the point that we need to emphasize to the greatest extent. Our service is absolutely free of charge, and our intention is first and foremost to try and find employment for students who seem serious about working, as well as to offer a free alternative to posting jobs in newspapers and ad agencies that could end up costing you an excessive amount of money through advertising ventures.

Working toward Precision: Wise Word Choices

As we have indicated throughout this text, most college and university writing assignments require formal writing, also known as formal diction. You may be more familiar with informal writing, which you probably use in social media and even used in your high school English courses. In informal writing,

- language may be close to speech or be chatty, with colloquialisms, idioms, or even slang;
- contractions are acceptable (e.g., *don't, can't, shouldn't, it's*);
- the first-person (*I, me*) and second-person (*you*) voice may be used;
- sentence fragments may be used occasionally for dramatic effect;
- short paragraphs are the rule rather than the exception; and
- citations for research sources are not given.

Formal writing follows the rules of formal usage and grammar. Therefore, unless you are quoting someone or your instructor tells you otherwise, avoid contractions, colloquialisms, slang, and jargon. For example, do not use any of the following in a formal essay:

do drugs	pan out
down-side	price tag
fall for	put a positive spin (on something)
give the green light	put on hold
go overboard	put (someone) down
go to great lengths	quick fix
grab the reader's attention	stressed (out)
mindset	the way to go
no way	tune out
obsess (about something)	upfront
okay	way more (of something—a lot is also
opt for	colloquial)

Avoid non-specific and merely qualitative words and phrases, such as *great*, *incredible*, *beautiful*, *terrible*, and the like. You also should refrain from using words and expressions that might suggest a gender, sexual, racial, cultural, or other kind of bias.

Of course, your word choices involve much more than thinking about the level of formality. Effective writers choose their words and phrases carefully. The following three examples from student essays demonstrate poor word choice:

> The mass production of plastics and ready-to-use products is growing at a *staggering* rate.

Formal writing features the rules of formal usage and correct grammar. **Diction** is related to word choices and level of language; formal and informal writing are examples of different kinds of diction. **Colloquialisms** are words and expressions acceptable in conversation but not in formal writing. An **idiom** is a phrase whose meaning is understood only within the context of the phrase. For example, *his bark is worse than his bite* can be understood only by looking at the overall meaning and not by the meanings of the individual words.

Avoid using informal verbs such as *saw, has seen*, etc., when you mean *resulted in* or *occurred* (e.g., The policy that was implemented two years ago *has seen* a 40 per cent drop in violent crime. Revised: The policy that was implemented two years ago *has resulted in* a 40 per cent drop in violent crime.).

Staggering is informal; the writer could have used *rapid, rapidly increasing*, or *exponential* or a specific rate, such as *doubling every five years*.

Exercise 16.7

Find uses of informal language in the following excerpt and then provide more concise wording.

> There was an article about a campaign that a group called Respect for Animals is waging to convince consumers to boycott Canadian seafood products. The magazine also carried two huge advertisements from the same organization.
>
> The Newfoundland seal hunt is transparently and demonstrably sustainable and humane. There are roughly half a million people in Newfoundland and Labrador, and nearly six million harp seals, which is almost three times as many seals as when I was a kid.
>
> Here's one of those obligatory disclosures: over the years, several environmental organizations—the Sierra Club, the David Suzuki Foundation, Greenpeace, etc.—have subsidized my preoccupation with things that move in the water by having me do research projects for them and so on. With that out of the way, I can now say, if it isn't obvious already, that it's the seal hunt's opponents who turn my stomach.
>
> Glavin, T. (2007). An enviro's case for seal hunt.
> http://thetyee.ca/Views/2007/03/07/SealHunt/

Writers usually don't make extreme blunders but choose a word that doesn't quite suit their purpose. These "near misses" can distract or confuse the reader. You should not let the search for the exact word prevent you from fully expressing your ideas in a first draft. But when revising, look up the meanings of all words you're in doubt about—even if you're only a little unsure. You can use a thesaurus to look for words similar in meaning to avoid repeating a word too often. Make sure you use a reliable dictionary as well; a thesaurus usually does not provide word connotations.

Some dictionaries help you to be precise not only by defining the main entry but also by providing distinctions among similar words. For example, the *Gage Canadian Dictionary*, which lists more than six meanings for the adjective *effective*, also defines two words similar in meaning but different in connotation:

> Writers often use words that have specific associations or implications. A word's connotation includes its possible meanings in its given context.

Syn. adj. 1. **Effective, effectual, efficient** = producing an effect. **Effective**, usually describing things, emphasizes producing a wanted or expected effect: *several new drugs are effective in treating serious diseases.* **Effectual**, describing people or things, emphasizes having produced or having the power to produce the exact effect or result intended: *his efforts are more energetic than effectual.* **Efficient**, often describing people, emphasizes being able to produce the effect wanted or intended without wasting energy, time, etc.: *A skilled surgeon is highly efficient.*

Similarly, the *Student's Oxford Canadian Dictionary*, which lists seven meanings for the adjective *nice*, offers the following examples of words that may be more appropriate or more forceful in certain contexts:

we had a delightful/splendid/enjoyable time
a satisfying/delicious/exquisite meal
a fashionable/stylish/elegant/chic outfit
this is a cozy/comfortable/attractive room
she is kind/friendly/likeable/amiable
our advisor is compassionate/understanding/sympathetic
a thoughtful/considerate/caring gesture

Precision and Logic

Imprecision sometimes results from illogical thinking or from writing down an idea quickly. To confirm that what you've written makes sense, you need to look carefully at the relationship among the parts of the sentence, especially at the relationship between the subject and predicate. A weak or non-existent relationship creates a logical error. For example, faulty predication occurs if a verb cannot be logically connected to its subject. In general, avoid *is when* and *is where* after a subject in sentences that define something. In the following sentence, *faulty predication* is illogically referred to as a time:

> **Faulty predication** occurs where a verb cannot be logically linked to its subject.

Incorrect: Faulty predication is when a verb cannot be logically connected to its subject.
Correct: Faulty predication occurs where [i.e., in a sentence] a verb is not logically connected to its subject.
or
Faulty predication is an illogical juxtaposing of a subject and a verb.

Consider this comment on the setting of Joseph Conrad's *Heart of Darkness*:

The Congo represents an inward journey for the character Marlow.

The Congo is the name of a country as well as a river. How can either represent a journey? Of course, a *trip through a country* or *on a river* would be a more logical phrase.

In one kind of faulty predication, an inanimate object is falsely linked to a human action.

> Some opponents claim that *PE programs* are unwilling to accommodate the needs of all students.

The programs aren't "unwilling," since this implies a will; teachers or administrators may be unwilling.

> Some opponents claim that *the administrators of PE programs* are unwilling to accommodate the needs of all students.

Sound should also play a role in word choice. You should avoid placing words with similar sounds in close proximity (e.g., *the echo effect*).

> Endorphins enable the body to heal itself and *gain pain* relief.

You should also be wary of unintentional puns in a work of scholarship:

> The first experiments in music therapy were *noted* during World War I.

An objective voice is the hallmark of both expository and argumentative writing. Though you may be tempted to write ironically or sarcastically, keep the **tone** objective. Remember, your reader may not share your attitude.

Tone shows the writer's attitude toward the subject.

> Inappropriate tone: It is well known that college students under stress need to exercise their livers on the occasional Friday night.

Exercise 16.8

Rewrite the following paragraph, replacing informal diction with formal. Note that a word or phrase might be colloquial but necessary due to context or not easily rephrased.

> Hosting the Olympic Games is a once-in-a-lifetime opportunity, and it seems like a great idea. It would create world recognition for a world-class city, helping to really put it on the map. On top of that, it would be a fun and exciting time for the citizens of the surrounding area. However, after sober second thought, it is clear

that while the Games might pay for themselves, who will pay for the upgrades necessary to get the city in good shape for the Games? Even with the government chipping in for a fair amount of the costs, because that city would be dealing in billions of dollars, even a small chunk of that cost is a lot of money. These small chunks would come from the pockets of the taxpayer, some of whom are not big fans of the Games at all. But although these direct costs are bound to be steep, it is the hidden costs of the Games that will be the real killer.

Verbs with Vitality

 Chapter 13 discusses verbs at length.

> When checking whether a subject fits with its predicate, ensure that the subject can perform the action that the verb describes.

> Verbs and nouns are the two most important parts of speech. The verbs you use can weaken or strengthen your prose. Choose them carefully, preferring active to static verbs and deleting forms such as *being* and *to be* when they are unneeded.

Look at the verbs in your sentences. Could you replace them with stronger, more descriptive ones? Could you replace *be* and *have*, which convey a state or condition, with verbs of action? Common verbs, such as *do*, *make*, *go*, and *get*, are not specific. Could you replace them with more precise or emphatic verbs?

The most common verb in English, *to be*, takes many different forms as an irregular verb—*am*, *is*, *are*, *was*, *were*, *will be*, etc.—and appears frequently as a helping verb. Your writing will be more concise if you omit these forms whenever they are unnecessary.

> The results of the study can be interpreted as ~~being~~ credible.
> She dreamed of a carriage ~~being~~ pulled by two fine horses.
> Hypnosis has been proven ~~to be~~ an effective therapy for some people.
> In 313 BCE Christianity was declared ~~to be~~ the official religion of Rome.

As people put on the spot by journalists and the public, politicians sometimes choose vague language to avoid committing themselves to statements they may regret later. A more cynical view suggests that abstract, indefinite language enables them to say little while appearing informed and in control. Notice the lack of specificity in the following comment by former American politician Colin Powell, made in an interview on *Fox News Sunday* on 16 May 2004:

> We knew that the ICRC had concerns, and in accordance with the matter in which the ICRC does its work, it presented those concerns directly to the command in Baghdad. And I know that some corrective action was taken with respect to those concerns.

Exercise **16.9**

Indicate which verbs in the following paragraph should be made more descriptive.

By the 1800s, inventions were beginning to put people out of work. One of the first inventions that resulted in rebellion was in the craft guild. In 1801, Joseph Jacquard became known as the inventor of the Jacquard loom. This loom was capable of being programmed by pre-punched cards, which made it possible to create clothing design patterns. This invention led to the creation of the Luddites, who were a group made up from the craft guild. These people were against any type of manufacturing technology and went about burning down several factories that were using this new technology. The Luddites were around only for a couple of years, but the name Luddite is still used to describe people who are resistant to new technologies. The Jacquard loom was, in effect, an invention that replaced people. It could do great designs quickly and without making any errors. The replacement of people by machines was beginning.

Exercise **16.10**

Suggest how the following passage could be improved by using more specific language and by omitting unnecessary words and phrases.

The time period between 1985 and 1989 was a difficult one for graffiti artists in New York City. This was a time when graffiti barely stayed alive because of the harsh laws and efforts of the Metropolitan Transit Authority, which is known as the MTA. This period was called the period of the "Die Hards" because of the small number of die-hard artists who were able to keep graffiti from dying out completely. As a result of the measures of the MTA against graffiti art and artists, there was a lack of paint available for use and the level of enforcement was extremely high. The only important thing that was happening during these years was the use of markers for tagging. These tags were usually small, of poor artistic quality, and were finished quickly by the artists. These tags can be seen today at some bus stops and in some washrooms throughout the city.

Prepackaged Goods: Clichés

Expressions considered **clichés** today were a veritable breath of fresh air in their prime. (Did you spot the clichés in the previous sentence?) If commentary on the cliché were to be made in clichés, the prose would be wordy and confusing:

> However, with the passage of time (more years than you can shake a stick at), they became the stuff of idle minds until after time immemorial they assumed the mantle of respectability and were accepted verbatim as par for the course. Writers worth their salt should avoid clichés like the plague or they will stop all readers with a good head on their shoulders dead in their tracks (to call a spade a spade and to give the devil his due).

Exercise 16.11

Although newspaper features use informal writing, it should be descriptive and concrete. How could you make this passage from a travel feature more interesting?

> We're up and about at the crack of dawn, and from outside our cabin we can see the peak of a small mountain looming in the distance. Our ship glides effortlessly over the fathomless blue sea, and soon the mountain's craggy features come into view.
>
> "It's breakfast, honey," my wife, Jen, sings from inside the cabin, and soon our impeccably dressed waiter knocks softly on our door. As we sit down to partake of the delectable repast, I feel as though I could pinch myself. Yes, here we are, aboard a luxurious liner, about to drop anchor off the coast of one of the world's most fabled isles.

Clichés are overworked and unoriginal phrases, dead metaphors that have been drained of their novelty through overuse. Inexperienced writers may reach for them in a vain attempt to "spice up" their writing. Although they may appear in some informal writing, they are poor substitutes for informative, imaginative words.

 # Common Words That Confuse

English has many word pairs that are confusing because the two words look similar (for example, *affect* and *effect*) or because they have similar, but not identical, uses (for example, *amount* and *number*)—or both. In most cases, the dictionary is the best resource for problems related to meaning and spelling (don't rely on a spellchecker), but **usage** can be more complicated. We will discuss the top 25 words that give student writers the most trouble. Hints and examples are provided.

> **Usage** is the customary and accepted way that a word is used.

1. **accept, except:** *Accept* is a verb meaning "to receive, to take what is offered." *Except* is a preposition meaning "other than" or "leaving out."

   Hint: Think of the "crossing out" connotation of "x" in *except* to remind you that the word means "leaving out."
   Example: The bargaining committee accepted all the terms except the last one.

2. **affect, effect:** *Affect* is a verb meaning "to influence or have an effect on." *Effect*, a noun, means "a result." As a verb, *effect* is used less often; it means "to bring about" or "to cause"—not "to have an effect on."

   Hint: Try substituting *influence* in the sentence; if it fits your intended meaning, *affect* is the word you want.
   Example: The news of Michael Jordan's return to basketball greatly affected his fans. The effect was also felt at the box office; an immediate hike in ticket prices was effected.

3. **allot, a lot:** *Allot*, a verb, means "to portion out"; *a lot* can be an adverb ("I sleep a lot") or a noun ("I need a lot of sleep") meaning "a great deal." *A lot* is too informal for most academic writing; you should use the more formal *a great deal*, *much*, *many*, or similar substitutes. The one-word spelling, *alot*, is incorrect.

   Example: My parents allotted me $500 spending money for the term, which was not a lot considering my shopping habit. [informal]

4. **all right, alright:** *All right* can be an adjective meaning "satisfactory, acceptable, or permissible" or an adverb meaning "satisfactory" or "definitely." *Alright* is not a word.

   Examples:

   The movie was *all right*.
   She was *all right* to drive.
   It was them *all right*.

5. **allude, elude:** Both are verbs, but they mean different things. *Allude* (*to*) means "to refer to something briefly or indirectly"; *elude* means "to avoid

or escape, usually through a clever manoeuvre or strategy." *Allude* should be followed by *to*: "In the poem, Hardy alluded to the end of the century."

Hint: *Allude* is the verb from which the noun *allusion* [a kind of reference, see *allusion*] is formed; you can associate the *e* in *elude* with the *e* in *escape*.
Example: In his prison memoirs, the bank robber alluded to the time in the desert when he eluded capture by disguising himself as a cactus.

6. **allusion, illusion:** You may have come across the literary use of *allusion*, a historical, religious, mythic, literary, or other kind of outside reference used to reveal character or theme in a work. An *illusion* is something apparently seen that is not real or that gives a false impression.

Hint: Since the most common mistake is misspelling *allusion* as *illusion*, remember that *allusion*, meaning an outside reference, always begins with *al*.

Examples:

The title of Nathanael West's novel *The Day of the Locust* is an allusion to the book of Exodus in the Bible.
Optical illusions often use graphics to fool our senses.

7. **among, between:** The simple distinction is that *between* refers to two persons or things and *among* to more than two.

Examples:

The senator found himself between a rock and a hard place.
Ms O'Grady stood among her adoring students for the school picture.

Between may be the obvious choice even if more than two things are involved. For example, "Interlibrary loans are permitted between campuses." Even though a number of campuses may be part of the interlibrary loan system, any exchange takes place between two campuses.

8. **amount, number:** Use *amount* to refer to things that can't be counted; *number* refers to countable objects.

Hint: Think of using numbers when you count.
Example: The number of errors in this essay reveals the amount of care you took in writing it.

9. **beside, besides:** *Beside* is a preposition meaning "next to or adjoining"; *besides* has several meanings as a preposition; as an adverb, it means "in addition (to)."

   Hint: Think of the extra *s* in *besides* as an additional letter to remind you of "in addition to."

   Example: Beside the cellphone was the charger, besides which she had her iPad.

10. **bias, biased:** *Bias* is a noun that refers to a "tendency to judge unfairly"; *biased* is an adjective that means "having or showing a preferential attitude." A person can have a bias (a thing); be a biased person (adjective modifying *person*); or can be biased (predicate adjective after a linking verb). A person cannot be bias. Also, a person is biased or has a bias against (not to or for) something or someone.

    Example: His bias against the Rastafarian lifestyle caused him to overlook some of its ideals.

11. **cite, sight, site:** *To cite*, a verb, is "to refer to an outside source." (The complete naming of the source itself is a citation.) *Sight* (noun or verb) refers to seeing, one of the five senses. *Site*, when used as a noun, is a location or place (usually of some importance). The most common error in essays is the use of *site* when *cite* is meant.

    Hint: Remember that *cite* is a verb referring to "the act of giving a citation"; *site* is "where something is situated or sits."
    Example: She said the ruins were excavated in 1926, citing as proof the historical plaque that commemorated the site.

12. **e.g., i.e.:** *E.g.* is an abbreviation for the Latin *exempli gratia*, meaning "for the sake of example"; *i.e.* is an abbreviation for the Latin *id est*, meaning "that is." Use *e.g.* before one or more examples; use *i.e.* if you want to elaborate on or clarify a preceding statement. In both cases, use a period after each letter and a comma after the abbreviation. Because they are abbreviations, they should be avoided in formal writing.

    Hint: The first letter in *example* tells you that examples should follow *e.g.*
    Example: J.K. Rowling defied the common formula for success in the children's book market by writing long novels (e.g., *Harry Potter and the Goblet of Fire* and *Harry Potter and the Order of the Phoenix*).

Some of Rowling's novels have episodic plots that contain many well-developed characters (i.e., they tend to be long).

13. **fewer, less:** *Fewer* is the quantitative adjective of comparison and refers to things that can be counted; *less* is the qualitative adjective of comparison, referring to amount and things that can be measured.

Examples:

Don't believe the notice on the mayonnaise jar: "Contains 40% less calories." Calories can be counted.
There were fewer than a dozen people at the nomination meeting.
The less said about his defection, the better.

14. **good, well:** *Good* may be an adjective, noun, or adverb. When used as an adjective, it should clearly modify a noun (e.g., *a good story*) or be used as a subject complement (predicate adjective, e.g., "The child was good until bedtime"). It cannot be used as a predicate adjective after verbs that express an action, although it is frequently heard in speech, especially in sports ("I was hitting the ball good").

Incorrect: She beat the batter good.
Correct: She is a good cook and beat the batter well.

As an adjective, *well* means "in good health" or "satisfactory." As an adverb, it has several meanings, including "thoroughly" and "satisfactorily."

Hint: Do not use *good* as a predicate adjective after an action verb; you may use it before a noun or right after an intransitive (linking) verb.

Examples:

Making a good donation to the Children's Hospital made the corporation look good. [i.e., "appear altruistic," not "appear good-looking"]
Although just having come out of the hospital, she looked well and continued to feel well during her recovery. [*Well* is used as an adjective after linking verbs and means "healthy."]

15. **its, it's:** *Its* is a possessive adjective meaning "belonging to it" and is formed from the personal pronoun *it*. Remember that personal pronouns are never spelled with an apostrophe. *It's* is the contraction for *it is*, the apostrophe indicating that the letter *i* is left out.

Hint: Try substituting *it is* if you're having problems identifying the correct form; if it fits, use *it's*; if it doesn't, use *its*. (*Its* is usually followed by a noun.)
Example: It's foolish to judge a book by its cover.

16. **lay, lie:** Both are verbs. *Lay* is a transitive verb, which must always be followed by a direct object (either a noun or a pronoun). It is incorrect to say, "I'm going to lay down to rest." *Lie* is an intransitive verb; it is not followed by an object.

    Hint: You always lay something down, as a hen does an egg. Then it lies there.

    Examples:

    He lay the baby in the crib before going to lie down.
    He had lain on the ground for 20 minutes before someone noticed him. [*Lain* is the past participle of *lie*.]
    Kim Campbell laid to rest the notion that a woman couldn't be prime minister. [*Laid* is the past participle of *lay*.]

17. **led, lead:** *Led* and *lead* are forms of the irregular verb *to lead* (rhymes with *weed*); the present tense is also *lead*. However, the past tense and the past participle are *led*. Writers may become confused by the noun *lead*, the metal, which looks like *to lead* but is pronounced like *led*. Therefore, when they come to write the past tense *led*, they may wrongly substitute the noun *lead* rather than the verb.

    Hint: Don't be led astray by thinking there is an *a* in *led*.
    Example: Although she led in the polls by a 2:1 margin three months ago, today she leads by only a slight margin.

18. **loose, lose:** *Loose* is an adjective meaning "not tight"; *lose* is a verb meaning "not able to find" or "to be defeated."

    Hint: When you lose something, it is lost. *Lost* is spelled with one *o*.
    Example: If you don't tighten that loose button, you're going to lose it.

19. **onset, outset:** Both are nouns that mean a "beginning." *Outset* means "setting out," for example, on a journey or to do something; you can also use the phrase *at the outset* to refer to the early events of a narrative or play. *Onset* refers to a force or condition that comes upon one.

Example: At the outset of my fourth decade, I experienced the onset of mild osteoarthritis.

20. **than, then:** *Than* is a conjunction used in comparisons ("He's happier than he knows"). *Then* is an adverb with temporal connotations meaning "consequently," "at that time," "after that," etc.

    Hint: If you're comparing one thing to another, use *than*. *Then* "tells when."
    Example: Warren said he was better at darts than Mark, and then he challenged him to a game to prove it.

21. **their, there, they're:** *Their* is a possessive adjective meaning "belonging to them"; *there* is an adverb meaning "in that place"; *they're* is the contraction of *they are*, the apostrophe indicating that the letter *a* is left out.

    Hint: If you're uncertain about *they're*, substitute *they are*; *there* (meaning "in that place") is spelled the same as *here* ("in this place") with the letter *t* added.
    Example: There is no excuse for the rowdy behaviour in there; they're supposed to be in their rooms.

22. **to, too:** *To* is a preposition indicating "direction towards"; *too* is an adverb meaning "also."

    Hint: *To* is usually followed by a noun or pronoun as part of a prepositional phrase; substitute *also* for *too*.
    Example: The next time you go to the store, may I come along, too?

23. **usage, use:** Many writers overuse *usage*, which refers to "a customary or habitual pattern or practice." It applies to conventions of groups of people, such as "language usage of the English." Usage shouldn't be used simply to mean a repeated action.

    Incorrect: The usage of email has allowed businesses to increase their efficiency.
    Example: I have no use for people who are always correcting my usage of *whom*.

24. **who's, whose:** *Who's* is the contraction of *who is*, the apostrophe indicating the omission of the letter *i*. *Whose* is the possessive adjective meaning "belonging to whom."

Hint: Try substituting *who is*. If it fits, *who's* is the correct form.

Examples:

Whose turn is it to do the dishes?
Who's going to do the dishes tonight?

25. **you're, your:** *You're* is the contraction of *you are*; *your* is a possessive adjective that means "belonging to you."

    Hint: Try substituting *you are*. If it fits, *you're* is the correct form.
    Example: You're going to be sorry if you don't take your turn and do the dishes tonight.

    Here is a list of 50 additional words that often give students trouble:

Don't say . . .	When you mean . . .
adolescents	adolescence (the time one is an adolescent)
aforementioned	this/previously stated
around	about (in reference to numbers)
associated to	associated with
attribute to	contribute to
avoid	prevent
base off/around	base on
conscience	conscious
continuous	continual
council	counsel
could of/would of	could have/would have
different than	different from
downfall	disadvantage
downside	disadvantage
entirety of	all
farther	further (farther applies to physical distance)
half to	have to
imply	infer
insure	ensure
irregardless	regardless
lifestyle	life
like	as
locality/location	place
majority of	most
man	human/humanity
manpower	resources

mindset	belief
misfortunate	unfortunate
multiple	many
none the less	nonetheless
obsess about	to be obsessed about
obtain	attain
overexaggerate	exaggerate
passed	past
popular	common
principal	principle
prior/prior to	before
references	refers to (references is a plural noun)
reoccur	recur
seize	cease
so	very
thanks to	due to
that	who/whom/where, etc.
thru	through
till	until
to transition	to change
upon	on
weather	whether
were	where
which	who/whom

As you progress through your course, you may have problems with other words. Add them, along with definitions and correct usage, to this list.

Exercise 16.12

From the lists provided in the previous sections, choose 10 words that give you trouble. Find their definitions and then write sentences using the words correctly.

Example:

Amount: the quantity of something; used for non-count nouns
The amount of rain that fell in June this year is equal to all the rain that fell last year.
Number: the quantity of something; used for count nouns
It is hard to count the number of raindrops that fall into a cup.

Providing Depth: Variety and Emphasis

When you revise an early draft to improve clarity, you will likely find opportunities to make your prose more interesting. Variety and emphasis in your writing make what is competent compelling. Thus, they are worthwhile goals in all forms of essays: personal, literary, argumentative, and expository.

Sentence Variety

Length

You can vary the lengths of sentences for rhetorical effect. Just as short paragraphs suggest underdeveloped points, short, choppy sentences could suggest a lack of content. On the other hand, several long sentences in a row could confuse a reader. That doesn't mean you should write only sentences that are between 15 and 20 words. Although sentence length alone is no measure of readability, consider revision if you find you have written more than two very short or very long sentences in a row.

> Avoid writing too many overly short or overly long sentences. Using proper grammar, combine short sentences or break longer sentences into shorter ones.

You can use appropriate conjunctions to connect short sentences. Join simple sentences with one of the seven coordinating conjunctions. If the idea in one sentence is less important than the idea in the sentence before or after it, use the subordinating conjunction that best expresses the relationship between them. Join independent clauses with a semicolon or a colon.

> Page 315 introduces coordinating conjunctions; pages 315–16 discuss subordinating conjunctions. See pages 347–52, 352–3, and 314–16 for more information on semicolons, colons, and joining sentences and clauses, respectively.

Exercise 16.13

The following paragraph has too many short sentences. Using the strategies mentioned in this section, revise the paragraph to make it more effective.

> During the earth's long history, there have been various periods of glaciation. This fact is well known. There is also evidence of one great glacial event. It is possible that the earth was once completely covered by ice and snow. Skeptics argue this is impossible. They say that the earth could never have become this cold. The idea of the tropics being frozen over is unlikely, they believe.

You can also join independent clauses with a conjunctive adverb or transitional phrase, but make sure that a semicolon precedes the connecting word or phrase. You may be able to connect phrases or clauses grammatically through a

> Pages 340 offers rules for punctuating appositives.

parallel relationship, such as apposition. The second phrase or clause could also modify the preceding word, phrase, or clause—for example, a relative (adjectival) clause could give information about a preceding noun clause.

Exercise 16.14

The following paragraph consists of sentences that are too long. Using joining strategies, revise the paragraph to make it more effective.

Finding a definition for "the homeless" is difficult, but the most common definition, which is used both in the media and in current research, defines the homeless as those who lack visible shelter or use public shelters. Literature about homelessness is sparse, and it was not until the 1980s that the incidence of homelessness began to be reported in the media, but homelessness has existed for centuries, and literature on the subject dates back to the feudal period in Europe.

Generally speaking, you waste space when you begin a new sentence by repeating part of the previous sentence or by beginning a new paragraph by recapitulating part of the previous one. Although repetition can be used to build coherence, it should not create redundancy.

In 1970, Gordon O. Gallup created the mirror test. This test was designed to determine whether or not animals are self-aware.
Revised: In 1970, Gordon O. Gallup created the mirror test, designed to determine whether animals are self-aware.

Page 382 discusses relative clauses.

When checking your work for overly long sentences, consider breaking up sentences with more than two independent clauses or one independent clause and more than two dependent clauses. See if the relationships between the clauses are clear. If they are not, divide the sentences where clauses are joined by conjunctions, transitional words and phrases, or relative pronouns.

Structural Variety

Pages 320–1 explain prepositional phrases.

You can also experiment with phrasal openings to sentences. Consider beginning the occasional sentence with a prepositional, participial, or absolute phrase instead of the subject. A prepositional phrase begins with a preposition followed by a noun or pronoun; it is adjectival or adverbial and modifies the closest noun (adjectival) or verb (adverbial). A participial phrase, which ends in *—ing*, *—ed*, or *—en*, is a verbal phrase acting as an adjective. An infinitive phrase, which is preceded by *to*, can act adjectivally or adverbially. An absolute phrase, consisting of a noun/pronoun and a partial verb form, modifies the entire sentence.

In this short excerpt from an essay about the death of a moth, Virginia Woolf uses the different types of phrases:

> After a time, tired by his dancing apparently, he settled on the window ledge in the sun, and the queer spectacle being at an end, I forgot about him. Then, looking up, my eye was caught by him. He was trying to resume his dancing, but seemed either so stiff or so awkward that he could only flutter to the bottom of the window-pane; and when he tried to fly across it, he failed.

Note the types of modifiers: the prepositional phrase *After a time*; the participial phrases *tired by his dancing* and *looking up*; and the absolute phrase *the queer spectacle being at an end*.

> Make sure that, when you use a participial phrase at the beginning of a sentence, you include the word it is intended to modify so that it does not dangle. See pages 389–91 for information on dangling modifiers.

Creating Emphasis

Writers can create **emphasis** by presenting main points or details in a particular order. Two kinds of sentences vary in the presentation of the main idea: periodic and cumulative sentences. Periodic sentences begin with modifiers before the independent clause. Cumulative sentences work the other way: they begin with an independent clause and are followed by modifying or parallel words, phrases, or clauses. While periodic sentences create anticipation by delaying the main idea, cumulative sentences develop the main idea by drawing it out. Many sentences are slightly or moderately periodic or cumulative, depending on whether the writer began or ended with modifiers. However, a writer can employ either type to create a specific effect. In the following examples, the independent clauses are italicized.

> **Emphasis** is the importance or stress that you place on an idea. A word or phrase has greater or less emphasis depending on where it appears in the sentence. You can begin a sentence with detail and follow with the main idea or begin with the main idea and follow with detail. These orders will produce contrastive effects.

Periodic:

> Unlike novelists and playwrights, who lurk behind the scenes while distracting our attention with the puppet show of imaginary characters— and unlike the scholars and journalists, who quote the opinions of others and take cover behind the hedges of neutrality—*the essayist has nowhere to hide.*
>
> Sanders, S. R. (1988). The singular first person.
> *The Sewanne Review, 96*(4), 658–672.

Cumulative:

The root of all evil is that we all want this spiritual gratification, this flow, this apparent heightening of life, this knowledge, this valley of many-colored grass, even grass and light prismatically decomposed, giving ecstasy.

Lawrence, D. H. (1990). *Studies in classic American literature.*
London, UK: Penguin, p. 76.

A writer can also delay the main idea and generate tension by beginning with a prepositional phrase:

Behind the deconstructionists' dazzling cloud of language lie certain more or less indisputable facts.

Gardner, J. (1991). *The art of fiction.*
New York, NY: Vintage, p. 88.

See Chapter 15 for more on agreement.

When the subject follows the verb and is thus delayed in this kind of construction, ensure that the verb agrees with the subject.

Other ways to emphasize parts of a sentence include parallel structures and repetition—techniques that also help in paragraph coherence—and rhythms that call the reader's attention to important ideas. The end of a sentence provides emphasis as well; a reader naturally slows down when approaching the last part of a sentence and pauses slightly between sentences.

The following two paragraphs employ parallel structures, repetition, and rhythm for emphasis.

A. My professors, many of whom were to become very famous, did not tend to be philosophic and did not dig back into the sources of the new language and categories they were using. They thought that these were scientific discoveries like any others, which were to be used in order to make further discoveries. They were very much addicted to abstractions and generalizations, as Tocqueville predicted they would be. They believed in scientific progress and appeared (there may have been an element of boasting and self-irony in this) to be convinced that they were on the verge of a historic breakthrough in the social sciences, equivalent to that scored in the sixteenth and seventeenth centuries in the natural sciences. . . . These teachers were literally inebriated by the unconscious and values. And they were also sure that scientific progress would be related to social and political progress.

Bloom, A. (2012). *The closing of the American mind.*
New York, NY: Simon & Schuster, p. 149.

Bloom employs the most common structural pattern of subject–verb–object in all his sentences, establishing a predictable rhetorical pattern that complements the predictability and uniformity of his professors that he wants to stress. Thus, *my professors*, the subject in the first sentence, is replaced by the pronoun *they* in the following three sentences; in the fourth sentence, *they* is the subject of two clauses. To avoid too many identical openings, Bloom continues with the same rhythm but varies the subject slightly: the last two sentences begin with *these teachers* and *and they*, respectively.

B. Tales about Pythagoras flew to him and stuck like iron filings to a magnet. He was said, for example, to have appeared in several places at once and to have been reincarnated many times. Taken literally, this idea can be consigned to the same overflowing bin which contains the story that he had a golden thigh; but taken figuratively, it is an under-statement. Pythagoras—or at least Pythagoreanism—was everywhere and still is.

Gottlieb, A. (2000). The dream of reason. New York, NY: Norton, p. 21.

The most obvious technique in this paragraph is the use of figurative language: Gottlieb uses a simile in the first sentence (*like iron filings to a magnet*) and a metaphor in the third (*overflowing bin*). He effectively uses sentence length and rhythm to make the paragraph more appealing. The paragraph is framed by short simple sentences that stress Pythagoras's importance. The middle sentences develop the main idea through examples. Gottlieb's final sentence, though the shortest, contains strong emphasis: the use of dashes allows the writer to repeat the name Pythagoras without seeming redundant, while heavy accents fall on the final two words.

Proofreading: Perfection *Is* Possible

In publishing, *editing* refers to the revising of a work before it is formatted, whether for a book, newspaper, magazine, journal, or other medium. *Proofreading* refers to the final check of the formatted material. While an editor is mainly concerned with improving a document, the proofreader looks for errors. He or she is the document's last line of defence before it is released. Ironically, poor proofreading may be the first thing noticed in the published document.

In spite of the importance of proofreading, student writers with an essay deadline usually neglect this stage. Exhausted from the final efforts of putting the essay together, students may think that tiny errors are unimportant compared to other parts of the process stressed throughout the term. However, distracting errors may strike your instructor in a completely different light. They could be

> When you edit or revise, you try to improve your work's structure and readability or solidify your ideas; when you proofread, you try to catch all mistakes to provide a clean copy for your reader.

> You may think that tiny errors are unimportant compared to other parts of the writing process. However, your instructor could see them as careless, a sign of a lack of effort.

seen as careless, a sign of a lack of effort. Your instructor could become annoyed by many small mistakes and even become more critical of other parts of the essay.

Whether or not proofreading is seen as tedious, it is best performed as a mechanical process. By taking a thorough and systematic approach to the essay at this stage, you can be more confident that the work of many hours, days, or even weeks will be more readable.

Proofreading Methods

Documents may be read in pairs, with one person reading his or her work aloud while the other follows the printed copy silently. This method works on the principle that two readers are twice as likely as one to spot errors—you will probably notice mistakes that you missed before. It may also be more enjoyable than working alone. Clearly, the approach works only if a second reader is available, both readers are knowledgeable about writing, and both are committed to the task.

The method of reading forward involves reading the paper aloud or to yourself but more slowly and carefully than you would usually do, paying attention both to the words and to the punctuation. Because it can be hard to concentrate solely on the words, it's best to read through the essay at least once for meaning and then at least once again for spelling and other errors.

Reading backward is the method of reading your essay from the end to the beginning, word by word or sentence by sentence. This technique forces your attention on the writing; it works well for catching spelling errors. However, it is time-consuming, and you may miss some punctuation and other "between the words" errors, as well as words that depend on their context.

Another type of proofreading is to read syllabically: you read from the beginning, breaking every word into syllables. This method is faster than reading backward, works well for catching internal misspellings, and is quite effective for catching missing and extra words and for correcting word endings (which may be overlooked when you read forward). However, it is a slower method than reading forward word by word, requires some discipline to master, and can be hard on the eyes if done for a long time.

Guidelines for Proofreading

Follow these tips when proofreading:

- Remember that the time not set aside for proofreading can undo the work of several hours.
- Plan to let at least a few hours pass before you look at the essay for the final time (overnight is recommended).
- Having someone else go over the essay can be helpful but is no substitute for your own systematic proofing. Instructors are not likely to be

sympathetic to the cry of baffled frustration, "But I had my roommate read it over!"

- As stated earlier, use a spellchecker but don't rely on it. A spellchecker will not catch the difference between "There house is over their two" and "Their house is over there too."
- Do not rely on autocorrect. Look carefully at the suggested words and chose the correct one. Many students have included the word *defiantly* in their essays rather than the intended *definitely*.
- Experiment with the different proofreading methods discussed in this chapter and use the one(s) that works best for you. However, when you start proofreading with one particular method, use it until you finish reading.

Common Errors

Here are categories of typical errors to watch for and correct in your writing.

- All areas that require consistency—spelling, capitalization, abbreviations, hyphenation, numbers, internal punctuation, and other places where choices pertaining to the mechanics of writing may be involved.
- Proper nouns (especially unfamiliar names), acronyms, etc. Are all references to authors and titles spelled correctly?
- Middles and endings of words, for spelling and for agreement.
- Small words, such as articles and prepositions.
- Words that have different spellings but the same pronunciation (homophones): *to/too/two, their/there/they're, role/roll, cite/site, led/lead, manor/manner*, etc.
- Font style. Are italics, bold, and roman applied correctly and consistently and to all necessary words? Have you used italics for the titles of complete works, such as books and films, and put quotation marks around the titles of works contained in larger works, such as essays, articles, short stories, and poems?
- End punctuation (periods and question marks).
- Quotation marks. Are they applied appropriately? Are both opening and closing quotation marks present? Have double and single quotation marks been alternated correctly? Are periods and commas inside and colons and semicolons outside? (Similar checks can be made for parentheses.)
- All citations, both in-text and in the reference or works cited list. Check both for accuracy (author, title, journal name, date, and page numbers) and for consistency. Are all citations documented according to the style of your discipline—including capitalization, punctuation, and other conventions?

Essay Presentation

Your audience and purpose are relevant to how you present your essay; for example, a scientific or engineering report probably would look quite different from an essay for English class—the former might have headings, whereas the latter would probably not. A research essay must conform to the documentation style of your discipline; presenting a personal essay may mostly be a matter of following directions for title, typeface, margins, spacing, indentation, page numbering, and identifying information.

Document design can vary. If your instructor asks you to format your essay a certain way, he or she will definitely check that you followed the instructions. Therefore, if you are unsure about essay presentation, ask for help. Unless you are told otherwise, you can refer to the following, which is based on MLA guidelines:

- Most instructors require essays to be typed. Use good-quality white paper; print on one side. If you wish to conserve paper by printing on both sides, check with your instructor first.
- Leave 1-inch margins (2.5 cm) on all sides. The first page should include identification information positioned flush left (i.e., starting at the left margin). List information in the following order: your name and student ID, if applicable; instructor's name (use the title that your instructor prefers—e.g., Professor Robert Mills, Dr M. Sonik, Ms J. Winestock, etc.); course number and section, if applicable; and submission date. Double-space, then insert the essay's title, centred.
- Double-space your essay, including notes, works cited, and block quotations; this practice makes it much easier for the instructor to correct errors and add comments.
- Indent each paragraph one half-inch (1.25 cm)—do not use additional spaces to separate paragraphs, and leave a single space (not two spaces) after each period before beginning the next sentence.
- Number pages using Arabic numerals in the upper right-hand corner preceded by your last name; place this line about one half-inch (1.25 cm) from the top and flush right (you can probably create this kind of header automatically using the **Insert** or a similar function on your computer). If you need to include prefatory pages such as a contents page or a formal outline, use lowercase Roman numerals (i, ii, iii) for them.
- A title page is usually optional, though some instructors require it. Position the essay's title down one-third of the page with your name about half-way down; include the course number, instructor's name, and submission date near the bottom of the page. All items should be centred. Begin your essay on the second page (numbered 1) under the centred title.

- Do not include any illustrations or colours other than black and white unless you use graphics directly relevant to your essay (e.g., charts or diagrams for a scientific study). Use a paper clip to attach the pages—some instructors ask for stapled pages—don't fold over a corner to keep them together. Don't use folders, clear or coloured, unless asked for. (If you do use a folder, the left-hand page margin should be slightly wider than the other margins to allow for the binding.)
- Prefer common fonts, such as Times New Roman, Arial, or Garamond (not Courier New or cursive ones). Use 10- to 12-point type size. Do not justify lines to the margins in academic papers or reports (i.e., set the paragraphing flush left and an uneven line at the right margin).
- Ensure that the text of your essay is easy to read. An essay printed in draft mode or from a cartridge that is almost out of ink will be difficult to read.

> Don't print your essay in draft mode; ensure that your cartridge has enough ink. Otherwise, your essay will be hard to read.

 ## Chapter Review Questions

1. Why is clarity important in writing?
2. Why is formal writing clearer than informal writing?
3. How is conciseness different from precision?
4. Find examples from business writing (such as advertising) that illustrate concepts discussed in this chapter, such as doubling up. Rewrite the samples so they are more formal and could be used in academic writing.
5. What are clichés? List examples other than those given in the chapter. Why should you avoid clichés in formal writing?
6. What is euphemistic language? Why are euphemisms confusing?
7. How are editing and proofreading different? Why are both important?
8. What are some things to look for when you proofread?
9. What message do you send to the reader if your paper has spelling mistakes or typos?
10. Why should you not rely solely on your spellchecker?

Appendix
Verb Tenses

Tense refers to the time when the action or condition expressed by the verb is taking, will take, or took place. There are four types of tense:

- simple
- progressive
- perfect
- perfect progressive

These forms further describe the aspect of the verb as to when its action began and its duration or completion.

The auxiliary (helping) verb for most forms determines the complete form of the verb. The auxiliary verb for the progressive tenses is *to be* (*is, was, will be*); for the perfect tenses, it is *to have* (*has, had, will have*).

 Present Tenses

Simple Present (action or situation exists now or on a regular basis):

I call	*we call*
you call	*you call*
he/she/it calls	*they call*

I usually *call* for the pizza; you *call* for it this time.

Present Progressive (action is in progress):

I am sending	*we are sending*
you are sending	*you are sending*
he/she/it is sending	*they are sending*

Mr Kahn *is sending* the package to you by courier.

Present Perfect (action began in the past and is completed in the present):

I have eaten   *we have eaten*
you have eaten   *you have eaten*
he/she/it has eaten   *they have eaten*

I *have eaten* the apple you gave me.

Present Perfect Progressive (action began in the past, continues in the present, and may continue into the future):

I have been hoping   *we have been hoping*
you have been hoping   *you have been hoping*
he/she/it has been hoping   *they have been hoping*

We *have been hoping* to receive news from the Philippines.

 ## Past Tenses

Simple Past (action or situation was completed in the past):

I saw   *we saw*
you saw   *you saw*
he/she/it saw   *they saw*

Garfield *saw* the moon rise last night over his burrow.

Past Progressive (action was in progress in the past):

I was talking   *we were talking*
you were talking   *you were talking*
he/she/it was talking   *they were talking*

James and Beth *were talking* about storms when the hurricane warning flashed onto their computer screen.

Past Perfect (action was completed in the past prior to another action in the past):

I had finished   *we had finished*
you had finished   *you had finished*
he/she/it had finished   *they had finished*

Alex *had finished* the second assignment when the storm knocked out power to his computer.

Past Perfect Progressive (action in progress in the past):

I had been practising	*we had been practising*
you had been practising	*you had been practising*
he/she/it had been practising	*they had been practising*

The golf team sophomores *had been practising* for the tournament all summer, but when school started, their coach announced his resignation.

 # Future Tenses

Simple Future (action will occur in the future):

I will see	*we will see*
you will see	*you will see*
he/she/it will see	*they will see*

I *will see* the Rocky Mountains on my way to Vancouver.

Future Progressive (action will be continuous in the future):

I will be walking	*we will be walking*
you will be walking	*you will be walking*
he/she/it will be walking	*they will be walking*

Norm and Martee *will be walking* in the Marathon of Hope next Saturday morning.

Future Perfect (action will be completed in the future):

I will have gone	*we will have gone*
you will have gone	*you will have gone*
he/she/it will have gone	*they will have gone*

Sally *will have gone* around the moon several times before the ship leaves its lunar orbit.

Future Perfect Progressive (actions are ongoing up to a specific future time):

I will have been studying	*we will have been studying*

you will have been studying   *you will have been studying*
he/she/it will have been studying   *they will have been studying*

With the completion of this assignment, they *will have been studying* verbs for 13 years.

Remember that verbs can reflect mood (conditional, subjunctive) and voice (active, passive), and auxiliary verbs can be used to indicate conditions, such as necessity ("I should go"), obligation ("You must go"), and possibility ("He may go").

Exercise

The verbs in the following passages are underlined; fix any that are incorrect.

A.

Nature <u>was</u> a precious gift. It <u>provide</u> energies that <u>affect</u> society today. Although it <u>is</u> a gift, nature <u>needs</u> our attention and care because it <u>is</u> fragile and easily destroyed. I never <u>paid</u> much attention to nature because I <u>thought</u> humanity's impact on the natural world <u>was</u> not important. A few years ago, an encounter with a squirrel <u>has changed</u> my view. I <u>walk</u> home one day, and I <u>saw</u> a gray squirrel picking up loose pine cones in the garden. I <u>am watching</u> the squirrel hopping joyfully around the yard. Suddenly, it <u>starts</u> to run across the street. But before it <u>reached</u> the other side of the street, a car <u>hit</u> it and <u>killed</u> it. I <u>am devastated</u> that the driver <u>didn't even slow down</u>, as if the life of a squirrel <u>is</u> worthless.

We <u>should always respect</u> what nature <u>has offered</u> us. The natural world <u>is</u> an important factor in maintaining a healthy life cycle. If this life cycle <u>is</u> not protected, the balance in the life cycle <u>is</u> destroyed, which <u>will bring</u> serious consequences to the lives of all human beings.

B.

I <u>remember</u> a camping trip that I <u>was going on</u> with a few of my friends. We <u>were</u> very unprepared and <u>run</u> into a few mishaps along the way. The trip <u>occurred</u> during the rainy season, and we <u>have not brought</u> any firewood. We <u>have</u> a hard time getting the fire to start, even after we <u>borrowed</u> wood and an axe from the campers next door. Of course, we <u>forgot</u> to bring a can opener, so we <u>had</u> to try stabbing at the tins with a Swiss army knife to get them open. We <u>spend</u> the night around our Coleman stove, trying to keep warm.

That night <u>made</u> us realize how much we <u>took</u> nature for granted. In our homes everyday we <u>had</u> many household appliances that <u>made</u> our lives easier for us. It <u>is</u> easy to forget that some people <u>live</u> in the world without these conveniences and <u>relied</u> on nature from dawn to dusk. This camping trip <u>occurred</u> a long time ago when I <u>am</u> much younger. But the memory of that long night in the nature <u>stays</u> with me ever since.

Appendix
A Checklist for EAL Writers

This appendix provides guidelines on some English idioms and the parts of speech. It also discusses articles, which can be confusing for EAL writers.

Adjectives

One-word adjectives usually precede the word(s) they modify, except predicate adjectives that follow linking verbs (see pages 312–13). However, relative (adjectival) clauses follow the noun they modify and present special challenges for writers.

Adjectives as Participles

When a participle ending in –*ed* or –*en* precedes a noun and acts as an adjective, keep the ending it requires as a past participle:

> Although Patrick lived a *fast-paced* [not *fast-pace*] life, he had the *old-fashioned* [not *old-fashion*] habit of stopping and reading a newspaper every day at work.

Adjectives and Present versus Past Participles

For verbs related to feeling or emotion, use the present particle (ends in –*ing*) when the subject causes the feeling and the past participle (ends in –*ed* or –*en*) when the subject experiences the feeling.

> The surprise ending of the football game was *exciting*; the few fans left in the stadium were *excited*.

When you want to refer to a time in the past and relate it to today, you can use the adjective *ago* after the noun. To refer to a specific point in the past, you can give the date preceded by *on*. (See "*Times and dates*" on page 464.)

> The first truly successful cloning of an animal occurred over *20 years ago*.
> The first truly successful cloning of an animal occurred *on 5 July 1996*.

Comparatives and Superlatives

Use the comparative of adjectives and adverbs when you want to compare one person or thing to another. Usually, the suffix *–er* is added if the quality being compared is one syllable, while *more* precedes a word of two or more syllables:

> In British Columbia, summers are usually *drier* than they are in Ontario.
> According to *the most recent* statistics, it is *more dangerous* to drive a car than to take an airplane.

Use the superlative of adjectives and adverbs when you want to compare more than two of something. The definite article is usually not used with comparisons, but it is used with superlatives (see "Articles—*A*, *An*, and *The*" on page 458).

> In my opinion, British Columbia is a *better* province than Alberta [there are two provinces]; in my friend's opinion, Alberta is *the best* of the western provinces [there are four].

Few versus *a Few*

Both terms can precede nouns that can be counted, but *few* means "not many," and *a few* means "some."

> *Few* Canadians know how to play cricket. However, *a few* people in my Facebook group said they would be interested in learning how to play it.

Much versus *Many*

Use *much* before nouns that cannot be counted and *many* before countable nouns.

> She didn't donate *much* money.
> Spotify features *many* different kinds of music.

Plurals as Adjectival Phrases Concerning Distance, Money, and Time

When these kinds of plural nouns appear in hyphenated phrases before other nouns, they drop the final *s*.

> a *10-kilometre* run [not a *10-kilometres* run], a *30-day* refund policy, a *70-year-old* man

Relative (Adjectival) Clauses

A relative clause modifies the noun it follows (known as the antecedent). These clauses begin with a relative pronoun (usually *who*, *whom*, *that*, or *which*). Make sure you include the relative pronoun at the beginning of the clause. In the example, the complete relative clause is underlined, the relative pronoun is bolded, and the antecedent is italicized:

> In China, there is a *high school* **that was painted green** because green is considered a relaxing colour.

When you use a phrase such as *in which* to introduce a clause, do not repeat the preposition at the end of the clause:

> Happiness for some people is measured by their success in the society *in which* they live *in*.

Agreement with Relative Clauses

The antecedent of the relative pronoun determines whether the verb in the relative clause is singular or plural. In the following example, the relative pronoun is bolded, the verb is underlined, and the antecedent is italicized:

> The Hyundai hybrid has a small *engine* **that** consumes less fuel than ordinary cars.

Adverbs

Adverbs with Adjectives

Adverbs can modify adjectives, other adverbs, or verbs. Ensure that you always use the correct adverbial form. In the example, *environmentally* is the adverbial form:

> The average Canadian household has become more *environmentally conscious* than in the past.

The few adjectives that end in –*ly* (e.g., *friendly, fatherly, cowardly*) cannot be made into adverbs.

Comparative and Superlative of Adverbs

See "Comparatives and Superlatives" on page 456.

Articles—*A, An,* and *The*

Indefinite articles precede some singular nouns, and definite articles precede some singular and plural nouns. Context often determines whether an article precedes a noun or whether it is omitted; idiom also can determine usage. Here are some guidelines for article use.

The Indefinite Article

Use the indefinite article *a* or *an* if you want to identify a general or nonspecific noun. Use *an* if the noun begins with a vowel that is not pronounced or with a silent *h*.

> When I was bird watching, I looked for *a* Rufus hummingbird. [no specific bird is referred to]
> When *the* hummingbird saw me, it darted into the trees. [a specific bird is referred to]

The indefinite article is not used before most uncountable concrete nouns, nor do these nouns form plurals. It is easier to remember these nouns if you divide them into categories:

- Kinds of liquids: *beer, blood, coffee, milk, oil, soup, water, wine,* etc.
- Kinds of food: *bread, cheese, corn, flour, food, fruit, lettuce, meat, pasta, popcorn, rice, sugar,* etc.
- Names of languages: *Arabic, Dutch, French, Japanese, Mandarin, Vietnamese,* etc.
- Names of areas of study: *biology, economics, geography, mathematics,* etc.
- Names of gases: *hydrogen, methane, oxygen, ozone,* etc. (*air, fire, smoke,* and *steam* also belong here)
- Sports and games: *baseball, bowling, football, hockey, jogging, surfing, tennis,* etc. (But *baseballs* and *footballs*—the objects—are countable.

- Others: *chalk, clothing, equipment, feedback, furniture, health, help, homework, housework, laughter, luggage, mail, money, research, scenery, soap, software, weather, wood, work,* etc.

However, if preceded by a word such as *piece* or *item*, such nouns may be countable: *a piece* (or *pieces*) *of chalk, an item* (or *items*) *of furniture, a glass of water.* As well, many nouns can be used adjectivally before countable nouns: *a cheese stick, a hockey game,* etc.

Some of the nouns in the list can be used in a countable sense if they can be divided into different types:

> Red *wine* in moderation can be beneficial to one's health. Different *wines* are classified by their place of origin.

Although *mail* is an uncountable noun, *email* can be used as a countable noun; thus, you can talk about receiving *an* email. As a noun, *email* can also be pluralized:

> Flora was shocked to see that she had received more than a hundred *emails* over the weekend; as a result, she vowed to get rid of her *email* by the end of the week.

See "Uncountable and Countable Nouns" on page 463.

The Definite Article

Nouns that refer to a specific person, place, or object are usually preceded by the definite article, *the*:

> Please give me *the* pen on *the* table.

A specific pen (distinct from other pens) on a specific table is requested.

> Please give me *a* pen on *the* table.

This request implies that there is more than one pen on the specific table.

> Please give me *a* pen.

Any pen from anywhere will do.

> Young children, especially in *the* 3–5 age group, are always asking questions.

Other age groups exist, making the reference specific.

Including Definite Articles before Nouns

a) *First versus second reference*: Use *a* when something is first mentioned, *the* when the same noun is mentioned again (it can now be identified).

> Mike found *a brown bottle* that had washed ashore. When he cleaned it up, he saw that *the bottle* had *a note* inside.

b) *Nouns that refer to a species or class of objects*: Use the definite article before this group; an example is *the definite article* in this sentence. Here is another example:

> In her English class, Izumi studied *the argumentative essay* before *the research essay*.

c) *Unique nouns*: If the noun has a unique identity, precede it by the definite article.

> Specific eras or time periods: *the Industrial Revolution, the Age of Reason, in the twentieth century*, etc.
> Unique celestial objects: *the sun, the moon, the North Star*
> Newspapers, museums, theatres, and hotels: *The* Vancouver Sun (newspaper), *the Royal Ontario Museum, the Imax theatre, the Banff Springs Hotel*

d) *Superlatives*: See "Comparatives and Superlatives" on page 456.

> I have found that *the best courses* at college are usually *the most challenging ones*, and they are taught by *the best teachers*.

e) *Ordinals*: Ordinal numbers are *first, second*, etc.; cardinal numbers are *one, two*, etc.

> Maria was *the first* to cross the finishing line; Linden was *the second*. They finished one and two, respectively.

Omitting Definite Articles before Nouns

When using nouns that fall into the following groups, omit the definite article in most cases.

a) *Before most plural nouns*:

If animals have no consciousness, it is meaningless to discuss whether eating meat is immoral.

Animals is a plural noun; *meat* is an uncountable noun.

b) *Before proper nouns*:

Canadians celebrate Thanksgiving in October; Americans celebrate this holiday in November.

This general rule has many exceptions. The article is used with some national, social, and cultural groups (*the English, the Japanese, the middle class, the Inuit peoples*) and with some geographical names (*the Pacific Ocean, the United States, the Philippines, the Arctic*).

Lonnie is a member of *the* Chipewyan First Nations and lives near Prince Albert in northern Saskatchewan.

c) *Before abstract nouns*: These nouns are usually uncountable and cannot be pluralized. Abstract nouns include *advice, anger, curiosity, employment, enjoyment, evidence, freedom, fun, health, information, intelligence, justice, knowledge, love, music, peace, pollution, reality, research, respect, truth, wealth, weather,* etc. The exception to this rule is that the article is used if a prepositional phrase follows the noun.

The reality of the situation, unfortunately, is that *justice* does not always prevail.

A prepositional phrase follows *reality* but not justice.

d) *Common nouns*: Using common nouns such *government, nature, society, Internet,* and *media* often result in errors in article use.

- *Government*: If you are referring to a specific government, use the definite article; otherwise, do not use *the*:

  The government [meaning, for example, the government of Newfoundland and Labrador] has no right to raise student tuition fees.

- *Nature*: If you are referring to the natural world, the noun *nature* is not preceded by *the*. If the sense is of a quality, essence, or habit, *the* may be required.

  It has been *the nature* of previous generations [their habit] to take *nature* [the natural world] for granted.

- *Society*: This term is not preceded by *the* if the reference is a general one. *Society* is usually singular and requires the singular verb form. If the reference is specific, *the* may be required (for example, if it is followed by a phrase that particularizes society):

Society does not look kindly on those who fail to respect *its* rules.

I find *the society of like-minded individuals* boring and unrewarding.

- *Internet/media*: When used as a noun, *Internet* is preceded by *the*, as is *media* when it refers to *the news media* as a form of mass communication, such as television, radio, newspapers, and magazines; it usually takes a singular verb form when used this way.

  With the rise of *the Internet*, *the media has* become even a more powerful influence on *society*.

For article use with gerunds, see "Gerunds" on page 463.

Nouns

The following nouns often give students trouble:

Human: This noun can be used in the singular or the plural, but possessive forms should be avoided.

It is a *human* [not a *human's*] need to aim for perfection.

Humanity: *Humanity* is not preceded by the definite article (or possessive adjective) unless it refers to an inner quality (see "*Nature*" on page 461).

One quality that *humanity* shares with other organisms is the need to solve problems.

She demonstrated *her humanity* [an inner quality] by forgiving her enemies.

Opinion; express an opinion: Don't say, "In my point of view," "As for myself," or "As far as I am concerned." The most direct way of stating your opinion is simply to say, "In my opinion" or "I believe that" and follow with a clause that states your opinion.

Every + Noun

Like *each one of, either one of*, etc., *every one of* is followed by a plural noun but a singular verb form. But when one of these words is followed directly by a noun, that noun and the verb will be singular, not plural:

Almost *every* drafting *course* in schools *involves* computers.

Using *every one of* would result in a plural noun in the *of* phrase: *Every one of the* drafting *courses.*

Gerunds

Gerunds are incomplete verb forms that act as nouns in a sentence (they end in *–ing*). They are always singular and are usually not preceded by articles.

> *Learning* many new skills *is* enjoyable if you have the time for *it.*

Kind(s) of/Type(s) of + Noun

A singular noun follows *kind of* and *type of*; a plural countable or an uncountable noun follows *kinds of* and *types of* because more than one kind/type is referred to. Often, a demonstrative adjective—*this* or *that* (singular); *these* or *those* (plural)—precedes *kind/type.*

> What *type of car* was Natalie driving?
> Many *kinds of cars* are on the market today.

Uncountable and Countable Nouns

The following uncountable nouns are responsible for many writing errors:

- *Clothing*: As an uncountable noun, *clothing* is never preceded by the indefinite article and never forms a plural. *Clothes*, however, is a countable noun.

  > People have used *clothing* to cover their body for thousands of years; however, we often choose our *clothes* for their fashion rather than their practicality.

- *Information, knowledge, evidence*, and *advice*: These words are uncountable abstract nouns. Thus, they are not preceded by *a* or *an* and are never plural.
- *Importance*: *An importance* or *importances* is incorrect. You can use *the importance* if a prepositional phrase beginning with *of* follows.
- *Research*: As an uncountable noun, it is never plural. However, *researcher*, a person who does or conducts research, is a countable noun. As a verb, *research* is usually followed by a direct object (not by *about*). As an adjective, *research* can be followed by a plural noun: *research projects, research studies.*

Some nouns can be either countable or uncountable depending on context.

In their youth, most people have at least 100,000 *hairs* on their head.

If you're determined, you could count the number of hairs!

Shaving your *hair* today is more often a matter of personal choice than of hygiene.

The sense here is of hair as a mass, therefore uncountable.

For examples of countable and uncountable nouns with articles, see "Articles—*A*, *An*, and *The*" on page 458.

Prepositions

***Despite, in spite of*:** Both act as prepositions, so a *noun*—not a clause—needs to follow each.

In spite of/Despite her best efforts to create interest in the performance, only a few people attended it.

***Times and dates, referring to*:** The preposition used for time expressions varies according to context: "I will be there *for* Christmas." ("I will arrive sometime *on* or *before* Christmas"); "I will be there *during* Christmas" ("I will be there for the entire time").

For specific times:
He will arrive *at* 9 a.m. *on* Tuesday, 24 December.

For less specific times:
He will arrive *in* the morning. [or *in* the evening, *in* December, *in* 2017, but *at* night]

See "Verbs and Prepositions" on page 466.

Verbs

The following verbs sometimes give students trouble:

***Conclude*:** There are a few ways to express a conclusion. In most cases, a clause should follow the verb:

One can *conclude that* commercialism destroys culture.
One can *come to the conclusion* that commercialism destroys culture.
One can *draw the conclusion* that commercialism destroys culture.

To announce the conclusion of your essay, use *In conclusion*, not *As a conclusion*.

***Remember*:** When you are recalling something (for example, when you're writing about a past incident), use the present tense of *remember* but describe the action in the past tense.

> I *remember* when I was little how I *thought* my parents *knew* everything.

Verbs as Modal Auxiliaries

Modals are a special category of helping verb that make the meaning of a main verb more precise. They are usually followed by the bare infinitive, without *to*. Here are some common uses of modals.

- *Can* expresses capability: Clothing *can* really say a lot about a person.
- *Could* expresses capability in the past tense: When she lived near a lake, Nina *could* swim every day.
- *Should* expresses necessity or obligation: There *should be* [or *must be*] stricter gun laws in the United States.
- *May* and *might* express possibility: *May* often conveys a stronger possibility than *might*.

  > Since she has the prerequisites, Bianca *may* enroll in the second-year course.
  > Although she worked late, she *might* decide to go to the party.

- *May* also expresses permission: Students *may* bring beverages into the study area but not food items.
- *Will* expresses probability: Since she has the prerequisites, Bianca *will* enroll in the second-year anthropology course.
- *Would* expresses a repeated action in the past: When she lived near a lake, Nina *would* swim every day.

Verbs and Nouns

Because nouns are sometimes formed from verbs and often look like them, they can be confused. Use a dictionary to ensure that you have used the required part of speech. Here are two sets of commonly confused words:

***Belief, believe*:** *Belief* is a noun; *believe* is a verb. *Believe* is often followed by *in* or *that*, depending on whether a word/phrase (*in*) or a clause (*that*) follows:

> She firmly *believed in* his innocence.
> She firmly *believed that* he was innocent; this was her true *belief*.

Breath, breathe: *Breath* is a noun; *breathe* is a verb. You can *take* or *draw a breath*, meaning "breathe in." Somewhat idiomatically, to *take a deep breath* can mean to prepare yourself for a difficult task (whether or not a deep breath is actually taken).

> The guest speaker, Madeleine, *took a deep breath* before she entered the crowded room. After she began speaking, she *breathed* normally again.

Verbs and Prepositions

The following alphabetical list includes verbs that may be confusing, usually due to idiomatic prepositional use.

Agree/Disagree with: You agree or disagree with someone or with a person's views or opinions on something. Other prepositions can follow both these verbs, but use *with* in most essays where you argue a thesis.

> I agree *with* space exploration in general, but I disagree *with* those who want us to spend billions of dollars per year on something with no practical benefit for humanity.

Agreed followed by *to* means "to consent (to)."

> I agreed *to* give a speech on the merits of space exploration to my philosophy class.

Apply for, apply to: You apply for a loan, scholarship, position, or job; you apply to a place (such as a school) or situation:

> Joshua *applied to* several colleges before he *applied for* a student loan.

Attend, study at: *Attend* means "to be present at," as in attend a university, class, concert, or wedding. *To study at* refers to a place, such as a college.

> Before he decided *to study at* Red Deer College he *attended* some classes at the University of Alberta.

See "*Graduate from*" on page 469.

Avoid, prevent: When you *avoid* something, you stay away from it; the verb is usually followed by a direct object (the thing that is avoided). When you *prevent* something, you take an action so that it does not occur; *prevent* can be followed by a direct object or by a direct object + *from* and a gerund phrase:

You should *avoid people* when you are sick as this will *prevent others from catching your* virus.

Call/draw attention to: This verb is followed by a noun and means "to point something out." A noun or possessive adjective often precedes *attention*.

> The Intergovernmental Panel on Climate Change (IPCC) was founded in 1988 in order to *draw* world *attention to* the link between climate change and human activity.

To *pay attention to* means "to take note of or to look at closely."

> All Canadians should *pay attention to* the next IPCC report.

To *get attention*, meaning "to attract notice," is not usually followed by a preposition:

> After failing to *get* the teacher's *attention* any other way, Harmon shouted "Fire!"

See "*Pay (for)*" and "*Point out*" on pages 470–1.

Care: To care *about* means "to be concerned about" (see "*Concern*" on page 468).

> She cares *about* good grades.

To *care for* or *take care of* means "to look after":

> Thomas *took care of* his sister when his mother was working.

Commit: A person can commit a crime, a murder, an error, but a person commits suicide (no article). Another meaning of the verb *commit* is "to dedicate to" or "resolve to do something"; it is often followed by the reflexive pronoun and the preposition *to*.

> After *committing a* serious crime, he thought briefly about *committing suicide*, but decided instead to *commit himself to* a life of helping others.

Compare, contrast: When you compare, you focus on similarities; when you contrast, you focus on differences. With either term, the direct object follows, then *with* or *to* and the indirect object.

In our class assignment, we were asked to *compare* the Canadian system of government *with* the system in another country.

In this construction, the grammatical subject (*Saskatoon*) is what is being compared:

Compared to the small town that I grew up in, Saskatoon seems like a big city.

The verb phrase *make a comparison*, uses the preposition *between*:

He *made a comparison between* one political system *and* another.

Compete for, compete against: *Compete for* is used with a thing; *compete against* with a person.

They *competed for* the honour of being named captain of the team. Mohammed *competed against* his friend to see who could get the higher mark.

Concern: The meaning you want determines the preposition to use. *To be concerned about* means "to be troubled or worried about something." *To be concerned for* means "to be worried about (or, occasionally, something)."

She *was concerned about* the implications of the new driving regulations; specifically, she *was concerned for* her daughter, who would soon be getting her licence.

When it is not followed by a preposition, *concern* means "applies to" or "is relevant to":

The matter I have to discuss, Yuto, *concerns* your future with this organization.

Consider, discuss, mention: When you consider something, you think carefully about it, usually in order to take some kind of action. *Consider*, like *discuss* and *mention*, is followed by a direct object—not by *about*. Unlike *discuss*, however, *consider* and *mention* may be followed by a clause beginning with *that*.

Before Yoshi decided to get married, he *considered the matter* by talking it over with his married friend Eizad. Then he *discussed it with* Sanjeet.

Before Yoshi *discussed* his marriage plans with his fiancée, he *mentioned* to Eizad and Sanjeet *that* he was considering marriage.

See "*Think*" on page 471.

***Depend, rely, count*:** These verbs can mean "have confidence in someone or something." They are followed by *on* + a noun that states who or what is depended/relied on and then may be followed by *for* + another noun that expands on the first:

Shaun *depends on* email *for* most of his business.
Maheen *relies on* her friend Amy *for* fashion advice.

***Discuss*:** See "*Consider, discuss, mention*" on page 468.

***Encourage/discourage*:** You encourage someone *to* do something, but you discourage someone *from* doing something.

Raising tuition may *discourage* students *from* enrolling in other courses.
The president of the students' union is *encouraging* all students *to* protest the tuition increase.

Note that an infinitive follows *to*, but a gerund follows *from*.

***Graduate from, to be a graduate of*:** In *graduate from*, *graduate* is a verb that refers to completing a program and receiving a diploma or degree. *To be a graduate of* is the noun form (the second *a* is a short vowel):

After Kasey *graduated from* college, she went to graduate school and became a *graduate of* UBC.

***Hire, hired by*:** To hire someone or a company is to give them a job or task. Employees are hired by their employers:

After applying for several positions during the summer, Teh *was hired by* another company.

See "*Apply for, to apply to*" on page 466.

***Know something, know someone*:** The former means to have information or expertise about something; the latter means to be acquainted with a person. When using *know someone*, follow the verb with the person's name.

When I got *to know Tey*, I learned about computers, and I now *know* everything *about* them.
Shelley *knows* that she has a test tomorrow.

Lack: As a verb, *lack* is followed by a direct object; as a noun, it is usually preceded by an article or other determiner (e.g., *its, that, this, your*) and followed by *of*:

The first thing she noticed about the bedroom was *its lack of privacy*.
The kitchen also *lacked* dishes and other utensils.

Lead to: This verb means the same as *result in* (see page 471). In both cases, a result or consequence follows the preposition.

The cloning of animals, according to many people, is certain *to lead to* the eventual cloning of humans.

Look at/around/for/into/over:

look at (examine): In my essay, I will *look at* solutions to the problem of homeless people.
around: Dazed by the accident, he slowly sat up and *looked around*.
for (search): Simon *looked for* his lost notes on his messy desk.
into (investigate): After being laid off for the second time this year, Natalie began to *look into* self-employment.
over (scan): She *looked over* her notes from the previous class.

Mention: See "*Consider, discuss, mention*" on page 468.

Participate in: You participate *in* something—activities, sports, etc.:

Dong Hun often *participates in* classroom discussions.

Pay (for): *Pay* means "to give (usually money) what is due for goods, services, work, etc." *For* + a noun may follow if you want to indicate what was purchased:

She *paid* less than $80 *for* all her textbooks since she bought them used.

Point out: This verb means "to call attention to (something)." It is generally followed by a noun/pronoun or a clause beginning with *that*. One of the meanings of *to point* is "to indicate, to single out, using a finger"; it is followed by *to*.

Ruji *pointed out* her sister among the bystanders.
Ruji *pointed out that* her sister was always late for a meeting.
Ruji *pointed to* her sister, who was standing in a crowd.

Refer: *Refer* is followed by *to* when the meaning is "to make a reference or to make mention of something." If a clause beginning with *that* follows, a noun such as *fact, idea*, etc., should intervene between the verb *refer* and the clause.

> In his letter of recommendation, he *referred to* the many occasions in which Duy had demonstrated his sense of humanity and compassion. Specifically, he *referred to the fact that* Duy had often volunteered for work in local hospices.

Result in/result from: When you use the verb *result*, you must be careful about the preposition you use after it. To result *in* means that what follows the verb is a result or consequence; to result *from* means that what follows the verb is a cause.

> Being convicted of the crime of murder *usually results in* long prison terms.

Prison terms are the consequence.

> Most murders in the United States *result from* the use of guns.

Guns are a cause.

Stress, emphasize: These terms mean the same thing and are usually followed by direct objects (not prepositions). But if you want to use the verb phrase *put stress/emphasis on*, note the preposition that is required. A *that* clause may also follow these verbs.

> The writer *emphasized* the main point of her argument by providing examples.
> The writer *put emphasis on* the main point of her argument by providing examples.
> The instructor *stressed that* all students should arrive on time for class.

Think: This verb has many uses. *To think about* means to "reflect on," and *to think over* means to "consider"; note the placement of *it* in the example. Use *think* + a clause beginning with *that* if you want to refer to a belief or opinion.

William originally *thought that he would take a commerce class* in the second term, but when he *thought about it* [or *thought it over*], he decided to enroll right away.

Verbs and Their Subjects (Subject–Verb Agreement)

Always ensure that you use the singular form of any verb that has a singular subject and a plural verb for any plural subject. Remember that the third-person singular form of a verb usually ends in *s*.

Appendix
Peer Edit Forms

 Formal Outline

The essay outline provides the structure for the essay. Therefore, as an editor, you should pay special attention to the relationship among the parts (introduction, body paragraphs, conclusion), to the order of arguments (weakest to strongest? strongest to weakest? some other logical order?), and to the strength and effectiveness of each main point (Is each adequately developed? Is the claim supported?).

Instructions

Use the checkboxes to indicate that you have considered and evaluated the criteria. Add suggestions, comments, questions, and advice in the space provided.

Introduction

- ❏ What kind of formal outline is used: topic, sentence, or other (such as graphic)?
- ❏ Does the introduction attract your interest?
- ❏ Does it announce the topic?
- ❏ Does it contain a two-part direct thesis statement announcing the topic and commenting on the topic?
- ❏ Is the claim one of fact, value, or policy?
- ❏ Is the thesis statement interesting, specific, manageable, and clearly expressed?
- ❏ Does each paragraph contain at least one main idea that can be easily identified as such? If not, which paragraph(s) doesn't do this?
- ❏ Does each paragraph contain at least two subpoints that help develop the main point? If not, which paragraph(s) doesn't?
- ❏ Has the writer provided support for his/her argument? If not, suggest ways that he/she could use kinds of evidence (e.g., examples, facts/statistics, personal experience, outside sources, etc.) to do so.

❏ Do the paragraphs appear to be organized using any of the rhetorical patterns discussed in Chapter 6 (e.g., definition, cause/effect, problem/solution, compare and contrast)?

❏ Are the main points ordered in a logical and persuasive way? If not, what is an alternative arrangement?

❏ Are there at least two levels represented in the outline (main points and subpoints)? Is parallel structure applied to main points and the levels of subpoints?

Conclusion

❏ Does it successfully summarize or restate the argument without sounding repetitious?

❏ Does it go beyond the introduction by enlarging on the implications of the thesis, urging a change in thought or call to action, or making an ethical or emotional appeal?

Final Comments or Suggestions

Writer's Name: _____

Editor's Name: _____

Argumentative Essay: First Draft

When editing a first draft, pay attention to its structure, argument, transitions, and grammar. Suggest ways for the writer to make his or her points stronger and clearer.

Instructions

Use the checkboxes to show that you have considered and evaluated the criteria. Use the space provided to add suggestions, comments, and questions. In addition, underline possible grammar, spelling, usage, and stylistic problems.

Introduction

❏ Does the introduction function successfully?
  ❏ Is it interesting?
  ❏ Does it announce the subject and contain a thesis statement? Is the claim arguable?

❑   Does it suggest the main way the argument will be organized (e.g., definition, cause/effect, time order, division, compare and contrast, question/answer, etc.)?

❑ Does the writer establish himself/herself as credible and trustworthy? How?

Body Paragraphs

❑ Does the argument seem complete, and does the order of the paragraphs appear logical?

❑ Look at paragraphs individually. Are any too short or too long?

❑ Is each paragraph unified (relates to one main idea)? If not, which ones aren't?

❑ Is each paragraph coherent? If not, which ones aren't?

❑ Do paragraphs contain topic sentences?

❑ Is the order of the sentences natural?

❑ Are there appropriate transitions between sentences, enabling you to see the relationship between consecutive sentences?

❑ Does the writer successfully use repetition, rephrasing, synonyms, or other devices to achieve coherence?

❑ Does each paragraph seem developed adequately?

❑ Are there different organizational methods used to develop the argument? Which ones? Are they effective?

❑ What kinds of evidence are produced? Are they used effectively? You don't have to refer to specific paragraphs—only note if they appear to be present to help support the thesis:
   ❑ examples, illustrations
   ❑ personal experience
   ❑ analogies
   ❑ precedents
   ❑ outside authorities/secondary sources
   ❑ other

❑ Are there points where the argument seems strained, weak, incomplete, and/or illogical? Are there any fallacies (e.g., cause/effect fallacies, fallacies of irrelevance, emotional/ethical fallacies)?

Conclusion

❑ Is the conclusion satisfying? Does it summarize and/or generalize?

Other Criteria

❑ Does the writer present himself/herself credibly?
   ❑ Conveys knowledge?

❏   Seems trustworthy and reliable?

❏   Appears to be fair?

❏   Is the opposing view acknowledged?

❏   Is the writer's voice objective?

❏   Are there any examples of slanted language?

❏   Is the opposing view successfully refuted (as in the point-by-point method)?

❏   Are specific argumentative strategies—common ground, appeal to reader interest, concessions, emotional appeals—used? If not, could any of these be helpful?

❏   Are there any places where the language seems unclear or where a point is unclear due to the way it is expressed?

❏   If the writer uses sources, are they integrated smoothly and grammatically? Are all direct quotations, summaries, paraphrases, and ideas acknowledged?

Final Comments or Suggestions

Writer's Name: _____

Editor's Name: _____

 # Research Essay: First Draft

As with the first draft of an argumentative essay, pay attention to a research essay's structure, argument, transitions, and grammar and suggest ways for the writer to make his or her points stronger and clearer. However, with this type of essay, you must also focus on the types of research used and the ways the writer integrates material from outside sources.

Instructions

Use the checkboxes below to demonstrate that you have considered and evaluated the criteria. Use the space provided to add suggestions, comments, and questions. Underline possible grammar, spelling, usage, and stylistic problems.

Introduction

❏   Is the introduction successful?

❏   Is it interesting?

❏ Does it announce the subject and contain a thesis statement with a claim of fact, a hypothesis to be tested, or a question to be answered?

❏ Does it suggest the main way the argument will be organized?

❏ Does the writer establish himself/herself as credible and trustworthy? How?

Body Paragraphs

❏ Does the essay seem complete, and does the order of the paragraphs appear logical?

❏ Look at paragraphs individually. Are any too short or too long?

❏ Is each paragraph unified (relates to one main idea)? If not, which ones aren't?

❏ Is each paragraph coherent? If not, which ones aren't?

❏ Do paragraphs contain topic sentences?

❏ Is the order of the sentences natural?

❏ Are there appropriate transitions between sentences, enabling you to see the relationship between consecutive sentences?

❏ Does the writer successfully use repetition, rephrasing, synonyms, or other devices to achieve coherence?

❏ Does each paragraph seem well developed?

❏ Has the writer used secondary sources effectively? Note any exceptions.

❏ Do all the sources seem reliable?

❏ Does the writer use a sufficient number of sources? Is there an overreliance on one source? If so, which one?

❏ Does the writer show familiarity with the sources used?

❏ Do the secondary sources appear to be relevant to the points discussed?

❏ Is each reference integrated smoothly into the essay, both stylistically and grammatically?

❏ Is the context made sufficiently clear in each instance?

❏ Do brackets and ellipses appear to have been used correctly?

❏ Are all sources cited? Identify any that may not be.

❏ Do the citations appear correct and consistent?

❏ Are any other kinds of evidence present in addition to secondary sources (for example, analogies, personal experience, illustrations, or examples)?

❏ Does the essay appear to be fundamentally focused on exposition (explaining) rather than argumentation (persuasion)?

Conclusion

❏ Is the conclusion satisfying? Does it summarize and/or generalize?

Other Criteria

❏ Has the writer presented himself/herself credibly?
    ❏ Conveys knowledge?
    ❏ Seems trustworthy and reliable?
❏ Is the writer's voice objective?
❏ Are there any places in the draft where the language seems unclear or where a point is unclear due to the way it is expressed?

Final Comments or Suggestions

Writer's Name: _____

Editor's Name: _____

Appendix
Partial Exercise Answer Key: Chapters 13–15

Exercise 13.2

1. The <u>children</u> built a large snow <u>fort</u>.
   common/concrete/count   common/concrete/count
2. The <u>doors</u> were slammed closed by the <u>wind</u>.
   common/concrete/count   common/abstract/count
3. The <u>women</u> present were all wearing <u>hats</u>.
   common/concrete/count   common/concrete/count
4. I would like five <u>glasses</u> of <u>water</u>, please.
   common/concrete/count   common/concrete/non-count
5. I bought a hard <u>drive</u> that has five <u>terabytes</u> of <u>memory</u>.
   common/concrete/count   common/abstract/count   common/abstract/
   non-count
6. I went to <u>Niagara Falls</u> yesterday.
   proper/concrete/count
7. I graduated from <u>Red River College</u> last summer.
   proper/concrete/count
8. My <u>job</u> as assistant <u>manager</u> is very challenging.
   common/concrete/count common/concrete/count
9. <u>King Arthur's</u> <u>Knights of the Round Table</u> were loyal and chivalrous.
   proper/concrete/count proper/concrete/count
10. <u>Learning</u> a new <u>language</u> is difficult.
    common/abstract/non-count   common/abstract/count
    <u>Learning</u> to speak <u>Chinese</u> is especially so for English <u>speakers</u>.
    common/abstract/non-count   proper/abstract/non-count common/
    concrete/count

Exercise 13.3

1. Incorrect: Abiha and I
2. Incorrect: Greg and I
3. Correct
4. Incorrect: its
5. Incorrect: us

Exercise 13.4

1. All students must submit <u>their</u> assignments on time.
2. Both Kenji and Thomas gave <u>their</u> approval.
3. A police officer must understand the laws <u>himself/herself</u>.
4. An employee must sign <u>his/her</u> contract before beginning to work at this company.
5. The members must cast <u>their</u> ballots before the deadline.

Exercise 13.5

1. linking
2. state of being
3. action
4. linking
5. action

Exercise 13.7

- Nouns: *Justin, Trudeau, Canada, prime minister, house, premier, background, son, Pierre, residence, 24 Sussex Drive, aspects, personality, lifetime, spotlight, fore, zeitgeist, comedian, John, Oliver, image, eve, election, search, choice, member, week, rehab, model, lobotomy, Johnny, Depp, twin, show, Last Week Tonight, March, 2012, psyche, fighter, senator, Patrick, Brazeau, match, opponent, nose, round*
- Pronouns: *who, he, his, you, him*
- Verbs: *is, has, was, are, lampooned, do, can, underwent, said, entered, beat*
- Adjectives: *elected, new, privileged, country, iconic, evolving, media, British, federal, Google, image, poor, boyband, sweater, model, evil, late-night, comedy, Canadian, much-loved, former, Conservative, charity, boxing, bloody, final*
- Adverbs: *newly, ahead, ever, literally*
- Prepositions: *in, of, after, to, on, from, before,*
- Conjunctions: *however*

Exercise 13.8

1. I slept.
   Parts of Speech (POS): pronoun, verb
   Sentence Elements (SE): subject (*I*), verb (*slept*)
2. Henry bought a ball.
   POS: noun, verb, adjective (article), noun
   SE: subject (*Henry*), verb (*bought*), adjective (article; *a*), noun (*ball*)
3. Mr Safi gave the test to Joshua.
   POS: noun, verb, adjective (article), preposition, noun
   SE: subject (*Mr Safi*), verb (*gave*), direct object (*the test*), indirect object (*Joshua*)
4. Stacey is homesick.
   POS: noun, verb, adjective
   SE: subject (*Stacey*), verb (*is*), subject complement (*homesick*)

Exercise 13.9
Complete subject = single underline; complete predicate = double underline

1. <u>Bob and Yan</u> <u>went to the movies</u>.
2. <u>They</u> <u>really enjoyed the new superhero movie</u>.
3. However, <u>they</u> <u>ate too much popcorn and drank too much pop</u>.
4. <u>They</u> <u>also spent too much money</u>.
5. <u>Bob and Yan</u> <u>are now poor</u>.

Exercise 13.10
Simple subject = single underline; simple predicate = double underline

1. <u>Bob</u> and <u>Yan</u> <u>went</u> to the movies.
2. <u>They</u> really <u>enjoyed</u> the new superhero movie.
3. However, <u>they</u> <u>ate</u> too much popcorn and <u>drank</u> too much pop.
4. <u>They</u> also <u>spent</u> too much money.
5. <u>Bob</u> and <u>Yan</u> <u>are</u> now poor.

Exercise 13.11

1. Tomorrow, (the class time) will be changed (for the rest)(of the semester).
             noun phrase   adjectival   adjectival
   S = *the class time*
2. (Some of the food) (in the fridge) (has spoiled).
           noun   adjectival   verb
   S = *Some of the food in the fridge*

3. The store (in the mall) (with the latest fashions) (has closed).
                        adjectival   adjectival   verb
    S = *The store in the mall with the latest fashions*

4. A search (of the abandoned house) (turned up) several cartons (of stolen goods).
                  adjectival   verb   adjectival
    S = *A search of the abandoned house*

5. (The 2018 hockey season) (will belong) (to the Leafs).
            noun   verb   adjectival
    S = *The 2018 hockey season*

Exercise 13.12
Independent clause = single underline; Dependent clause = double underline

1. I will meet you at the airport before the flight.
2. Because Stan likes ginger ale, I bought two flats of it.
3. Yesterday, while I was reviewing my finances, I noticed that I forgot to pay my electric bill.
4. I had to pay the bill with my credit card and I am now at my credit limit.
5. I need to go to the bank to apply for a loan, and I need to visit my parents because I need more money this month.

Exercise 13.13

1. I will meet you at the airport before the flight.
2. Because Stan likes ginger ale, I bought two flats of it.
3. Yesterday, while I was reviewing my finances, I noticed that I forgot to pay my electric bill.
4. I had to pay the bill with my credit card and I am now at my credit limit.
5. I need to go to the bank to apply for a loan, and I need to visit my parents because I need more money this month.

Exercise 13.14

1. S
2. P
3. Complete sentence
4. Complete sentence; question structure
5. Complete sentence; command

Exercise 13.15
Italics show material added to make complete sentences. Other options exist for turning the fragments into complete sentences.

1. The store that I missed *had a really great sale today.*
2. The brilliant idea that came to me in the middle of the night *was lost when I woke up.*
3. A marching band that is able to rouse everyone *is needed for the Canada Day parade.*
4. The kind of doughnut that doesn't have a hole in the middle *is often called a Bear Claw or a Dutchie.*
5. The rugby towel that was on the ground *was used by my hero, Tim.*

Exercise 13.16

Italics show material added to make complete sentences. Other options exist for turning the fragments into complete sentences.

1. The empty cup on the bench *belongs to Todd; I was surprised to see* the empty cup on the bench.
2. *The irate parent* signed his name to the bottom of the petition.

Exercise 13.17

Italics show material added to make complete sentences. Other options exist for turning the fragments into complete sentences.

1. Completing the test on time *is very important.* [*–ing*]
2. Huge tears rolled down his cheeks. [complete sentence]
3. Being that she worked late, *she had to make sure the office was securely locked.* [*–ing*] [A better sentence: Because she worked late, she had to make sure the office was securely locked.]
4. He promised to call her tomorrow *to* see if she was still all right. [add-on]
5. A murder of crows, along with a flock of sheep, blocked the road. [no predicate]
6. He must be guilty *since* he's already confessed. [dependent clause]
7. Walking beside the tracks, he eventually reached the town. [complete sentence]
8. Introducing our next prime minister. [*–ing*]
9. For example, the reboot of the famous TV show *The X-Files.* [add-on]
10. Swimming on her back, *she eventually reached the shore.* [*–ing*]

Exercise 13.18

[1.]<u>When considering college or university</u> [dependent]. Many students must decide where to live. If they are going to school close to home, they may decide to continue living with their families. [2.]<u>Listening to their parent's advice.</u>[*–ing*] However, if the school is far away and commuting is not possible, students must decide whether to live in the school residence or in an apartment. Residences are convenient. [3.]<u>Especially if there is a meal plan</u>

available. [add-on] <u>Meal plans that are nutritious.</u>[4] [add-on] Apartments might be a better idea though, especially if students need to work. Not all residences are close to where jobs are. Privacy might be an issue in residence. Not all students can get their own rooms. Apartments may provide privacy, but only if there is no need for roommates. Many factors need to be considered when choosing where to live.

Corrections:

1. When considering college or university, many students must decide where to live.

2. If they are going to school close to home, they may decide to continue living with their families, often listening to their parent's advice.

3 & 4. Residences are convenient, especially if there is a nutritious meal plan.

Exercise 13.19

1. They intended to eat at Benny's Bistro, but they saw a long line-up outside Benny's, so they went to Kenny's Kitchen instead. [compound]

   Alternative with minor changes: As soon as they saw a long line-up outside Benny's Bistro, they went to Kenny's Kitchen instead, even though they had intended to eat at Benny's. [complex]

2. Although there may be nearly two million kinds of plants in the world, and there are likely at least as many different kinds of animals, no one can know how many species have evolved, flourished, and become extinct. [compound-complex]

Exercise 13.20

1. I read two books in two days. I did nothing else but read. [run-on]
2. I couldn't use my laptop today. I forgot to plug it in before the battery was dead. [comma splice]
3. I was frightened during my first driving lesson: the instructor yelled at me. [run-on]
4. It's easy to punctuate sentences: just put a comma whenever you pause. [comma splice]
5. She finished watching the movie then took the bus home. [correct]
6. Magazines are available for digital download. This is better for the environment. [comma splice]
7. Technology continues to evolve, but we can't always predict whether this is good or bad. [correct]
8. Humans are imitators. Conforming is something they are good at. [comma splice]

9. Many immigrants want to learn about Canadian culture. They take courses about it. [run-on]

10. Binge drinking is a serious problem. Many students engage in this behaviour. [comma splice]

Exercise 13.21

1. Problem: comma splice

   Correct: He managed to pass the year though he seldom did his homework. What will happen to him next year is anyone's guess.

2. Problem: fragment

   Correct: The opening ceremonies were delayed on account of rain.

3. Problem: fragment

   Correct: She has decided to work at a fast-food restaurant: not a great place for tips.

4. Problem: comma splice

   Correct: Movies provide entertainment for people; different people prefer different genres such as horror.

5. Problem: fragment

   Correct: She's been very happy since she bought the new tablet.

6. Problem: fragment

   Correct: The only way a person can learn is to pay attention to what is going on in class.

7. Problem: fragment

   Correct: He was too tall and thin to excel at sports—except basketball, of course.

8. Problem: comma splice

   Correct: The concept that "bigger is better" is part of our culture. It is promoted by both advertisers and the media these days.

9. Problem: fragment

   Correct: I have trouble understanding the theory of relativity and its impact on our daily lives.

10. Problem: comma splice

    Correct: Justin Trudeau may eventually be as well known as his father. Pierre had charisma and charm.

Exercise 13.22

The "Freshmen 15" is not a recent phenomenon this refers to the weight students typically gain during their first year at college or university. [run-on]

What concerns doctors now is the amount of weight gained during this time. In the 1970s and 1980s, students typically gained 5 pounds, now it is up to 15. [comma splice] This is a very unhealthy weight gain. Once the weight is gained. [fragment] It is very hard to lose. Because of this. [fragment] Cafeterias are starting to offer more nutritional meals with fewer calories. Student councils are beginning to be proactive and inform students of the dangers of excess weight gain. School gyms are offering more classes to help students battle this weight gain. In the future, many hope that the "Freshman 15" becomes non-existent.

Corrections:

The "Freshmen 15" is not a recent phenomenon. This refers to the weight students typically gain during their first year at college or university. What concerns doctors now is the amount of weight gained during this time. In the 1970s and 1980s, students typically gained 5 pounds, but now it is up to 15. This is a very unhealthy weight gain. Once the weight is gained, it is very hard to lose. Because of this, cafeterias are starting to offer more nutritional meals with fewer calories. Student councils are beginning to be proactive and inform students of the dangers of excess weight gain. School gyms are offering more classes to help students battle this weight gain. In the future, many hope that the "Freshman 15" becomes non-existent.

Exercise 14.1

1. After her inaugural speech, several members of the House rose to congratulate her. [independent clause: introductory phrase]
2. The optional package includes bucket seats, dual speakers, and air conditioning. [items in a series]
3. We have collected more than $20,000, and there is a week remaining in our campaign. [independent clauses]
4. Metaphors, similes, and personification all are examples of figurative language. [series]
5. As one can see, the tower is leaning some 4.5 metres to the south. [independent clause: introductory dependent clause]
6. Hardly daring to breathe, Nelson took a quick look at the valley far below him. [independent clause: introductory phrase]
7. Although many are called, few are chosen. [independent clause: introductory dependent clause]
8. The magnificent country estate is hidden behind a long, elegant row of silver birches. [miscellaneous: coordinate adjectives]
9. "We can't achieve peace in our time if we assume war is inevitable," he said. [miscellaneous: quotations]
10. Her house was a newer one with dark wood trim and large, open rooms. [miscellaneous: coordinate adjectives]

Exercise 14.2

1. I had planned to go to Calgary, but my bus was delayed for more than four hours, so I decided to go back home.
2. Juliet studied medicine at Dalhousie University in Halifax, Nova Scotia, before becoming a doctor near Prince Albert, Saskatchewan.
3. Like Jane Austen's character, Emma, the heroine of *Clueless*, Cher, is less superficial than she first appears. [If the context suggested that the reader would know what Austen character is being referred to, *Emma* would be considered non-essential information (an appositive); if not, only the comma after *Emma* would be correct.]
4. Nick and Nicole were married on 20 April 1995, but they separated two years later.
5. Jessica Julep, the mayor of Anytown, Nova Scotia, provided inspirational leadership.
6. The simple sentence, as we've seen, is easily mastered by students, but compound sentences necessitate an understanding of various forms of punctuation.
7. The waste of our resources, including the most precious resource, water, is the major environmental problem that Canada is facing today.
8. British general Sir Frederick Morgan established an American–British headquarters, which was known as COSSAC.
9. The book with the fine red binding on the highest shelf is the particular one I want.
10. Agnes Campbell Macphail, the first woman elected to Canadian Parliament, served for 19 years, beginning her career in 1921.

Exercise 14.3

1. If you asked people to name the most gruelling and challenging race in the world, most of them would probably say that it was an auto race, such as the Indianapolis 500. Few people would name the Tour de France, which is a bicycle race. Thousands of cyclists, however, vie for an elite position in this annual event. Even with the modern advances in bicycle technology, cyclists still find the course very challenging. It offers a variety of climbs, including slight inclines, hills, and steep grades. The Tour de France has a history that dates back about a hundred years. In the years to come, the race will continue to challenge, inspire, and glorify new riders.
2. Autism is a much misunderstood problem. Often, children with autism are viewed as a "handful" and "hyperactive." Very little is known of its causes, and characteristics can vary, making a diagnosis difficult. In children, it is even harder because other children can

exhibit some of the characteristics associated with autism. Although autism can cause many behavioural difficulties, autistic children can still live near-normal lives if they are surrounded by understanding caregivers. Working with autistic children can change a person and make one realize the need for better understanding and education. Treating autism can be difficult because often there is no feedback from the patient. Over the years, there have been many ideas of how to treat autism, but not all were correct and have at times made treatment problematic.

Exercise 14.4

1. One of my roommates rode her bicycle to school most of the time; *as a result*, she was more physically fit than my other roommate, who didn't even own a bicycle.
2. SPCA officers work for but are not paid by the government; *in fact*, it is donations that provide their salary.
3. If homelessness continues to increase, it will be costly for taxpayers; homelessness, *moreover*, affects downtown businesses.
4. Many professional golfers have used the same caddy for years; Steve Williams, *for example*, caddied for Tiger Woods from 1999–2011.
5. Scientists tend to strongly support stem-cell research. *However,* most evangelical Christians just as strongly oppose it.

Exercise 14.5

1. April showers bring May flowers; May flowers bring on my asthma.
2. A developing salmon goes through four stages: the alevin, the fry, the smolt, and the adult.
3. Every essay needs three parts: an introduction, a body, and a conclusion.
4. He paused to admire the splendid sight before his eyes: the ruins of Montgomery Castle.
5. Mayumi tended to look on the good side of things; Glenn usually saw the bad side.
6. The following is not a rule for comma use: put a comma wherever you pause.
7. It is probable (though not certain) that she will be promoted to the rank of corporal next year.
8. It was the best of times; it was the worst of times.
9. Marselina has a fine ear for music; unfortunately, she can't sing a note.
10. In my health sciences class, we studied the four main food groups: dairy products, meats, carbohydrates, and fruits and vegetables.

11. Whenever I order designer clothing for my boutique, I shop in Toronto, Ontario; Buffalo, New York; and London, England.

12. The Online Dictionary defines animal cruelty this way: "treatment or standards of care that cause unwarranted or unnecessary suffering or harm to animals."

13. The tuition increase has affected many lower income families; therefore, there is an even greater demand for student loans.

14. Brian never tired of misquoting Shakespeare: "The quality of mercy is not stained."

15. Virginia Woolf had this to say about the essay: "Of all forms of literature it is the one which least calls for the use of long words."

Exercise 14.6

1. Cocaine, an alkaloid obtained from coco leaves, is a stimulant to the nervous system; unfortunately, it is one of the most addictive drugs, and it is possible to overdose and die on first use. Among the 3 million users today, 500,000 are highly addicted. Cocaine users describe the high as a euphoric feeling: they feel energetic and mentally alert; however, this feeling wears off in as little as 20 minutes. User responses to the drug vary but may include the following: hyperactivity, elevated blood pressure and heart rate, and increased sexual interest. Large amounts of cocaine, such as more than 100 milligrams, can cause bizarre, erratic, and violent behaviours.

2. Labour shortages during the late nineteenth century in Canada became an impediment to progress, and something had to be done to fix this problem. For white politicians and business owners, the solution seemed obvious: exploit cheap labour. Chinese immigrants provided exactly what was needed to boost the labour scene; they were male, unskilled, and cheap. Between 1881 and 1885, approximately 17,000 Chinese immigrants arrived in Canada. Chinese men were employed in masses; their jobs included those in mining, forestry, canning, and, above all, railroad construction. Sir Matthew Begbie, the chief justice of British Columbia, said: "Chinese labourers do well what white women cannot do and what white men will not do."

Exercise 14.7

1. In South Africa, the current crime rate is using up much of the country's GDP.

2. Parents and teachers often complain about television's influence in today's society.

3. The Crosses' house is up for sale, and its list price is $179,000.

4. One's education should not depend on the financial resources of one's parents.
5. The school's biggest draw for new students was the brand new recreation complex.
6. The course I took required two hours' homework a day.
7. The mayor's biggest asset is her commitment to the city's future growth.
8. In anorexia nervosa, a patient's fingernails and teeth may be damaged due to a lack of calcium.
9. Ryan's and Jessica's birthday is on the same day.
10. Apples, oranges, mangoes, and tomatoes are the store's specials today.

Exercise 14.8

Corrections to the first two paragraphs are provided here.

Reader reaction was swift and impassioned. The site's traffic, which averages 65 to 70 million views each month, experienced an additional 50,000 page views within the first 10 days of the posting. The investigation drew more than 400 letters to the editor, hundreds of emails to the message boards, and more than 16,000 responses to an online poll.

The intensity of the response surprised veteran investigative journalist Wayne MacPhail, the article's author. Although the sheer volume of letters was unexpected, it proved to him that there was an audience for online journalism in Canada. MacPhail has experimented with hypertext reporting since the late 1980s, but, outside of "Spin Doctors," he believes that, by and large, newspapers have done a "woeful job" of building an audience for Web-based investigative reporting. . . .

Exercise 15.1

If a child begins to perform poorly at school nowadays, he or she [option 1] will likely be sent to a school counsellor to deal with the situation. Everyone assumes that attention deficit disorder is the culprit, and ~~they~~ [option 3] just as automatically assume that drugs are the answer. On the other hand, perhaps the child is just not interested in a particular subject, or he or she does [option 1] not understand the material. Parents, in turn, treat their children as if they are [option 2] the problem instead of listening to them [option 2] to find out how they [option 2] can be helped.

Exercise 15.2

1. Those who supported the motion raised their hands.
2. Neither the film's director nor its producers were on hand to receive their prestigious award.

3. The instructor, as well as the students, thinks the room is too small.
4. It is unfortunate when a person no longer cares what others think about him or her.
5. One should never expect to succeed unless one is willing to persist—even against the odds.
6. It is the tried and true that provides the ultimate refuge in mediocrity.
7. Everyone who works during the year is obliged to file an income tax return.
8. Her set of baby teeth was complete when she was only 18 months old.
9. He was one of those few candidates who was able to win re-election.
10. None of the company's products require testing on animals.

Exercise 15.3

1. Every person in the community should have the right to attend university and create new opportunities for himself or herself.

   or

   All people in the community should have the right to attend university and create new opportunities for themselves.
2. No errors.
3. The tonal quality of Amati's violins is excellent but not perfect.
4. During the past week, there have been some unexplained occurrences on the girls' floor of the residence.
5. Small class sizes and a low student population mean few opportunities to meet new people.
6. A typical poem by Emily Dickinson leaves the reader searching for another line or even another stanza to satisfy his or her craving for closure.

   or

   A typical poem by Emily Dickinson leaves readers searching for another line or even another stanza to satisfy their craving for closure.
7. No errors.
8. A coalition of neighbourhood organizations, students, and unions is currently forming to oppose the university's proposed plan.
9. Everyone who has purchased tickets is eligible for the grand prize, but he or she must be a resident of Canada to claim his or her prize.

   or

   Everyone who has purchased tickets is eligible for the grand prize but must be a resident of Canada to claim the prize.

   or

   Those who have purchased tickets are eligible for the grand prize, but they must be residents of Canada to claim their prize.

10. If a child is denied the opportunity to play, how can he or she develop emotionally and physically?

or

If children are denied the opportunity to play, how can they develop emotionally and physically?

Exercise 15.4

Alex and his lawyer, Alan, left in Alex's limousine for Loonies Unlimited to buy Alex's landlady, Alice, a litre of light lemonade. She told them to also buy a litre of light lemonade for her long-time lodger, Alison. When they alighted at Loonies Unlimited, they were alarmed that Alex had left his loonie in his loft. So Alphonse, of Loonies Unlimited, allowed them only one litre of lemonade, along with a length of limp licorice, and he loudly lamented their laxness.

Exercise 15.7

1. According to my textbook, pronouns should always have a clear referent. [no reference]
2. Whenever a staff meeting is called, employees are required to attend. [no reference]
3. Racism is a disease that will continue to plague society until the disease is cured. [ambiguous reference]
4. Sixty per cent of our pesticides, our major ground water pollutant, are used on cotton. [ambiguous reference]
5. During Roosevelt's Pearl Harbor speech, the president identified the United States as a peaceful and tolerant nation.
   or
   During his Pearl Harbor speech, Roosevelt identified the United States as a peaceful and tolerant nation. [no reference]
6. I know the sign indicated "No Parking," but I went ahead and parked there anyway. An officer gave me a $20 fine. [no reference in both sentences]
7. Her second novel, set in the remote Hebrides, was far different from her first one. [ambiguous reference]
8. Previous Afghan successes were significant victories; for example, the country last waged war against the powerful Soviet Union. [no reference]
9. Some psychologists and researchers believe in the "innate" theory of prejudice. According to this theory, ingrained prejudice is cross-cultural and awareness of race is one of the earliest social characteristics to develop in children. These findings may help account for the theory's popularity. [remote reference]

10. During the dinosaur age, dinosaurs lived in a rapidly changing environment. [no reference]

Exercise 15.8

1. Management often forgets about the needs of us wage earners.
2. Who should run for office this election?
3. I have no intention of speaking to them.
4. The person who finishes first will be rewarded.
5. You recommend whom for the position?
6. As she entered the room, a mysterious feeling came over her.
7. Margaret Laurence was a novelist who entertained her readers with well-developed plots and realistic characters.
8. People who use memory aids tend to be better spellers.
9. The instructor explained the different pronoun cases to Gail and me.
10. "Hey, whom did you mean to refer to when you used that insulting term?"

Exercise 15.9

Informal: You can definitely learn a lot from educational TV; you can learn things that cannot be learned from written texts. If you are a major in commerce, for example, and if you watch the business news, you can understand the commerce textbook better by applying what you learn from the news. Similarly, watching sports programs can be exciting and can also give you a better understanding of the game. On the other hand, if you choose to watch comedy all the time, you are not going to gain any real benefits. In general, I think that comedies are meaningless.

Formal: Educational TV has many benefits and can teach people things they cannot learn from written texts. If a person is a major in commerce, for example, and watches the business news, he or she can understand the commerce textbook better by applying what is learned from the news. Similarly, watching sports programs can provide people with excitement and also give them a better understanding of the game. On the other hand, if people choose to watch comedy all the time, they will not gain any real benefits as comedies, generally, are meaningless.

Exercise 15.10

1. Problem: misplaced
   Correct: A striped, pointed hat was on his head.
2. Problem: misplaced
   Correct: As we were leaving, he tearfully promised to visit us.

3. Problem: dangling
    Correct: Although Sam is unambitious and downright lazy, I have never known him to break his word.
4. Problem: dangling
    Correct: His ego was further inflated when he was awarded first prize in the Ben Affleck look-alike contest.
5. Problem: misplaced
    Correct: Every character has a purpose, big or small, in Shakespeare's play.
6. Problem: misplaced
    Correct: When asked what my favourite sport is, without any hesitation I usually say that it is running.
7. Problem: dangling
    Correct: Stepping out of the airplane, she thought the fresh air was most invigorating.
8. Problem: misplaced
    Correct: In his book, Gabriel Kolko describes peace in Vietnam after the war.
9. Problem: dangling
    Correct: As he opened the door unexpectedly, his eyes fell upon two of his employees sleeping in front of their computers.
10. Problem: misplaced
    Correct: Teacher Laurie McNamara posed for the photographer in the Cloverdale Elementary School hallway with Principal Dan Saunders, who gave her a kidney last month.

Exercise 15.11

1. In our city, shady characters who offer a variety of drugs lurk on quiet corners.
2. Over the years, several world-class cyclists, such as Eddy Merckx and Greg LeMond, have had spectacular careers.
3. As he ran down the street without a care in the world, two pedestrians had to quickly move out of his way.
4. As I am a member of the Sikh community, my paper will be given a strong personal focus.
5. You will have a fully interactive website, built in mere minutes, for your business or for your personal use.
6. Benefits will result only from a smoke-free environment.
7. Germany has built an extensive network of highways, known as the Autobahn, through its countryside.
8. When they look for employees today, employers are stressing verbal and written communication skills more than ever before.

9. If people are caught in criminal behaviour, their rights to privacy should be forfeited.
10. In captivity, this species of snake will eat frogs, mice, and small pieces of meat.

Exercise 15.12

1. I like toe socks because they are warm and comfortable, come in many colours and designs, and are the latest in sock fashions.
2. Yoga offers many benefits: it enables you to relax and reduce stress, to exercise regularly, and, through yoga classes, to meet people with similar interests.
3. Computers are important to students as they provide entertainment, cut down on homework time, and enable them to obtain a wealth of information quickly.
4. Disadvantages of having roommates are that they can create a lot of mess and invade your personal space, but having a roommate gives you someone to talk to about your problems.
5. The benefits of coffee include helping you wake up, improving your mood, and improving your concentration.

Exercise 15.13

1. A good journalist is inquisitive, persistent, and attentive. [series]
2. Music can directly affect your thoughts, emotions, and feelings. [series]
3. In this essay, I will be looking at and writing about the role of women in the military. [compounds]
4. Tiddlywinks is a game not only of considerable skill but also of strategy. [correlative conjunctions]
5. Television can affect children in a variety of negative ways since children often lack judgment, are naturally curious, and are easily influenced. [series]
6. There are three main qualities that a leader must possess: a leader must be enthusiastic, organized, and creative. [series]
7. Aman never has been and never will be good at golf. [compounds]
8. She not only was the best teacher I have ever had but also was very modest. [correlative conjunctions]
9. Tremors may occur on either side or both sides of the body. [compounds]
10. There are many reasons why people choose to watch or enjoy watching television. [compounds]

Exercise 15.16

1. *Identify the problems*: In my family, my father and sister play video games as much as me [c]. They [h] have become very complex, [b] and can even improve problem-solving in children. By progressing through increasing difficulty levels, it [e] can help childrens [g] thought processes. On the one hand, if the child goes straight to the hardest setting, they [f] may feel discouraged, [a] on the other, if the child tries to systematically progress through increasing levels, they [f] can learn the mechanics of the game step by step. This [d] can help in the study of math, as the child may be more likely to persevere with a problem until he [i] finds the solution.

   Rewritten with corrections: In my family, my father and sister play video games as much as I do. Video games have become very complex and can even improve problem-solving in children. Progressing through increasing difficulty levels can help children's thought processes. On the one hand, if the child goes straight to the hardest setting, he or she may feel discouraged; on the other, if the child tries to systematically progress through increasing levels, he or she can learn the mechanics of the game step by step. This method can help in the study of math, as the child may be more likely to persevere with a problem until a solution is found.

2. *Identify the problems*: Having a job and earning one's livelihood is [b] a necessary goal in life, [h] it is one of the reasons you [g] acquire an education. At the place where I work [a] however, many people come in expecting to find a job lacking presentation skills [e]. Many are poorly dressed, do not know how to behave, and they may not speak grammatically [d]. Untidy, disorganized, and unprepared, [f] I still have to match them with a prospective employer. They lack the skills to present themselves to others and knowing [d] what to do in public. Although they may be highly intelligent people. [c]

   Rewritten with corrections: Having a job and earning one's livelihood are necessary goals in life. They are one of the reasons one acquires an education. At the place where I work, however, many people lacking presentation skills come in, expecting to find a job. Many are poorly dressed, do not know how to behave, and may not speak grammatically. They are untidy, disorganized, and unprepared, yet I still have to match them with a prospective employer. They lack the skills to present themselves to others and to know what to do in public, though they may be highly intelligent people.

Exercise 15.17

1. a. dangling modifier
    Correct: Written through the eyes of a young boy, the narrative shows us the perspective of the Indigenous peoples.
2. c. more than one error (subject–verb agreement: the subject, *stresses*, should agree with the verb, *teach*; pronoun inconsistency: *you* is not the same person as the noun antecedent, *students*.)
    Correct: The daily stresses of students, such as project or assignment due dates, teach them to manage their time wisely.
3. b. pronoun reference error
    Correct: Parents sometimes push their children so hard to excel that these children lose interest altogether.
4. c. comma error
    Correct: My roommate thinks it would be better for society if all drugs were decriminalized.
5. d. parallelism error
    Correct: Contributors to homelessness include the lack of good-paying jobs, increasingly large families and, probably the most important factor, the cost of living in a large city.

Exercise 15.18

1. c. their
    Correct: Anorexia starts when a person decides to take control of his or her body weight.
2. b. the semicolon
    Correct: There are three types of turbine engines used in aircraft: the turbojet, the turbofan, and the turboprop.
3. b. vendors
    Correct: Work songs and street vendors' cries are examples of traditional African-American music styles.
4. c. to extend
    Correct: Reforms of the UN Security Council include abolishing the veto or extending the Council beyond the current five members.
5. c. who listened . . .
    Correct: Results from a recent study showed that patients suffering from osteoarthritis reported a 66 per cent reduction in their perception of pain by listening to music for 20 minutes each day.

Appendix
Essay Templates

The templates for expository and argumentative essays are reprinted here for easy reference. See Chapter 5 for more about different types of expository essays and Chapter 9 for more on the argumentative essay.

EXPOSITORY ESSAY TEMPLATE

Introductory paragraph with thesis statement	Supporting idea	1. 2. 3.
Body paragraph 1	Topic sentence Point 1 Explanation/Illustration Point 2 Explanation/Illustration Point 3 Explanation/Illustration Conclusion	(quotation, personal observation, etc.)
Body paragraph 2	Topic sentence Point 1 Explanation/Illustration Point 2 Explanation/Illustration Point 3 Explanation/Illustration Conclusion	
Body paragraph 3	Topic sentence Point 1 Explanation/Illustration Point 2 Explanation/Illustration Point 3 Explanation/Illustration Conclusion	
Concluding paragraph	Main ideas to summarize Clincher	Idea to leave reader with

ARGUMENTATIVE ESSAY TEMPLATE

Introduction	• gain reader's attention and interest • include your claim • suggest the primary developmental method (if there is one) • establish your credibility (knowledge, reliability, and fairness)
Body paragraph 1: Background	• present background information, if relevant
Body paragraph 2: Lines of argument	• present good reasons (logical, emotional, and ethical appeals) in support of your thesis • use all relevant evidence—facts, statistics, examples, views of experts/authorities • present reasons in specific order related to argument
Body paragraph 3: Rebuttal	• consider opposing points of view • note both advantages and disadvantages of opposing views; may use concessions or common ground • argue that your thesis is stronger than the opposing view and more beneficial to the reader
Conclusion	• summarize your argument • elaborate on the implication of your thesis • make clear what you want the reader to think or do • possibly make a final strong ethical or emotional appeal

Glossary

abstract 5, 10 An overview of a work's purpose, methods, and results; can include key phrases or whole sentences from the full work.

adjectival modifier 15 A word or phrase that functions as an adjective.

adjective 13 A word that describes a noun or pronoun; usually precedes the word it modifies but can also follow a linking verb, where it modifies the subject.

adverb 13 A word that modifies a verb, adjective, adverb, or sentence.

adverbial modifier 15 A word or phrase that functions as an adverb.

agreement 15 The principle that a verb must agree with (i.e., match) its subject in number and that a pronoun must agree with its antecedent in number, person, and gender.

American Psychological Association (APA) style 12 A citation style used in the social sciences and some sciences; uses parenthetical in-text citations (that include the author's surname, year of publication, and page number) and a reference list.

analogy 4, 8 A comparison between two dissimilar things; this device helps the reader better understand the original object or ideas.

anecdote 7 An interesting or striking story about an incident or event.

annotated bibliography 5 A list that appears at the end of an essay or article and that summarizes similar works in the field of study. It includes a concise version of the content, focusing on the thesis statement and major points or findings, and can also include an appraisal of the study's usefulness.

antecedent 13, 15 The noun that appears earlier in the sentence and that a pronoun replaces. The term can also refer to a preceding event, condition, or cause.

antecedent-consequent 4 A method of paragraph or essay organization that includes an antecedent and its consequence.

apostrophe 14 A mark of spelling that indicates the possessive or shows where letters have been omitted in a contraction.

appeal 9 A call on reason, ethics, or emotion to persuade a reader that an argument is valid.

argument 5, 6, 9 The main position of a work; the viewpoint that a writer tries to make the audience see and/or accept.

article 13, B A word such as *a*, *an*, or *the*, which precedes and modifies a noun.

audience 2, 10 The intended recipients of a piece of writing or oral presentation, as well as their expectations, knowledge of, interest in, or opinions on the subject. Other considerations include the diction, tone, sentence structure, and format used.

authority 8 An expert's findings or opinion that can be used for support.

block quotation 11 A method of setting off a large quotation (4 or more lines or 40 or more words) from the rest of the essay's text. The quotation is set in its own paragraph and indented half an inch from the left margin.

body paragraphs 2 The middle paragraphs of an essay that help prove the thesis by presenting facts, arguments, or other support. Many college or university essays have at least three body paragraphs, each having one main point expanding on the thesis.

Boolean operators 10 Terms such as AND, OR, and NOT, which are used to customize an online or database search.

brainstorming 2 A pre-writing strategy that involves writing words, phrases, or sentences associated with a particular subject.

case study 8 A carefully selected example that is closely analyzed in order to provide a testing ground for the writer's claim.

cause–effect 4 A method of paragraph or essay organization in which a writer looks at why or how something happened (causes) and the outcomes (effects) of those causes.

chronology 4 A method of paragraph or essay organization in which a writer traces a topic's development over time.

circular conclusion 7 A conclusion that reminds the reader of the thesis.

citation 10, 11, 12 An acknowledgement of the source of a quotation, paraphrase, or summary; includes the author name, publication date, title, publisher name and location, and/or page numbers. Parenthetical in-text citations point to a complete citation in a reference or works cited list.

claim 8, 9, 10 An assertion about the essay's topic that appears in the introduction, usually in the form of a thesis statement. A claim can be tentative or conclusive and can be based on fact, value or opinion, or policy. See also *factual claim, value or opinion claim,* and *policy claim.*

clarity 16 In writing, work that is grammatical, concise, direct, precise, and specific.

classification 4 A method of paragraph or essay organization in which a writer organizes a large number of items into manageable groups and analyzes them. See also *division.*

clause 13–16 A group of words containing both a subject and a predicate; can be independent or dependent. See also *independent clause* and *dependent clause.*

cliché 16 A word or phrase that, though often true, has become overused (e.g., *green with envy*).

clustering (or mapping) 2 A pre-writing strategy that involves graphically linking ideas or thoughts by circling words and phrases and connecting them to other words; enables a writer to visualize the interrelations among thoughts.

coherence 3 The principle that ideas should be expressed clearly and be connected to one another.

collective noun 15 A noun that may be singular or plural, depending on context. If in doubt, consider it singular.

colloquialism 16 A word or an expression acceptable in conversation but not in formal writing.

comma splice 14 A major grammatical error in which a comma alone is used to separate two independent clauses.

common ground 9 An argument strategy that shows an opponent that a writer shares similar concerns or basic values.

comparison and contrast 4, 6 A method of paragraph or essay organization in which a writer analyzes similarities and differences between things according to selected bases of comparison. The two major patterns of a comparison and contrast essay are point-by-point and block.

complete sentence 13 A sentence that contains at least one subject and one predicate and expresses a complete thought.

complete subject 13 The subject of a sentence plus its modifiers.

complex sentence 13 A sentence that contains an independent clause joined to a dependent clause by a subordinating conjunction.

compound 15 Two of the same parts of speech acting as one grammatical unit, usually joined by a coordinating conjunction.

compound-complex sentence 13 A compound sentence joined with a complex one.

compound sentence 13 A sentence that contains two or more independent clauses joined by a coordinating conjunction.

compound subject 15 Two nouns, two pronouns, or a noun and a pronoun acting as one subject.

concession 9 An argument strategy that acknowledges that an opposing point is valid.

conclusion 7 The final paragraph of the essay that sums up what was said in the body paragraphs. See also *circular conclusion, spiral conclusion,* and *wrap.*

conjunction 13–16 A word that joins words, phrases, or clauses. See also *coordinating conjunction, correlative conjunction,* and *subordinating conjunction.*

conjunctive adverb 13 An adverb such as *however, therefore,* or *thus* that joins two independent clauses. It is preceded by a semicolon and usually followed by a comma.

connotation 1, 16 The feeling or idea that a word creates for a person. Compare *connotation.*

consequence 4 A result.

coordinate adjective 14 An adjective that can be placed in a different order within a list without changing the meaning of the sentence.

coordinating conjunction 13 A conjunction that joins equal units, such as two independent clauses. These conjunctions are known as FANBOYS (*for, and, nor, but, or, yet, so*).

correlative conjunction 13 A conjunction that joins parts of a sentence. It is a two-part grammatical unit; both must be used to complete the sentence.

cost-benefit 4 A method of paragraph or essay organization in which a writer analyzes a topic's pros and cons.

credibility 8 A reader's sense that a writer can be believed. Three factors contribute to credibility: knowledge of the topic, reliability/trustworthiness, and fairness.

critical response 2 A type of essay in which a writer analyzes and shares his or her views on a piece of writing.

critical thinking 1   A series of logical mental processes—including weighing the evidence, analyzing, comparing, evaluating, questioning, and rethinking—that lead to a conclusion.

dangling modifier 15   A grammatical error in which a word or phrase is meant to modify a noun or pronoun that doesn't appear in the sentence and thus modifies the closest noun, often giving the sentence an unintended meaning. See also *dangling participle* and *misplaced modifier*.

dangling participle 15   A dangling modifier that is a verb ending in *–ing* or *–ed*. See also *dangling modifier*.

database 10   A collection of related data organized for quick access. College and university databases include journals in searchable interfaces that allow users to search by specific criteria, such as title, author, or keyword.

deductive reasoning 9   A method of reasoning that includes a general statement and a specific statement to arrive at a conclusion. Compare *inductive reasoning*.

definition 1, 4, 6, 7   A method of paragraph or essay organization in which a writer explains the characteristics of a subject or term, such as an abstract concept.

delayed subject 15   A sentence construction in which the subject appears after a prepositional phrase and the verb.

demonstrative pronoun 15   A pronoun that makes the reference to a noun clearer (e.g., *this book* vs. *that book*).

denotation 1   The literal meaning of a word; a word's dictionary definition. Compare *denotation*.

dependent clause 13   A clause that contains a subject and a predicate but expresses an incomplete thought and thus cannot form a complete sentence. The clause needs information found in the sentence's independent clause. Compare *independent clause*.

description 4, 8, 9   A method of paragraph or essay organization in which a writer uses concrete, physical details to enable the reader to understand an object.

development pattern (or organizational pattern) 4   The principle or method that determines how an essay or a paragraph will be organized.

diction 16   The style and tone of a piece of writing; related to word choices and level of language. Formal and informal writing are examples of kinds of diction. See also *usage*.

digital object identifier (DOI) 10, 12   A number–letter sequence that begins with the number 10 and is often found with documents obtained electronically through databases; used in citations.

direct object (DO) 13   The receiver of the action of the verb; also called the object of the verb.

direct quotation 11   An exact reproduction of a source; requires a citation. See also *block quotation*, *brackets*, *citation*, and *ellipsis*.

division 4   A method of paragraph or essay organization in which a writer breaks a subject into parts in order to better understand the whole. See also *classification*.

dramatic approach 7   A method of writing an introduction; attempts to catch the reader's attention in an interesting or thought-provoking way.

ellipsis (. . .) 11   A punctuation mark that indicates the omission of one or more words within a direct quotation. A fourth dot is added if the words up to and including the final period are omitted.

emphasis 16   The importance or stress placed on an idea. A word or phrase has greater or less emphasis depending on where it appears in the sentence.

empirical 8   Related to observing and measuring data under controlled conditions in order to reach a conclusion about a phenomenon.

euphemism 16   A word or phrase substituted for the actual name of something, usually to make it more acceptable or to give it dignity; an example of indirect writing.

evidence 8   Information, such as that gathered from books, journals, or personal experience, used to support a claim. See also *hard evidence* and *soft evidence*.

example 4, 8, 10, 11   A method of paragraph or essay organization in which a writer uses concrete details to translate an abstract claim into something the reader can more easily understand. An example, which is considered soft evidence, is also one of the best ways to support a point and clarify an abstract idea.

expanded thesis statement 7   A thesis statement that provides details such as the main points of an essay. Compare *simple thesis statement*.

expert 10   A specialist in a subject, who has published or produced significant work about that subject. See also *authority*.

exposition 6-7   Informing, explaining, describing, or defining a topic. An expository essay uses claims of fact.

factual claim 8   A claim that is proven by facts and figures or the results of relevant studies.

fallacy 9   A misleading or unsound argument or a misuse of an appeal to emotion.

faulty predication 16   The problem that occurs where a verb cannot be logically linked to its subject.

faulty reasoning 9   An error in thinking that can result from an invalid argument, a lack of proof for a claim, or an opinion that is not clearly separated from fact.

focused reading 1   A close and detailed (i.e., word-by-word) reading of a specific, relevant passage. See also *selective reading*.

formal writing 16   Writing that features the rules of formal usage and correct grammar and does not use colloquialisms and contractions.

freewriting 2   A pre-writing strategy that involves writing without stopping—and without editing or censoring ideas—for a specified time.

gender-inclusive language 15   Terms and grammatical forms that include all genders.

generalization 9   A statement applied to all people or things in a large category. If there are many exceptions to the statement, the generalization is considered invalid.

hard evidence 8   Evidence that provides direct support to a claim; includes facts, statistics, and results of studies.

helping (or auxiliary) verb 13   A verb that combines with a main verb to indicate tense, mood, and voice.

hypothesis 8   A prediction or expected result of an experiment or other research investigation.

idiom 16   A saying whose meaning is understood only within the context of the phrase, not by the meaning of the individual words.

illustration 8   A detailed example that usually takes the form of an anecdote or a brief narrative.

imperative sentence 13   A sentence that issues a command. Its subject, *you*, is always understood even though it is not expressed.

incomplete verb form (or base verb form) 13   A verb form ending in *–ing* or *–ed/en*; requires a helping verb to join it to a subject.

indefinite pronoun 13, 15   A pronoun that can be used in place of a noun for an unspecified individual or group (e.g., *each, either, one,* or *everyone*). It is usually considered singular and takes a singular verb.

independent clause 13   A group of words that has a subject and a predicate and can therefore stand alone as a complete sentence. Compare *dependent clause*.

indirect object (IO) 13   The noun that is found in a prepositional phrase and usually tells for whom the action in the sentence is done; also called the object of the preposition.

indirect source 12   A source that is cited in another work. This second-hand information requires specific methods of citation in APA and MLA styles.

inductive reasoning 9   A method of reasoning that produces a general conclusion from several specific facts of examples. It is sometimes called scientific reasoning because scientists and other researchers use it to answer questions about the natural world and make predictions about natural phenomena. Compare *deductive reasoning*.

inference 1   A conclusion based on the evidence presented; the corresponding verb is *infer*.

interrogative pronoun 15   A pronoun, such as *who, which,* and *what*, that introduces a question.

introduction 7   The opening of an essay that presents the main idea (the thesis statement) and the main organizational pattern. An introduction is meant to create reader interest and can be developed through several means (see *logical approach, dramatic approach,* and *mixed format*).

jargon 1, 16   Language that is specific to a field or a group and may not be understood by other people.

journal 10   A periodical that publishes the results of experts' research.

keyword 10   A word identified by an author or a cataloguer as important in an article and used in online and database searches.

linking verb 13   A verb that joins a subject to a noun or adjective that follows the verb.

logical approach (or inverted pyramid approach) 7   A method of writing an introduction; begins with the general aspect of the topic and moves to the more specific (i.e., moves from a broad to a narrow focus).

looping 2   A pre-writing strategy that occurs after a round of freewriting; involves identifying potentially useful words, phrases, or sentences and choosing the best one as a focus for more freewriting.

mechanics 2, 16   In formatting, matters such as margin size, spacing between sentences, font size and type, and page numbers; in writing, abbreviations, capital letters, hyphenation, and numbers.

misplaced modifier 15   An adjective, adjectival phrase, adverb, or adverbial phrase that is too far away in the sentence from the word it should modify, possibly giving the sentence an unintended meaning. See also *dangling modifier*.

mixed quotation format 11   A combination of a direct quotation (using the significant words of the source) with paraphrasing.

modal verb 13   A verb that appears before the main verb to express necessity, obligation, possibility, or probability.

Modern Language Association (MLA) style 12   A citation style used in the humanities; uses parenthetical in-text citations (that include the author's last name and page or paragraph number) and a works cited list.

narration 4   A method of paragraph or essay organization in which the writer relates a scene, incident, or anecdote. Narration may include dialogue.

non-coordinate adjective 14   An adjective that cannot be moved within a list without changing the meaning of the sentence.

non-restrictive clause 14   A clause that contains information that can be left out of the sentence without affecting the meaning.

noun 13   The name of a person, place, thing, or idea. See also *subject*.

noun phrase 13   A group of words that acts as a noun in a sentence and can be either the subject or an object.

outline 2, 6–7, 9–11   An organized representation of an essay's points and supporting material. Three types of outline types are scratch, graphic, and formal.

parallelism 15   The principle that the elements in a sentence that have the same grammatical function are expressed in parallel structures. It applies to lists of three or more items, compounds, items joined by correlative conjunctions, and comparisons.

paraphrase 5, 10–12   Restate a source's meaning using different words; paraphrased text includes all of the original thought and is approximately the same length.

parentheses 11, 13   A form of punctuation that encloses less important text that explains or expands on something and, in documentation, encloses in-text citations. Parentheses are used in pairs.

passive construction 15   A construction in which the subject of the sentence does not perform the action; the noun that receives the action is the subject and is placed at the beginning of the sentence.

peer reviewed 10   The assessment of an article by experts in the field; occurs before the article is published.

periodical 10   A publication that is issued regularly, such as newspapers, magazines, journals, and yearbooks.

personal essay 4   An essay that focuses on an aspect of the writer's life or a relevant experience.

personal experience 8   A type of example that takes the form of direct experience or observation, which can often be effective in supporting a value or opinion claim.

personal pronoun 15   A pronoun that refers to persons. The first person refers to the one doing the speaking or writing; second person refers to the one spoken to; and third person refers to the one spoken about.

phrase 13   A group of grammatically linked words that lacks a subject, predicate, or both; functions as a single part of speech. See also *prepositional phrase*.

plagiarism 11   The intentional or unintentional use of someone else's work as if it were one's own; includes borrowing someone else's words or ideas without acknowledging the source, not placing quotation marks around a direct quotation, or following the source's wording or structure too closely when paraphrasing.

policy claim 8   A claim that is usually a call for action to fix a problem or improve a situation.

possessive 13–16   The case that indicates relationships, such as ownership, between two nouns. For most singular nouns, the possessive is shown with an apostrophe + s; plural nouns ending in s take an apostrophe alone. Some pronouns have a separate possessive case (e.g., *my* books, *their* dinner).

precedent 8   An example that refers to the way a particular situation was handled in the past. Precedents are often used in argument to suggest similar treatment for the matter under discussion.

predicate 14   The part of the sentence that contains the verb and object (and indirect object) or subject complement. It tells what the subject is doing or what is being observed about it.

premise 8   A statement assumed to be true. In deductive reasoning, the major premise is a generalization that must be true in order for the conclusion to be valid.

preposition 13   A short word or phrase that often refers to place or time and that joins a noun or pronoun to the rest of the sentence, adding information to the subject or predicate.

prepositional phrase 13   A group of words that consists of a preposition and a noun or pronoun (the object of the preposition). The phrase can act as an adverb to modify a verb or as an adjective to modify a noun or pronoun.

pre-writing (or inventing) 2 A group of strategies that help clarify thoughts about a subject, generate useful ideas, create a thesis, and possibly determine main points. Pre-writing involves *questioning, brainstorming*, and/or *clustering* or *mapping*.

primary sources 8 Original sources, including literary texts, historical documents, surveys, questionnaires, and interviews. Compare *secondary sources*.

problem-solution 4 A method of paragraph or essay organization in which a writer focuses on a problem, a solution to a problem, or both a problem and solutions.

process 4 A method of paragraph or essay organization in which a writer focuses on the steps in a sequence.

pronoun 13 A word that takes the place of a noun in a sentence. See also *antecedent, agreement, pronoun reference, pronoun case, pronoun consistency*, and *relative cause*.

pronoun-antecedent agreement 15 The principle that a pronoun must agree with its antecedent in number, person, and gender.

pronoun case 15 The principle that a pronoun changes its form depending on its function in the sentence (e.g., *I/me, she/her, they/them*).

pronoun consistency 15 The principle that a pronoun must agree in number, gender, and person with its antecedent.

pronoun reference 15 The principle that each pronoun must refer clearly to its antecedent.

proofreading 16 The final stage of writing an essay, in which the writer corrects all errors in order to provide a clean copy for the reader. See also *revising*.

proposal 10 A description of a planned essay that announces the work's topic, purpose, and research sources.

purpose 2 The reason for writing and the method for approaching the task. It can encompass the skills that the assignment is intended to develop or the desired effect on the audience.

question-answer 4 A method of paragraph or essay organization in which a writer poses questions (Who? What? When? Where? Why? and How?) and explains their answers.

questioning 2 A pre-writing strategy that frames a possible thesis as a specific question or series of questions that the writer will try to answer.

rebuttal 9 The part of an argument that raises the other side's points, usually to strengthen the argument and to appear fair.

reference 12 A citation that gives complete retrieval information for a source used in an essay.

reflexive pronoun 13 A pronoun that uses –*self* at the end (e.g., *himself*); can be used only if the person has already been referred to earlier in the sentence.

relative clause 15–16, B A dependent clause that functions adjectivally, modifying the preceding noun. The clause usually begins with a relative pronoun.

relative pronoun 14 A pronoun that introduces a dependent clause and connects it to the rest of the sentence (e.g., *who, which*, or *that*).

research 1, 10–12 A stage of essay writing that involves exploring a topic to discover what others (especially experts) have written or said about it, which can serve as background information and supporting evidence. Research requires using library resources and/or reliable online sources.

restrictive clause 14 A dependent clause that contains information that is necessary for the reader to understand the sentence.

revising 16 A process that involves editing to achieve a polished final version. See also *proofreading*.

run-on sentence 13 A major grammatical error in which a sentence has two independent clauses with no punctuation separating them.

scanning 1 A reading strategy in which the reader looks for key words or sections of a text.

secondary sources 10 Works that comment on primary sources; include authoritative written sources (e.g., books and journal articles), oral presentations, and conference papers.

selective reading 1 A reading strategy with a goal, such as scanning for main points or reading for details.

sentence adverb 14 An adverb that modifies the complete independent clause that follows it.

sentence fragment 13 A major grammatical error that consists of an incomplete clause or a dependent clause on its own.

signal phrase 5, 11, 12 A phrase that indicates what follows is taken from another source; the phrase contains the original author's name and a signal verb.

simple sentence 13 A sentence that contains one subject and one predicate.

simple thesis statement 7 A thesis statement that announces the essay's topic and makes a comment on it. Compare *expanded thesis statement*.

slanted language 9   Language that reveals the writer's bias, affecting his or her credibility; should be avoided in most writing.

soft evidence 8   Evidence that indirectly supports the writer's points and helps the reader understand them; includes examples, anecdotes, case studies, and precedents.

spiral conclusion 7   A conclusion that restates the thesis and leads the reader beyond it.

square brackets (or brackets) 11   Punctuation marks that, when used in a direct quotation, indicate a change or addition to the original passage.

style 16   Specific aspects of a text, such as document formats or citation methods; also refers to the way someone writes, including his or her tone and diction.

subject 2, 13, 15   The field of study that an essay is about; in grammar, the part of the sentence containing a noun that performs the action of the verb.

subject complement (SC) 13   A noun or pronoun that follows a linking verb and gives more information about the subject.

subject-verb agreement 13   The principle that a sentence's verb must match its subject in number (i.e., a singular subject requires a singular verb, and a plural subject requires a plural verb).

subordinating conjunction 13   A conjunction that joins a dependent clause, which contains less important information, to an independent clause, which contains more important information.

summary 5, 11   A shorter rephrasing of an original work; restates only the main ideas of the source.

support 8   Facts and other evidence that help prove a claim and make it believable.

synonym 1   A word that means the same thing as, and can therefore replace, another word. See also *connotation* and *denotation*.

syntax 15   The way words are put together into sentences in a language.

synthesis 10   The process of putting together ideas from different sources.

thesis statement 1, 7   The main point of an essay, or what the writer is trying to prove in it, usually stated in the introduction. See also *simple thesis statement* and *expanded thesis statement*.

tone 1, 16   The writer's attitude (e.g., subjective, objective, formal, or informal) toward the subject matter.

topic 2   The general idea that an essay is about. A topic is narrower and more focused than a subject but less focused than a thesis statement.

topic sentence 3   Usually the first sentence in a paragraph; introduces the paragraph's main idea.

transition 3   A word or phrase that contributes to an essay's coherence by connecting ideas from one sentence or paragraph to the next.

uniform resource locator (URL) 10, 12   The address of specific Internet content.

unity 3   The principle that a paragraph should focus on one central idea announced in the topic sentence and that all sentences in the paragraph should relate to that idea.

usage 16   The customary and accepted way that a word is used. See also *diction*.

value or opinion claim 8   A claim that appeals to one's principles or moral system.

verb 13   A word that conveys an action, state of being, or condition.

verb phrase 13   A group of words that acts as the verb in a sentence.

working bibliography 10   A list of sources consulted while working on an essay.

wrap 3   The last sentence of a paragraph; sums up the main point and recalls the topic sentence.

Index

sentences, 317–19; cumulative, 443; errors, 323–34, 386–99; fragments, 24, 323–7, 426; length, 441–2; logical order, 68; opening, 153–4; parallel structure, 69; patterns, 319–23; periodic, 443; run-on, 329–30; transitions between, 69–70; variety, 441–3
series: and parallelism, 394–7; punctuating, 336–7, 350, 352–3
several, 369
Shakespeare, William, 395
shall, 312
should, 312
sic, 253
sight/site/cite, 435
signal phrase, 107–8, 251–2; and citations, 265–7, 282
simile, 445
since, 327
slang, 426
slanted language, 193
so, 69, 315
social sciences writing, 45, 88, 173, 175, 264
society, 461–2
software for research, 231
sources: and bias, 173–4; electronic, 229, 235–40; evaluating, 10, 14–16, 173–4, 238; finding, 224–5; hyperlinking, 178; indirect, 266–7, 275, 282; non-textual, 241, 269, 277, 285, 292–4; primary, 173, 223, 233; and publication dates, 229–30; reference, 229, 233; researching, 233–41; secondary, 223, 233–4, 248–54; summarizing, 107; *see also* documentation
spellchecker, 433, 447
spiral conclusion, 162
splice, comma, 24, 330–2, 346
square brackets, 253, 287
squinting reference, 376
statistics, 173–4
Statistics Canada, 237
Stock, Ian, 150
straw man argument, 191
stress, 471
structure: essay, 54, 225–7; parallel, 69, 127, 393–9, 444; sentence, 386–99, 441–3
Strummer, Lindsay, 137–40, 173
Student's Oxford Canadian Dictionary, 428
Stutt, Bree, 89
style: writing, 414; documentation, 263–5
subject (in a sentence), 317–19; complement, 312, 318; delayed, 364; empty,

421; missing, 323–4; in passive constructions, 402–5; pronouns, 309–10
subject–verb agreement, 308, 364–9, 444, 472
subject *vs* topic, 43
subordinating conjunction, 315, 320, 326–7, 350, 441
summary, 55, 104–21, 248; *vs* paraphrase, 113, 115–16
superlatives, 456, 456
support, *see* evidence
synonyms, 21, 69
syntax, 387
synthesis, 223, 225–7

television, citing: APA style, 269, 277; MLA style, 285, 293
templates: for argumentative essay, 211–13; for expository essay, 147–8; in PowerPoint, 218
than/then, 399, 438
that, 339–40, 419
the, 313, 458–62
their/there/they're, 438
therefore, 332, 341, 349, 350
thesaurus, 24, 427
thesis statement, 7, 42–3, 48, 152; checklist, 158
thesis, types of, 125, 154–8
they/their, 376; as singular pronoun, 311, 371
think, 471–2
though, 327, 339
thus, 332
time, 457, 464
time management, 136–7
title page, 448
to be, 312, 322, 430
to have, 312, 322
to/too, 438
tone, 16, 41, 429
topic, 33, 43, 81
topic-based rebuttals, 200
topic sentence, 64, 87
track changes function, 52
tradition, as argument, 192
transitions, 232, 348–9; in oral presentations, 216; between paragraphs, 65–6; between sentences, 69–70
translated sources, 233; APA style, 267, 270; MLA style, 288
types of, 463
Tyre, Robert, 87

unified paragraph, 66–7, 80
URL (uniform resource locator), 230, 238–9, 275, 291
usage/use, 438

vague reference, 377
Vahlis, Julianny, 61–2
value claim, 170–1, 194
Van Horne, Jordan, 64–5
verbs, 312, 464–72; base form, 325; incomplete, 325–6; phrase, 321; and precision, 430; and prepositions, 466; tenses, 450–4; weak, 421
Verhulst, Graeme, 174–5
visualization of ideas, 47
visuals, in oral presentations, 217–18
vocabulary, 23–4, 68; *see also* word choice

what, 383
when, 327
whereas, 327, 339, 350
which, 339–40
while, 327
who/whom, 339–40, 382–4
who's/whose, 438–9
Wikipedia, 240
will, 312, 465
Windsor, Hillary, 166–8
Woolf, Virginia, 443
word choice, 5, 68, 193, 426–32
word meanings, 21–3
word-processing programs, 52, 231
working bibliography, 229
workplace communication, 41–2, 117–19, 215, 218
works cited, MLA style, 285–94; *see also* bibliography, documentation
WorldCat, 238
would, 312, 465
wraps, paragraph, 64–5
writer's block, 46
writing: direct, 420–1; formal *vs* informal, 35, 426; free, 45–7; on computer *vs* by hand, 51–2; process of, 2–5, 31; purpose of, 4, 32–4, 41–54; reader-based, 35–6; style, 414; subjective *vs* objective, 5; for the workplace, 41–2

Yaworski, Bev, 141–5
yet, 69, 315
you, 35, 322–3, 380
your/you're, 439

Some **Irregular Verb** Forms

Basic form	3rd-person singular	Past tense	Past participle	Present participle
be	is	was, were	been	being
bear	bears	bore borne,	born	bearing
beat	beats	beat	beaten	beating
begin	begins	began	begun	beginning
bite	bites	bit	bitten	biting
bleed	bleeds	bled	bled	bleeding
blow	blows	blew	blown	blowing
break	breaks	broke	broken	breaking
bring	brings	brought	brought	bringing
broadcast	broadcasts	broadcast	broadcast	broadcasting
build	builds	built	built	building
buy	buys	bought	bought	buying
catch	catches	caught	caught	catching
choose	chooses	chose	chosen	choosing
come	comes	came	come	coming
cost (have as a price)	costs	cost	cost	costing
cut	cuts	cut	cut	cutting
deal	deals	dealt	dealt	dealing
dig	digs	dug	dug	digging
dive	dives	dived, dove	dived	diving
do	does	did	done	doing
draw	draws	drew	drawn	drawing
drink	drinks	drank	drunk	drinking
drive	drives	drove	driven	driving
eat	eats	ate	eaten	eating
fall	falls	fell	fallen	falling
feel	feels	felt	felt	feeling
fight	fights	fought	fought	fighting
find	finds	found	found	finding
fly	flies	flew	flown	flying
forbid	forbids	forbade	forbidden	forbidding
forget	forgets	forgot	forgotten	forgetting
get	gets	got	got, gotten	getting
give	gives	gave	given	giving
go	goes	went	gone	going
grow	grows	grew	grown	growing
have	has	had	had	having
hear	hears	heard	heard	hearing
hide (conceal)	hides	hid	hidden	hiding
hit	hits	hit	hit	hitting
hold	holds	held	held	holding
hurt	hurts	hurt	hurt	hurting
input	inputs	input, inputted	input, inputted	inputting
keep	keeps	kept	kept	keeping
know	knows	knew	known	knowing
lay	lays	laid	laid	laying
lead	leads	led	led	leading
learn	learns	learned, learnt	learned, learnt	learning
leave	leaves	left	left	leaving
lend	lends	lent	lent	lending
let	lets	let	let	letting